# Dedication

For my wife Janice, with love, thanks, and ttcc:
*In your eyes*
*I am complete*
*in your eyes*
*the resolution of all the fruitless searches*
*—Peter Gabriel*

# About the Author

**Chris Sherman** is President of Searchwise LLC, a Boulder, Colorado–based web consulting firm, and Editor of *SearchDay,* a daily newsletter from SearchEngineWatch.com. Chris is also conference chair and organizer of Jupitermedia's Search Engine Strategies conferences in Bangalore, Beijing, London, Stockholm, and Toronto.

Chris is a Web Search University faculty member and an honorary inductee of the Internet Librarian Hall of Fame. His previous books include *The Invisible Web: Uncovering Information Sources Search Engines Can't See* (with Gary Price) from CyberAge Books, *The McGraw-Hill CD-ROM Handbook,* and *The Elements of Basic, The Elements of Cobol,* and *The Elements of Pascal,* from John Wiley & Sons.

Chris has more than 20 years of experience in developing multimedia and Internet applications. Early in his career, he worked on prototypes of many products and concepts that are now commonplace, such as CD-ROM multimedia technologies and interactive cable television. Later, he was Vice President of Technology for a global management consulting firm based in Amsterdam.

Chris has written about search and search engines since 1994, when he developed online searching tutorials for several clients. His clients have included International Data Corporation, Accenture, Motorola, Levi-Strauss, Ortho Biotech, Porsche, United Technologies, and the Scripps Clinic. From 1998 to 2001, he was the Web Search Guide for About.com. Chris holds a master's degree in Interactive Educational Technology from Stanford University and a bachelor's degree in Visual Arts and Communications from the University of California, San Diego.

# Contents

# Acknowledgments

I owe a huge debt of gratitude to the many people who helped me with *Google Power*. As people who know me well will attest, one of the major reasons I'm fascinated with search engines is that they help me compensate for what some have kindly described as "terminal absentmindedness." I've undoubtedly overlooked very important contributors, and if I've neglected to mention you by name here, my sincere apologies—but please know that I appreciate your support.

People attracted to the field of web search seem to invariably share two characteristics: extreme curiosity and a collegial graciousness that manifests itself with an open, generous willingness to share information, swap ideas, and help each other keep abreast of the constantly changing landscape of web search. I'm most grateful to colleagues Gary Price, Mary Ellen Bates, Danny Sullivan, Genie Tyburski, Susan Feldman, Tara Calishain, Ran Hock, Greg Notess, Marydee Ojala, and Nancy Blachman for sharing their thoughts, insights, and learnings about Google and other search engines.

I've also been fortunate in having an excellent relationship with Google over the years. I owe a special debt of gratitude to "Google Guy," a senior engineer at the company who was unstinting with both time and patience in answering my many questions for the book. Thanks also to all the Googlers I've had the good fortune to work with on a wide variety of projects, including Tim Armstrong, Sergey Brin, Matt Cutts, Daniel Dulitz, Jen Fitzpatrick, Debbie Frost, Urs Holtze, Omid Kordestani, David Krane, Ema Linaker, Marissa Mayer, Michael Mayzel, Cindy McCaffrey, Craig Nevill-Manning, Peter Norvig, Larry Page, John Piscitello, Jim Reese, Eileen Rodriguez, Jonathan Rosenberg, Wayne Rosing, Sheryl Sandberg, Barry Schnitt, Craig Silverstein, and Nate Tyler—and a hat tip to Google corporate chef Charlie Ayers for the excellent food every time I've visited the Googleplex.

Thanks to the power searchers who contributed their expertise to several chapters of this book: Mary Ellen Bates, Alexander Holt, Irene McDermott, Gary Price, Cynthia Shamel, Danny Sullivan, and Genie Tyburski. Thanks also to the capable crew at McGraw Hill/Osborne for guiding this book to fruition, especially Jane Brownlow, Agatha Kim, and the ever-patient and capable Patty Mon. The book also benefited enormously from Bart Reed's deft copy editing.

Gary Price played the invaluable role of technical editor for the book. In addition to ensuring accuracy, Gary offered numerous suggestions for enhancing and improving the book. *Google Power* would have been a lesser work without his careful eye and important suggestions—though I must also issue the standard disclaimer that any errors in the book are mine and mine alone.

To my children, Skylar and Sonya: Many thanks for patiently tolerating the too-frequent weekends and evenings your father spent working on this book. Now that *Google Power* is finished, that backyard play area we've been planning together is my top priority.

And finally, to my wife Janice: It's impossible to thank you enough for your unfailing support, high level of tolerance to my incessant blatherings, and most especially for your encouragement when I hit the overload wall that's an inevitable part of writing a book like this. It's a timeworn cliché, but very true: I couldn't have done it without you.

# Introduction

In January 1996, two Stanford University graduate students (who were "not terribly fond of each other when they first met" the previous year) began collaborating on a search engine they called "BackRub." Larry Page and Sergey Brin worked on their project steadily for the next year, building a "data center" in Larry's dorm room at Stanford. This was the era of virtually free venture capital for all things "dotcom," but the pair had little interest in building a company of their own around the technology they had developed. Instead, they began calling on potential partners who might want to license the fledgling search engine.

Yahoo! co-founder David Filo took a look and said encouraging things but told the duo to come back once the search engine had grown up. Others were less kind. "I wasn't impressed with their demo at all," said Doug Cutting, senior architect for then high-flying search engine Excite. "I didn't have the authority to sign a check anyway," said Louis Monier, AltaVista's chief technical officer. "I told them to go pound sand," said Infoseek founder Steve Kirsch.

Undaunted, Page and Brin decided to strike out on their own. They wrote up a business plan, invented a name for their new company, and paid a visit to an "angel" investor who was a friend of one of their Stanford faculty advisors. According to Brin, "We gave him a quick demo. He had to run off somewhere, so he said, 'Instead of us discussing all the details, why don't I just write you a check?' It was made out to Google Inc. and was for $100,000."

This initial funding posed a problem, however: The pair had not yet incorporated their new company, so they couldn't deposit the check. It sat in Page's desk drawer for a couple of weeks while the duo set up a corporation and raised additional money from family and friends.

Page and Brin continued to work on their search engine, rechristened it "Google," and by early 1999 were ready to invite the world to its virtual doors. Here's one of the first articles ever published about the then virtually unknown search engine.

## Do You Google?

by Chris Sherman
Originally published on June 29, 1999 on About.com.

As search engines go, Google (to borrow a phrase) thinks different. And Google's co-founder and CEO, Larry Page, thinks big.

Take Google's name. A "googol" is a huge number: 10 to the power of 100—more than the number of atoms in the universe. Google aims to index the huge number of documents that make up the vast universe of the Web—but differently. Google aims to *understand* what it finds. And: "We liked the spelling 'Google' better," says the company info page. "It sounds cool and has only six letters."

Unlike the other major search services, Google is a "pure" search engine. No news, email, chat, stock quotes, or other trappings offered by the major portals. And Page says that Google intends to keep it that way, focusing the company's energies strictly on search.

Google also takes a unique approach to determining what results you see for search queries. "Google measures link importance" to determine relevance, says Page. A page is important if other pages with high importance link to it, and especially if *lots* of pages with high importance point to it.

This may sound circular, and it is, but it also makes sense. A link to a Web page is the online equivalent of a citation in a book. Web page authors generally only link to pages they think are important. "It's almost like a peer review process for the Web," says Page.

The beauty of this approach is that it's virtually impossible for spamdexers to scam the search engine with bogus techniques. It's also highly scalable, meaning Google will actually get better over time. As the Web grows, more links are created and Google can be more certain about the importance of documents. That's good news, because the Web is doubling in size every nine months, according to Page.

## Google's Other Unique Features

Google has a number of other neat features, such as the "I'm feeling lucky" button. Clicking this button skips search results altogether and takes you directly to the page Google thinks is the best match for your search. And it works so well it's almost scary.

Google's results page includes the page title, the URL, and an "importance" score (called a PageRank). The PageRank takes the form of a red bar graph, and it's also a link. Clicking it shows you all of the important pages that have links pointing to the page.

In essence, clicking the PageRank bar lets you do an "Oh, Yeah?" test on the results, to see what sources Google used to compute the importance of the document. No other search engine provides this kind of transparency to show you how relevance is calculated.

The description of each document in the results list is also customized to your search terms. "Words in the description will match what's found in the document," says Page. The description is an excerpt of the text that matches your query, with your search terms in bold. "We can do this because we have the documents stored in cache" on Google's computers.

"On every query, we do a calculation on the exact distance between words, and use that to rank results," says Page. And *all* of your search terms must appear on a document for it to be considered a match. In Boolean terms, Google has no "or" operator.

These are just a few of the features that set Google apart from other search engines.

## Ambitious Plans

Google is the third major search service spawned by Stanford University, and by all indications it will be soon joining Excite and Yahoo as a major player in the search engine arena. Google recently secured $25 million in venture-capital funding. "Even by Internet standards, Google has attracted an unusually large amount of money for a company still in its infancy," said the Wall Street Journal.

Google is not wasting any time putting the money to work. "We've hired a lot of really smart people" to enhance and improve Google, says Page. "We think we can make search a lot better than it is now. To do the best job, it requires artificial intelligence. The search engine must understand the question being asked, and understand everything on the Web."

Last week, Netscape unveiled its new search engine, using Google's technology as its core. It's possible that Google may adopt an Inktomi-like strategy, selling its search technology to others instead of competing directly with the major search services. For a time, Inktomi had a search site, before it went undercover as the primary index underlying HotBot, MSN, and other search sites. Page declined to comment on Google's future strategic plans.

## Tips on Using Google

I asked Larry for some tips on getting the best results from Google. He made several helpful suggestions.

*Use fewer words in your query.* "Google tends to do the right thing even if you type short queries," says Page.

*Use cached, not direct links.* "Cached links tend to be fast. Use them if you're not looking for something time-critical. You'll get faster results."

*Go for an exact match.* "Google doesn't do stemming," says Page. Stemming is when search engines add variants to the root of a word. With Google, "house doesn't get you houses," just as "search" doesn't equate to "searching."

These are exciting times for Web searchers. The major players are feeling increasing competitive pressure to improve and expand their capabilities. And with hungry new players like Google pushing search technology into the next generation, things can only get better.

If you don't Google, you're missing out on something truly different—and something really, really big.

# Google Today

Everyone knows how this story played out: Google gained unprecedented popularity, grew rapidly into one of the most profitable businesses ever launched, and had a spectacular initial public offering in August 2004, vaulting co-founders Page and Brin on to the *Forbes 400* list of the world's wealthiest people.

I've been following and reporting on Google since that first article I wrote in 1999. The book you hold in your hands represents the distillation of everything I've observed, experimented with, and been captivated by through those six amazing years of growth. It's my hope that in reading *Google Power* and trying out the tools, strategies, and techniques it lays out that you, too, will become a Google power searcher, able to take full advantage of this most remarkable information-seeking machine.

# Why You Want to Read This Book

Learning to be a Google power user involves more than just geeking out on all the search engine's advanced tools and capabilities. Google's simplicity and its uncanny ability to provide reasonable answers at a moment's notice are the keys to its success. But Google's spare, streamlined interface masks the search engine's extreme power—power that's available to anyone with just a bit of extra effort.

That's important, because as good as Google is, research firm IDC says that upwards of 50 percent of all searches fail because people don't know how to use search engines effectively. If your searches aren't producing the results you expect, it's not necessarily because Google can't find the information you're seeking. Google is designed to do the best job possible for the widest range of people possible with the least amount of effort. In practice, that means Google finds good results most of the time, but may not always find the best answers to satisfy *your* information need—unless you have the keys to unlocking Google's secrets.

For example, did you know that there's a set of "magic keywords" that makes it a snap to sleuth out both personal and professional information about people? Or that certain power commands can surface inside information on companies—sometimes confidential information that businesses *don't want to be found?*

Throughout the book, the emphasis is not just on finding information but on finding *really useful* information. Some of the Google power-searching strategies and techniques you'll learn include:

- How to do a "checkup" on your doctor, examining his or her past record, disciplinary history, and other vitals.

- How to locate travel deals that can save you hundreds or thousands of dollars, some of which you'll never find elsewhere.

- How to set up automated tools that automatically search while you sleep and send you alerts whenever new information that's important to you is found.

- How to find and listen to *legal* music and other streaming audio files located all over the world.

- How to find content that has been removed from the Web and is no longer available at its original source.

■ How to find elusive government information that's often hidden away in the "invisible web."

■ How to discover what kinds of personal information Google collects about you (whether you realize it or not), and most importantly, how to regain control of that personal information.

These are just a few of the hundreds of tips and techniques you'll find in every chapter of the book.

# How the Book Is Structured

*Google Power* takes you under the hood and shows you how to turbo charge your Google searching for maximum results, no matter what you're looking for. Google's advanced features and capabilities are explained in plain language, with numerous examples demonstrating a wide variety of practical web search techniques.

The book has two parts, each with a different focus and purpose.

Part I, "Going Under the Hood to Supercharge Google," focuses on Google itself, describing the advanced capabilities the search engine makes available. This is a hands-on, nuts-and-bolts look at the search engine, how it works, and its wide array of power tools mostly hidden beneath the surface of Google's clean, simple home page. The emphasis in Part I is on the practical applications of power-searching features—why they're useful, not just how they work.

Part II, "Power Searching with Google," shifts the focus to using Google to uncover specific types of information. The advanced techniques you learn in Part I can and should be applied in different ways, depending on whether you're looking for people, advice about a medical condition, business intelligence, or other types of information. Part II is packed with practical, real-world-tested tips and techniques that will help you dramatically improve your searching.

Each chapter starts off by focusing on how to use Google to accomplish a specific task. As good as Google is, sometimes it's not the best tool for the job, so each chapter also features a "Beyond Google" section that offers high-quality alternatives that significantly enhance your web search tools arsenal.

# A Final Word about Google's Dog Policy

Full disclosure: I must admit to a very strong bias that favorably influences my opinion of Google. This bias has nothing to do with search, technology, Google employees, or any other matter relevant to this book. Nonetheless, I would be remiss in not making my bias perfectly clear. This has to do with Google's Dog Policy, which is summarized in the company's official Code of Conduct:

*"Google's respect and affection for our canine friends is an integral facet of our corporate culture. We have nothing against cats, per se, but we're a dog company, so as a general rule we feel cats visiting our campus would be fairly stressed out."*

You've got to love a company like that.

## Companion Web Site

Readers of *Google Power* have access to the companion web site for this book, which includes links to all the sites and web services mentioned in the book, at http://www.googlepower.net.

# Part I

## Going Under the Hood to Supercharge Google

# Chapter 1

## How Google Works

Search engines are magical machines. They're mysterious black boxes that accept our requests for information and somehow manage to locate relevant content regardless of where on the Web (or in the world) it's located. But all too often, we tend to approach search engines as we would a slot machine: Punch in a few words, pull the handle, and pray for a jackpot. While this slot-machine approach works more often than not, you'll get far better results if you have a basic understanding of how search engines work, and what goes on "under the hood" to bring you search results.

Google was built by some seriously smart people and the company employs more than 200 PhDs. Its data centers were even built by a brain surgeon (really! See Appendix B for details). However, you needn't be a neurosurgeon or have a doctorate to have good working knowledge of what goes on behind the scenes at Google. This chapter sets the stage for the rest of the book, offering a look under the hood at the inner workings of the search engine.

Fear not: To the extent possible, I've avoided using tech gobbledygook to describe how Google works. Technical terms are clearly defined, and knowing them will help you become a better searcher.

I've also put together two different overviews of how Google works. If you simply want a picture of how Google works painted in broad strokes, read the next section and then skip to other chapters in the book. For a more thorough look at the inner workings of the search engine, including an overview of how Google "thinks," be sure to read the entire chapter.

# How Google Works: The High-level Version for the Information Overloaded

Although we say we're "searching the Web" with Google, that's not really an accurate statement. What we're really doing is searching Google—specifically, a massive database of web pages that the search engine has collected, indexed, and made easily accessible through the familiar search box on Google's home page.

Why does Google go to all the trouble of creating its own database of web pages, rather than simply searching the Web itself? Because searching the Web in real time is an impossible task, at least for today's technologies. Let's examine the reasons why.

Start with the Web itself. The Web is a loosely affiliated federation of *web sites,* each identified by a unique *domain name.* In 2005, there are roughly 45 million unique domains located throughout the world, conceptually residing on computers called *web servers.* These web servers are home to billions of web pages, as well as other types of content, such as PDF files, audio and video files, and databases stuffed with all kinds of information.

We access information on the Web with a *browser* such as Internet Explorer, Opera, or Firefox. Browsers can easily reach all these varied types of information on the Web thanks to a common *protocol* (set of rules) known as *Hypertext Transfer Protocol (HTTP),* which hides the complexity of information exchange between far-flung computers and makes accessing information as simple as clicking a link.

When you click a link, your computer sends a request to the web server that hosts the information you're interested in. This request is routed from computer to computer on the Internet, sometimes passing through a dozen or more way stations before it finally ends up at the web server where the content resides. In most cases, the web server graciously responds to the request by packaging a complete copy of the web page or other requested content and sending it back to you. The package is automatically routed through numerous computers on the Internet until it reaches your own computer, where it is then displayed by your web browser. This process is illustrated in Figure 1-1.

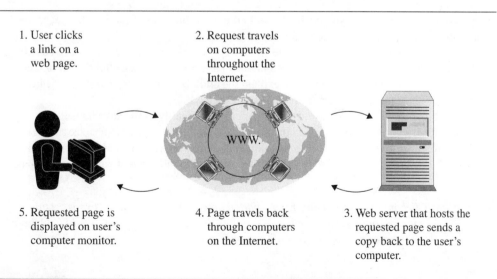

1. User clicks a link on a web page.

2. Request travels on computers throughout the Internet.

WWW.

5. Requested page is displayed on user's computer monitor.

4. Page travels back through computers on the Internet.

3. Web server that hosts the requested page sends a copy back to the user's computer.

**FIGURE 1-1**    Clicking a link is a simple process that initiates a complex series of events behind the scenes to bring you the content you've requested.

Now consider Google. The search engine handles hundreds of millions of requests per day. If Google had to simultaneously search all 45 million web servers for each of the hundreds of millions of search requests it handles each day, this prodigious activity would snarl the Internet with a massive virtual traffic jam.

Instead of attempting to go out and search the Web in real time, Google takes the opposite tack, discreetly visiting as many web servers as possible over a period of several days, collecting as much content as possible from all those servers and saving it into a single database—in essence, a full-scale copy of the Web.

When you "search the Web" with Google, you're actually searching this copy of the Web stored in Google's data centers. Instead of trying to solve the impossible task of real-time web searching, Google's engineers designed and built the search engine for speed and efficiency, solving the bottleneck problem described earlier by applying dozens of innovative techniques that work behind the scenes to give you high-quality search results without creating an Internet traffic jam.

When you enter a *query* (search terms) into a Google search form, Google first analyzes your words to attempt to understand what you're looking for. Then the search engine performs over 100 calculations, comparing your search terms with those in the database of web pages it has vacuumed up. Each of these calculations is designed to ferret out the web content that best matches your query and filter out everything else found in the billions of pages Google knows about.

When it has finished cogitating, Google assembles a page containing the "best" results for your query, sends it to your computer, and then effectively goes away. When you click a link on a Google search result page, your computer sends a request to the web server where that page is stored, not to Google (unless you click the **Cached** link, discussed in Chapter 3). That server, in turn, responds by sending your computer a copy of the requested content.

That's the high-level view of how Google works. The key point is that when you're searching Google, you're searching a *copy* of the Web, and one that is always at least slightly out of date. In most cases, this doesn't matter, but it can explain the odd occasion when you click a search result link and see a page that differs from what you expected.

Google's broad appeal comes from its simplicity and the quality of the search results it provides. But just as you can transform an ordinary automobile into a powerful stock car racer, you can also rev up your Google searches by taking a look under the hood and taking control of the powerful tools and services the search engine provides to those who take the time to learn how to use them.

POWER SEARCHER TIP  *Clicking the **I'm Feeling Lucky** button on Google's home page bypasses the search result page altogether and simply displays the page that would have been the number-one search result for your query.*

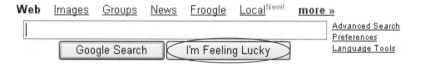

# How Google Works: The Bells-and-Whistles Version for Everyone Else

As you can imagine, search engines are complex systems. Google is made up of hundreds of software routines running on thousands of computers, handling tasks such as finding and saving web pages, cataloging their contents, processing search requests, and so on. Describing these systems and processes in all their technical glory would fill an entire book, and probably appeal only to those of us (raising my hand here) who are truly nerdy geeks.

Nonetheless, having a good grasp of how Google works on a fundamental level really can help you become a better searcher. For this book, I've created a simple model that accurately describes Google's operations without going into excessive technical detail. This model is designed to help you get a clear top-level overview of search engine mechanics so you understand conceptually how Google works. You won't be able to get a job as a Google engineer once you've completed this chapter, but you'll have a good idea of what's going on behind the scenes when you use Google to locate information on the Web.

At the most basic level, Google is a massive web harvesting machine that stores content and makes it searchable by millions of people simultaneously. To accomplish this remarkable feat, Google relies on three core parts, each responsible for handling a different aspect of the overall search process. While these three parts typically are made up of numerous subsystems that handle specialized tasks, their basic operation is essentially the same for Google, Yahoo!, Ask Jeeves, and every other search engine.

The three parts of a search engine are:

- **The crawler**   Responsible for finding and harvesting all content discovered on the Web
- **The indexer**   Responsible for cataloging and storing information about web content
- **The query processor**   The system you interact with to get search results

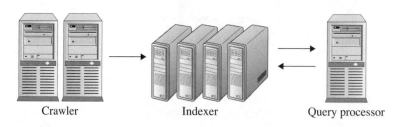

Crawler          Indexer          Query processor

**FIGURE 1-2**    The three fundamental parts of every search engine, including Google

Each part works with the others (as shown in Figure 1-2), ultimately delivering the results you see when you use Google to "search the Web."

Let's take a look at each of these parts in detail, first by exploring what the parts do, and then examining how they work together to help you navigate the Web.

## The Crawler: Discovering the Web

A search engine crawler is a software program responsible for exploring the Web, finding content and retrieving it for indexing and storage. Crawlers are automated programs (sometimes called *spiders* or *robots*) that work in much the same way as a web browser such as Internet Explorer or Firefox, but on a much more vast and speedier scale.

When you click a web page link displayed in your browser, your computer sends a request to the server where that page is stored. The server responds by sending a copy of that page back to your computer to be displayed in your browser window. Crawlers work in much the same way, requesting copies of web pages from the servers that host them. But crawlers are orders of magnitude more powerful than browsers—think of them as browsers on steroids. While your browser can request only a single page at a time, crawlers are capable of requesting thousands of pages from hundreds of web servers simultaneously—an important capability that allows Google to find and regularly revisit the billions of pages of content distributed throughout the web.

Google's crawlers run on dozens of computers working together using a "divide-and-conquer" strategy to download pages from all over the Web, without overwhelming any single web server with a massive number of requests. Google's primary crawler, called GoogleBot, typically crawls the entire Web once per month. Even with hundreds of computers working full-out around the clock, a complete crawl of the eight billion plus pages Google knows about typically takes days to complete.

How do Google's crawlers find web pages? Initially, crawlers are given a list of URLs (web pages) that are known to exist. The crawlers then request and download each one of those web pages to hand off to the indexer for cataloging. Before the crawler turns over a page to the indexer, however, it scans the page looking for links to *other* web pages. If it finds additional links, the crawler adds these URLs to its master list of pages to visit. Then the crawler requests another URL on its list, endlessly repeating this process until all the URLs on the master crawl list have been downloaded and indexed in Google's massive database of web pages. Figure 1-3 illustrates how crawlers work.

This strategy of scanning pages to discover new links is a clever way to discover new content, but isn't without problems. One problem is that popular pages have hundreds or even thousands of links pointing to them. To avoid repeatedly requesting popular pages that have already been fetched, the crawler will check to see if and when a page was previously crawled. Most pages that were crawled relatively recently are skipped in favor of new pages or pages that haven't been visited for some time.

There is an exception to this general rule of thumb, and that's for pages that change frequently. Google uses a crawler called FreshBot to visit these pages often to ensure its index stays as current as possible. FreshBot crawls millions of pages per day, and these pages are added immediately to Google's main database, which is completely updated every 30 days or so.

Another problem with the strategy of relying on links to discover new information is that it's random and somewhat self-referential, in that Google's crawler relies on itself to discover new links to crawl. In addition, some web pages have no links pointing to them, and other types of links are virtually impossible for Google to crawl. I'll talk more about this problem in the "Invisible Web" section at the end of this chapter.

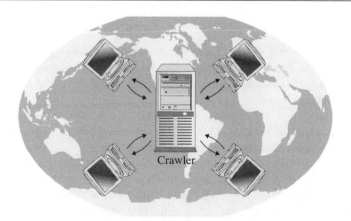

**FIGURE 1-3**    Crawlers are harvesting programs, responsible for vacuuming up as much of the Web as possible into Google's data centers.

# The Indexer: Organizing the Web

The indexer has a simple but very important function: To catalog all the words and their positions on every page that the crawler fetches. These catalogs serve as maps for the search engine, allowing it to match the words in your search requests to specific web pages and to pinpoint the exact locations of those words on web pages returned as search results.

A search engine's web index is similar to the index found at the back of this book, though much more granular and, obviously, much more vast in both size and scope. Search engine indexes record every instance of every word on a web page, noting its specific location as well. Google stores this index, as well as a copy of every crawled page, in a massive database that's essentially a complete copy of the entire visible Web. More than one copy, actually—for efficiency and reliability Google stores literally *dozens* of copies of the Web in its data centers.

Remember, when using Google, you're actually searching its database of web pages, *not* the Web itself. The search engine's index and copy of web pages is highly tuned and optimized for fast performance under the load of thousands of queries per second. The advantage to this approach is that you get search results quickly. The disadvantage is that you're searching an out-of-date copy of the Web. Your results may include pages that the search engine last crawled and indexed more than 30 days previously.

# The Query Processor: Delivering Search Results

While the crawler and indexer operate behind the scenes, the query processor is your direct interface to Google, and it's what most people think of as the "search engine." The moment you click a Google "search" button, your search terms are sent to the query processor and the real fun begins. Figure 1-4 is Google's illustration of the "life of a query," which illustrates how your search request is processed.

I've been referring to Google's collection of web pages and its index as a "database." While this is accurate at a high level, Google actually stores information in a number of different locations, using data structures that are optimized for specific tasks. Let's take a look at these systems in a bit more detail.

First, the Google web server sends your query to *index servers,* which contain the lists of all the words found on all pages, as mentioned earlier. The real heavy-lifting occurs here, as Google weighs your search terms and chooses pages that will provide the best match for what you're looking for. Your query then travels to the *doc servers,* where the actual pages that match your search request are retrieved. Google then creates a result page for you by extracting the titles of matching pages and linking these titles to the actual pages on the Web itself. Google creates a description for each page, called a "snippet," by extracting parts of the page that are the most relevant to your search terms. This is done on the fly, and each snippet is created to reflect your specific search terms as closely as possible.

Finally, Google sends your custom-built result page to your computer for your perusal. All this activity usually takes place in less than a second. And, if Google has correctly interpreted your query, your search results will lead you to click a link that requests a high-quality web page that satisfies your information need just scant moments later.

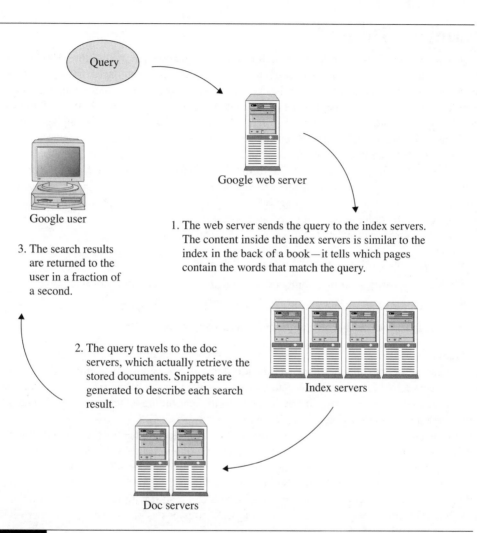

Query

Google web server

Google user

3. The search results are returned to the user in a fraction of a second.

1. The web server sends the query to the index servers. The content inside the index servers is similar to the index in the back of a book—it tells which pages contain the words that match the query.

2. The query travels to the doc servers, which actually retrieve the stored documents. Snippets are generated to describe each search result.

Index servers

Doc servers

**FIGURE 1-4**    A high-level view of how your search requests are processed by Google

Of course, there's a lot more going on behind the scenes when you search than this high-level description suggests. You don't really need to know a lot more about the crawler or the indexer to be an effective searcher. However, to really exploit Google's strengths, it's helpful to know more about how the query processor handles your search requests. Let's take a closer look at this process, examining how Google "thinks."

# How Google "Thinks"

To present you with a list of relevant search results, Google considers more than 100 factors (called *metrics*) related to both your search terms and its index of web pages. Google performs specialized computations with each of these metrics, distilling results of these computations into a single *score* for every web page that's a candidate for your search results. In the end, the page with the highest score is presented as the first result. The page with the second-highest score is listed next, and so on. Each metric is represented by a number, and the ultimate score a particular page receives as being relevant or not for your query is simply the sum of all the metrics.

Your search terms, of course, are one of the most important factors in these relevance calculations. Google favors pages where *all* your search terms appear on the page. Pages where your search terms are near each other are even better, and best of all are pages where your search terms appear in the order you typed them, as a phrase.

Other important metrics related to your search terms include:

- Search terms appearing in the title of a web page
- Search terms appearing in unique font elements, such as boldface or italic type
- Search terms appearing in other "prominent" areas of a page, such as a bulleted list
- The frequency with which your search terms appear on a page

Google considers other "on-the-page" metrics, such as synonyms for your search terms, and many other factors beyond the scope of this introduction. It's important to realize that while Google places a lot of importance on finding pages containing your search terms, this isn't the only, or in some cases even the primary factor used in determining which web pages contain the most relevant information to satisfy your query.

For instance, Google also considers "off-the-page" metrics. The most important of these metrics has to do with links pointing to a web page. Google considers a link to a page to be a "vote" for that page. The reasoning here is that if someone thinks highly enough of a web page to link to it, they are essentially saying, "I like this page enough to recommend it, and I'm making it easy for you by creating a link so you can read it with just the click of a mouse." In essence, Google views web authors creating links to pages as participating in a peer review process of the Web.

Google does more than simply count the total number of links pointing to a page, however. Overall popularity is certainly important, but as with any type of voting, measures need to be put into place to avoid "ballot box stuffing." On the Web, anyone can "vote" repeatedly for a page by creating hundreds, thousands, or even millions of links to the page. This is easily done with simple software programs, and it's a common (though discredited) technique for increasing the apparent popularity of a web page.

Google takes this potential vote fraud into account by also considering the *reputation* of the page that's voting for another page by linking to it. Votes cast by pages with a good reputation count for more than votes cast by pages with lesser reputations. Google determines reputation in a number of ways. Some web sites receive a high reputation by default, such as those run by government agencies, well-known or prominent companies, and universities (at least on the faculty side of the sites). Google considers some other sites to have a good reputation if other sites with good reputation link to them—in other words, allowing reputation to be transferred from a known reputable site to an unknown site, all through the mechanism of linking (voting).

Yes, this is circular logic (or a *recursive process,* in geekspeak), but it works. This intelligent link analysis is called PageRank, a pun on Google co-founder Larry Page's name. PageRank lies at the core of Google's web page evaluation system, and it plays a very important role in determining the quality of search results.

For example, when factoring reputation into the overall relevance equation, Google considers a link from a government web page, or from the Yahoo! directory or another highly reputable site, to count for much more than a link from Uncle Billy Bob's True Trout Fishing Stories page. That is, unless Uncle Billy Bob is regarded by the web community as the ultimate expert on trout, which Google would know by the computed reputation of his site. Figure 1-5 illustrates how Google uses "shared" reputation to ensure that more important pages get higher ranking than less important pages.

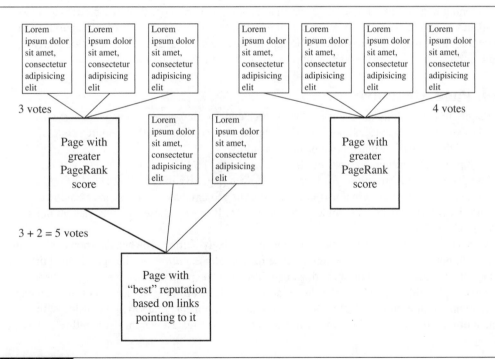

**FIGURE 1-5**     Google considers both the quantity and quality of links to be important factors in ranking a page.

It's important to note that PageRank is *query independent*. What that mouthful means is that Google calculates a PageRank score for every web page at the time the page is indexed, and this score has nothing to do with the actual words appearing on the page. PageRank is concerned only with the relative *importance* and *reputation* of a web page relative to *all* other pages on the Web, regardless of the content of the page. This means that the PageRank score can be used in combination with other ranking metrics as a third-party validation mechanism of a web page's quality. In essence, it allows Google to say, "We think this page is a pretty good match based on analyzing the words and other factors on the page. If the PageRank score is also high, the Web itself is confirming our analysis."

Another very important off-the-page factor Google considers in ranking calculations is link text used to describe a page (called *anchor text*) found on other web pages. A link has two parts: the URL pointing to a page, and the anchor text that describes the link. URLs are fixed, but a web author can write anything they please as the anchor text for a link. Google has found that anchor text often provides a concise summary of the page the link points to—it's sometimes an even better description than the title of a page itself. In fact, Google will occasionally display a search result for a page that doesn't contain your search terms at all—because your search terms appear only in links pointing to the page.

These are just a few of the metrics Google uses to determine the relevance of a web page as a potential match for your query. To summarize: Google uses more than 100 metrics to rank web pages as potential results for your search queries. Using a combination of text analysis and reputation-based link popularity allows Google to provide a useful and relevant list of search results for any query, no matter how complex, typically in a fraction of a second.

## Web Page Structure

It's helpful to look behind the scenes at the "source code" of a typical web page, to see what Google sees when it crawls and indexes the page. Figure 1-6 shows both the source code of a page and the page as displayed in a browser window.

Web pages are written in *Hypertext Markup Language (HTML)*. This language uses *tags* (codes) that contain instructions for formatting a web page. By interpreting HTML tags, a browser knows when to format text in columns, when to emphasize words using boldface or italic characters, and so on. Google also "reads" HTML tags and uses them as factors in its ranking calculations.

Web pages have two parts: the head portion and the body portion. The head portion can contain many tags, but only one has major significance for Google: the *title tag*. The aptly named title tag contains the title that the author of the document has given the page. When a web page is displayed in a browser, the title appears in the title bar at the top of the browser, not as part of the web page itself, as shown in Figure 1-6. Of all the on-the-page components that Google considers, the content of the title tag is the most important and carries the greatest weight in overall relevance ranking.

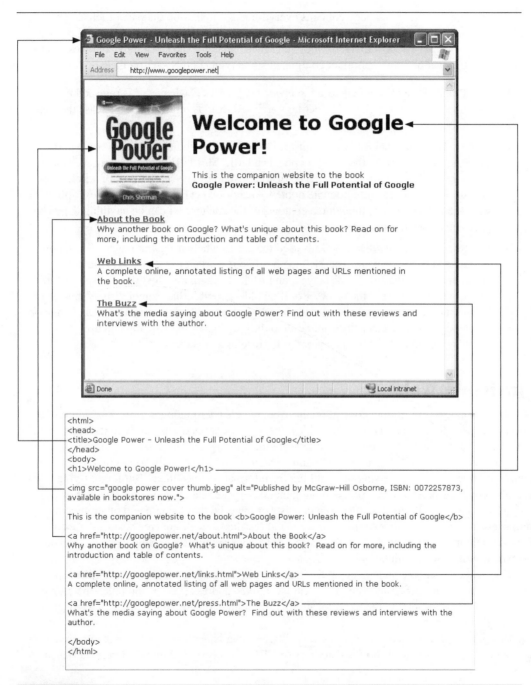

**FIGURE 1-6**    The source code for a web page specifies how a page is formatted in your browser.

The body portion of a web page contains everything that makes up the page, such as text and images, that are displayed in your browser window. Google indexes everything in the body portion of the web page except images—they're crawled and indexed separately, a process that's discussed in Chapter 6. Some important components of a typical body section include:

- **Headings**    Headings are enclosed in *header tags* (`<Hx>`, where "x" is replaced by a number from 1 through 6). Header tags are used to add emphasis and increase the font size of headings.

- **Links**    Links are enclosed in *anchor tags* (`<A Href>`) and typically have two parts. The first part, following the `href=` code, is a URL. This URL can point to a web page, an image, a PDF file, or any other type of web resource. The second part of a link is the *anchor text,* enclosed within double quotes. Anchor text is typically a brief description of what the URL points to, though the contents of the anchor text can be anything the web page author decides to write.

- **Images**    The *image tag* (`<IMG>`) is used to specify where a separate image file should be included on a web page. The `IMG` tag has two important parts: `SRC=` is the name of the image file that's to be displayed, and `ALT=` is alternative text that's displayed if images are turned off in the browser or if an older browser that cannot display images is being used. Alternative text is also displayed when you move the cursor over an image on a web page. Google pays close attention to the contents of the `ALT` tag and uses it as one of the factors in computing the overall relevance of a document.

# The Invisible Web

As good as Google is at finding content on the Web, there's a vast amount of information you'll never find using Google or any other search engine, because it resides squarely in the realm of the *invisible Web*. Much like the purloined letter in the famous story by Edgar Allen Poe, content residing in the invisible Web is largely in plain sight. You and I can easily access this content by simply visiting sites and browsing or searching for information once there. But forget trying to find this content using Google—or any other general-purpose search engine for that matter.

Why? In a nutshell, the invisible Web consists of material that Google and other general-purpose search engines either cannot (for technical reasons) or will not (for business reasons) include in their web indexes. In Google's case, the reasons are mostly technical and have to do primarily with crawling limitations.

Google's crawlers are quite adept at finding web pages, images, PDF files, and other types of *static* content on the Web. This type of content has a fixed address (URL), and unless it's moved, the URL will always point to the exact location of the content on the Web, making it a trivial task for Google to fetch the page.

By contrast, *dynamic* content poses a very different challenge for Google. Dynamic content is stored in databases and has no fixed address or URL. To access dynamic content, you typically run a search or create customized pages that tailor content to your particular tastes or needs. Because dynamic content typically lacks a fixed URL, it's difficult for people to link to it, and without links, crawlers cannot locate content.

Google's crawlers can typically find the home page or the search form for a database or other dynamic content site on the Web. But a crawler cannot take the same actions humans can when visiting a database, such as entering search terms, using drop-down menus, selecting radio buttons or check boxes, and clicking buttons. Simply put, crawlers can't type. When a crawler encounters a database, it's as if it has come across the front door of a vast library of information—but the door is securely locked.

For you as a searcher, this isn't a trivial problem. In the book I co-authored with Gary Price, *The Invisible Web: Uncovering Information Sources Search Engines Can't See* (CyberAge Books, 2001), we estimate that the invisible Web is 2 to 50 times larger than the visible Web—estimates that have been confirmed by Google engineers. That's a ton of information you simply cannot directly access using Google.

And that's unfortunate, because the lion's share of information secreted away in the invisible Web is produced by reputable publishers, including universities, governments, and other organizations offering very valuable information. For many types of searches, it's exactly the type of information that provides the most satisfactory results.

Google is aware of this problem and has a number of initiatives under way to access this valuable content. I once spoke on a panel with Google's chief technology officer, Craig Silverstein, and I asked him when he thought the company would solve the problem. His estimate at the time was that it would take Google engineers 50 years to fully crack the invisible Web problem— despite having one of the most powerful brain trusts of any company on the planet working on the problem!

Don't despair, however. As said, Google can find the home pages and search forms for many dynamic database-driven sites. Many of the advanced commands and operators discussed throughout the book can also help you find invisible Web resources. The key point to keep in mind is that as good as Google is, it's not omnipotent.

# Go Forth and Google

This chapter has focused on the technical aspects of Google's operation, providing the "view from 30,000 feet." The rest of the book comes down to earth and focuses on specific, actionable strategies and tactics for getting the most out of Google in your day-to-day searching.

If you'd like more technical information about how Google works, be sure to read Appendix B. This appendix provides more details about Google's engineering and operations, and it also provides links to further reading that gets into the serious nitty-gritty of the search engine's architecture, construction, and performance.

Now that you've had an introduction to how Google "thinks," it's time to take the plunge and really get the most out of the search engine.

# Chapter 2

## Google Power Searching Essentials

From the outset, Google was designed to be simple to use and fast to respond with high-quality results for just about any type of query. Most of the time, entering two or three search terms will generate an acceptable result in the top ten returned, and this usually happens in less than one second. Simplicity, ease of use, and speedy, relevant results are the key factors that have contributed to Google's success and appeal.

Hewing to these core principles has a downside, however. Google must be all things to all people, and in doing so has made some tradeoffs that sacrifice features and tools that power searchers find useful. The good news is that most of these features lie just beneath the surface, easily accessible and in some cases available as default options that override the basic interface and output seen by most users.

Like a good race horse, Google responds best when urged on by a knowledgeable user who understands how to play to its strengths and coax out the best performance, using a variety of techniques. This chapter shows you how to configure Google for best results, how to use its basic power searching tools, and offers strategies for maximizing your effectiveness as a searcher.

# Make Your Preferences Known

The very first thing any power searcher should do is to investigate the preferences Google offers, and permanently select those that help get the best results. The **Preferences** link is ubiquitous—it's on Google's home page and appears next to the search box on every result page.

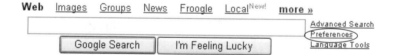

Clicking the **Preferences** link displays the Preferences page, shown in Figure 2-1. When you change your preferences, the new settings apply to most Google services, including web search, news search, Google groups, and Froogle.

## Interface Language

Google has two language options. The first, **Interface Language**, is what you see on Google itself in everything other than search results. The interface language is the language used on the Google home page, on commands, buttons, and messages, for the text of the Preferences page,

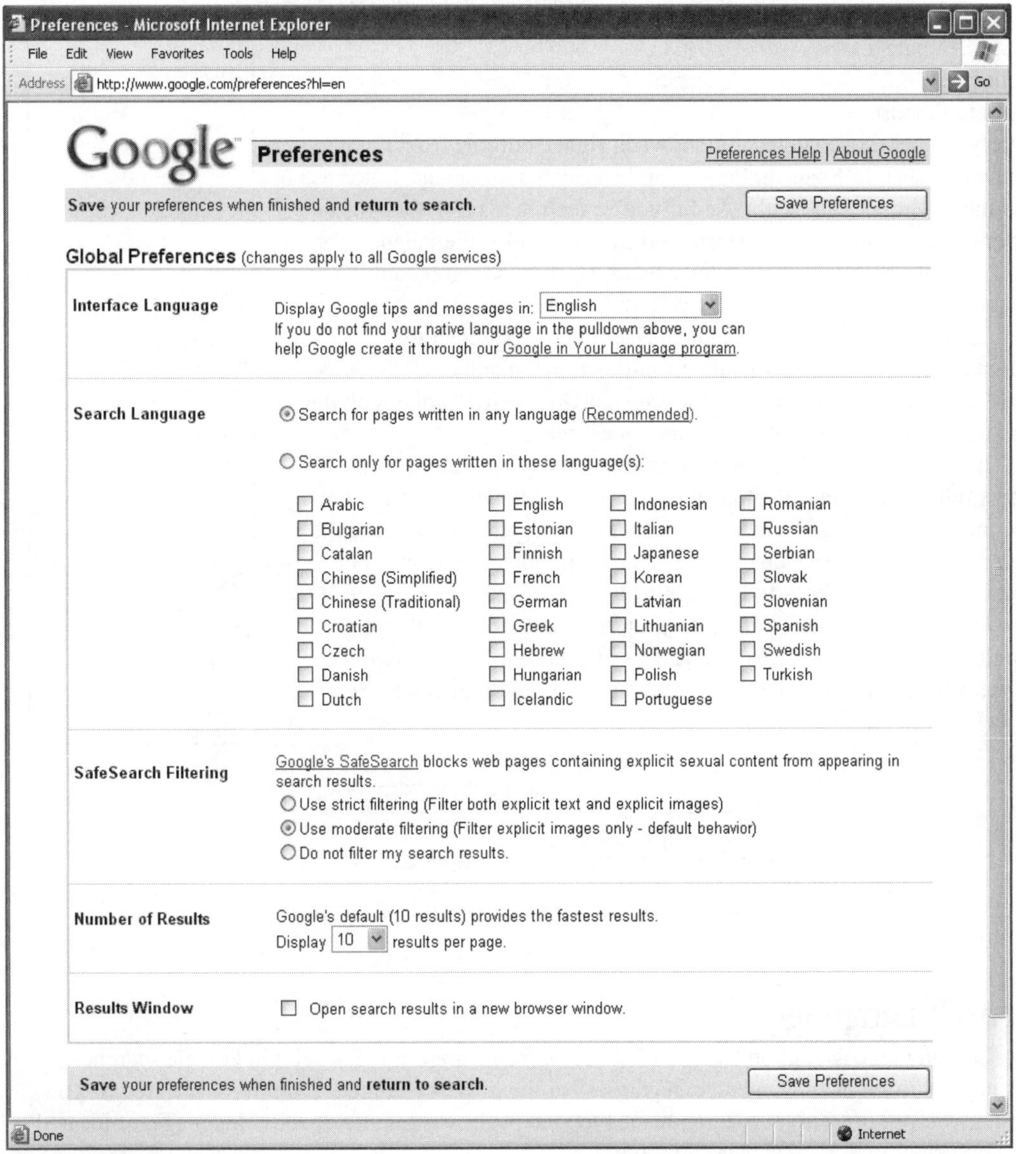

**FIGURE 2-1**    The Preferences page lets you permanently change options to all Google services.

and, for many languages, the text of Google's help files. Google supports nearly 100 interface languages (shown at right), ranging from common languages such as Spanish, French, and German, to languages such as Amharic, Marathi, and Zulu. And if you're feeling playful, Google also offers silly language interfaces in Bork! Bork! Bork! (the language of the Muppets' Swedish chef), Elmer Fudd, Hacker, Klingon, and Pig Latin.

Interface Language

Display Google tips and messages in: English
If you do not find your native language help Google create it through our Goog

English
Esperanto
Estonian
Faroese
Filipino
Finnish
French
Frisian
Galician
Georgian
German
Greek
Guarani
Gujarati
Hacker
Hebrew
Hindi
Hungarian
Icelandic
Indonesian
Interlingua
Irish
Italian
Japanese
Javanese
Kannada
Klingon
Korean
Kurdish
Kyrgyz

Changing the interface language is simple—just select the language of your choice from the drop-down menu and click the **Save preferences** button. Figure 2-2 shows what Google looks like with the Traditional Chinese and Klingon interfaces selected.

Be careful when changing your interface language to one you don't fully understand! If English is your default language, changing the interface language back to English can be a challenge, because the word "English" doesn't directly translate in all other languages. For example, to change back to English from the Frisian language, you'll need to select "Ingelsk." Fortunately, there's an option on all non-English Google home pages to select Google.com in English (shown next), which will also reset your preferences to the English language interface.

Google - hoe en het - Google.com in English

Tenei altyd fuort de Google-side werjaan at jo jo Internetprogramma derfoar klikke? Klik hjirre!

©2004 Google - Google hat 4,285,199,774 websiden yn syn argyf

## Search Language

The second language option Google offers is **Search Language**. By default, Google searches for pages written in any language, regardless of the interface language you have selected. If you prefer, you can restrict your search results to web pages written in a specific language, or located in a particular region, as shown in Figure 2-3.

Google's search language feature currently supports more than 30 languages, with additional languages added on an ongoing basis. You may select as many or as few as you want in search results by simply ticking the check box next to a language on the Preferences page. To resume getting results in all languages, just select **Search for pages written in any language**, and all the individual language selections will be cleared.

FIGURE 2-2    Two flavors of the Google home page

POWER SEARCHER TIP
*Restricting results to a specific language means Google is searching only a small portion of the Web. In most cases, you'll get better results by searching for pages in any language and then using Google's translation tools (explained later in this chapter) to translate pages in unfamiliar languages.*

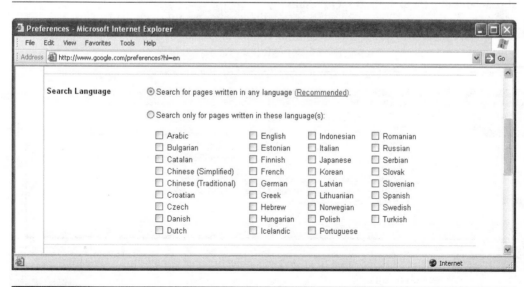

FIGURE 2-3    Google's search language options

## SafeSearch Filtering

The Web is wild and wooly, and there's a lot of content out there that's objectionable or offensive to some. Google's SafeSearch filter (shown in Figure 2-4) provides three levels of filtering, for both text and images.

By default, Google applies moderate filtering to images, and no filtering to text. Moderate filtering screens most pornography and explicit sexual content from search results. Strict filtering applies to both images and text results. Google's filter uses proprietary technology that checks words and phrases on a page, URLs, and Open Directory categories for potential offensive content. To turn off filtering altogether, select the **Do not filter my search results** option.

While the SafeSearch filter works reasonably well, no filtering technology is 100-percent accurate. Occasionally, objectionable content will slip through the filter and appear in your search results. Should you find this troublesome, you should look into a third-party adult content filter such as NetNanny or Cyber Patrol that offers greater control over the display of Internet content.

*If you find offensive content in your results, even with SafeSearch turned on, Google wants to know about it. Send an e-mail with the URL of the objectionable page to safesearch@google.com, and Google will investigate.*

## Go for Maximum Results

Google returns ten results by default for any query, but allows you to set the number of search results to 10, 20, 30, 50 or 100 results per page, as shown in Figure 2-5. Even if you're using a relatively slow dialup connection, you should go for the maximum and set your number of search results to 100. Why, when study after study has shown that most people don't go past the first search result page to the next set of results?

Because real gems are often found beyond the first ten results. When Google is forced to decide which ten pages to display in search results out of thousands or millions of possibilities,

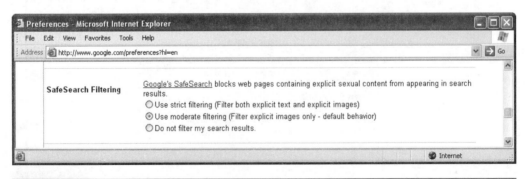

**FIGURE 2-4**   Google's SafeSearch filter prevents objectionable content from appearing in search results.

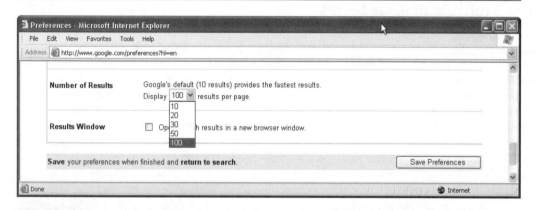

FIGURE 2-5   Change your preferences to display 100 search results at a time.

it's bound to overlook high-quality pages that might have just the information you're looking for. There's also the problem of spammers or aggressive search engine optimizers elbowing their way into top result positions, relegating perfectly acceptable content to lower positions. Setting your results to 100 gives you both the option and leisure to scan ten times the number of results on a single page. Though you may see a very slight delay in performance, the increased variety of results makes the wait well worth it.

# Choose Your Words Carefully

Google's simplicity almost invites us to casually toss words into a search box and expect good results. And in most cases, Google does a relatively good job with just about any query you throw at it. But you can really maximize the quality of your search results if you take a moment to think about what you're looking for, and choose the search terms that give Google enough to chew on to bring you the best results possible.

## Don't Make a Case of It

Google is not case-sensitive. All characters in your search words, whether capitalized or not, are treated as lowercase letters. This means that searches for "FedEx," "fedex," and even "FeDeX" will all return the same results. Save yourself some effort—type all your queries in lowercase because Google ignores uppercase letters anyway.

**POWER SEARCHER TIP**   *If capitalization is really important to you, check out the Google Alert service described in Chapter 11. In a nutshell, this service lets you know whenever something new has been added to Google's search index, and you can specify which characters in your search strings must be uppercase.*

## Use Multiple Search Terms

Google says that most searches consist of just two or three words. Google does the best it can with these cryptic queries, but adding more words to your query will usually provide better results.

Think of how you interact with a librarian, seeking help finding information about the Chinese alternative medicine known as *qigong*. Imagine treating the librarian as a search engine and demanding "qigong!" Most librarians would think you were a stark-raving lunatic. But unlike a compliant search engine that simply gives you results based on your single word command, a good librarian will ask you questions, ferreting out your information need, gradually honing in on what you're really looking for and pointing you to the best sources of information.

Google can't do this—it can't ask you for clarification or further details. It has to guess what you're looking for. But if you provide more clues in your query, such as "qigong chinese medicine internal exercises asthma," Google can zero in much more closely on what you're looking for, surfacing relevant documents and, more importantly, weeding out thousands of less-relevant documents.

## Use Thirty-Two Words or Less

Using more search terms almost always improves your results, but there's a limit. Google only pays attention to the first thirty-two words in your query—any words beyond that limit are ignored. Most queries will safely fall within that limit, but there's a catch: Google counts advanced search commands used in a query toward the thirty-two-word limit. These commands are described in detail in Chapter 4. As a rule of thumb, just be sure that the total number of words and commands in any query is thirty-two or fewer.

## To Quote Is Divine

Chapter 1 described the various methods search engines use to determine relevance. One of the most common techniques is basic word matching that simply looks for occurrences of your search terms anywhere on the page. But this is not helpful if you're searching for words that belong together, in the order you type them, with no other words between them. This is known as a *phrase,* and you can force Google to treat your search terms as a phrase by enclosing your query in double quotes (e.g., "*query*").

Try entering the query **John Smith** without quotation marks. Google returns more than 8.5 million results, as shown in Figure 2-6. Some of these results are relevant, about men named John Smith. Other results, however, have the words John and Smith anywhere on the page, as shown here.

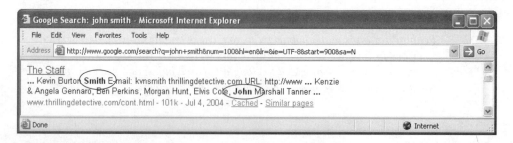

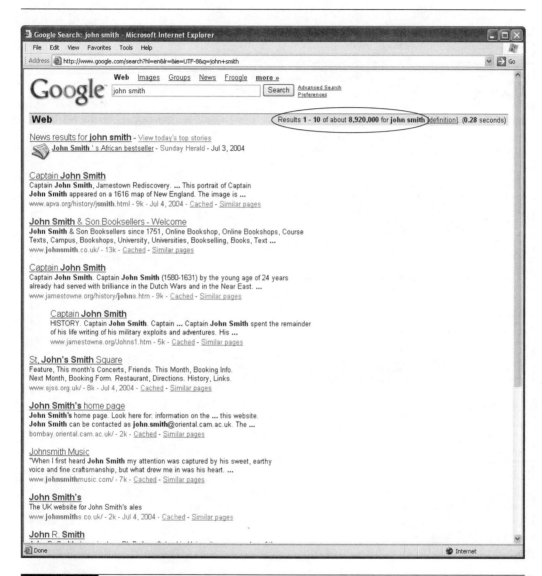

**FIGURE 2-6**   A query for John Smith returns millions of results.

Contrast these results with those returned when "John Smith" is enclosed in double quotes, as shown in Figure 2-7. Although the top ten results are similar, the total number of results has been pruned by more than 90 percent.

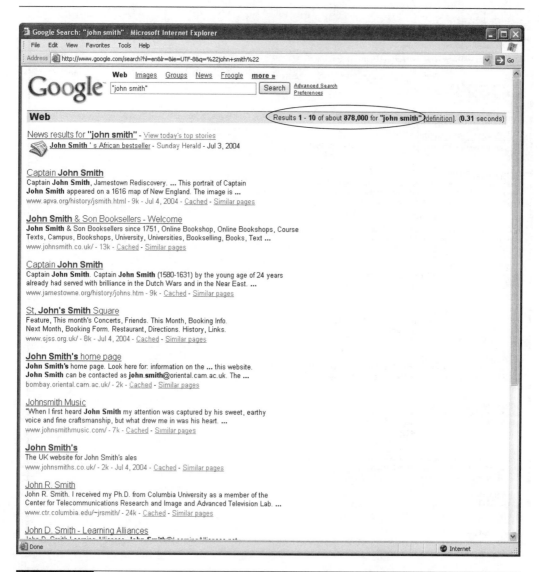

Enclosing a query in double quotes can drastically reduce the total number of results.

# Don't Stumble on Stop Words

Careful—Google ignores some words altogether, as well as certain single letters and digits. These are called *stop words,* and Google ignores them because they are either too common to generate meaningful results or are parts of speech such as adverbs, conjunctions, prepositions, or forms of "be" that mean nothing unless they're part of a phrase with more "important" nouns and verbs. In other words, they are ignored because they convey no meaning in and of themselves, but rather modify the meaning of words they are used with.

Examples of stop words include "the," "be," "or," "from," "about," and so on. Although Google doesn't publish a list of all stop words, it will alert you when you've used a stop word in your query, as seen in Figure 2-8.

**FIGURE 2-8**   Pity poor Shakespeare! Hamlet's famous question is completely ignored by Google.

If stop words are crucial for getting good results for your query (for example, "to be or not to be"), you have two options for forcing Google to include them in your search rather than ignoring them. Your first option is to enclose your query in double quotes, telling Google you want it treated as a phrase. Contrast the results of Figure 2-8 with those in Figure 2-9, which shows the result of enclosing the query "to be or not to be" in double quotes.

The other option is to use the inclusion operator in front of each stop word. This operator is described later in this chapter.

# Speaking in Tongues: Google's Language Tools

You've seen how to change Google's search and interface language via the Preferences page. Google also offers a set of language tools that lets you selectively change your search and interface language, limit your results to pages located in a particular country, and translate text or entire web pages from one language to another. Click the **Language Tools** link on Google's home page to access all of Google's language functions on a single page.

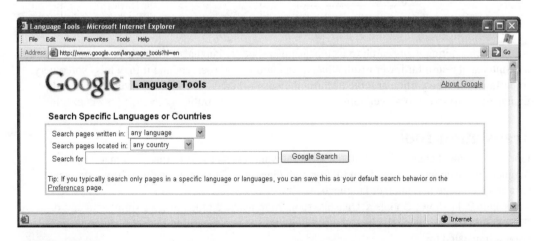

## Search Specific Languages or Countries

The Search Specific Languages or Countries form allows you to change your language preferences for each individual search (see Figure 2-10). Use the drop-down menus to select a search language and/or a specific country and then enter your query in the search box.

**FIGURE 2-10**    This form makes it easy to limit your search to specific languages or countries.

As with limiting your search to web pages in a specific language, limiting your search to a country will return far fewer results than a standard Google search, and it may miss some very important sites on a particular topic because they use a ".com" or other top-level domain rather than the country-code top-level domain, such as ".au" for Australia or ".co.ve" for Venezuela.

## Translation Tools

Google's normal behavior is to find the most relevant results for your query no matter what language the web pages are written in. For many languages, Google has the ability to translate text or a web page into another language.

Figure 2-11 shows Google's Translate tool. To translate a block of text, simply cut and paste the text into the box, and tell Google what language the text is written in and what language you want it translated to.

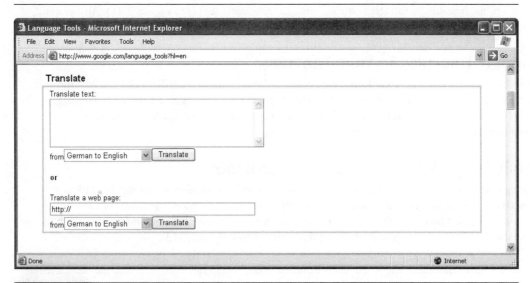

**FIGURE 2-11**    Google's translation tool works on text or entire web pages.

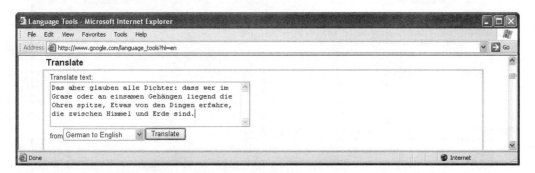

Translating a web page works the same way. Enter the URL of the page you want translated and select the translation languages, and Google will fetch and translate the page, maintaining the format of the page to the extent possible.

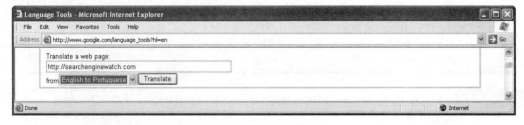

Translation isn't perfect. Google uses sophisticated machine translation programs, but no program can translate text with the skill of a human being, so there will likely be grammatical errors in the translation. Google is also limited to translating text (see Figure 2-11). Any graphic images that contain text will not be translated.

## Google Interface in Your Language

The **Google Interface in Your Language** option (shown in Figure 2-12) works just like the **Interface Language** option on the Preferences page, but only changes the interface language until you close your browser window. When you start your browser again, your interface language is determined by your preferences settings.

## Visit Google's Site in Your Local Domain

Google operates in nearly 100 countries around the world. In addition to having the language interface enabled in the local country's dominant language, the regional versions of Google also have a radio button on the home page that lets you select whether you want your search to include the whole Web or just pages from that country (see Figure 2-13).

**FIGURE 2-12**    Changing the interface language only lasts for the duration of your browser session.

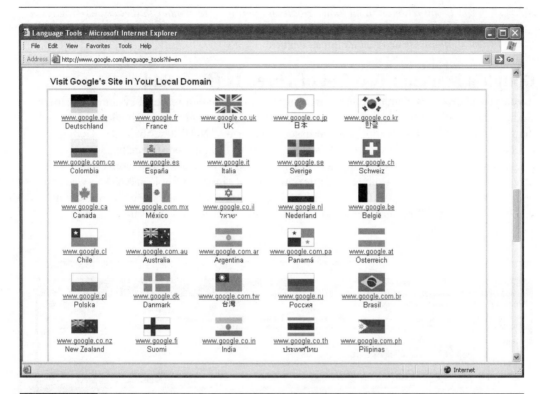

**FIGURE 2-13**    Google offers nearly 100 local versions in countries throughout the world.

# Avoid Bungling with Boolean

All search engines use Boolean logic, based on mathematician George Boole's work with logic and algebra. Boolean logic is deceptive in its simplicity, made up of three simple words: AND, OR, and NOT. Each of these simple words has radically different meanings, and when used with a search engine, they can produce significantly varied effects.

AND essentially means *all*. When a search engine applies a Boolean AND operator to a query, it is looking for pages that have *all* the search terms appearing somewhere on the page. Pages with some but not all the words on the page are excluded from further consideration.

OR essentially means *any*. When a search engine applies a Boolean OR operator to a query, it is looking for pages that have *any* of the search terms appearing somewhere on the page.

NOT means just what it says. When a search engine applies a Boolean NOT operator to a query, it is looking for pages *without* the search term.

Boolean operators seem simple, but in practice they can be tricky to use, because they require a good understanding of logic to be used effectively. While all search engines offer some degree of control using Boolean queries, Google provides relatively little support for user-specified Boolean queries.

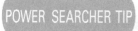  *If you're determined to use Boolean operators, remember that each search engine implements Boolean differently. Be sure to read the help pages to see how Boolean operators work with a given engine.*

## Google's Boolean: Two Out of Three Is (Not) Bad

If you've had experience with another search engine or information-retrieval system with strong Boolean capabilities, you'll be disappointed with what Google has to offer. Google supports only the AND and the OR Boolean operators. It has a weak form of NOT, described later. Google offers no additional Boolean support, such as the ability to form nested statements.

Google uses the AND operator by default with any query of two or more words. This happens behind the scenes. Although Google automatically inserts a Boolean AND between all your search terms, you'll never see the word AND in search results unless you type the word yourself—and that will prompt Google to display a message that the word is unnecessary, as shown in Figure 2-14.

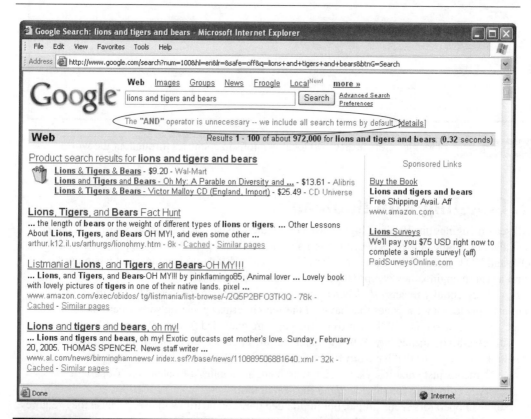

**FIGURE 2-14**    Google automatically puts the Boolean AND operator between your search terms.

Google also supports the Boolean OR operator, used to return pages in search results that contain the search terms on either side of the OR operator. The OR operator *must* be typed in uppercase or Google will treat it as a stop word and ignore it. Unlike the AND operator, which is automatically used for all queries and cannot be explicitly included in your queries, OR will work on any query. Figure 2-15 shows the results of an OR query.

## To OR Is Human

Perhaps no other "advanced" search technique causes more trouble than the incorrect use of the Boolean OR operator. This simple little word, which seems so harmless, can wreak havoc on your search results.

Here's a trick question: What does the word "or" mean? Let's consider two scenarios.

FIGURE 2-15    Search results with the Boolean OR operator

Say you're ordering breakfast, and you ask for the #4 special. Your server asks, "Would you like your eggs fried or scrambled? Toast or biscuit? Coffee or juice?"

In each case, you'd specify one OR the other. You might choose scrambled eggs, toast, and coffee. Or perhaps fried eggs, biscuit, and juice. But for each type of food, you'd get just one of the two possible choices. Simple and straightforward, right?

Now try those same combinations with a search engine. The Boolean OR operator tells the search engine to return results that have either or both of the words in the query. With a search engine as chef, your eggs could be both fried and scrambled, you'd have some mutant pastry that was both toast and biscuit, and your beverage would be a blend of coffee and juice. What a mess!

The simple, seemingly straightforward little word "or" has nearly opposite meanings to people and to search engines. Why? Whereas people think of "or" as being exclusive, excluding all but one option, search engines do the opposite, using the Boolean inclusive OR to return results that include one or all of the terms in a query.

As a rule of thumb, think of "any terms" as the equivalent of OR, and "all terms" as the equivalent of the Boolean AND. "Any terms" will almost always return many more results than "all terms" simply because it's a much looser requirement. In practice, this means that most OR queries return many more results than other types of searches. Bottom line: Unless you're absolutely certain using the OR operator will get you better results, you're better off not using it at all.

# Fun with Other Word Operators

Google supports four other word operators that are useful for controlling search results. Two are similar to the Boolean operators AND and NOT. The other two automatically expand your query to include additional search terms. These four operators are:

- The inclusion operator (+)
- The exclusion operator (−)
- The wildcard (*)
- The "fuzzy" or synonym operator (~)

All these operators work on single words, with the exception of the wildcard operator. They must be typed immediately before the word with no spaces between the word and the operator (for example, +kangaroo, −osmosis, ~photography). The wildcard operator is used by itself to stand in for other words, as shown later in this section.

## Count Me In: The Inclusion Operator

The inclusion operator, the plus sign (+), has one purpose: to force Google to consider stop words in a query that it would otherwise ignore. You've already seen how enclosing a query in double quotes forces all the stop words in a phrase to be included in the search. The inclusion operator works the same way, but on a word-by-word basis rather than on a complete phrase. Figure 2-16 shows an example of this.

It's important to note that using the inclusion operator with all your search terms is not the same as enclosing your search terms in double quotes as a phrase. If you compare the results of Figure 2-8 and Figure 2-16, you'll see that they're not the same, even though the results include all the words in the queries. Why? While the inclusion operator makes sure that all the words in the query are considered, it doesn't make any difference whether they appear together on a result page or not. By contrast, when these words are used in a query as a quoted phrase, they must appear on result pages as that phrase, in exactly the order you typed them.

*Using the inclusion operator is unnecessary for any words other than stop words.*

**POWER SEARCHER TIP**

**FIGURE 2-16**   The inclusion operator forces Google to use stop words that Google otherwise ignores.

## Count Me Out: The Exclusion Operator

Google doesn't support the Boolean NOT operator, but the exclusion operator, the minus sign (–), provides similar functionality, as shown in Figure 2-17.

The exclusion operator is very powerful, especially for queries where you have a common or popular word that takes on very different meanings when used with other words. For example, the word "palm" refers to the inner surface of the hand. It's also a common type of tree. Do a Google search on **palm**, however, and all your results refer to the Palm personal digital assistant, as seen in Figure 2-18.

Using the exclusion operator to remove words such as "pda," "pilot," and "handheld" changes the results dramatically, as Figure 2-19 shows. Of course, your results would be even more relevant if you add additional words to your query, such as "tree," "date," and so on.

You can mix and match search words using the inclusion and exclusion operators together with quoted phrases to fine-tune your search results for maximum effectiveness.

**FIGURE 2-17**    The exclusion operator allows you to eliminate pages containing specific words from search results.

A search for palm returns no trees or hands.

 *The exclusion operator is particularly useful when you're searching for people. Use it to exclude the first names of people you don't want appearing in search results—for example, Barbara Bush −George −Jeb.*

## Match Any Word: The Wildcard Operator

The wildcard operator, the asterisk (*), will match *any* word in a quoted phrase in a query. Figure 2-20 shows how the asterisk was replaced by the words "world," "waves," and so on.

Two important things to note with the wildcard: First, it only works in a quoted phrase. Google ignores the asterisk character if it's used in a query outside of a quoted phrase. Second, results can be unpredictable, as shown in Figure 2-21.

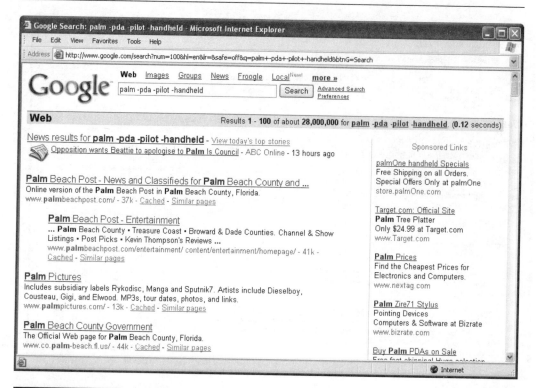

**FIGURE 2-19**    The exclusion operator lets you filter out dominant words that can skew results toward one meaning of a word over another.

**POWER SEARCHER TIP**    *Use the wildcard operator when searching for complex words that are difficult to spell. For example, the query "governor Arnold *" returns very good results for the rather muscular name "Schwarzenegger" (see Figure 2-22).*

## Use Synonyms: The Fuzzy Operator

Google doesn't have an official name for the tilde symbol operator (~), which finds synonyms for a word and includes them in your query. But Google co-founder Sergey Brin called it the "fuzzy" operator in an interview at a Search Engine Strategies conference, so we'll follow his lead.

The fuzzy operator is very useful for surfacing information when you're not exactly sure what search terms will produce the best results. Say you're helping a student with a research

**FIGURE 2-20**    The wildcard can be substituted for any whole word in a query.

project about dinosaurs. You want a broad range of information about dinosaurs. What are the best search words to use? Figure 2-23 shows the results of a search for **dinosaur** and **facts** preceded by the fuzzy operator. This causes Google to look both for the word "facts" as well as related synonyms. In the results, Google has returned results for dinosaur *information,* dinosaur *data,* dinosaur *trivia,* and other synonyms for the word "facts."

The fuzzy operator can also be used as a selective wildcard, saving you the trouble of running multiple searches with different search terms. For example, using the fuzzy operator with the search term "meat" returns results including recipes for beef, pork, lamb, and so on.

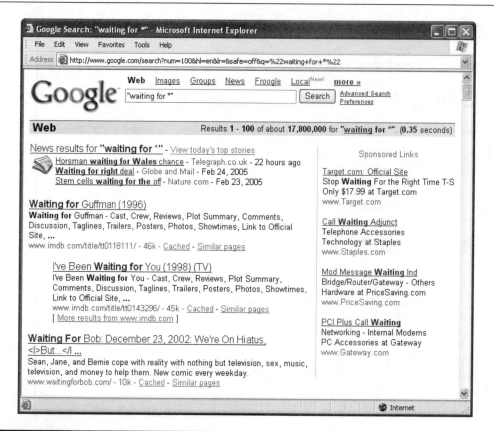

**FIGURE 2-21**  You're never sure what results you'll get with the wildcard operator.

## A Note About Word Variations (Stemming)

In its effort to fully understand your information need, Google expands some queries by using variations of some or all your search terms. This process is called *stemming*. Simple stemming takes the singular form of the word and adds all the plural forms. More complex stemming takes into account the present and past tense forms of words.

When appropriate, Google performs simple stemming on your query, including both the singular and possessive forms of search terms. It will also pick up possessive forms as shown in Figure 2-24.

**FIGURE 2-22**    The wildcard operator is a good substitute for finding difficult-to-spell words.

If you don't want Google to stem your search terms, you can turn stemming off with the inclusion operator. Putting a plus sign before a search terms tells Google you want an exact match for the word, without any variations that may arise from stemming. Using the inclusion operator to turn off stemming is the one exception to the rule that you never need use the inclusion operator on any word other than a stop word.

# Power Searching Strategies

Successful searching requires tuning Google for best performance and using the power tools that it offers. But the best searchers go beyond these mechanics, applying a number of strategies to maximize results. Strategies for finding specific types of information will be offered throughout

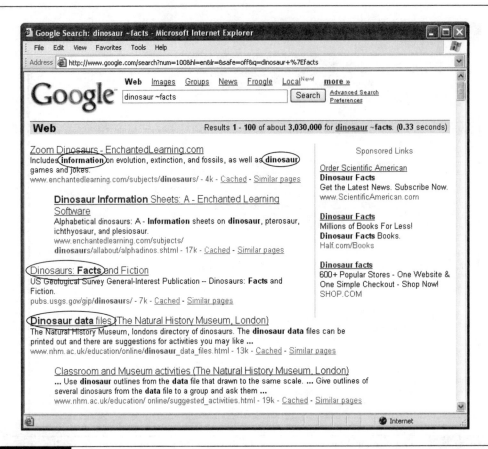

**FIGURE 2-23**   The fuzzy operator matches a wide range of words with similar meanings.

the rest of the book. The following strategies are more general, applicable to any type of searching for virtually any type of information.

## Fill-in-the-Blank Searching

Rather than agonizing over formulating the perfect query, take advantage of Google's ability to "fill in the blank" for the answer to many types of questions.

As you've seen, using explicit phrases can improve your general search results, especially when you're searching for a person's name, the title of a book, song, or other creative work, a famous quotation, and so on.

**FIGURE 2-24** Stemming allows Google to automatically search on singular and possessive forms of words, such as "plutarch" and "plutarch's."

You can go even further with the strategy by searching for phrases already written by other people. Rather than taking the usual approach of "querying" (literally, asking) the search engine, try the opposite. To do this, enter an incomplete phrase into the search box that, if matched, will provide a specific answer. Be sure to enclose your phrase in double quotes.

Remember those "fill-in-the-blank" quizzes you took in school? For example, "RNA stands for _____." If you filled in "ribonucleic acid," your answer would be correct. Well, the Web is so huge that the odds are quite good that someone, somewhere, has written a page with the phrase "RNA stands for" and has "filled in the blank" with an answer. In fact, Figure 2-25 shows just the result we're looking for.

Good writers explain things in ordinary language. For your part, the trick is to create a phrase that someone has likely written and published on the Web. If you do that, and enclose your phrase in double quotes, you'll be surprised how often Google will find documents with the answer you're looking for.

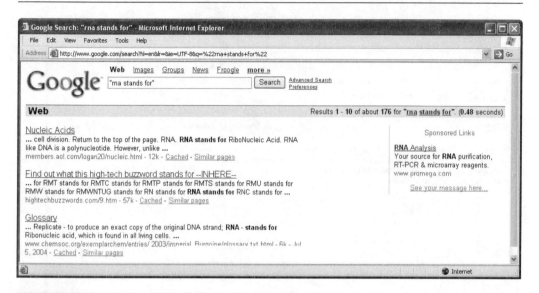

Fill-in-the-blank searching looks for pages where someone has already written most of the words in your search phrase.

It's easy to do. Just change any question into an answer and leave the information you're searching for as the "blank" part of the query. Here are some examples:

■ To find out the name of the current president of Uzbekistan, search on the phrase "the current president of uzbekistan."

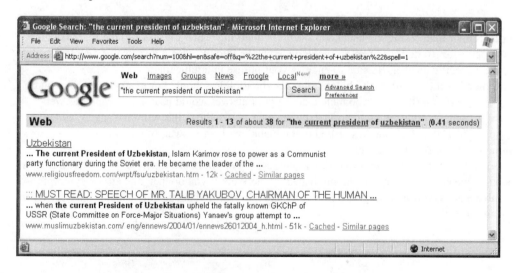

■  To learn which bird species is the most intelligent, search on the phrase "the most intelligent bird species."

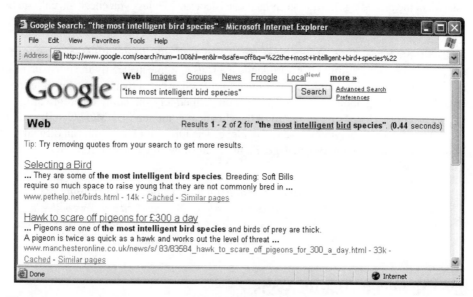

■  To discover the dates that the explorer Magellan circumnavigated the globe, search on the phrase "magellan circumnavigated the globe in."

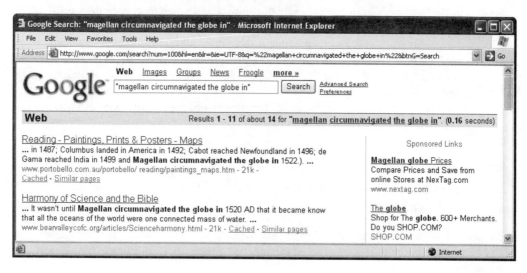

This technique works best for finding factual answers. Be careful, though. Not all "facts" found on the Web are accurate. Note the two different dates reported for Magellan's famous voyage shown in the preceding illustration. Which one is correct? Unless you check an authoritative reference, you can't be certain. (According to the Columbia Encyclopedia, Magellan was killed in 1521.)

As you try these types of "fill-in-the-blank" queries, you'll also discover that the Web is rife with satire, where seemingly straightforward language is used to mean exactly the opposite of its literal meaning. You'll also find multitudes of misinformation, written by people who either don't know what they're talking about or, worse, are bent on deliberately spreading misinformation.

Here's an example. Have you ever heard of the chemical compound DHMO? Google reports nearly 50,000 results for a query on the acronym alone. The top result looks to be an official web site, with some alarming cautionary language. Figure 2-26 shows the home page of this supposed deadly chemical. What is it? Water!

 *Lists can be a great source for finding famous people, the most profitable companies, lists of tips—just about anything. You can find lists by combining a number such as 10 or 100 with a search term and the wildcard symbol—for example, "100 famous *" or "10 poker *" (see Figure 2-27).*

## Beware the Seven Deadly Nyms

Virtuous searching takes more than hard work and clean thinking—you must keep constant vigilance against the seven deadly nyms, which can play the devil with your search results.

When was the last time you thought—really thought—about how you choose the words you enter into search engine query boxes? Did you know there are literally hundreds of words that are virtually guaranteed to produce the worst possible results, no matter how good the search engine?

We've seen how stop words in your queries can cause problems, but there are far more insidious culprits that you should avoid like the plague. These words are the class of search terms I call the "seven deadly nyms."

The first deadly nym is a set of words called *contronyms,* or Janus words. A contronym is a single word that has multiple meanings that contradict the others. Some common contronyms include:

- ■ **Fast** Moving quickly vs. firmly stuck in place
- ■ **Hysterical** Overwhelmed with fear vs. outrageously funny
- ■ **Root** Establish something new vs. dig out completely

The second deadly nym is a group of words known as *heteronyms*—words that are spelled identically but have different meanings when pronounced differently (for example, bow, desert, object, refuse).

Heteronyms can sometimes be the result of melioration, or the acquisition of a positive meaning by a word that has traditionally had a negative meaning. "Bad" is an example. In its original sense, bad means nasty, spoiled, broken, and so on. But pronounced "baad" it takes on the slang meaning that's just the opposite: good, cool, or fashionable.

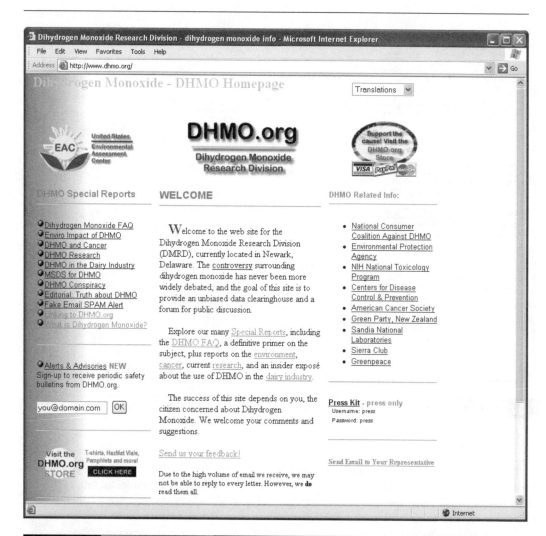

**FIGURE 2-26**    Be careful—some serious-looking web pages are actually parody pages.

A particularly insidious example of a melioration is the word "factoid," which means "a piece of unverified or inaccurate information that is presented in the press as factual, often as part of a publicity effort, and that is then accepted as true because of frequent repetition," according to Dictionary.com.

Watch out for the opposite of heteronyms: polyonyms. These are different words with the same meaning (for example, Jupiter, Zeus, Oden). Depending on what you're looking for, you might miss some important information if you use only one variant of a polyonym. For best results, find and use them all.

**FIGURE 2-27**   The wildcard symbol provides broader results for fill-in-the-blank searches.

For the spelling-challenged, homonyms are the most pernicious deadly nym. Homonyms are words that have the same sound but a completely different meaning (for example, to, too, two). Some homonyms are also contronyms—words that are spelled and pronounced like another word but have a different origin and meaning.

The fifth deadly nym: capitonyms, words that change pronunciation or meaning when capitalized. Capitonyms are common words that become proper nouns when capitalized: For example, amber is a yellow, orange, or brownish-yellow fossil resin; Amber is the eighth-grade softball team captain. You polish silver with ammonia and silicon, though you'd never dream of applying the same to a Polish sausage.

Next up: caconyms. A *caconym* is an erroneous name, especially in taxonomic classification. While caconyms might be useful for tracking down archaic or outdated usage, you're likely to end up with inaccurate information if you use them in search queries.

The seventh deadly nym is the obscure but lethal exonym, especially if you're searching for nonlocal information. An exonym is a place name that foreigners use instead of the name that natives use (for example, Cologne/Köln, Florence/Firenze, Morocco/Maroc). Beyond provoking a chuckle from locals, using exonyms as search terms will likely net results biased toward foreign information, which may not be as accurate as homegrown content.

The next time you're tempted to nym, think before you type. Abstain from nyms and you'll likely end up choosing far better query terms and be blessed with the fruits of a virtuous search.

## Use the "Three Strikes" Rule

Don't let the similarity between the appearance and apparent function of search sites fool you into thinking they are all alike. They aren't. Search sites not only cover different parts of the Web, they use different rules and procedures to analyze your queries and decide what results you will see.

If you've tried a query a few times on Google and aren't getting anywhere, switch to another search engine. Don't waste time thinking up keyword variants or constructing elaborate Boolean queries.

Give a search engine the same number of chances a baseball batter or a convicted criminal gets: Three strikes and it's out.

## Don't Play Favorites

Just as you have favorite foods, people, cars, and so on, it's natural to have a "favorite" search engine. Since you're reading this book, odds are good that yours is Google. In one sense, this is good, because regular practice helps you master a search tool.

But don't succumb to the temptation to rely solely on one search engine for all of your needs. Instead, try to use several search sites on a regular basis, to get a feel for which ones work best for specific types of searches. Over time, it will become automatic for you to select the "best" search engine for each query from among several that you know well.

Although the focus of this book is Google (with good reason), Google isn't always the best choice. For that reason, I'll show you dozens of alternatives to Google that will give you good results for certain types of queries—often much better than Google itself. It's fine to use Google as your favorite search engine, but just remember that there are literally hundreds, if not thousands, of alternatives that might provide just the results you're looking for.

# Chapter 3

## Deconstructing Google Search Results

Like just about everything with Google, search results are clean, sparse, and straightforward. In many cases, all you need to do is take a quick glance at a result page, click a promising link, and you'll be transported to a web page that provides the information you're looking for.

For all its simplicity, a Google result page offers a wealth of understated information, providing valuable clues that can save you time and help you select the best results *before* clicking any links. Even if you consider yourself a Google expert, take the time to skim through this chapter—you'll likely be surprised at what you'll learn.

# Anatomy of a Search Result

Figure 3-1 shows a typical Google search result page. All Google search result pages have four essential parts:

- **Organic search results**    "Natural" results found from crawling the Web
- **Sponsored links**    Paid advertisements
- **Statistics**    Information about your search
- **Controls**    Links, buttons, and other navigation aids

Depending on your search terms, result pages may also include "one-box" results, with information drawn from Google's news, product, image, or other catalogs.

Notice that your search terms are highlighted in boldface on a result page. This is true regardless of whether the terms appear in organic results or sponsored links. Boldface type makes your search terms stand out, allowing you to quickly grasp the context of each result.

Most Google users focus on the organic search results—and with good reason. Organic search results are what most people expect from a search engine: pages discovered on the Web containing specific content that has the most relevance to a particular query. But the other parts—sponsored links, statistics, and controls—each have a valuable function as well. Let's take a closer look at each of these components in more detail.

## Organic Search Results

Organic search results (sometimes called *algorithmic* or *editorial results*) are links to web pages, images, news stories, and other online content that Google has discovered on its own and has determined represent the best matches for your search terms. Google displays organic search results on the left side of a result page, and they are by far the most prominent part of the page (see Figure 3-2).

Organic results are "pure" in the sense that Google has not accepted any money from web page authors, advertisers, or anyone else to include these web pages in search results, or to give one result a higher ranking than another. Organic results are the product of Google's objective approach to discovering content by crawling the Web and assessing the relevance of content using the dozens of techniques described in Chapter 1.

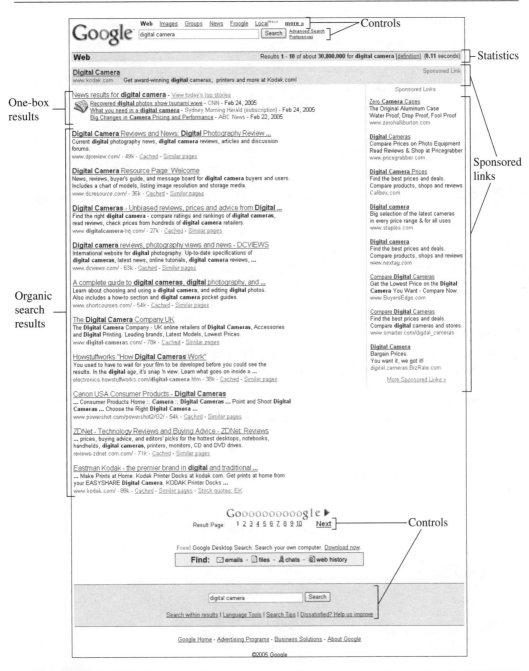

**FIGURE 3-1**   A typical Google search result page

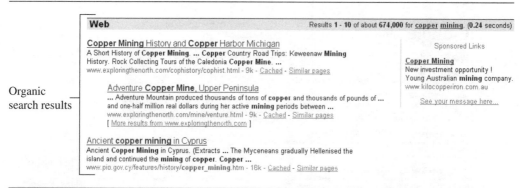

Organic
search results

**FIGURE 3-2**   Organic results are displayed prominently on the left side of a search result page.

Most searchers gravitate to organic search results. If you're searching for information, facts, or an answer to a specific question, organic results typically are the best source for finding what you're looking for. But if you're looking to buy a product or service, or are researching options before you buy, you should consider looking at the sponsored links, as well.

## Sponsored Links

Sponsored links are *advertisements*. Just like graphical banner or pop-up ads, sponsored links are purchased by advertisers who hope to get your attention, your click, and ultimately your business.

Sponsored links can appear in two places on a search result page. Most commonly, they appear to the right of organic search results, in a much narrower column, as shown in Figure 3-3.

Sponsored links

**FIGURE 3-3**   For most queries, sponsored links appear in a narrow column to the right of organic search results.

For certain queries that have a very clear commercial (as opposed to informational) intent, Google will also display up to two sponsored links directly above the organic search results, with a shaded background to differentiate them, as shown in Figure 3-4. Ads that get placed in the top one or two spots above organic results have been reviewed and approved by Google, and they meet an additional level of performance based on the relevance of the ad to the search terms.

Google's advertising policy requires the content of sponsored links to be relevant to the search terms for which they appear. Although they are usually relevant for your search terms, and are visually similar to organic search results, sponsored links are completely different, in a number of ways.

The first difference lies in how Google determines what results are displayed and the order in which they appear. Organic results represent Google's assessment of the most relevant content found on the Web for your query, regardless of source and without any financial consideration for inclusion or position of the result. By contrast, sponsored links are displayed solely because they match one or more of your search terms, and their position on a result page is largely determined by the amount an advertiser is willing to pay when someone clicks the sponsored link.

Anyone can purchase a sponsored link—all it takes is a credit card and a $5 registration fee, and you, too, can create a listing that will be displayed on Google search result pages for just about any search terms you choose. Google claims more than 100,000 unique advertisers use its sponsored links program, called AdWords.

To purchase a sponsored link, an advertiser signs up for Google's AdWords program and then selects the search terms that will trigger the display of the advertisement. The advertiser then places a bid representing an amount of money they are willing to pay Google any time a searcher

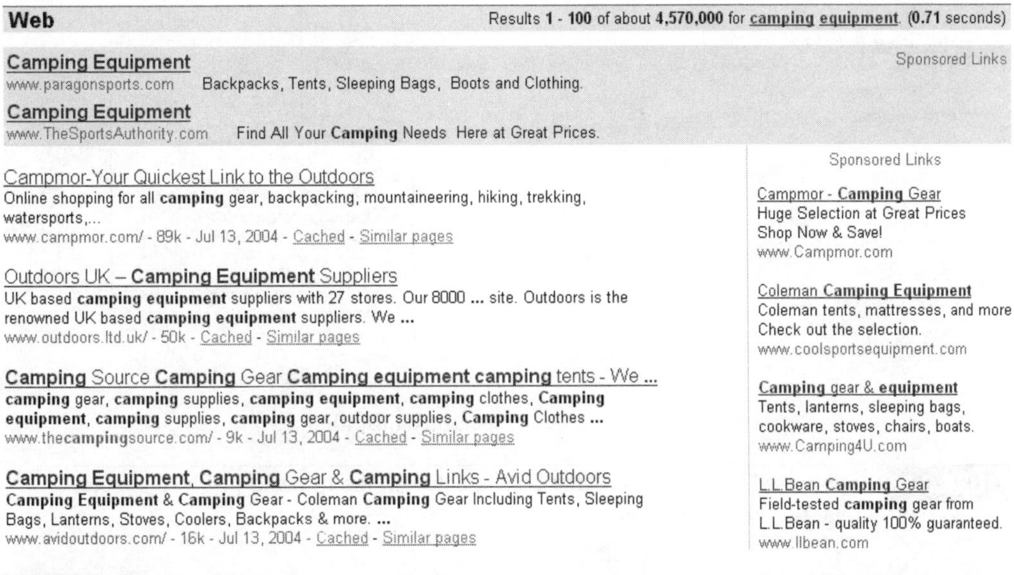

---

**Web**                                          Results **1 - 100** of about **4,570,000** for <u>camping equipment</u>. **(0.71 seconds)**

**Camping Equipment**                                                              Sponsored Links
www.paragonsports.com    Backpacks, Tents, Sleeping Bags, Boots and Clothing.
**Camping Equipment**
www.TheSportsAuthority.com    Find All Your **Camping** Needs Here at Great Prices.

Campmor-Your Quickest Link to the Outdoors                            Sponsored Links
Online shopping for all **camping** gear, backpacking, mountaineering, hiking, trekking,
watersports,...                                                    Campmor - **Camping** Gear
www.campmor.com/ - 89k - Jul 13, 2004 - Cached - Similar pages       Huge Selection at Great Prices
                                                                     Shop Now & Save!
                                                                     www.Campmor.com
Outdoors UK – **Camping Equipment** Suppliers
UK based **camping equipment** suppliers with 27 stores. Our 8000 ... site. Outdoors is the    **Coleman Camping Equipment**
renowned UK based **camping equipment** suppliers. We ...              Coleman tents, mattresses, and more
www.outdoors.ltd.uk/ - 50k - Cached - Similar pages                  Check out the selection.
                                                                     www.coolsportsequipment.com
**Camping** Source **Camping** Gear **Camping equipment camping** tents - We ...
**camping** gear, **camping** supplies, **camping equipment**, **camping** clothes, **Camping**    **Camping** gear & **equipment**
**equipment**, **camping** supplies, **camping** gear, outdoor supplies, **Camping** Clothes ...    Tents, lanterns, sleeping bags,
www.thecampingsource.com/ - 9k - Jul 13, 2004 - Cached - Similar pages    cookware, stoves, chairs, boats.
                                                                     www.Camping4U.com
**Camping Equipment, Camping** Gear & **Camping** Links - Avid Outdoors
**Camping Equipment** & **Camping** Gear - Coleman **Camping** Gear Including Tents, Sleeping    L.L.Bean **Camping** Gear
Bags, Lanterns, Stoves, Coolers, Backpacks & more. ...                Field-tested **camping** gear from
www.avidoutdoors.com/ - 16k - Jul 13, 2004 - Cached - Similar pages    L.L.Bean - quality 100% guaranteed.
                                                                     www.llbean.com

**FIGURE 3-4**    Sponsored links with the highest relevance (measured by actual click-through rates) can appear above organic search results.

clicks the sponsored link. Google does not charge to display a sponsored link—an advertiser pays only when a searcher clicks a sponsored link. In general, the greater the amount of the bid, the higher up a sponsored link will appear on a result page (though Google also counts how often people click sponsored links, and boosts the positions of those that get more clicks even if others have higher bids). The Google AdWords program is described in more detail in Chapter 19.

**POWER SEARCHER TIP** *To learn more about Google's advertising programs, and how to sign up as an advertiser, see http://www.google.com/ads/.*

Sponsored links differ from organic results in another very important way. For organic results, Google analyzes the full text of a web page, looks at its link popularity, and considers dozens of other factors to try to come up with the best possible results for your search terms. By contrast, Google does almost no analysis of sponsored links (other than a brief editorial review to make sure the listing is relevant to the search terms). There's no full-text analysis—sponsored links are limited to a single line title of 25 characters and two lines of description no longer than 35 characters each, as shown in Figure 3-5.

Furthermore, clicking a sponsored link takes you to any page of the advertiser's choosing. Your search terms may or may not appear on this "landing page." The only connection between your search terms and the page you see after clicking a sponsored link is that the advertiser is willing to bet you'll find it relevant enough to pay Google a finder's fee for getting you to the page.

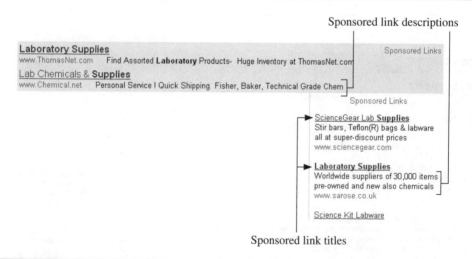

**FIGURE 3-5** Sponsored links are limited to 25 characters in the title and just 70 characters total for the description.

## Statistics

The pale shaded bar below the search box and immediately above the results is called the Statistics Bar. The left side of the Statistics Bar shows you which catalog results have been drawn from: Web, Images, Groups, News, Froogle, and so on. On the right, Google reports the number of results being displayed (based on your preference), an estimate of the total number of results found for your query, your search terms (linked to dictionary definitions; see Chapter 5), and the amount of time taken by the search. The following illustration shows the Statistics Bar.

| **Web** | Results **1** - **10** of about **1,290,000** for <u>south beach</u> <u>diet</u>. **(0.29** seconds) |
|---|---|

While these statistics are interesting, they're really not very useful. In fact, they can be misleading. It's increasingly common to see newspaper or magazine journalists use the total number of search results as a proxy for popularity. For example, a Google search for **south beach diet** returns more than 1 million results, but that doesn't mean a million web pages have information about the nutritional program. Rather, it means that the words "south" and "beach" and "diet" were found on most of those pages, anywhere on the page, and not necessarily together or even near one another. For some of those results, in fact, the search words don't appear at all—they only appear in links pointing to pages. In short, the number of results reported by Google as an indicator of popularity is a flawed measure at best, and completely misleading at worst.

POWER SEARCHER TIP *A large number of search results can be an indicator that your search terms are too general or too broad. Whenever Google reports millions of results and you can't find good information, consider running your search again with more specific, focused search terms.*

## Controls

Controls on a result page allow you to navigate to additional result pages, or alter your search to get different results. Let's start with the controls that let you get additional search results beyond the first page.

At the bottom of the result page, beneath the stretched out "Goooooooooogle" logo, are links to ten additional result pages, as shown next. Click one of these links and you'll see additional result pages.

**South Beach Diet|**Information about the **diet**
**South Beach Diet**. Information about the **South Beach Diet** and links to the webs best weight loss resources. ... **South Beach Diet** Information. ... The **South Beach Diet**. ...
www.thecolumn.org/**south-beach-diet**.asp - 11k - Jul 11, 2004 - <u>Cached</u> - <u>Similar pages</u>

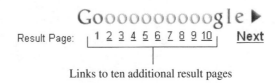

Result Page:  1 2 3 4 5 6 7 8 9 10  **Next**

Links to ten additional result pages

By default, Google displays links to ten result pages at a time. Click link 10 and you'll see a new set of links for result pages 11-19. Click link 19 and the list expands to include result pages 20-28, and so on, as shown in Figure 3-6.

POWER SEARCHER TIP

*To see more than ten search results per page, click the **Preferences** link and change the number of search results setting to a higher number.*

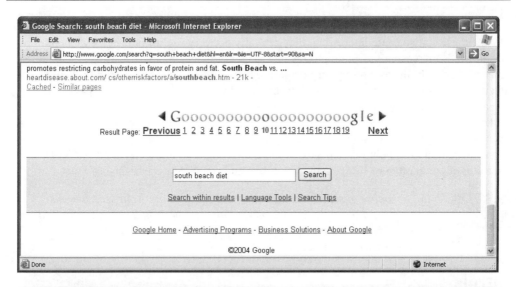

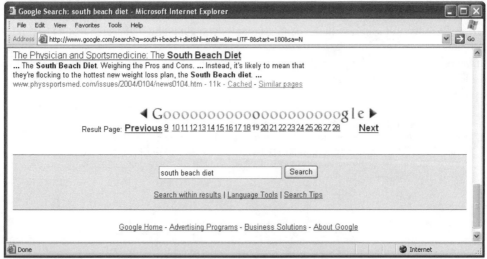

FIGURE 3-6    Click the rightmost link to access an additional set of ten result pages.

Google places a limit on the total number of results you can see for a query, typically somewhere in the range of 700–900 results. This is true even if Google reports thousands or millions of results for your query on the Statistics Bar. Take the search term "travel," for example. Even though Google reports 170 million results for **travel**, clicking through to the last result page with the results display set to 100 (the maximum settings), you'll run into a roadblock. Despite reporting such a massive number of web pages found for the query, Google will only display the first 900 or so—this number will vary based on a number of factors, and it will rarely be the same even from day to day.

Why the limitation? Because most people never click past the first page of search results. Still fewer make it past the second or third page of results. Virtually nobody takes the time to slog through up to 900 results. By limiting total results, Google eliminates costly processing time that is better used making searches faster for everyone.

You can get past this apparent limit on the number of results displayed, however. Another control at the bottom of the result page allows you to search within results.

Click the link and you'll see a new search form, as shown in Figure 3-7.

Enter additional search terms in this form that will help Google narrow your search. No need to repeat your original search terms; Google remembers them and adds your new search terms to the original query.

Google also provides a number of controls on a result page that let you easily run your search in one of Google's other catalogs without having to retype your query. By default, Google will always run your search against its catalog of web pages. Would you rather see pictures, or get the latest news? At the top of the page is a set of "top links" that let you quickly access Google's different catalogs.

Top links

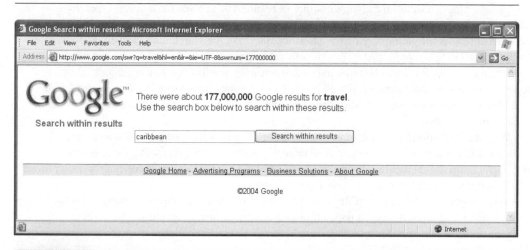

**FIGURE 3-7**    Searching within results is a good way to refine your query.

Whenever you enter a query and run a search, your search terms are always carried along and displayed in the search box of a result page. Clicking one of the top links runs your search in that catalog.

Still not happy with your search results? A control to the right of the search button on all result pages takes you to an advanced search page (shown next), described in detail in the next two chapters.

**POWER SEARCHER TIP**    *Be sure to click the **more** » top link to explore more than a dozen different Google catalogs and services.*

## Message from Google

Sometimes your particular choice of search terms will trigger a message from Google. These messages can appear directly under the search box or at the top of search results. In Chapter 2, you saw the message Google generates when your search terms are stop words: *The following words are very common and were not included in your search.* Two other common messages, displayed above search results, are triggered when Google has a spelling suggestion or has a tip to help you potentially improve your search.

"Did you mean" messages are spelling suggestions. Google doesn't look up search terms in a dictionary. Rather, it looks at the occurrences of words on actual web pages and will suggest alternate spellings when one version of a word appears more frequently on the Web than another.

"Tip" messages appear when Google detects that your search might be more effective if you were to try a different approach to your query. For example, if your query is a very long, quoted phrase, Google might offer the following tip: *Try removing quotes from your search to get more results*. Other tips suggest using different catalogs, such as Google Images for finding pictures.

**Web**        Results 1 - 100 of about **106,000** for **disneyland** <u>address</u> <u>anaheim</u>. (**0.52** seconds)

Tip: Find maps by searching for a street address with city or zip code

# The Parts of Organic Results

Organic web results are links to web pages that Google has selected as the most relevant pages on the Web for a particular query. In these results, Google provides numerous clues about what you can expect to find on a web page, along with a number of useful tools that can really help you narrow your options, even before you click a link.

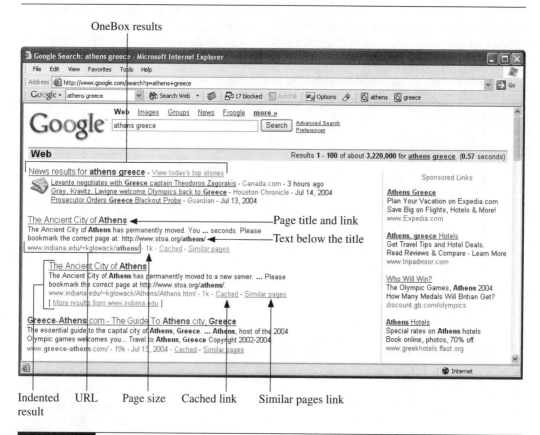

OneBox results

Page title and link

Text below the title

Indented result    URL    Page size    Cached link    Similar pages link

**FIGURE 3-8**    The parts of organic search results

Figure 3-8 shows a typical set of organic search results, with the major parts labeled. Let's take a closer look at the wealth of information Google has provided in these search results.

## OneBox Results

As mentioned, Google searches its catalog of web pages by default. However, for many queries, Google also looks beyond its catalog of web pages to other sources of information, attempting to locate relevant results. In some cases, OneBox results will be drawn from multiple sources, as shown in Figure 3-9.

Google will often find OneBox results when your search terms suggest you're looking for news, stock quotes, airport conditions, local web sites, and various other types of specialized information. These additional links are called OneBox results because they are automatically

OneBox results

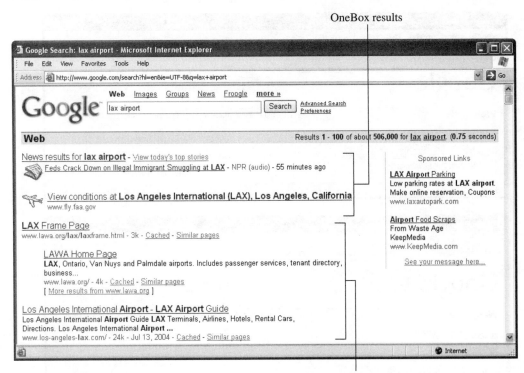

Organic search results

**FIGURE 3-9**    OneBox results for this query show both news headlines and travel conditions at Los Angeles International Airport.

included in web results—you don't have to search from a special box to see them. Figure 3-10 shows a composite of several of these types of OneBox search results.

OneBox results are effectively shortcuts to other sources of information beyond what Google found from searching its index of web pages. More types of OneBox results are described in Chapter 5.

# Page Title and Link

The first line of a result is the title of the underlying web page. This is the HTML title created by the author of the page. It's important to understand that the HTML title is a special component of a web page that isn't actually displayed in your browser window. Rather, the title is displayed in the title bar at the very top of your browser. Figure 3-11 shows the underlying code of an HTML title on a web page and how it is displayed in the title bar of the browser.

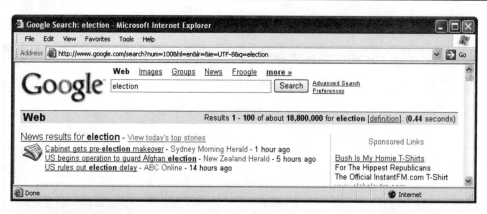

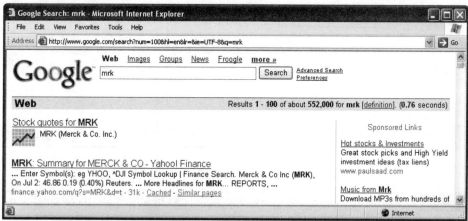

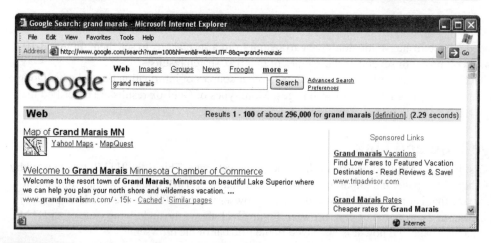

**FIGURE 3-10**    OneBox results for news, stock quotes, and local information

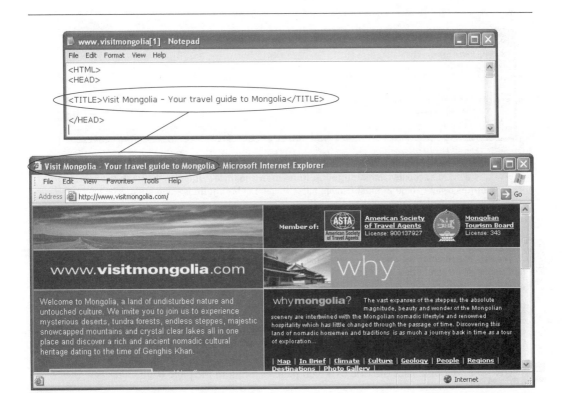

FIGURE 3-11    An HTML title is displayed in the browser's title bar, not as part of the web page itself.

Google uses page titles as hyperlinks for organic results. Clicking a link will cause your browser to request a page directly from the web server where the page is stored, and the page will then be downloaded to your computer. As mentioned in Chapter 1, whether the page you see matches what you expect from the search result depends on when Google last crawled the page. Figure 3-12 shows how Google uses the page title as a hyperlink.

Sometimes a result appears as just a bare-bones, hyperlinked URL without a descriptive title. In these cases, Google has not indexed the page at all. Instead, it has found the URL of the page elsewhere on the Web. By analyzing pages that link to the URL, particularly the anchor text in links that describes the page, Google can confidently display the URL as a relevant search result, even without having a copy of the page itself. Figure 3-13 shows an example of a result that Google has not indexed.

FIGURE 3-12    Google uses the title of a web page as a link to the page itself.

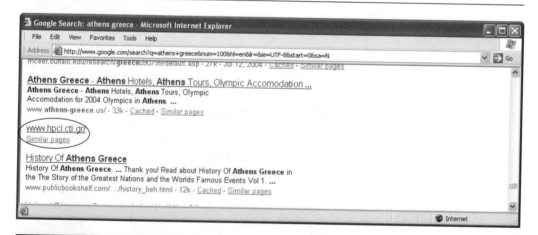

FIGURE 3-13    An unindexed search result, displaying only a hyperlinked URL

3

*The telltale sign that a page has not been indexed by Google is the absence of a **Cached** link in the search result. All pages that have been indexed are cached. The cache feature is described in more detail later in this chapter.*

Why wouldn't Google index a URL that it knows about? The crawler may have technical problems accessing a page, particularly if the URL is complex or the page is served by a content management system that's difficult for Google's crawler to access. Occasionally, the web page author may have forgotten to give the page a title, or deliberately omitted it. Lacking a title to display, Google uses the URL of the page as a link instead. In other cases, the page author may have used the special `noarchive` meta tag mentioned in Chapter 16 to prevent Google from indexing the page.

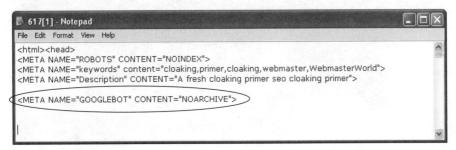

## Text Below the Title

Immediately below the title, you'll typically see two lines of text describing the web page. This text is a snippet that Google has created to describe or summarize the page. Snippets are created dynamically, based on your search terms, and can come from several different sources.

First, Google tries to locate your search terms on the web page. If it can find a meaningful chunk of text that uses any or all of your search terms in context, this text is extracted from the page and used as a snippet (see Figure 3-14). It doesn't matter where the snippet text is located on the page—it can be near the top, in the middle, or even at the bottom of the page, as long as it's relevant to your search terms.

Sometimes several chunks of text are used. When multiple snippets are used, they are separated by an ellipsis. Occasionally, Google will extract a snippet from the meta tags in the head portion of the page and may combine it with text extracted from the body of the page.

Google also has the ability to create snippets for pages that have little or no text in either the meta tags or on the page body. How? By using descriptive text from other pages found elsewhere on the Web that link to the page.

Sometimes you'll see a search result that has no snippet at all. Similar to results showing just a URL, these results are pages that typically have no descriptive text anywhere on them and, furthermore, may have no external links pointing to them. Lacking this information, how does

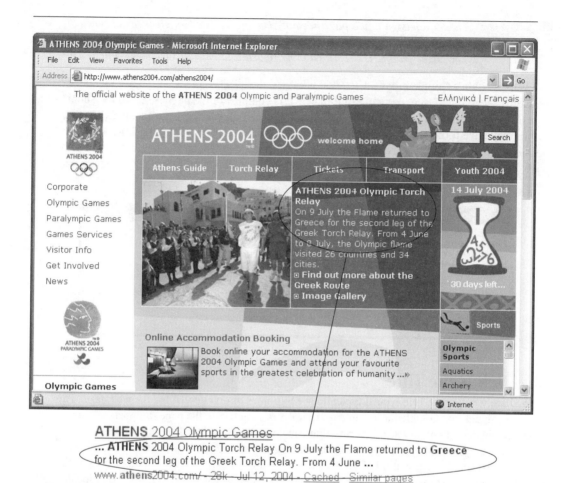

FIGURE 3-14   Google extracted text from the middle of the page to form this snippet.

Google know they are good results? Typically these pages will be interior pages of authoritative web sites that Google already has plenty of information about. The ranking of other pages on the site has, to a degree, been inherited by these pages.

## URL of a Result

For savvy searchers, the URL of a search result provides some of the most revealing information about a page, offering even more clues about the potential value of the page than the title or snippet description. Why? Because a URL often reveals the source and authority of the information—or lack of it.

3

The result for **The Ancient City of Athens** (www.indiana.edu/~kglowack/athens/) is located on the web servers of Indiana University. By convention, a tilde (~) symbol in a URL suggests that this is a personal page created by a faculty member, rather than being official content from an academic department. Google returned this as the number one result for the search terms **Athens Greece**, so it's likely a very good source of information. But the URL tells us two very important things, even before we look at the page itself—that it is a personal page and that it's located in the United States. If you're looking for information directly from a source in Greece, you should look elsewhere.

The Ancient City of **Athens**
The Ancient City of **Athens** has permanently moved. You ... seconds. Please
bookmark the correct page at: http://www.stoa.org/**athens**/
www.indiana.edu/~kglowack/**athens**/ - 1k - Cached - Similar pages

The result for **Athens 2004 Olympic Games** (www.athens2004.com) is the official site of the Olympic Games. In the past, official sites for major events typically registered with .org top-level domain names, but it has become increasingly common for nonprofit or community-oriented organizations around the world to create sites using the .com top-level domain.

**ATHENS** 2004 Olympic Games
02 July 2004. 42 days left... The official website of the **ATHENS** 2004
Olympic and Paralympic Games, ... **ATHENS** 2004 Tickets. The Olympic ...
www.**athens**2004.com/ - 28k - Cached - Similar pages

The following illustration shows an example of a result for a web site that's actually located in Greece—the URL is part of the top-level ".gr" (Greece) domain. If you're looking for sites within a particular country, looking for country codes in a URL is a good way to quickly identify native sites. Not all sites use country code top-level domains. In fact, anyone located anywhere in the world can register sites with other top-level domains, such as .com and .org, so the country code domain is not a flawless indicator of a web site's location.

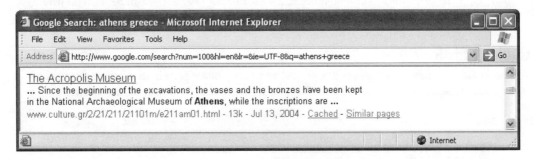

POWER SEARCHER TIP

*Sometimes a top-level country code domain has little to do with a country. For example, the country Tuvalu has licensed its ".tv" top-level domain, and many sites using it are involved in the television industry and have no physical presence in Tuvalu at all.*

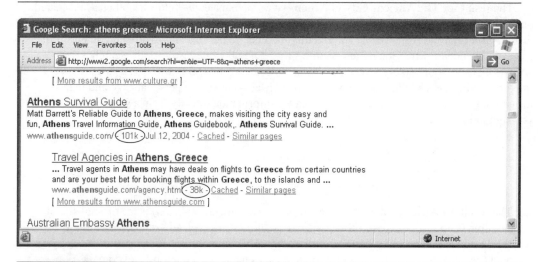

FIGURE 3-15   The page size offers a good clue about the substance (or lack thereof) of a web page.

## Page Size

Next to the URL, Google reports the size of the text portion of a web page in kilobytes (see Figure 3-15). This can be a useful indicator of what to expect—larger numbers generally indicate pages with richer content, or pages that have lots of links for further exploration. Smaller numbers indicate less text.

*Google indexes only the first 101K of text on a web page and the first 120K of PDF files, so although the size indicator isn't perfect, it can be a useful way to filter out skimpy pages that might have little or no value for your purposes.*

## Cached Link

Whenever Google crawls and indexes a page, it stores a copy of the page in its database, also known as the *cache*. In search results, the **Cached** link appears next to the page size, as shown here:

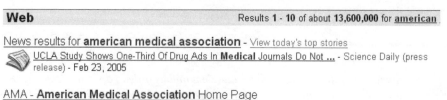

The **Cached** link is useful for several reasons. Clicking the **Cached** link shows you an exact copy of the page that Google indexed (see Figure 3-16). This means that even if you get an unexpected page when you click a result link, you'll still be able to see the page that Google saw at crawl time. The cached page remains available until Google reindexes the page, anywhere from a day or two to 30 days later.

Cached pages are displayed with a header with several useful tidbits of information. Perhaps most importantly, Google tells you when the page was retrieved for indexing and provides a reminder that the page may have changed since Google last crawled and indexed it. Want to see the latest version? Click the link to see the current version of the page. Google recently introduced a new command that displays the contents of a cached page showing only the text of the page, without any images (see Figure 3-17). Examining the cached copy of a page without images is a good way to study how Google "thinks," because the indexing process looks primarily at the text on the page when calculating relevance.

Your search terms are also highlighted on a cached copy of a page, making it easy to locate them on the page itself.

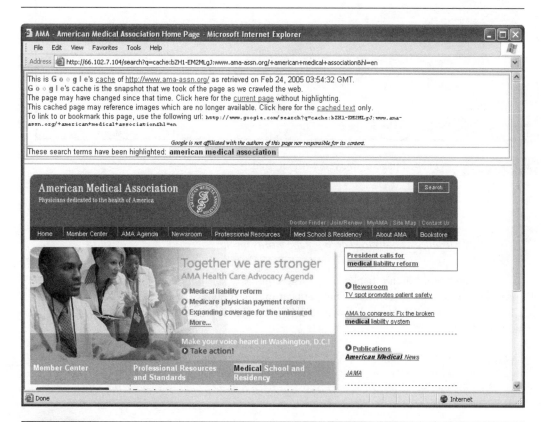

**FIGURE 3-16**    This is the page that Google's crawler fetched for indexing.

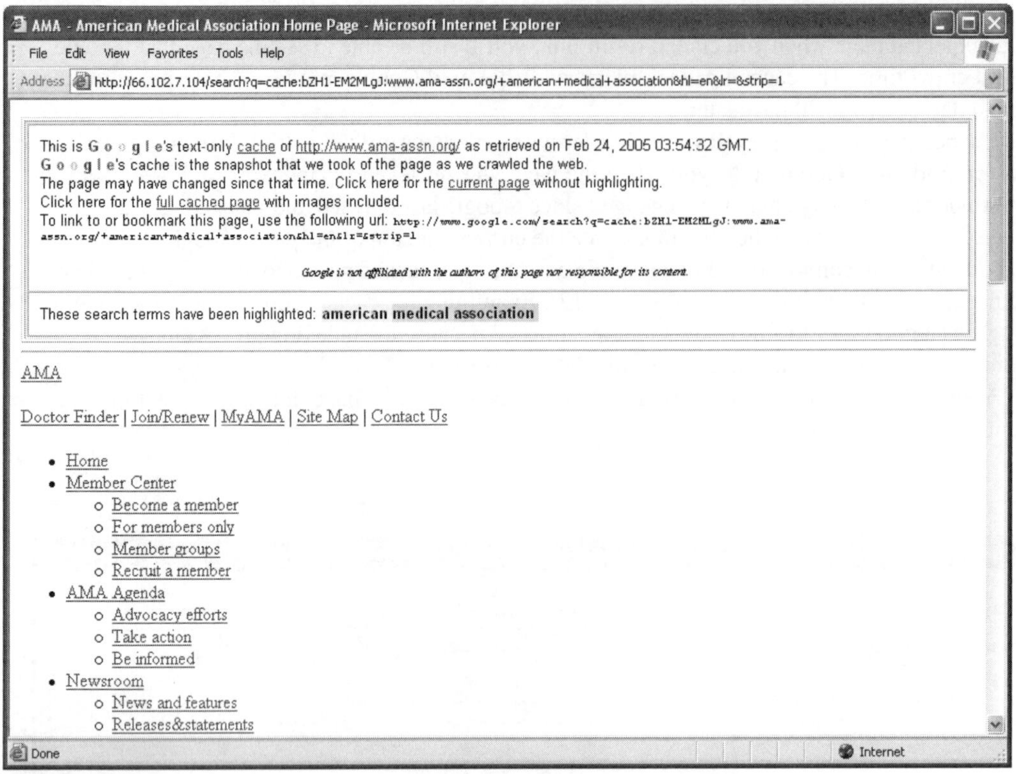
AMA - American Medical Association Home Page - Microsoft Internet Explorer
File Edit View Favorites Tools Help
Address http://66.102.7.104/search?q=cache:bZH1-EM2MLgJ:www.ama-assn.org/+american+medical+association&hl=en&lr=&strip=1
This is Google's text-only cache of http://www.ama-assn.org/ as retrieved on Feb 24, 2005 03:54:32 GMT.
Google's cache is the snapshot that we took of the page as we crawled the web.
The page may have changed since that time. Click here for the current page without highlighting.
Click here for the full cached page with images included.
To link to or bookmark this page, use the following url: http://www.google.com/search?q=cache:bZH1-EM2MLgJ:www.ama-assn.org/+american+medical+association&hl=en&lr=&strip=1
Google is not affiliated with the authors of this page nor responsible for its content.
These search terms have been highlighted: american medical association
AMA
Doctor Finder | Join/Renew | MyAMA | Site Map | Contact Us
Home
Member Center
Become a member
For members only
Member groups
Recruit a member
AMA Agenda
Advocacy efforts
Take action
Be informed
Newsroom
News and features
Releases&statements
Done
Internet

**FIGURE 3-17** A cached page displayed without images

**POWER SEARCHER TIP** *To locate search terms on a long web page, use your browser's "Find" command (usually* CTRL-F*) to search for the words on the page.*

If your search terms aren't displayed anywhere in the title, snippet, or URL of a search result, it's probably because the search terms only appear in links pointing to the page. In these cases, you'll see a message in the header of a cached page that your search terms only appear in links pointing to the page.

**POWER SEARCHER TIP** *Because Google is optimized for speedy performance, clicking a **Cached** link is often a faster way to access a page than clicking the title link, especially if the Internet is slow or you're trying to fetch a page from a server on the other side of the world.*

# Similar Pages Link

Google automatically finds and recommends pages that are similar or related to those appearing in search results. Click the **Similar pages** link (shown next) and you'll see a list of pages that are conceptually related to a particular page.

| Web | Results **1 - 100** of about **378,000** for **louvre museum** |
|---|---|

**Louvre Museum** Official Website - [ Translate this page ]
**Louvre Museum** Official Website.
www.**louvre**.fr/**louvre**a.htm - 2k - Cached - Similar pages

For example, if you want to find pages that are similar to the home page of the Louvre Museum, clicking the **Similar pages** link will display results for web sites of several other notable art museums around the world, as well as a number of links to art information resources.

This function can be a useful way to find related content, but you'll find that results vary considerably depending on your starting page. You'll get the best results from prominent pages, such as home pages or pages that have many other pages linking to them. These pages tend to have a higher PageRank, allowing Google to make recommendations with more confidence than it can by comparing less prominent pages.

# Indented Results

Google always tries to present a broad section of results from across the Web. To provide this broad set of results, Google usually only includes one page from any given site in search results. However, when it finds more than one highly relevant result from a web site, Google will display two results from that site, with the "best" result listed first, and the "next-best" result indented immediately beneath it.

| Web | Results **1 - 100** of about **199,000** for **solar flare** |
|---|---|

**Solar Flare** Theory
... a glance into the future of **solar flare** research. In these pages we address the general questions: ... next arrowNext: What is a **Solar Flare**? ...
hesperia.gsfc.nasa.gov/sftheory/ - 12k - Cached - Similar pages

> **Solar Flares**
> What is a **Solar Flare**? A **flare** is defined ... Full Disk Corona with **Flare** Soft x-ray image of a **solar flare** on the Sun. As the magnetic energy ...
> hesperia.gsfc.nasa.gov/sftheory/**flare**.htm - 9k - Cached - Similar pages
> [ More results from hesperia.gsfc.nasa.gov ]

In this case, Google also adds a **More results from...** link at the end of the indented result, which lets you see a full list of pages from that site that are relevant to your search terms. This approach strikes a good balance between breadth and depth, showcasing sites with lots of high-quality content without overwhelming results from sites that may have just a single relevant page that matches your search terms.

POWER SEARCHER TIP    *You can restrict your results to a single web site using the Advanced Search page described in the next chapter.*

## Omitted Results

Because Google returns only a maximum of two results per site for any search, it often leaves out many results that are similar to those displayed. These omitted pages typically are duplicates or nearly identical copies of pages that already show up in results. By omitting them, Google is helping you save time by filtering out redundant information. Google will often indicate in the Statistics Bar when it is only displaying partial results (see Figure 3-18).

You can override this filtering by clicking to the very last page of the search results, where you will see the message and link shown in Figure 3-19. Click the link to repeat the search with the omitted results included.

In most cases, this is a waste of time, because you'll only be seeing duplicate content. But in some cases, you'll find that Google has omitted results that might be quite useful.

As a rule of thumb, you're probably better off letting Google omit duplicate results rather than repeating the query, unless you're really stuck. Varying your search terms, or even trying another search engine, is a better strategy than wading through duplicate results.

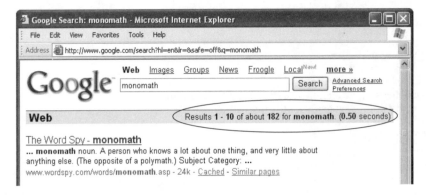

FIGURE 3-18    Google is omitting more results than it is showing for this query.

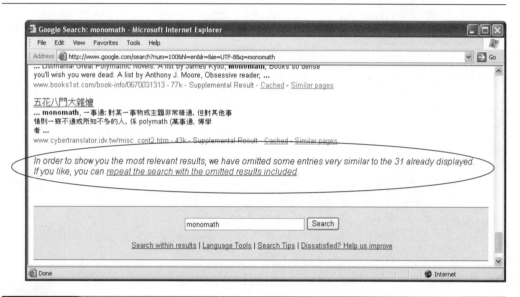

**FIGURE 3-19**   Google tells you when it is omitting results, and it provides a link to repeat the search with the omitted results included.

# File Types

The majority of pages both on the Web and in Google's index are HTML web pages. But there are many other types of files that Google has discovered and indexed. These file types include:

- Adobe PDF and PostScript files
- Microsoft Office documents, such as Word, Excel, and PowerPoint
- Rich Text Format documents
- Macromedia Flash files
- Other file types, including those with the following extensions: ASP, JSP, HDML, SHTML, XML, CFM, WKS, LWP, and WRI

When Google includes a non-HTML file in search results, it indicates the file type with a small icon to the left of the title, as shown in Figure 3-20.

Google displays the file type for a very good reason. Many browsers will attempt to open a non-HTML file type with the appropriate program, running Word for files of type DOC, Adobe Acrobat for PDF files, or in some cases, installing file readers in your browser. These programs can take time to load. What's more, if you don't have the underlying program installed on your

FIGURE 3-20    Google displays an indicator for non-HTML files in search results.

machine, an error message or a dialog appears asking you which program to use to view the file. To expedite viewing the files, Google adds a **View as HTML** link to non-HTML results.

> [PPT] A **Distributed Web Crawler** over DHTs
> File Format: Microsoft Powerpoint 97 - View as HTML
> ... Generalized **crawler** for querying **distributed** graph structures. ... **WebCrawler** over PIER, Bamboo DHT, up to 80 PlanetLab nodes. ... 78244 different **web** servers. ...
> www.cs.berkeley.edu/~boonloo/ classes/cs294-4/p2pwebcrawl.ppt - Similar pages

Google automatically converts the file to HTML, stripping out formatting codes and allowing the document to be easily and quickly displayed in your browser. Documents may be somewhat difficult to read without their native formatting, but using the **View as HTML** link is a fast way to get information quickly.

## Supplemental Results

On rare occasions, typically when your search terms are unusual or obscure, you'll see what Google calls a "supplemental result." Supplemental results are pages Google keeps in a separate index that it uses when it fails to find good results in its main index. From a practical standpoint, it makes no difference whether a result is labeled with the "supplemental result" tag or not. About the only difference you'll notice is that searches including supplemental results may take longer than ordinary searches, though we're talking maybe an additional second or two, which is really no big deal.

[DOC] Embleton, Gerry; Howe, John (1994): The Medieval Soldier: 15th ...
File Format: Microsoft Word 97 - View as HTML
... knitted woollen caps (not illustrated) which are the earliest examples of headgear
in the **collection**, or describing the single 15th-century **poulaine** owned by ...
www.verso.org/clothing/Tudor-Stuart.doc   Supplemental Result - Similar pages

## Translate This Page

One of Google's strengths is that it can find relevant documents in just about any language, regardless of the language of your search terms. Google initially determines your language settings based on the language configuration of your browser and the Google domain that you're accessing. So if your browser is configured for Spanish and you're accessing Google in Mexico, your Google default interface is Spanish. You can override the default by changing the search language option on the Preferences screen (Chapters 2 and 16 have much more on customizing Google's extensive language capabilities).

POWER SEARCHER TIP    *You can change your browser language in Internet Explorer through the Internet Options dialog on the Tools menu.*

Some search terms will surface high-quality results in languages other than your default language. In the following illustration, the top result for **Picasso** is "Pablo Picasso: Le site officiel," which is in French and hosted on a site located in France. If your default language is not French, Google often will add a **Translate this page** link next to the title of this result. Clicking the link will automatically translate the page into your default language, or the interface language you've selected on the Google Preferences page.

**Web**                                                          Results **1 - 100**

News results for **picasso** - View today's top stories
     Thieves 'missed **Picasso**' - Melbourne Herald Sun - Jul 11, 2004

Pablo **Picasso** : Le site officiel - ( Translate this page )
Le site officiel sur Pablo **Picasso**. ... Demandes d'autorisations en ligne pour l'utilisation des
oeuvres, de l'image et du nom **Picasso**. ...
www.**picasso**.fr/ - 3k - Cached - Similar pages

Because the translation is automatically performed by Google's computers, it's often not perfect. If you aren't happy with the translation, simply click the **View Original Web Page** link at the top of the translated page. Google is somewhat selective about the pages it offers to translate. You won't see a **Translate this page** link when multiple languages appear on a page, or for pages with too few words for Google to be confident of doing an adequate job of translation. And because Google cannot index text within images, images are not translated either. Google offers English translation from French, German, Italian, Spanish, and Portuguese web pages.

## Date Crawled

On some results, you'll see a date. This date shows the last time Google crawled and indexed the web page. It's important to realize that a date on a result page does not correspond to the date that the page was created or updated. Rather, dates are an indicator of freshness in the index. Google displays dates only for pages it has crawled within the past few days.

| **Web** | Results **1 - 100** of about 586,000 |
| --- | --- |

The **Straits Times** Interactive
The **Straits Times** Interactive - Singapore news.
Find the latest news reports here. ...
straitstimes.asia1.com.sg/home/0,1869,,00.html - 36k - Jul 13, 2004 - Cached - Similar pages

# Organic Results vs. Sponsored Links

As a searcher, should you have a preference one way or another for organic results vs. sponsored links? It depends largely on what you're searching for and whether your ultimate need is for information or to purchase something.

Sponsored links have come under fire from critics for not being clearly labeled as advertisements, and looking confusingly similar to organic, unpaid results. In fact, the U.S. Federal Trade Commission issued a letter of recommendation to a number of major search engines in 2002 recommending that they improve their labeling and disclosure of sponsored listings. Google avoided most of this controversy because it has always been upfront in clearly labeling sponsored links.

The advertising program has been a smash financial success for Google, moving the company from a small struggling startup to one of the world's most profitable companies. This success has allowed Google to reinvest its profits in research and development, arguably improving the quality of organic search results as a direct benefit.

The bottom-line issue for a searcher is whether sponsored links provide relevant results. Google works hard to ensure that sponsored links are relevant, publishing extensive editorial guidelines and employing numerous quality-control staff members to make sure advertisers adhere to guidelines. For the most part, sponsored links do provide relevant results for most queries.

But the reality is a sponsored link has one purpose: to get you to "convert" (buy, register, or take some other tangible action). Sponsored links can be very useful if you're researching a product or a service, because they'll generally provide you with exactly what you're looking for with minimal fuss, especially if your query is focused and specific.

If you're seeking information or facts, sponsored links are likely to be less helpful than organic results. The bottom line: Both organic results and sponsored links offer valuable information. It's up to you as a searcher to decide, on a query-by-query basis, which are likely to give you the payoff you're seeking.

**POWER SEARCHER TIP** *It's worth checking out Google's extensive advertiser guidelines to understand what is and is not allowed in sponsored links. These guidelines can be found at http://adwords.google.com/select/guidelines.html.*

3

# The Hidden Manipulators:
# Search Engine Optimization Experts

An entire industry has evolved to help site owners boost their page rankings in Google and all the other major search engines. Search Engine Optimization (SEO) is the part-art/part-science of crafting web pages that are "search engine friendly," potentially boosting their positions on search result pages.

There's nothing inherently wrong or illegal with SEO. Some SEO techniques focus on simple tasks that actually make it easier for Google to understand the content of a page. These techniques include writing a clear, descriptive title, and focusing the text of a page on a specific subject. What does an "optimized" page look like? Figure 3-21 is a Google search result for the query **diamond jewelry**. Even without clicking through to view the page, a close examination of the second result reveals that this site has likely been optimized to attract the attention of search engines for the search terms "diamond jewelry." How can you tell?

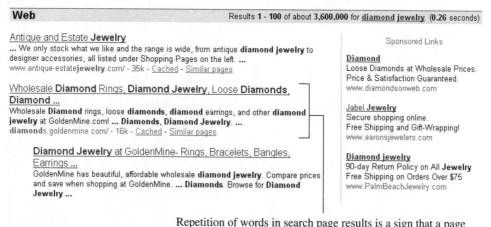

**Web**                                                Results **1 - 100** of about 3,600,000 for <u>diamond jewelry</u>. (0.26 seconds)

Antique and Estate **Jewelry**
... We only stock what we like and the range is wide, from antique **diamond jewelry** to designer accessories, all listed under Shopping Pages on the left. ...
www.antique-estate**jewelry**.com/ - 35k - Cached - Similar pages

Wholesale **Diamond** Rings, **Diamond Jewelry**, Loose **Diamonds**, **Diamond** ...
Wholesale **Diamond** rings, loose **diamonds**, **diamond** earrings, and other **diamond jewelry** at GoldenMine.com! ... Diamonds, **Diamond Jewelry**. ...
**diamond**s.goldenmine.com/ - 16k - Cached - Similar pages

    **Diamond Jewelry** at GoldenMine- Rings, Bracelets, Bangles, Earrings ...
    GoldenMine has beautiful, affordable wholesale **diamond jewelry**. Compare prices and save when shopping at GoldenMine. ... **Diamonds**. Browse for **Diamond Jewelry** ...

Sponsored Links

**Diamond**
Loose Diamonds at Wholesale Prices. Price & Satisfaction Guaranteed.
www.diamondsonweb.com

Jabel Jewelry
Secure shopping online. Free Shipping and Gift-Wrapping!
www.aaronsjewelers.com

Diamond jewelry
90-day Return Policy on All **Jewelry** Free Shipping on Orders Over $75
www.PalmBeachJewelry.com

Repetition of words in search page results is a sign that a page may have been optimized to rank well for those words.

**FIGURE 3-21**   Repetition of search terms is a common tactic used by SEOs.

Repetition is a key tactic used by SEOs. Look at the number of times the search terms are repeated: twice in the title, twice in the body (at least twice—Google is showing us two snippets where the terms are repeated, more than usual for "unoptimized" pages). Both terms also appear in the URL. Clicking through to the page shows both terms repeated dozens of times, as seen in Figure 3-22.

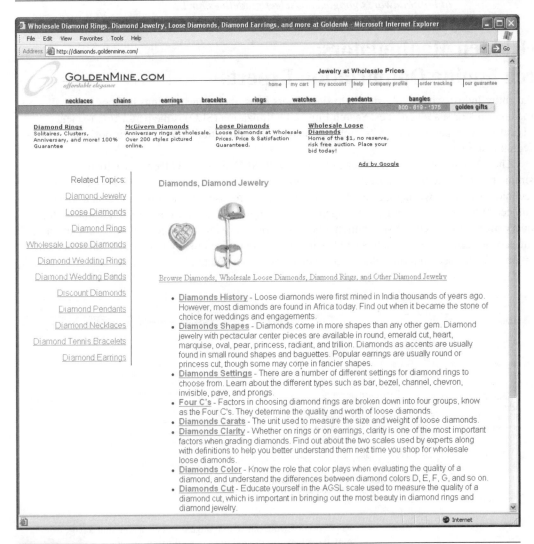

**FIGURE 3-22**    Some optimized pages have very relevant content for a query.

When a search result shows these telltale clues of optimization, should you avoid it? Not necessarily. Remember that Google also considers links to a page and many other factors when calculating its rank. The page shown in Figure 3-22 is actually quite relevant for the query **diamond jewelry**, even though the page has been optimized. Unless a number of other reasonably high-quality sites link to a page, it's unlikely that the page will rank well. In most cases, the signs of optimization may or may not tell you anything about the page's quality, but almost always indicate that you can expect a highly commercially oriented page once you click through.

Google has an ambivalent attitude toward SEOs. On the one hand, "ethical" SEOs focus on improving the overall content of a site, making it search engine friendly in this process. Google actually encourages this, publishing a set of "Webmaster Guidelines" at http://www.google.com/webmasters/guidelines.html.

Some SEO tactics are designed to trick Google and subvert its indexing and ranking processes. Google takes a harsh view of these "black hat" SEO tactics, and if it catches sites using them, Google can and will demote page rankings or even ban the site altogether. What are some of these nefarious SEO tactics?

Google publishes a list of some of the most common abuses it encounters, along with tips for site owners who are considering hiring the services of an SEO firm (http://www.google.com/webmasters/seo.html). Some of the tactics Google looks askance at include:

- Use of "shadow domains," designed to funnel users to a site they didn't intend to visit by the use of a deceptive technique called *redirection*

- Doorway pages, heavily optimized to catch the attention of a search engine but comparatively worthless for a human reader

- Cloaking, a bait-and-switch technique that involves feeding a crawler one page and serving a completely different page to a human user

- Link farms, using dozens or hundreds of sites to cross-link to one another, attempting to create the illusion of link popularity

- Hidden text or hidden links, created by using the same foreground and background color so these items are essentially invisible to the human eye but perfectly visible to a crawler

- Pages loaded with irrelevant words or excessive repetition

- Multiple pages, subdomains, or domains with substantially duplicate content

These are just a few of the techniques used by black hat SEOs (more appropriately known as *search engine spammers,* of the same Neanderthal species as their e-mail kin). A detailed discussion of SEO is beyond the scope of this book. For an excellent guide to legitimate and ethical techniques, see *Search Engine Visibility*, by Shari Thurow (New Riders, 2002).

# Does Google Censor Results?

Google takes a harsh line when it discovers spammers, particularly those who use the technique of cloaking. Google's Webmaster FAQ states the following: "To preserve the accuracy and quality of our search results, Google may permanently ban from our index any sites or site authors that engage in cloaking to distort their search rankings." (See http://www.google.com/webmasters/faq.html.) Google also encourages users to report suspected spam through a form at http://www.google.com/contact/spamreport.html.

Despite this aggressive attitude toward spam and deceptive tactics, Google does not actively censor most search results. Again, from the Webmaster FAQ: "Google prefers developing scalable and automated solutions to problems, so we attempt to minimize hand-to-hand spam fighting. The spam reports we receive are used to create scalable algorithms that recognize and block future spam attempts."

Google has been accused of removing offensive, politically charged content from its index, but has denied the allegations. In a statement responding to an outcry over results related to a religious search term, the company wrote: "Our search results are generated completely objectively and are independent of the beliefs and preferences of those who work at Google. Some people concerned about this issue have created online petitions to encourage us to remove particular links or otherwise adjust search results. Because of our objective and automated ranking system, Google cannot be influenced by these petitions. The only sites we omit are those we are legally compelled to remove or those maliciously attempting to manipulate our results." (See http://www.google.com/explanation.html.)

The bottom line is that while Google can act swiftly and surely to remove the sites of known spammers, it considers all other content on the Web to be valid for inclusion in its index. Whether this content is ever seen by searchers depends both on the search terms used and on the hundreds of ranking algorithms that are applied to all web pages, regardless of content.

# Chapter 4

# Maximizing Google with Advanced Search

If you're like most people, you view Google as something of a slot machine for the Web. Punch a few search terms into the box, pull the lever, and—voila!—you're often rewarded with a jackpot. But this isn't always the case. In fact, recent user surveys have shown that people feel that their searches fail between 50 and 80 percent of the time.

Some people blame themselves. Others blame the search engine. But the reality is that most search failures could turn into successes if only people took full advantage of the tools and capabilities the search engine has to offer.

In Google's case, this means mastering its wide array of advanced search features. Even though Google's clean, sparse interface invites us to keep things simple with just a few search terms, if you look under the hood you'll find that Google's engineers have provided a full set of industrial-strength tools that allow you to fine-tune the engine's performance to meet your specific needs. You've already had a glimpse of some of these capabilities in Chapter 2. Now we're going to dive into the full set of Google's advanced search tools.

I know, you probably think you're a pretty good searcher already. And you're probably right. But let me share a little story with you.

# An "Expert's" Parable

When I first started college, I was eagerly looking forward to studying photography with a professor who had been Ansel Adams' apprentice. On the first day of courses, I presented myself to him and suggested that I skip all the introductory classes, since I had been doing serious photography for years. He listened politely as I boasted about being the staff photographer for my high school yearbook. How I had won numerous contests. Hey, I had even been the photography editor for a metro-wide magazine (circulation 120,000) for high school students!

At the end of my pitch, he smiled and simply said that he'd see me in Photography 101. "But I know the basics!" I spluttered. I wanted to go deep into the really sophisticated techniques! He just smiled again and walked away.

I grudgingly showed up for my first introductory class, prepared to snooze the hour away. Within ten minutes, I realized how little I really knew, and how much I had to learn. That introductory photography course laid the foundation for my first profession, and it has left me with invaluable skills I still use today.

So, yes, I realize you know Google. But bear with me through this chapter on Google's advanced search tools. Get to know them inside out, and I guarantee you'll be a far better, more skillful searcher than you've ever imagined.

# The Advanced Search Page

Google's Advanced Search page (shown in Figure 4-1) is a control console into the heart of the machine. There are four major groupings of search boxes and controls on this page, each with its own unique set of functions and capabilities.

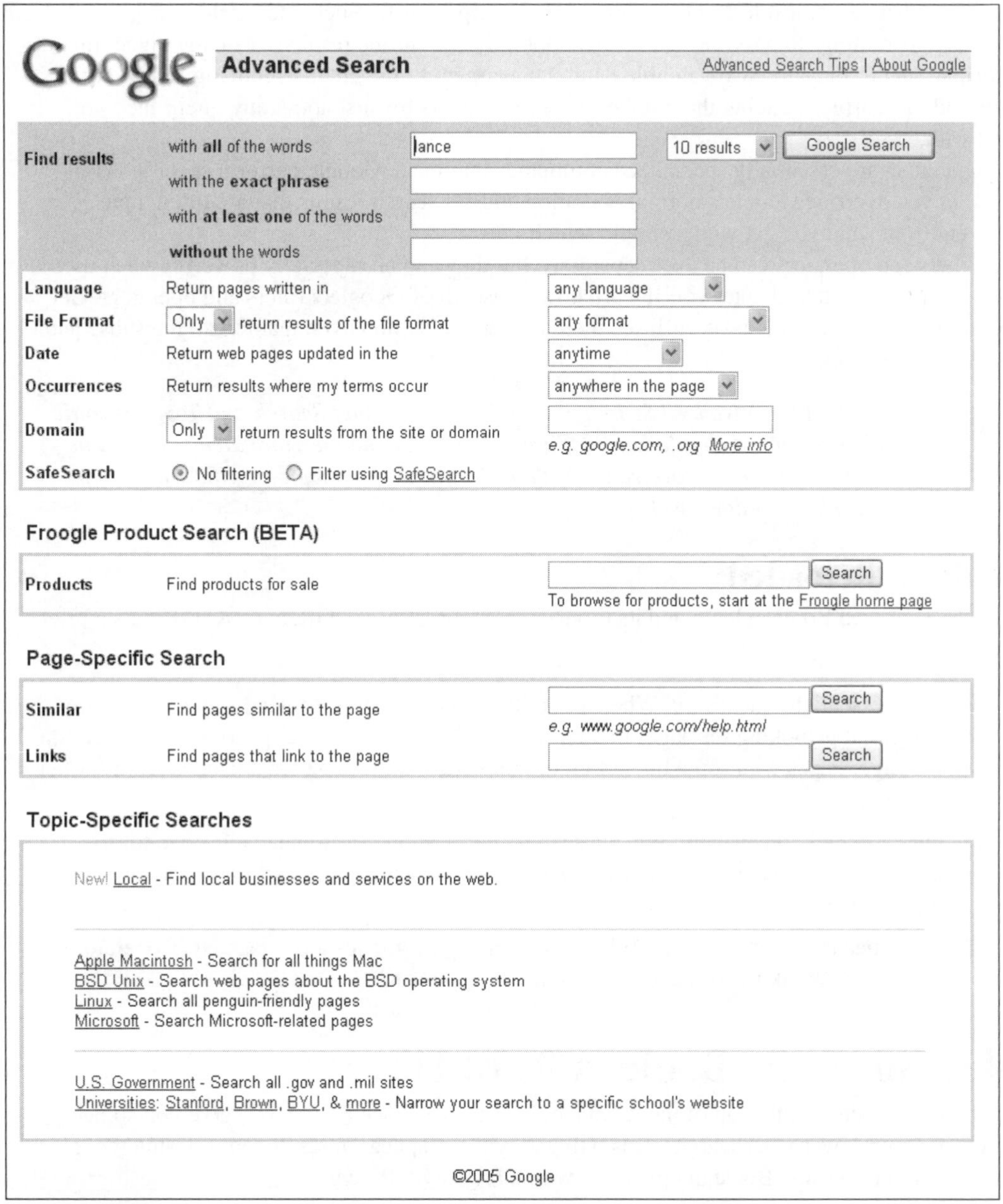

Google™  **Advanced Search**                    Advanced Search Tips | About Google

| | | | |
|---|---|---|---|
| **Find results** | with **all** of the words | lance | 10 results ▾  Google Search |
| | with the **exact phrase** | | |
| | with **at least one** of the words | | |
| | **without** the words | | |

| | | |
|---|---|---|
| **Language** | Return pages written in | any language ▾ |
| **File Format** | Only ▾ return results of the file format | any format ▾ |
| **Date** | Return web pages updated in the | anytime ▾ |
| **Occurrences** | Return results where my terms occur | anywhere in the page ▾ |
| **Domain** | Only ▾ return results from the site or domain | |
| | | e.g. google.com, .org *More info* |
| **SafeSearch** | ◉ No filtering ○ Filter using SafeSearch | |

**Froogle Product Search (BETA)**

| | | |
|---|---|---|
| **Products** | Find products for sale | Search |
| | | To browse for products, start at the Froogle home page |

**Page-Specific Search**

| | | |
|---|---|---|
| **Similar** | Find pages similar to the page | Search |
| | | e.g. www.google.com/help.html |
| **Links** | Find pages that link to the page | Search |

**Topic-Specific Searches**

New! Local - Find local businesses and services on the web.

Apple Macintosh - Search for all things Mac
BSD Unix - Search web pages about the BSD operating system
Linux - Search all penguin-friendly pages
Microsoft - Search Microsoft-related pages

U.S. Government - Search all .gov and .mil sites
Universities: Stanford, Brown, BYU, & more - Narrow your search to a specific school's website

©2005 Google

**FIGURE 4-1**    Google's Advanced Search page

Two key concepts underlie Google's advanced search capabilities: *filters* and *operators*. Google's filters work just like you'd expect—their purpose is to block undesirable things while allowing good things to pass. Google's filters not only help refine results, surfacing higher quality information, but they are also valuable data management tools, greatly reducing information overload by sharply reducing the number of search results for just about any query they are used with.

Operators are essentially specialized commands that make Google perform specific tasks. They let you override Google's normal operation and get search results that are often quite different from what you get with a simple search.

Filters and operators can be used separately, but they can be especially powerful when used in combination. In this chapter you'll learn how to use all of Google's filters and operators. Get good and familiar with them—you'll see them in action over and over again in all the subsequent chapters of the book.

**NOTE**    *Two parts of the Advanced Search page—**Froogle Product Search** and **Topic-Specific Searches**—aren't really "advanced" search features and therefore aren't covered in this chapter. Froogle is covered in depth in Chapter 15, and topic-specific searches are explained in the following chapter.*

## Boolean, Reloaded

Chapter 2 covered Boolean logic and its three simple words: AND, OR, and NOT. Here's a brief review:

- AND essentially means *all*. When a search engine applies a Boolean AND operator to a query, it is looking for pages that have *all* of the search terms appearing somewhere on the page. Pages with some but not all of the words on the page are excluded from further consideration.

- OR essentially means *any*. When a search engine applies a Boolean OR operator to a query, it is looking for pages that have *any* of the search terms appearing somewhere on the page.

- NOT means just what it says. When a search engine applies a Boolean NOT operator to a query, it is looking for pages *without* the search term.

# Google's Not-Quite-Boolean Word Filters

The four word filters at the top of the Advanced Search page (see Figure 4-2) give you some degree of control over what search terms will and will not appear in result pages. Using these filters is similar to using Boolean operators, with a few key differences.

## Find Results with All of the Words

Google uses the AND operator by default with any query that you type. This happens behind the scenes. Entering your search terms in the **with all of the words** search box on the Advanced

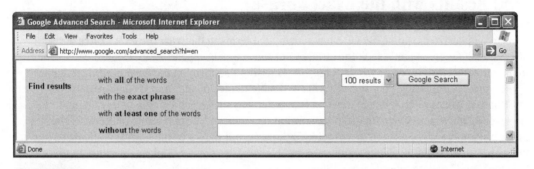

**FIGURE 4-2**   Google provides four basic word filters in forms at the top of the Advanced Search page.

Search page is the equivalent of using the Boolean AND operator, requiring all of the words in your query to appear on search result pages or in links pointing to those pages.

Although Google automatically inserts a Boolean AND between all of your search terms, you'll never see the word AND in results unless you type the word yourself—and that will prompt Google to display a message that the word is unnecessary, as shown in Figure 4-3.

The catch here is that Google ignores common words and characters—the *stop words* described in Chapter 2. To force Google to consider stop words, put the inclusion operator (the plus sign) in front of them. You must do this even when using the **with all of the words** search box.

You may wonder what the difference is between the **with all of the words** search box on the Advanced Search page and a regular Google search box. The answer is none! The only time you would want to use the **with all of the words** search box on the Advanced Search page is when you need to use other filters or operators on the page as well.

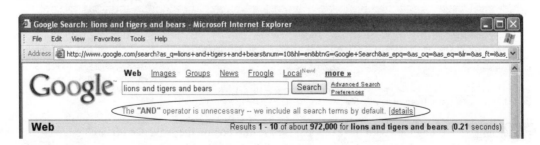

**FIGURE 4-3**   Google displays a message that the word AND is not necessary when you use it in a query.

## Find Results with the Exact Phrase

Google does a pretty good job of recognizing when search terms make up a phrase, but it never hurts to emphasize the point. By entering your search terms in the **with the exact phrase** search box, you tell Google to only look for instances of those words appearing adjacent to one another, in the order that you typed them (see Figure 4-4). Using this form on the Advanced Search page is equivalent to enclosing your search terms in double quotes in a regular Google search box.

Entering your search terms in this box is another way of forcing Google to pay attention to stop words. It's not necessary to use the inclusion operator with search terms in the **with the exact phrase** search box. Google will include them even if they are stop words. Notice also that in this particular example, Google did not treat the word "and" as a Boolean operator. In this case the word "and" was an integral part of the phrase.

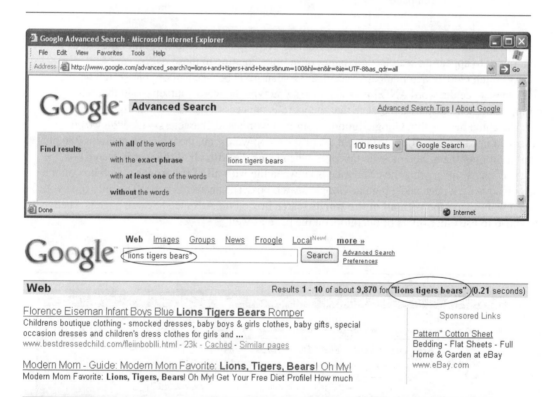

**FIGURE 4-4**    Using the "with the exact phrase" search box on the Advanced Search page is equivalent to enclosing your search terms in double quotes.

## Find Results with at Least One of the Words

On the Advanced Search page, entering your search terms in the **with at least one of the words** search box is the equivalent of using the Boolean OR between each of the terms, as shown in Figure 4-5.

On the result page, notice how Google has indicated that it has put the Boolean OR between the search terms, even though they weren't explicitly included with the query.

## Find Results Without the Words

Google doesn't support the Boolean NOT operator, but the exclusion operator (the minus sign) provides similar functionality. On the Advanced Search page, you can specify words that should not appear in results by entering them in the **without the words** search box, which is the equivalent of putting an exclusion operator in front of each, as shown in Figure 4-6.

It's important to note that of all the four word search filters on the Advanced Search page, the **without the words** filter does not work alone. You must also put at least one search term in one of the other three word filter search boxes. Why?

| **FIGURE 4-5** | Using the "with at least one of the words" search box on the Advanced Search page is equivalent to using the Boolean OR operator between each of your search terms. |

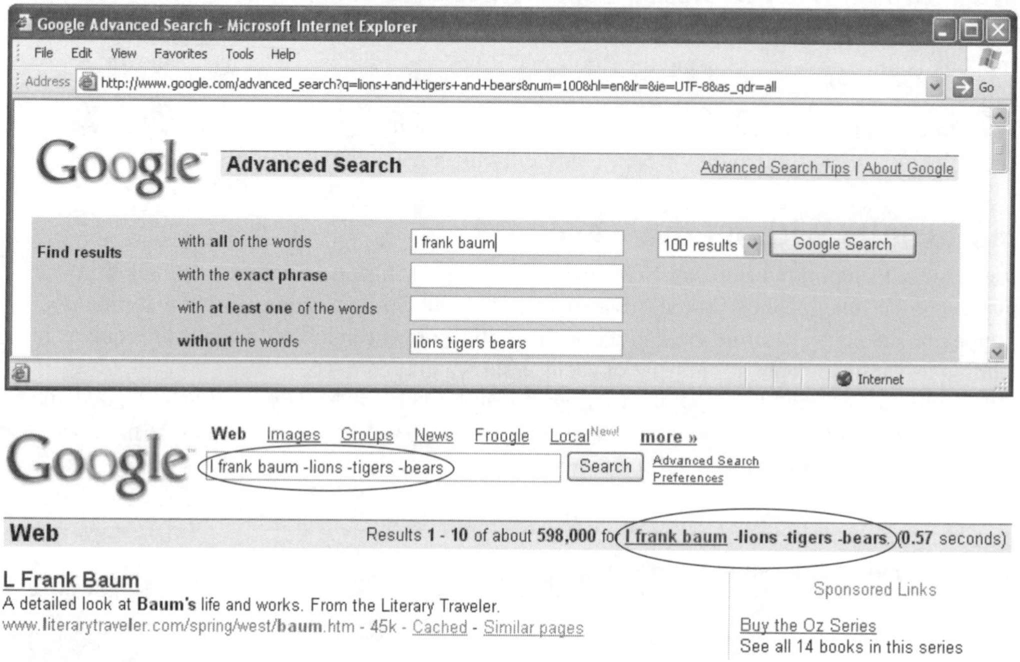

**FIGURE 4-6**   Using the "without the words" search box on the Advanced Search page is equivalent to using the exclusion operator in front of each of your search terms.

Google needs to know what you're looking for before it can begin to exclude pages with words that you don't want included in the results. In other words, Google will start with a set of web pages that match your search terms, and only then will it eliminate pages containing the words you've put in the **without the words** search box. Putting a query in the **without the words** search box without indicating the other search terms you want to find leaves Google with the hundreds of thousands of words that you didn't exclude, which makes no sense.

**POWER SEARCHER TIP**   *Each of the four word filters on the Advanced Search page can be invoked from any Google search box. The value of the filters on the page comes when you combine them, or use them with other filters or operators on the Advanced Search page.*

## Combining Word Filters

The real power of the word filters on the Advanced Search page lies with using them together. For example, the **without the words** filter works with any of the other three filters, and it's a very powerful way to limit search results. Another good combination is the **all of the words** and **exact phrase** filters. For example, the exact phrase "truths to be self evident" combined with all of the words "Jefferson Franklin Adams Livingston Sherman" will effectively limit results to documents related to the authors of the U.S. Declaration of Independence, excluding the thousands of other web pages that simply refer to the document (see Figure 4-7).

Sometimes using two filters together seems counterintuitive, but in fact really focuses your results. For example, combining a query in the **exact phrase** box with search terms in the **at least one of the words** box may seem paradoxical—looking for an exact phrase OR other search terms. Remember, though, that Google automatically inserts an AND between your search terms. So, for the query illustrated in Figure 4-8, Google is really performing the following operation:

((worthless OR revolutionary) AND "bluetooth networking")

The outcome is a list of web pages that has *both* the phrase "bluetooth networking" and the words "worthless" or "revolutionary" appearing together.

**POWER SEARCHER TIP**   *These four word filters appear at the top of most Google Advanced Search pages (Images, Groups, and so on). Get to know how to use them here and you'll have mastered them elsewhere.*

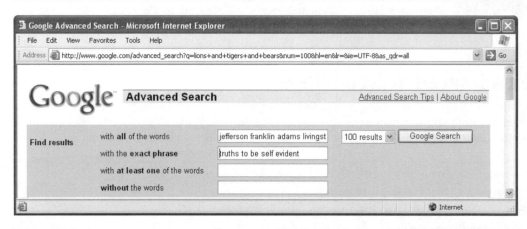

**FIGURE 4-7**    Using the "all of the words" and "exact phrase" filters together is a powerful combination.

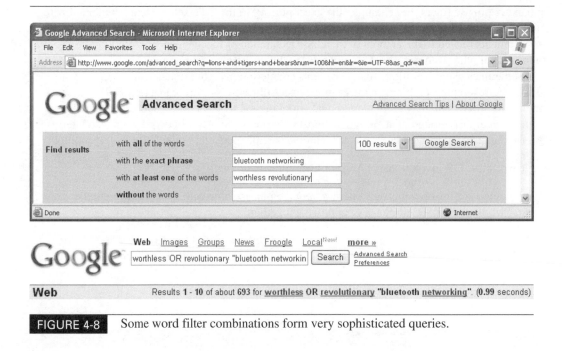

**FIGURE 4-8**    Some word filter combinations form very sophisticated queries.

# Other Advanced Search Filters

While word filters are the most common and all-around useful mechanisms that Google provides to refine search results, a number of other filters are handy when you've got specific information needs. Controls for these filters appear immediately beneath the word filters, as shown here:

| Language | Return pages written in | any language |
| --- | --- | --- |
| File Format | Only ⌄ return results of the file format | any format |
| Date | Return web pages updated in the | anytime |
| Numeric Range | Return web pages containing numbers between [    ] and [    ] | |
| Occurrences | Return results where my terms occur | anywhere in the page |
| Domain | Only ⌄ return results from the site or domain | [    ]  e.g. google.com, .org *More info* |
| SafeSearch | ◉ No filtering  ○ Filter using SafeSearch | |

## Language Filter

You've already seen Google's language capabilities in action in Chapter 2. The Advanced Search page language filter allows you to specify the language for search result pages. This filter lets you limit your results to pages written in up to 30 languages—you can expect more to come. Alone, this filter works just like the **search pages written in** filter on the Language tools page. Its inclusion on the Advanced Search page allows you to construct sophisticated queries in any language, and then limit result pages to a particular language.

To limit your search results by language, simply use the drop-down menu to select a language and then type your search terms in the appropriate word filter boxes.

> *Google understands the special characters and symbols used by many languages. You can increase the precision of your results by using symbols, accent marks, and other special characters as appropriate in your search terms.*

POWER SEARCHER TIP

## File Format

Most web pages are composed using the Hypertext Markup Language (HTML). But documents in a variety of other formats can also be found on the Web, and sometimes these alternate formats will offer the best results for what you're looking for. For example, a lot of government information is published in the Adobe Acrobat PDF format. Statistical information is often found in Microsoft Excel spreadsheets. Microsoft PowerPoint is the preferred format for presentations. And so on.

The **File Format** filter allows you to limit your results to a particular file format or to exclude a format from your search results. To use the filter, first select either **Only** or **Don't return results of the file format** from the drop-down menu.

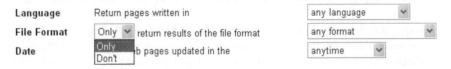

Next, select the file format. Use the drop-down menu to select Adobe Acrobat PDF, Adobe Postscript, Microsoft Word, Excel, or PowerPoint, or Rich Text Format documents.

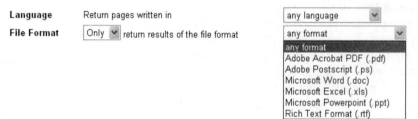

Once you've set the filter, type your search terms in the appropriate word filter boxes above and run the search.

 *Google allows you to limit your searches to several other file types than those available on the Advanced Search page. The "Advanced Search Operators" section, later in this chapter, shows you how.*

## Date Filter

The **Date** filter lets you limit search results to pages that have been modified in the past three months, six months, or year. To use this filter, simply select the appropriate timeframe from the **Date** drop-down menu, as shown next, and then type your search terms in the appropriate word filter boxes above.

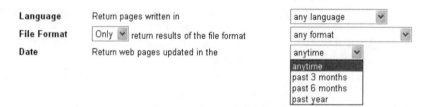

In theory, the **Date** filter should be very useful for making sure your results are comparatively fresh and up to date. In practice, however, the **Date** filter is unreliable—and not through any fault of Google's.

The problem is that the date Google uses to determine when a page was last modified is provided by the server that hosts the page. Each page on a web server has a special "Last-Modified" field that stores a date. However, the date stored in that field is not standard and isn't consistently applied on all web servers. In some cases, the last modified date represents when the page was originally uploaded to the server. In others, it's when the page was most recently updated. But just because a page was recently updated doesn't necessarily mean that its content has changed since it was first published. Some web servers routinely replace all web pages on a regular basis as part of a maintenance routine. Other pages are created on the fly, pieced together by content management systems from parts of other web pages, database records, or other components, and these pages typically show a very recent "last-modified" date.

Figure 4-9 shows an example of a result that refers to a page published in 2001 and hasn't changed since then. However, the web server hosting the page uses a content management system that reports the current date whenever the page is requested by Google's crawler. Therefore, Google assumes that this page was modified within the past three months, when in fact it hasn't changed since it was originally published.

| FIGURE 4-9 | An example of a page that hasn't changed in years, returned in search results by Google as modified within the past three months |

The bottom line is that the **Date** filter can be useful for some purposes, but it's not one that you can rely on to give you consistent results.

# Occurrences Filter

The **Occurrences** filter lets you specify that your search terms must appear in specific parts of a web page, or the links pointing to a page. These parts include:

- The title of a page
- The text on a page
- The URL of a page
- Links pointing to a page

Use the drop-down menu shown in the following illustration to activate the filter.

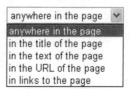

Why would you want to narrow your search to these parts? Because they each play a unique role in all of Google's relevance calculations. With a normal search, Google considers search terms appearing in all of these page parts. By limiting your search to one of these components, you can get interesting results that might not otherwise turn up. Let's look at each component more closely:

- **The title of the page**   Google considers the HTML title to be one of the most important parts of any page. The title is essentially a nutshell description of the entire page, a condensed abstract of the main idea or content appearing on the page. By limiting your search to the title, you're only going to get pages that use your search terms in this important tag, in most cases drastically reducing your total number of search results.

   Remember, though—just as you can't judge a book from its cover, you can't rely entirely on a title to judge the quality of an underlying page. You also need to examine factors such as the snippet and the URL, and in many cases you must actually view the page itself before determining whether the page is a good one or not.

- **The text of the page**   Google uses dozens of factors to calculate the relevance of the page, and it looks at much more than just the text on the page itself, including text in the header portion of the page, links pointing to pages, and so on. If you want to exclude all factors other than the text on a page, limiting your search to the **in the text of the page** is the way to go.

- **The URL of the page**   URLs for many pages use descriptive keywords that hold clues to the entire contents of a web site. It's pretty easy to guess what you'll find at sites with URLs such as shoes.com, gardenweb.com, and chemistry.org. Limiting your search to words appearing in the URL is a great way to find "birds of a feather" sites, all related to the same topic.

*Limiting your search to words in a URL won't always give you the results you may expect. When an original domain owner abandons a site, the name can be picked up by advertisers, cybersquatters, or worse, spammers who put completely unrelated content on the site, hoping to lure the unsuspecting with an innocent-sounding domain name.*

4

- **Links to the page**   Google's PageRank technology, which analyzes links to web pages, plays a key role in how the search engine determines relevance for web pages. Link analysis involves not only looking at the number and quality of links pointing to a page, but also at the text in the links themselves. This is called *anchor text,* and the **in links to the page** filter looks only at this type of text.

  Unlike a URL for a page, which is fixed, anchor text for a link is written by the person creating the link. The anchor text in the link can be anything that person wants it to be. A link pointing to page A will always have the same URL, but the anchor text could be "a page about wildebeests," "African wildlife," or even the nondescriptive but ubiquitous "click here." Searching for text in links to pages tends to favor pages where there is a great deal of agreement among web page authors who have collectively used the same language in their anchor text to describe a page.

## Domain Filter

The **Domain** filter allows you to either limit your results to a particular domain or exclude a domain from your search results. In the first instance, you are effectively using Google as a site search tool, limiting results to web pages found on a particular web site. In the second, you are excluding all pages from a particular site from results.

To use the filter, first select either **Only** or **Don't return results from the site or domain** from the drop-down menu shown next. Then enter a domain name, such as researchbuzz.com or harvard.edu. Finally, enter your search terms in the word filter boxes and run your search.

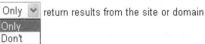

Domain    Only ▾ return results from the site or domain          e.g. google.com, .org *More info*
          Only
          Don't

**POWER SEARCHER TIP**    *The **Domain** filter is particularly powerful. It can be used to restrict results to a particular domain and even a subdomain of a site.*

The **Domain** filter can be used even more broadly than limiting or excluding results from a particular site. You can also enter a top-level domain, such as .com or .org, and all results from those top-level domains will also be filtered appropriately. Table 4-1 shows a list of the current top-level domains that have been approved by the Internet Assigned Numbers Authority (IANA) and what types of organizations are eligible to register for each type of domain.

In addition to the top-level domains listed in Table 4-1, most countries have their own top-level domains. Many U.S. state and local governments also have their own domains. Table 4-2 lists a few of the hundreds of government-controlled domains throughout the world.

**POWER SEARCHER TIP**    *A complete listing and description of all top-level domains is available at http:// en.wikipedia.org/wiki/List_of_Internet_TLDs. Links to listings and descriptions of second-level domains (for example, .nv.us and .ac.uk) are also available by clicking TLD links.*

| Domain | Registration Requirements or Restrictions |
|---|---|
| .aero | Reserved for members of the air-transport industry |
| .biz | Restricted to businesses |
| .com | Open to any individual or organization |
| .coop | Reserved for cooperative associations |
| .info | Open to any individual or organization |
| .museum | Reserved for museums |
| .name | Reserved for individuals |
| .net | Open to any individual or organization |
| .org | Open to any individual or organization |
| .pro | Restricted to credentialed professionals and related entities |
| .gov | Reserved exclusively for the United States Government |
| .edu | Reserved for postsecondary institutions accredited by an agency on the U.S. Department of Education's list of Nationally Recognized Accrediting Agencies |
| .mil | Reserved exclusively for the United States Military |
| .int | Used only for registering organizations established by international treaties between governments |

**TABLE 4-1**    Top-level Domains and the Organizations Eligible to Register for Them

| Domain | Registered Government Entity |
|---|---|
| .ac | Ascension Island |
| .bf | Burkina Faso |
| .it | Italy |
| .sa | Saudi Arabia |
| .va | Holy See (Vatican City State) |
| .zw | Zimbabwe |
| .nv.us | Nevada State |
| ci.roswell.nm.us | City of Roswell, New Mexico |

**TABLE 4-2**    A Small Sample of Government-Controlled Domains Throughout the World

## SafeSearch Filter

The **SafeSearch** filter settings can be changed on the Advanced Search page, overriding your preferences on a per-search basis. Select the **No filtering** or **Filter using SafeSearch** option and your results will be filtered accordingly for the current search.

**SafeSearch**        ○ No filtering  ◉ Filter using SafeSearch

**POWER SEARCHER TIP**    *Changing the SafeSearch settings on the Advanced Search page affects only the current search. Your global preference settings are not affected.*

# Page-Specific Search Filters

Most of the advanced search features described so far work with a small set of keywords, or they focus on specific components of web pages. The two page-specific filters work very differently. These filters don't look so much at the content of a particular web page, but rather focus on the relationship of a page to other pages on the Web.

It's important to realize that the page-specific filters do not work together with the other functions on the Advanced Search page, or with each other. It is possible to combine these functions, but only using the advanced search commands described later in this chapter.

## Similar Pages

The **Find pages similar to the page** filter is designed to make it easy to find pages that are conceptually related to a specific web page. To use it, simply enter the URL of a web page. Your results are links to other pages that are similar or somehow related to that page.

For example, if you enter **www.worldbank.org**, your results may include home pages for International Monetary Fund, the Organisation for Economic Co-operation and Development, and similar organizations. This filter produces results identical to what you get clicking the **Similar pages** link that appears on most ordinary Google search results.

## Links to Pages

The **Find pages that link to the page** filter does exactly what it says. To use the filter, type in the URL of a web page, and your results will be limited to pages that link to the URL. These pages may or may not have anything in common with the URL—Google is simply looking at links, ignoring the anchor text of the link and the text found on the linking page.

It's important to note that Google does not show you *all* the pages that link to a particular page. It's a good indicator, but it's not comprehensive.

 *Use the **Find pages that link to the page** filter to discover who on the Web is linking to your own web site.*

# Advanced Search Operators

Many of the advanced search functions available on the Advanced Search page have corresponding operators that work from any Google search box. These operators make it easy to harness the full power of the search engine without having to go to the Advanced Search page and use the forms to construct a query.

Each of these operators consists of a single character, or a single word followed by a colon. Table 4-3 shows a summary of Google's advanced search operators.

You've already seen many of these operators in action—they power the functions on the Advanced Search page. Let's look at each operator in more detail.

## cache:

Use the **cache:** operator to see the page Google crawled and fetched for indexing. The **cache:** command is useful when a page turning up in normal search results mysteriously lacks the information you were looking for—the page may have changed since Google crawled it, and the cached copy will likely have the information you're looking for. Using the **cache:** command in a Google search box produces results identical to clicking the **Cached** link in search results.

POWER SEARCHER TIP *Cached pages are also useful for ferreting out spam. If a page you're viewing differs completely from what you'd expect from a search result, the web page author may have used a spam technique called cloaking to feed Google one page for indexing while serving a completely different page to human users. Comparing the cached page with the actual page can often uncover this chicanery.*

| Operator and Example | Function |
| --- | --- |
| cache:<br>**cache:www.archive.org** | Show the most recently crawled version of a page stored in Google's cache. |
| related:<br>**related:www.northpole.com** | Show pages that are similar to a particular URL. |
| link:<br>**link:www.searchengineguide.com** | Show all pages linking to a specific URL. |
| info:<br>**info:www.sina.com** | Show information about a specific URL. |
| filetype:<br>**"burning man" filetype:ppt** | Restrict results to pages of the specified file type. |
| ext:<br>**"employee memo" ext:doc** | Restrict results to pages of the specified file type (alias for filetype:). |
| site:<br>**goliath frog site:www.ssarherps.org** | Limit results to a particular web site or domain. |
| allintext:<br>**allintext:dromedary arabia water** | Show pages where all search terms appear in the body (visible text) portion of the page. |
| allintitle:<br>**allintitle:combinatorial mathematics** | Show pages where all search terms appear in the title. |
| intitle:<br>**intitle:funicular** | Show pages where a single search term appears in the title. |
| allinurl:<br>**allinurl:crazy eights** | Show pages where all search terms appear in the URL. |
| inurl:<br>**inurl:Ouagadougou** | Show pages where a single search term appears in the URL. |
| allinanchor:<br>**allinanchor:issaquena county** | Show pages where all search terms appear in the text of links pointing to the page. |
| inanchor:<br>**inanchor:Neanderthal** | Show pages where a single search term appears in the text of links pointing to the page. |

**TABLE 4-3**   Google's Advanced Search Operators

## related:

The **related:** operator performs the same function as the **Find pages similar to the page** filter on the Advanced Search page. The **related:** operator also gives you the same results as clicking a **Similar pages** link in regular search results. Why Google decided to use two names for the same function (related and similar) is one of those unsolvable mysteries that shouldn't make you loose sleep at night.

## link:

The **link:** operator performs the same function as the **Find pages that link to the page** filter on the Advanced Search page, limiting results to pages that link to the specified URL. Note that the **link:** operator looks only at URLs pointing to a page, not at the anchor text of the links.

POWER SEARCHER TIP *The **link:** operator cannot be combined with any other advanced search command.*

## info:

The **info:** operator shows you the Google search result for the specified URL, and it provides preconfigured links to run four additional operators:

- Google's cache of the page (**cache:**)
- Web pages that are similar to the page (**related:**)
- Web pages that link to the page (**link:**)
- Web pages that contain the term (exact phrase search)

For publicly traded companies, the **info:** operator will also provide a link to show stock quotes and other financial information for the company, as shown in Figure 4-10.

POWER SEARCHER TIP  *The **info:** operator is redundant—you get exactly the same result if you type a URL without the **info:** operator into a Google search box.*

## filetype: and ext:

The **filetype:** operator performs the same function as the **File Format** filter on the Advanced Search page, limiting results to pages in the specified file format.

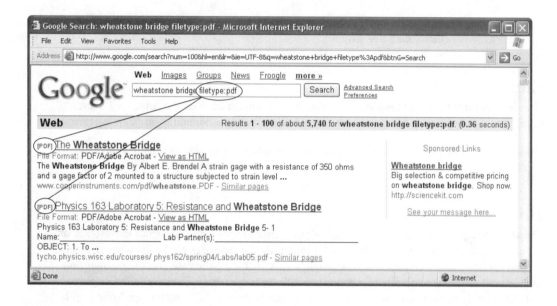

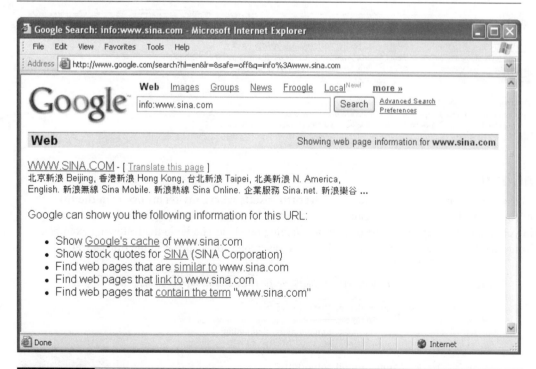

**FIGURE 4-10**    The **info:** operator creates links to automatically run other advanced search operators on the specified URL.

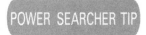

*The **ext:** operator is an undocumented alias for the **filetype:** operator and works in exactly the same way.*

## site:

The **site:** operator performs the same function as the **Domain** filter on the Advanced Search page, limiting your results to a particular domain or excluding a domain from your search results.

*The **site:** operator will often provide better search results than a web site's own site-search tool.*

## allintext:

The **allintext:** operator makes sure that all of your search terms actually appear in the body of the web page. For some searches, this can be important, because Google looks in many places beyond the body of a web page for your search terms, including the title, meta tags, image alt tags, as well as in links pointing to a page. The **allintext:** operator essentially tells Google to make absolutely certain that your search terms appear in the body of a web page. Your search terms can also appear in other areas, as long as they appear in the text as well.

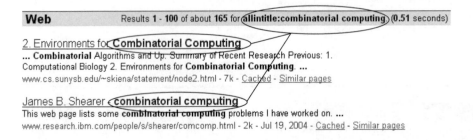

## allintitle:

The **allintitle:** operator is identical to the **Return results where my terms occur in the title of the page** filter in the **Occurrences** section of the Advanced Search page. Each search term in your query must appear in the title for a matching result, as shown in the following example. Your search terms can also appear in other areas, as long as they appear in the title as well.

# intitle:

The **intitle:** operator is similar to the **allintitle:** operator, but it only works with a single word following the operator. All other search terms in your query are treated normally. Putting an **intitle:** operator in front of all search terms is equivalent to using the **allintitle:** operator.

**Web**        Results **1 - 100** of about **1,580** for intitle:funicular (0.33 seconds)

Vesuvius **funicular** railway and chairlift
**Funicular**, railway and chairlift. Mt. Vesuvius **funicular**. Only plant in
the world climbing up on an active volcano at that time, transported ...
www.vesuvioinrete.it/funicolare/e_funicolare.htm - 14k - Cached - Similar pages

**Funicular** History
Vesuvius **funicular** was the only plant in the world clambering up
on an active volcano, at that time. In 1870, when Vesuvius was ...
www.vesuvioinrete.it/funicolare/e_funicolare_storia.htm - 17k - Cached - Similar pages
[ More results from www.vesuvioinrete.it ]

**POWER SEARCHER TIP**    *Use the **intitle:** operator when you want to find an important keyword in the title of a page, but you want the other words to appear in the text of the page or in the anchor text of links pointing to the page.*

# allinurl:

Like the **allintitle:** operator, the **allinurl:** operator requires all of your search terms to appear in the URL of a web page. This operator works only with words; punctuation is ignored. The order of the words in your query is also irrelevant—if the words appear anywhere in the URL, there will be a positive match.

**Web**        Results **1 - 100** of about 557 for allinurl:crazy eights (0.55 seconds)

Fun **Crazy Eights** - Download Fun **Crazy Eights** - Modern version of ...
Fun **Crazy Eights**, Fun **Crazy Eights** 1.05.1. ... File Size: 1.42 MB. Screenshot: Fun **Crazy**
**Eights** screenshot. Rating: Rating of Fun **Crazy Eights**. Support: ...
www.topshareware.com/Fun-Crazy-Eights-download-8238.htm - 15k - Cached - Similar pages

     Download Fun **Crazy Eights**
     Fun **Crazy Eights** Download. ... Fun **Crazy Eights** 1.05.1 Description: Fun **Crazy Eights** is
     the modern version of world famous '**Crazy Eights**' card game. ...
     www.topshareware.com/Fun-Crazy-Eights-transfer-8238.htm - 11k - Cached - Similar pages
     [ More results from www.topshareware.com ]

Sponsored Links

**Crazy Eights**
Family fun. Kids love to play. Go
Fish, **Crazy** 8's, Old Maid & more.
www.alwaysbrilliant.com

See your message here...

# inurl:

The **inurl:** operator is similar to the **allinurl:** operator, but it only works with a single word following the operator. All other search terms in your query are treated normally. Putting an **inurl:** operator in front of all search terms is equivalent to using the **allinurl:** operator.

**POWER SEARCHER TIP**   *Use the **inurl:** operator where you want to find an important keyword in the URL of a page, but you want the other words to appear in the text of the page or in the anchor text of links pointing to the page.*

# allinanchor:

The **allinanchor:** operator is the complement of the **link:** operator. This operator matches the words in anchor text of links.

# inanchor:

The **inanchor:** operator is similar to the **allinanchor:** operator, but it only works with a single word following the operator. All other search terms in your query are treated normally. Putting an **inanchor:** operator in front of each search term is equivalent to using the **allinanchor:** operator.

# Combining Advanced Search Operators

Some advanced search operators can be used together to greatly improve results. But some, when used together, cancel each other out. Others cannot be combined. There are literally thousands of possible combinations when using advanced search operators, so it would be impossible to provide a full set of rules and recommendations for using them. Keep in mind these rules of thumb:

- ■ Operators that work with URLs, such as **cache:**, **related:**, **link:**, and **info:**, cannot be combined with other operators.

- ■ Operators beginning with "**allin**" generally work best when not combined with each other.

- ■ Remember that, by default, Google ANDs search terms together. Some operators will work together only if you use a Boolean OR in your query to override the automatic AND.

When in doubt about whether operators work together, your best bet is to experiment. Then look carefully at your results to assure yourself you're really seeing the effect you intended.

## Additional Google Operators

The operators described in this chapter are specialized commands to filter and control your web search results. Google has a number of other operators that perform various functions, such as looking up information or in some cases providing links for additional information from third-party content providers. These operators are covered in depth in the next chapter.

*In the book* How to Do Everything with Google *(McGraw-Hill/Osborne, 2003), authors Fritz Schneider, Nancy Blachman, and Eric Fredricksen list a number of additional undocumented (and unsupported) advanced Google operators. See http://www.googleguide.com/advanced_operators.html for details.*

4

# Chapter 5

## Hidden Google Tools

A fundamental philosophy driving all development work at Google is to make sure something "intelligent" happens when a user types literally anything into a search box. Most of the time, people type in words related to information they are seeking, and Google responds by suggesting a list of web pages that contain relevant information.

But just beneath the surface of Google's Spartan interface lies a gaggle of hidden tools that go far beyond searching the Web for relevant pages of information. These tools are "hidden," not because Google is secretive about them, but rather because they work automatically whenever a user enters a special type of query.

Some of these hidden tools generate specialized Google search results. Others create links to information on partner web sites. The bottom line is that they can be real timesavers if you know what these tools do and how to use them.

# Definitions

What's the meaning of life? Ask Google, and you'll not only get web search results, but a link to a definition of the word "life" from Answers.com.

Click this link and you'll see a page with multiple definitions of the word from a number of sources, including the *American Heritage Dictionary*, Princeton University's *Word Net* database, *The American Heritage Stedman's Medical Dictionary,* and several others.

If you enter more than one search term, the **definition** link is replaced with hyperlinks for each word. Clicking any of these links will also take you to a definition page on Answers.com.

For many words, you'll also see synonyms from *Roget's II: The New Thesaurus, Third Edition.* You may also see encyclopedia entries from the *Columbia Electronic Encyclopedia* and the volunteer-compiled Wikipedia; common misspellings from the *Misspeller's Dictionary*, as well as translations of the word into other languages. As you can see, it's far more than a simple definition!

Google also offers what it calls "web definitions" of most words. To get a web definition, type the word **define**, a space, and the word you want defined, as shown here:

At the top of your result page, the first result is a web definition for your word, next to an icon of a book, as shown in the following illustration. Web definitions are extracts taken from sources such as online glossaries or frequently asked questions pages. The source web page is indicated, and there's a link to see the definition in context. It's important to keep in mind that these web definitions may not have the same authority as dictionary definitions. Their real value lies in the different perspectives on a topic that they offer.

Web definition

**Web**                                  Results **1 - 10** of about **6,690** for <u>define</u> <u>latitudinarian</u>. **(0.09** seconds)

<u>Web definitions for **latitudinarian**</u>

 a person who is broad-minded and tolerant (especially in standards of religious belief and conduct)
www.cogsci.princeton.edu/cgi-bin/webwn - <u>Definition in context</u>

<u>Definition of **Latitudinarian** from dictionary.net</u>
Free online English dictionary. We **define latitudinarian** as
NLatitudinarian \Lat`i*tu`di*na'ri*an\, a. [Cf. F.latitudinaire.]1. Not restrained;
not confined ...
www.dictionary.net/**latitudinarian** - 9k - <u>Cached</u> - <u>Similar pages</u>

<u>Thesaurus.com/**latitudinarian**</u>
Synonyms of **latitudinarian** at Thesaurus.com. ... Definition:, progressive.
Synonyms:, advanced, avant-garde, big, broad, broad-minded, catholic, detached, ...
thesaurus.reference.com/search?q=**latitudinarian** - 14k - <u>Cached</u> - <u>Similar pages</u>

<u>Thesaurus.com/liberal</u>
... Definition:, abundant. Synonyms:, ample, aplenty, bounteous, bountiful, ...
impartial, indulgent, inexact, intelligent, interested, **latitudinarian**, ...
thesaurus.reference.com/search?q=liberal - 24k - <u>Cached</u> - <u>Similar pages</u>
[ <u>More results from thesaurus.reference.com</u> ]

Clicking the **Definition in context** link often displays the WordNet database entry for the word. Occasionally, however, clicking the link simply displays the page on which the word was defined, and you'll have to hunt on the page to find the word in context.

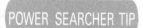 *To find a word on any web page, use your browser's "Find" command (CTRL-F), which will highlight the word on the page.*

There are two ways to see all the web definitions Google has found for a particular word. At the top of every web definition is a link that reads **Web definitions for....** Clicking this link will give you the full list of web definitions for that word, as shown here:

**Web**

Tip: Try <u>Google Answers</u> for help from expert researchers

Definitions of **latitudinarian** on the Web:

a person who is broad-minded and tolerant (especially in standards of religious belief and conduct)
<u>www.cogsci.princeton.edu/cgi-bin/webwn</u>

free-thinking: unwilling to accept authority or dogma (especially in religion)
<u>www.cogsci.princeton.edu/cgi-bin/webwn</u>

Alternatively, you can cut to the chase and get a full list of web definitions immediately by using the special **define:** operator with no space between the colon and the word you want defined. Results using the **define:** operator omit web page results. Depending on the word, you may see dozens of definitions that Google has found on the Web.

## Beyond Google: Online Dictionaries

Although Google provides both web definitions and links to other online dictionaries, other authoritative dictionaries can provide even more comprehensive definitions.

As one of the most authoritative online dictionary publishers, Cambridge offers its Cambridge Dictionaries Online site, at http://dictionary.cambridge.org/. This site has several online dictionaries, including idiom dictionaries as well as French/English and Spanish/English dictionaries.

The OneLook Dictionary Search (http://www.onelook.com/) is a huge "one-stop" reference source, with definitions of more than six million words drawn from an index of nearly 1,000 online dictionaries, including dozens of specialized subject-specific dictionaries. Be sure to try the reverse dictionary, which lets you describe a concept and get back a list of words and phrases related to that concept.

# News

Google has a very powerful news-search service that's described in detail in Chapter 19. But you don't have to use Google News to get headlines. In keeping with the philosophy of "do something intelligent" with every query, Google always analyzes your search terms to see if there are any current news stories related to your query. If so, headlines for up to three relevant stories are displayed at the top of the result page next to an icon of a newspaper, as shown in Figure 5-1.

Clicking a headline link takes you directly to the source of the news story. Two other links provide direct access to the full Google News service. The **News results for...** link reruns your query in Google News, changing your results from web pages to news stories. The **View all the latest headlines** link takes you to the top-level page of Google News.

# Stock Quotes

Google offers two ways to get direct information about U.S. stocks and mutual funds. You can enter one or more NYSE, NASDAQ, AMEX, or mutual fund ticker symbols directly into any Google search box. The topmost result link, **Stock quotes for...**, provides stock quotes for the symbols you entered (see Figure 5-2).

Clicking this link will take you to a framed result page, with financial information from a number of providers on the company or mutual fund you searched for. Click the tabs to see different perspectives from each of these providers.

The second way to get stock quotes is to search using the name of a publicly traded company. In most cases, the company's home page will be in the top web results. Look for the **Stock Quotes:**

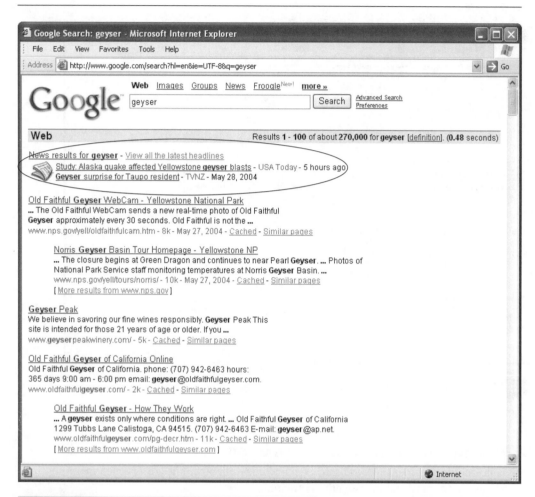

**FIGURE 5-1**   Google scans all your queries looking for relevant news headlines.

link on the final line of this result, next to the **Cached** and **Similar pages** links. Clicking the **Stock Quotes:** link displays the same framed result page from multiple providers, as described earlier.

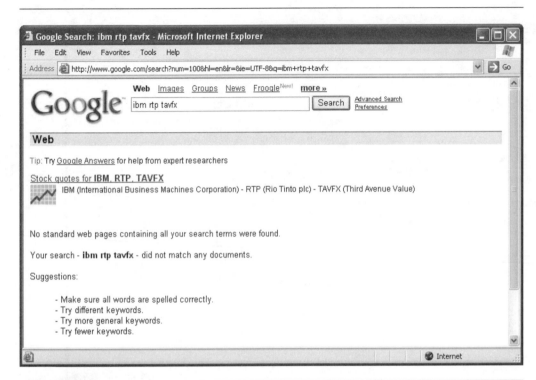

**FIGURE 5-2**    Google provides links to financial information when you search for company names or ticker symbols.

## Beyond Google: Financial Information

Although Google provides links to basic stock information, other sites offer much more comprehensive financial and investment information.

MSN Money's Create Your Own Stock SearchTool (http://moneycentral.msn.com/investor/finder/customstocksdl.asp) is a screening tool that allows you to find stocks that fit specific criteria, allowing you to filter results by industry, market cap, price/earnings ratio, and a number of other metrics. Be sure to check out the additional financial research links on the left side of the screen—these are very powerful tools for investment research.

Big Charts (http://bigcharts.marketwatch.com/) is a comprehensive investment research web site offering professional-level research tools such as interactive charts, quotes, industry analysis, market news, and commentary.

# Street Maps

To find a street map of most locations in the U.S., Google needs only an address and a city name to recognize a query as a map request. Results include links to Google Maps, Yahoo! Maps and MapQuest, which display a map of the location you entered.

Of these three mapping services, Google Maps (http://maps.google.com) is the best. Maps are colorful, accurate, and you can easily zoom in or out using the slider to the left side of the map. Arrows at the top of the slider let you scroll the map in any direction, as shown in Figure 5-3. You can also hold down your left mouse button and drag the map into a new position. Unlike other mapping services that reload an image when you use these interactive features, Google Maps updates instantly, making this a seriously cool tool.

A floating bubble pinpoints the street address you typed, and it provides options to get step-by-step directions "to there" or "from there" for any other location. Just click the appropriate link and a dialog box appears—simply type your start or destination address, click the **Get Directions** button, and a new map appears showing your route on the map, together with detailed driving directions.

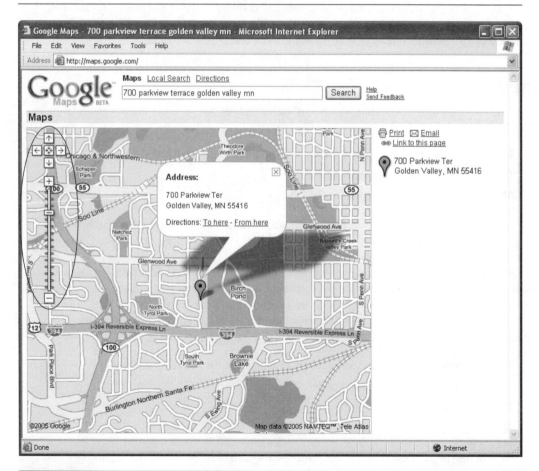

FIGURE 5-3   Use sliders, arrows, or just drag a Google Map around to update the locations it displays.

Street maps are also a prominent feature of Google Phonebook and local business listings results. The Google Maps home page has a link to Google Local above the search box, but if you're looking for local information, you can type a query directly into the Google Maps search box and you'll often see local search listings displayed next to a map.

POWER SEARCHER TIP *Use the words "in" and "near" in Google Maps queries to narrow your search. For example, "new york deli near santa fe" returns a list of New York-style delicatessens in the Santa Fe, New Mexico area.*

## Beyond Google: Aerial Images

Want to see an aerial photograph of a location, rather than a two-dimensional map? Try the TerraFly site (http://www.terrafly.com).

TerraFly lets you search by coordinates, city, ZIP code, or address, and it displays aerial or satellite images of your specified location. Images offer options to overlay road names, places and Census information with aggregate annual income and population counts.

# Phonebook

Looking for a phone number? Google can look up listings for both U.S. businesses and residences. You have three ways to find listings for a U.S. business:

- Type the business name, city, and state into the Google search box.
- Type the business name and ZIP code.
- Type a phone number with the area code.

Results from Google's Business Phonebook show listings of businesses that match your search terms, with phone numbers, addresses, and links to maps from Yahoo! or MapQuest (see Figure 5-4).

Notice that the search box at the top of the result page is subtly different from regular web search results. Instead of a single "search" button next to the search form, there are two buttons—one to search the phonebook, and the other to search the Web.

You have a few more options for finding listings for a U.S. residence. From any Google search box, you can type any of these combinations:

- First name or initial, last name, and either city, state, area code, or ZIP code
- Phone number, including area code
- Last name, city, state
- Last name, ZIP code

Be sure to type your query using the word order shown here. Searching for a state, city, and last name will not give you phonebook results.

**FIGURE 5-4**   Results from Google's Business Phonebook

For relatively common names, Google only shows two names in the phonebook result. Click the **Phonebook results for...** link to see additional phonebook listings. If Google isn't sure whether you're searching for a business or residential listing, it will show results from both, as you see in Figure 5-5. To expand the listings from either source, click the **More business listings** or **More residential listings** link.

To bypass web and local results and force Google to return only phonebook listings, use the undocumented **phonebook:** operator with your search terms.

Although Google does a fairly good job of looking up business and residential phonebook listings, it relies on third-party data that's notoriously incomplete and out of date, so you may not always get satisfactory results. Google's local search results, described in detail in the next section, are typically much better than business phonebook results, both in terms of accuracy and the amount of detail provided.

# Beyond Google: Internet Yellow and White Pages Search

Although Google provides quick-and-dirty phonebook lookups, other services offer much more sophisticated White and Yellow Pages listings.

For example, Argali White & Yellow (http://www.argali.com/) searches multiple online telephone and e-mail directories and then combines and displays results as if they came from one integrated directory. Because it uses multiple sources, Argali's results are often better than most other online directories.

**FIGURE 5-5**    Phonebook listings for both businesses and residences

# Local Business Information

Google's local business information service combine the best of the phonebook and street maps features, and it adds additional information that Google has compiled from analyzing the Web. Google's approach to local search involves using Yellow Page and business directory information from third-party providers, and integrating this with information about individual businesses from Google's main web page index.

Google also applies its ranking algorithms to local search results, rather than listing results in alphabetical order or by distance, as do most other online business directories. This means Google is attempting to show you the most relevant local results for each search, rather than those that are closest to your location.

As with the Maps and Phonebook features, Google Local currently only searches for locations within the U.S., but plans are in the works to expand the service to other locations throughout the world in the near future.

*You can use Google Local to find noncommercial local attractions, such as parks, recreation centers, and other community landmarks.*

There are two ways to access local business information. The easiest is to simply enter your search terms and a city name or ZIP code into any Google search box. The topmost results will feature up to three links to local businesses in the city or area you've specified, as shown in Figure 5-6.

Clicking the **Local results for...** link will provide a full listing of local business results related to your query.

A more direct method of getting local results is to start from the Google Local home page, at http://local.google.com/ (see Figure 5-7).

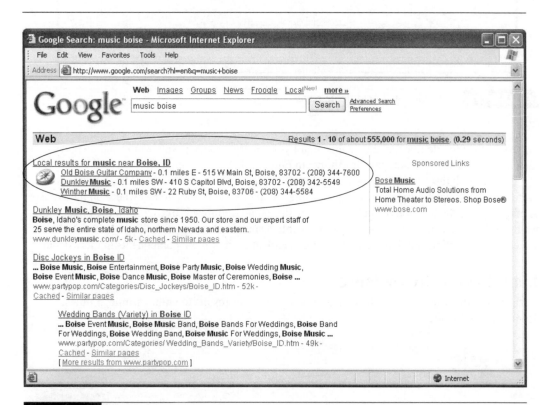

Local search results appear at the top of normal web search results.

**FIGURE 5-7**    The Google Local home page

Using the Google Local home page to enter your query bypasses web results and displays a local business search result page, as shown in Figure 5-8.

Local search results are displayed in columns, including business name, address, and links to "references," which are pages about each business that Google has found elsewhere on the Web. A map displays the location of each business with a small thumbtack-like icon. At the top of the result page are links that limit your results to within a specific distance as well as **Show only** links, which can help refine and limit your query. Let's look at each of these components in more detail.

## Limit Results by Distance

At the top of the result page are links that let you limit your results to within 1 mile, 5 miles, 15 miles, and 45 miles.

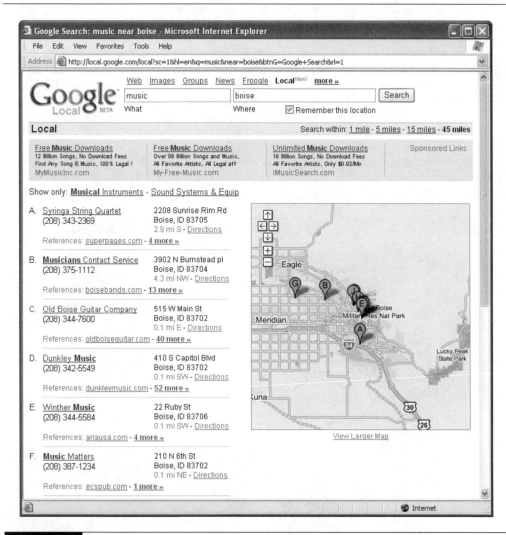

**FIGURE 5-8**    A local business search result page

By default, all results are displayed. To narrow results, click the **1 mile**, **5 miles**, or **15 miles** link. To restore all results, click the **45 miles** link.

## Refine and Limit Local Results

In addition to filtering your results by distance, Google also provides suggestions for narrowing your query to find more specific results, as shown here:

Show: **All Results** - Music: Musical Instruments Instruction - Books: Sheet Music - Miscellaneous Other Publishing: Music Publishers - *None of these*

Clicking one of these links will typically greatly reduce the number of results, making it easier to find a local merchant that can satisfy your needs. To restore all results, click the **All Results** link.

POWER SEARCHER TIP    *With Google Local, you might want to experiment with your search terms to get the best results. For example, searching for "lawyers" vs. "attorneys" offers different results. A search for "cell phone" found no stores closer than 20 miles away. Changing the search to "wireless phones" found numerous locations within a few miles of the starting location.*

The map display is also updated when you use the refinement links. Try clicking the links to show results within 1 or 5 miles, and you'll see the scale of the map shrink, showing much more detail of a particular area, as shown here:

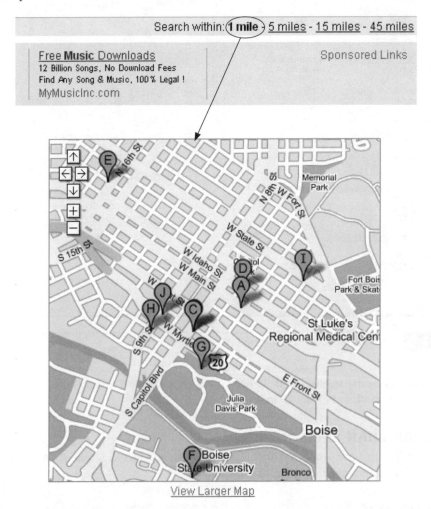

View Larger Map

Alternatively, you can select one of the category filters, and you'll see the proximity of businesses offering similar products or services to one another.

 *If you always want your local search results to be relative to a specific location (such as your home or office address), check the **remember this location** box on any local search page. To change the location, simply enter and save a new location. To delete a saved location, use the URL http://local.google.com/local?sl=1.*

## Business Reference Pages

Clicking a link to a business name displays what Google calls a "business reference page" with lots of additional information about the business. Figure 5-9 shows a typical business reference page.

At the top of each business reference page, the business name, address, and telephone number are listed. Next to this listing is a map, with an icon representing the location of the business in the center of the map. Links beneath the map allow you to easily zoom in or out or get driving directions.

 *By default, the city name or ZIP code you used in your query appears in the search box—not very useful for most of us. To get accurate driving directions, enter the full street address and city name of your starting point before clicking the **Get Directions** button.*

Beneath the business listing and map is a list of the types of products or services Google thinks the business offers, as well as links to other web pages related to the business. At the bottom of the page are links to pages related to the business found in Google's main index. Using an elaborate process of cross-referencing information, Google tries to identify the company's web site in its index and, if it can, makes this the topmost link in this **References** list of web sites.

 *More information about Google Local can be found in the FAQ at http://local .google.com/help/faq_local.html.*

## Beyond Google: Local Search

Google's local search is sparse compared to other sources of local information on the Web. All the major search services offer a local search, each with its own flavor and strengths. Just as it's important to use multiple search engines when searching for information, it's worth trying out the various features of the other local search services on the Web. And although Amazon's A9 search isn't yet considered a major search service, its novel approach to local search, displaying photographs of storefronts in search results is a fascinating and often useful alternative. Table 5-1 shows you where to find these services.

 *Many online Yellow Pages are now also offering web search, product search, and other features, thus blurring the line between search engines and Yellow Pages. One of the best is Superpages, at http://superpages.com/.*

**FIGURE 5-9**   A business reference page for a Boise, Idaho company

| Local Search Service | Web Address |
| --- | --- |
| Amazon A9 Yellow Pages | http://a9.com/a=oyp |
| AOL Local Search | http://localsearch.aol.com |
| Ask Jeeves Local | http://local.ask.com/local |
| MSN Local Search | http://search.msn.com |
| Yahoo! Local Search | http://local.yahoo.com/ |

**TABLE 5-1**   Local Search Services Provided by the Major Search Engines

# Travel Information

You're about ready to catch a flight—what are the conditions at the airport? Is the weather affecting airline schedules? Or are there delays for other reasons? To find out, you can enter the three-letter U.S. airport code followed by **airport**, and the topmost link in your results will be to airport status information provided by the Federal Aviation Authority, as shown here:

You can also get the status of many flights in the U.S. by entering the name of an airline and flight number. At the top of your result page, you'll see a link that gives you the option of tracking the flight on Travelocity, Expedia, or fboweb.com.

Links for flight tracking information

# Beyond Google: Flight Information

Have you ever flown on a plane that displays real-time flight tracking information on the video monitors? That same information is available on the Web.

Cheap Tickets FlightTracker (http://www.cheaptickets.com/trs/cheaptickets/flighttracker/flight_tracker_home.xsl), shown in Figure 5-10, tracks the status and arrival time of airborne flights in North America, and to and from North America and other parts of the world for some airlines, in real time using data from air traffic control computer systems.

Current Airport Traffic (http://www.flightview.com/TravelTools/ProcessFTQuery.asp?qt=at) provides a visual map of real-time flight traffic for ten major U.S. airports.

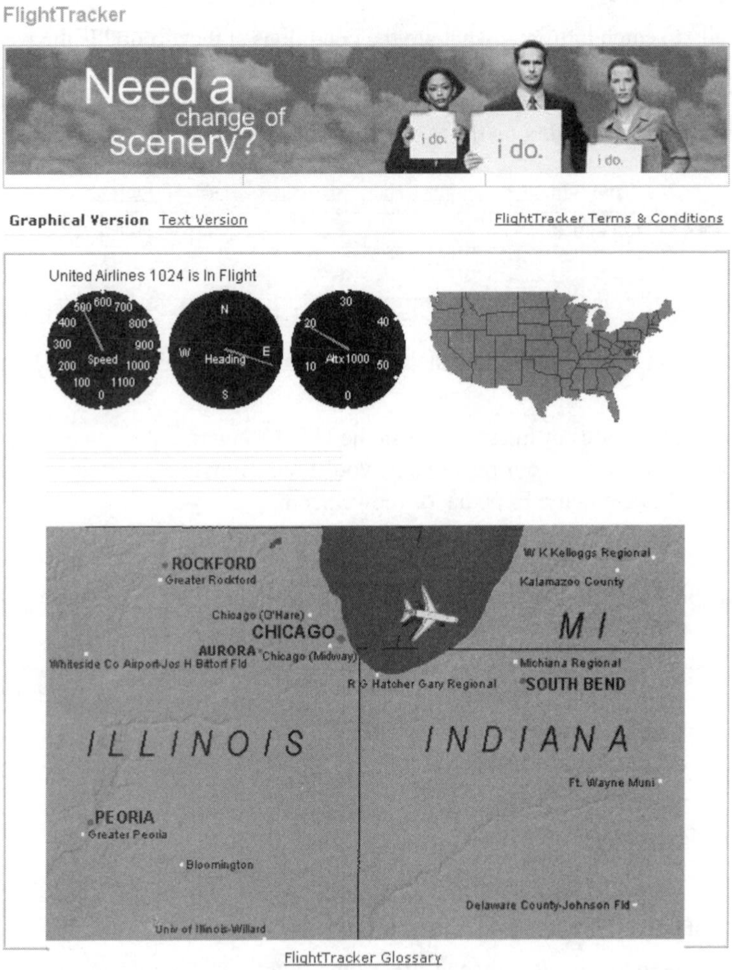

FlightTracker

Graphical Version  Text Version                                FlightTracker Terms & Conditions

United Airlines 1024 is In Flight

FlightTracker Glossary

**FIGURE 5-10**   In-flight information from FlightTracker includes an accurate estimated arrival time.

# Weather Information

Want to know what the weather is like in any U.S. city? Simply type the command **weather:** followed by a city name or a ZIP code into any Google search box, and you'll see current conditions as well as a forecast for the next few days at the top of search results.

---

**Web**

Tip: Find maps by searching for a street address with city or zip code

**Weather** for **Juneau, AK**

| | Mon | Tue | Wed | Thu |
|---|---|---|---|---|
| **41°F** Overcast Wind: E at 12 mph Humidity: 93% |  44° \| 37° |  45° \| 37° |  44° \| 36° |  46° \| 36° |

# Movie Reviews and Show Times

"Here's looking at you, kid." Those immortal words, made famous in... in... what movie was that, again? There's an easy way to find out. Simply use the **movie:** command followed by a phrase or keywords related to a movie you remember, and Google will attempt to name the movie for you, as shown in Figure 5-11. Search results also include reviews and ratings for movies, all gathered automatically.

Click a movie's name, and you'll see a page with all the reviews of the movie Google has found, as well as links to frequently mentioned terms in the reviews, such as actor names, soundtrack information, and so on.

The **movie:** command also works to locate movies currently showing in theaters. It works just like the **weather:** command described earlier. Simply enter **movie:** followed by a U.S. city or ZIP code, and you'll see listings of all movies currently showing in theaters near that city.

---

 **Web** Images Groups News Froogle Local^New! **more »**

movie:here's looking at you kid       Search   Advanced Search
                                                Preferences

**"at"** is a very common word and was not included in your search. [details]

**Movies**

★★★★★
19 reviews     Casablanca (1942)

> Review: Casablanca
> ... It contains a slew of recognizable lines ("**Here's looking** at **you, kid**", "Of all the gin joints in all the towns in all the world, she walks into mine", ...
> Reelviews - James Berardinelli
>
> BBC - Films - review - Casablanca
> "**Here's looking** at **you, kid**". "Casablanca" has often been called the best film of all time. Probably because it is. Unrequited love, midgets, some of the ...
> BBC - William Mager - Dec 4, 2000

---

**FIGURE 5-11**   Google's **movie:** command finds reviews and show times.

# Web Page Information

In the last chapter, you learned about a number of operators designed to provide additional information about a specific web page, providing information about similar pages, pages that link to the page, pages that contain the URL of the page, as well as an operator that displays the cached page that Google has stored.

Although you can use each of these operators separately, there's an easier way to get all this information: Just type the URL of a page into a Google search box. Your results will contain a link to the page and its description, as well as links that run the four operators described previously without any additional typing, as shown in Figure 5-12.

## Beyond Google: Web Page Information

The Whois Source site (http://www.whois.sc/) provides more extensive information about a web page than what Google provides.

Enter a domain name into the Whois Source search box (omit the "http://www" part of the URL), and you'll get a thumbnail image of the web page, domain ownership information, and much more.

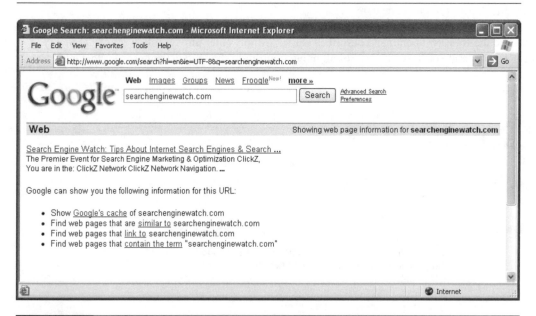

**FIGURE 5-12**   Using a URL as a query returns information about that page rather than web results.

# Search by Number

Part of Google's effort to "do something intelligent" with queries is the addition of a search-by-number capability that lets you enter package-tracking numbers, area codes, patent numbers, and other numeric strings, and get sensible results. Table 5-2 shows several examples of the search-by-number feature. The search-by-number feature is still relatively limited at this point, but you can expect to see Google expand this capability in the future.

Search-by-number results are not Google web search results; rather, they are links to external providers of information.

# Calculator

By just about any reckoning, Google is one of the world's largest supercomputers. Little wonder, then, that an enterprising Google engineer rigged up a way to use Google as a calculator (and incidentally did so while he was supposed to be working on Google's spell-checking software). The calculator can solve math problems involving basic arithmetic, more complicated math, units of measure and conversions, and physical constants. Even better, the calculator tries to understand your problem without requiring you to use special symbols or commands. Tables 5-3 through 5-5 show the types of problems Google's calculator can solve.

Calculator results are often displayed without web search results, though Google will provide a link to search for the equation you entered, if you're interested in seeing web documents where the equation occurs.

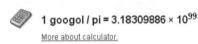

1 googol / pi = $3.18309886 \times 10^{99}$

More about calculator.

**POWER SEARCHER TIP** *The calculator understands many different units, as well as many physical and mathematical constants, in both their long and abbreviated forms.*

| Search For: | Example |
| --- | --- |
| UPS tracking numbers | "1Z9999W99999999999" |
| FedEx tracking numbers | "999999999999" |
| USPS tracking numbers | "9999 9999 9999 9999 9999 99" |
| Vehicle ID (VIN) numbers | "AAAAA999A9AA99999" |
| UPC codes | "073333531084" |
| Telephone area codes | "650" |
| ZIP codes | "55416" |
| Patent numbers | "patent 5123123" (the word "patent" must precede the number) |
| FAA airplane registration numbers | "n199ua" |
| FCC equipment IDs | "fcc B4Z-34009-PIR" (the word "fcc" must precede the number) |

**TABLE 5-2** Google's Search-by-Number Feature

| Operator | Function | Example |
|---|---|---|
| + | Addition | 9+77 |
| − | Subtraction | 1901–17 |
| * | Multiplication | 12*7 |
| / | Division | 109/3 |
| ^ or ** | Exponentiation (raise to a power of) | 5^2 |
| % | Modulo (finds the remainder after division) | 13%7 |
| choose | **X choose Y** determines the number of ways of choosing a set of Y elements from a set of X elements | 13 choose 5 |
| th root of | Calculates the $n$th root of a number | 5th root of 94 |
| % of | **X % of Y** computes X percent of Y | 25% of 1500 |

**TABLE 5-3**    Calculator Operators That Combine Two Numbers

The calculator works with decimal, hexadecimal, octal, and binary numbers. Prefix hexadecimal numbers with **0x**, octal numbers with **0o**, and binary numbers with **0b**.

Use the **in** operator to tell Google how you want an answer to be expressed. Here are a few examples of the kinds of things you can do with the Google calculator:

- 500 miles in roman numerals
- 5 terabytes in gigabytes
- 16 tons in kilograms
- 427 kilometers in rods

**POWER SEARCHER TIP**    *More information about the Google calculator can be found in the FAQ at http://www.google.com/help/calculator.html.*

| Operator | Function | Example |
|---|---|---|
| sqrt | Square root | sqrt(64) |
| sin, cos, tan, etc. | Trigonometric functions (numbers are assumed to be radians) | sin(pi/5) |
| | | tan(30 degrees) |
| ln | Logarithm base e | ln(13) |
| log | Logarithm base 10 | log(10,000) |

**TABLE 5-4**    Calculator Operators That Work on Single Numbers

| Operator | Function | Example |
|----------|----------|---------|
| ! | Factorial | 15! |

**TABLE 5-5** The Factorial Operator Comes after the Number

## Beyond Google: Online Calculators

Want a calculator to help with fire engine design? How about one for dating ancient mummies? You'll find them in Martindale's Calculators On-Line Center (http://www.martindalecenter.com/Calculators.html), a huge directory of more than 18,000 online calculators, covering just about every subject imaginable.

# Special Searches

Google has a number of special search pages that automatically limit your search results to web sites related to a specific topic. These include:

- Apple Macintosh
- BSD Unix
- Linux
- Microsoft
- U.S. Government
- University Search

## Apple Macintosh

The Apple Macintosh specialty search (http://www.google.com/mac.html) limits results to sites focusing on Apple computer products, services, reviews, and so on, including Apple itself as well as sites such as Apple Insider, We Love Macs, Mac Rumors, Apple-History.com, and many others.

## BSD Unix

The BSD Unix specialty search (http://www.google.com/bsd) limits results to sites focusing on BSD, the version of Unix developed at the University of California, Berkeley. These include Bsd.org, freebsd.org, Oreilly's BSD Dev Center, and many others.

## Linux

The Linux specialty search (http://www.google.com/linux) limits results to sites focusing on the open-source operating system. These include Linux.org, companies that sell Linux (such as Red Hat), online news and discussion forums (such as Slashdot), and many others.

## Microsoft

The Microsoft specialty search (http://www.google.com/microsoft.html) limits results to sites focusing on Microsoft and its products and services. These include Microsoft itself, Windows Annoyances, most of the online Windows-oriented magazines, Security Focus, and many others.

## U.S. Government

The U.S. Government specialty search (http://www.google.com/unclesam) limits results to sites focusing on federal, state, and local government information and services. Although these are mostly government web sites, there are also results from non-governmental sites such as Findlaw.

## University Search

Google's University Search (http://www.google.com/options/universities.html) let's you narrow your search to a specific school's web site. It's fundamentally similar to limiting your search to the domain of a particular university using the Advanced Search page or the **site:** operator. However, the home page for University Search features a handy alphabetized listing of all schools that can be searched.

# Chapter 6

## Searching for Images

A picture is worth a thousand words, and that poses a problem for Google—and every other general-purpose search engine, for that matter. Why? Because Google is highly tuned and optimized to understand *words*. Words on a web page are called *text strings,* made up of individual characters, and characters are stored in computer memory as unique numbers. It's easy for Google to recognize and manipulate text strings, because they form recognizable patterns that can be compared to one another.

By contrast, images on the Web are made up of hundreds or thousands of discrete points, each with its own color and brightness, which together make up a gestalt whole that our brain perceives as a picture. Like alphabetic characters, each point in an image is also represented by a number, but these numbers don't form the same kind of recognizable patterns that text strings do, because each picture is unique.

So in essence, although Google can recognize the format of an image, it can't "see" it or know what the picture represents. Google overcomes this "blindness" by some clever detective sleuthing that does a pretty good job in most cases of correctly guessing what a picture is about.

# How Image Search Works

To fully understand how Google's Image Search feature works, you need to know a bit about the most common formats used for web graphics and also how Google pieces together various clues to form an educated opinion about what an image represents.

## Web Image Formats

Images on the Web are typically stored in one of two formats:

- **GIF (file extension .gif)**    The most common image format on the Web, the GIF (Graphics Interchange Format, pronounced like *jiff,* but with a hard *g*) format is used for illustrations and simple graphics that use 256 colors or less. Most artwork, banners, and buttons on web pages are created using the GIF format, because its limited color palette allows graphics to be compressed into small files that can be downloaded quickly from a web server. Figure 6-1 shows an image in GIF format.

- **JPEG (file extension .jpg)**    This format is commonly used for photographs or complex artwork that uses more than 256 colors. The JPEG (Joint Photographic Experts Group, pronounced *jay-peg*) format has a variety of compression options, allowing images to be saved as very small, low-resolution images, very large, high-resolution images, or anywhere in between. Figure 6-2 shows the same image as Figure 6-1, but in JPEG rather than GIF format.

Understanding the differences in these formats and when they are commonly used can really help you improve your search results, especially if you use Google's advanced Image Search capabilities discussed later in this chapter.

°FIGURE 6-1    GIF format graphics are for simple illustrations. (Photo by Chris Sherman)

## How Google Uses Clues to "See" Images

Because images are made up of bits rather than text, Google cannot directly compare your search terms with the actual contents of the image. Instead, Google relies on a number of indirect techniques that provide useful clues about what the image represents.

One of the most important clues is the filename and file type of the image. Figure 6-3 is a picture of Sydney's famous opera house at sunset. The picture's filename is opera-house.jpg. Right away, Google knows that because the file type is .jpg, the image is likely a photograph or complex illustration. Google also knows that the picture probably represents an opera house, though the filename isn't specific enough to allow Google to guess that it's in Sydney.

FIGURE 6-2    The JPEG format is commonly used for photographs and complex artwork. (Photo by Chris Sherman)

**FIGURE 6-3**    Sydney's opera house at sunset  (Photo by Chris Sherman)

Google also analyzes the text surrounding the image. In many cases, the text immediately above or below an image is a caption describing the image. In the case of Figure 6-4, the web page author created a caption that reads "A picture of the Opera House taken from the Botanic Gardens at Sunset." In addition to verification that the image is a picture of an opera house, Google now has two more clues to work with: the opera house is near a botanic garden, and the photograph was taken at sunset.

Still more clues are available. The full text of the page is analyzed for conceptually related information, or for words that occur together elsewhere in Google's vast index. Other photographs on the page show images from the Taronga Zoo and from picturesque Rose Bay. Even if the web page author doesn't use the word "Sydney" anywhere on the page, Google can infer that all these pictures are probably of Sydney, because other pages on the Web link Taronga Zoo, Rose Bay, and the opera house to Sydney harbor (the technical term for this is "co-citation").

Two HTML tags can also offer important clues. The title tag may explicitly describe the contents of the page, such as "Sightseeing trip on Sydney ferries." Each image also has an optional ALT tag, which lets the page author write a description of the image that will be displayed in browsers that don't support images or that have the image display function turned off.

Web page title ——————►

**FIGURE 6-4**    The caption and page title provide valuable clues about an image.

Google also uses link analysis to help understand the content of images. Links pointing to the page with the Sydney opera house photo might use anchor text describing either the image itself or the general contents of the page: "Check out this photo of the Sydney opera house at sunset," or "This is a great collection of photos taken around Sydney harbor."

These are the most important of what Google says are "dozens" of factors it uses to determine image content. So even though Google can't "see" an image in the way a human being can, in many cases there are enough clues for Google to confidently determine that a particular image is a likely match for your search terms.

# Basic Image Search

Google has indexed nearly 1.2 billion web images. To use Google's Image Search, click the **Images** top link above any search form.

Watch carefully when you do! Unlike the other primary Google search services, such as News, Groups, and Froogle, the Image Search page, shown in Figure 6-5, looks virtually identical to Google's home page. But there are subtle differences, such as links for **Advanced Image Search** and **Image Search Help**.

Image Search results differ radically from web search results. Rather than a list of links and descriptions of web pages, Image Search results consist of a page of 20 thumbnail images, with image dimensions and filenames listed beneath (see Figure 6-6). Notice the message beneath the search box, which tells you the status of the SafeSearch filter described in Chapter 2. The default for Image Search is moderate filtering, unless you have previously set your preferences for no filtering or strict filtering. You can change your preference from any Image Search result page by clicking either the SafeSearch message link or the **Preferences** link.

POWER SEARCHER TIP

*Remember, Google's SafeSearch filter only works with the English language interface.*

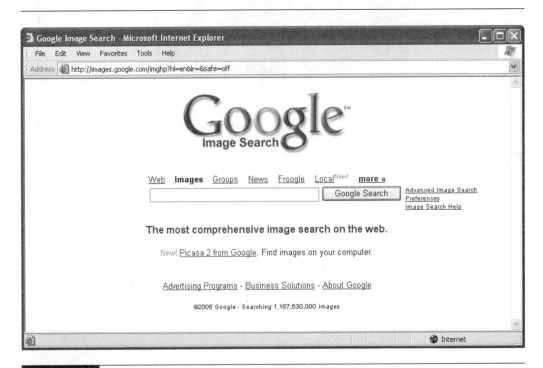

FIGURE 6-5    Google's Image Search page

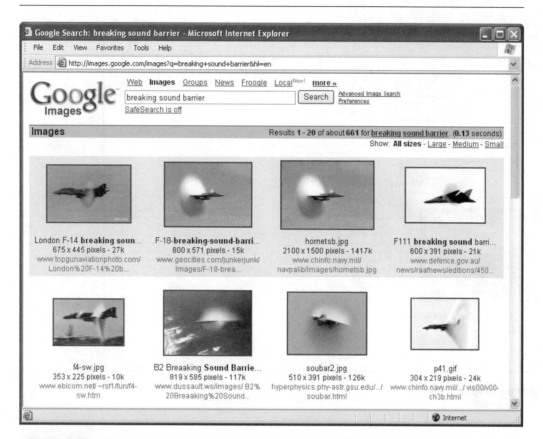

**FIGURE 6-6**    Image Search results display 20 thumbnail pictures.

To see a full-size version of any image, simply click the image itself. This brings up a split-screen page, in which the thumbnail version of the image is displayed in the top frame, and the page on which the image was found is displayed in the bottom frame (see Figure 6-7). The top frame also contains filename and size information, as well as a message that indicates whether the thumbnail is actual size or has been scaled down. In either case, there's a link next to the message titled **See full-size image**. Clicking this link causes the image alone to be displayed in the bottom frame.

Two other links appear in the top frame. One removes the frame, displaying only the full page on which the image was found. The other works just like your browser's Back button, taking you back to your initial search result page.

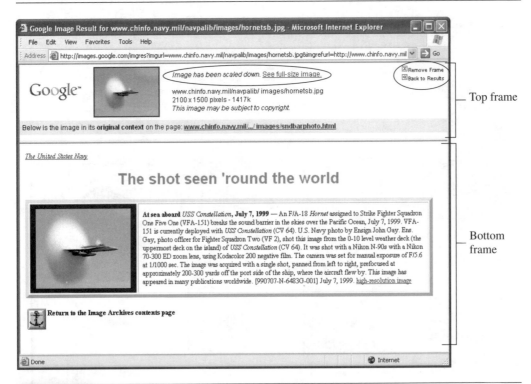

**FIGURE 6-7**    Single-image result pages are divided into a split screen.

The page displayed in the bottom frame is the actual web page that the image was found on—unlike the information in the top frame, it is not coming from Google's index. In most cases, you need to scroll down the page to locate the image. Occasionally, when you scroll you won't find the image on the page. This isn't a bug with Google—rather, it means that the web page has been modified and the image removed in the time since Google last crawled the page. If you can't find the image on the page, you're out of luck.

**POWER SEARCHER TIP**    *To save an image, place the cursor over it, right-click with your mouse, and select the **Save Image** command. Remember, many images on the Web are protected by copyright.*

Google provides a basic filter that lets you select the size of the images displayed in search results (this refers to the size of the images themselves—thumbnail results will always be small). By default, all sizes are shown. In the upper-right corner of each search result page are links that let you select large, medium, or small images (height and width, not file size). Click one of these links, and the other sizes will be filtered out. You'll also see a new link that restores all results.

## Image Search and News Photos

When you run an image search, Google automatically checks Google News for relevant images. If news photographs related to your search terms are found, these are automatically placed at the top of the search results. Unlike other images, news photographs are time sensitive. News images that you see one day may not appear in Image Search results the next day. In fact, you may see different news images each time you search on the same subject.

# Advanced Image Search

Many of the special operators described in Chapter 4 work in the basic Image Search box, including the exclusion operator, the Boolean OR operator, and quoted phrases. For even more control over your Image Search results, Google provides the Advanced Image Search page.

Google's Advanced Image Search page, shown in Figure 6-8, is deceptively sparse, but behind the apparent simplicity are some very powerful image-finding tools. Because Google relies on far fewer clues for finding images than finding text, using Advanced Image Search can almost always help dramatically improve your results.

**6**

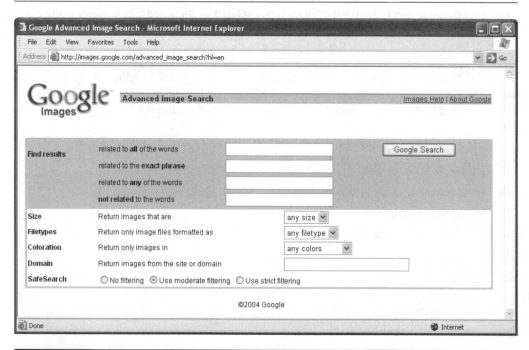

FIGURE 6-8    Google's Advanced Image Search page

## Advanced Image Search Word Filters

Like all Google Advanced Search pages, the top portion of the Advanced Image Search page consists of four search boxes that serve as word filters. Again, Google can't directly associate search terms with images, so each of these search boxes lets you enter words *related to* images that Google has indexed.

The four Image Search word filters let you limit your search results to images related to all of the words, an exact phrase, any of the words, or images *not* related to the words you enter into the respective search forms.

Each of these filters has a corresponding operator that works directly in any Google Image Search form:

- **All of the words** is the equivalent of putting the inclusion operator (+) in front of each search term.

- **Exact phrase** is the equivalent of enclosing your search terms in quotation marks.

- **Any of the words** is the equivalent of using the OR operator.

- **Not related to the words** is the equivalent of putting the exclusion operator (–) in front of each search term.

Probably the most useful of all these filters is **not related to the words**. This is especially true when your search term is a common word with multiple meanings. Say, for example, you are looking for pictures of London, Kentucky, home of the renowned World Chicken Festival. A simple image search using the word "London" returns more than 700,000 results, most of which are pictures associated with London, England and the author Jack London. The simple addition of the words "Kentucky" to the **all the words** search box and "England" and "Jack" to the **not related to the words** search box changes the results dramatically, as you can see in Figure 6-9.

Here are some other examples where excluding terms can improve search results:

- Orlando Bloom –Florida

- Apple computer –fruit

- Beagle mars explorer –snoopy –Darwin

- De Gaulle airport –president

The **any of the words** filter is useful when there are multiple possible results and you'd like to have a sampling of all of them, rather than letting the most popular or important instance of the word dominate the search results. Search results for **Fonda**, for example, are dominated by pictures of Jane Fonda. Simply adding the names of her relatives to the **any of the words** search box changes the results significantly, adding photographs of Henry and Peter.

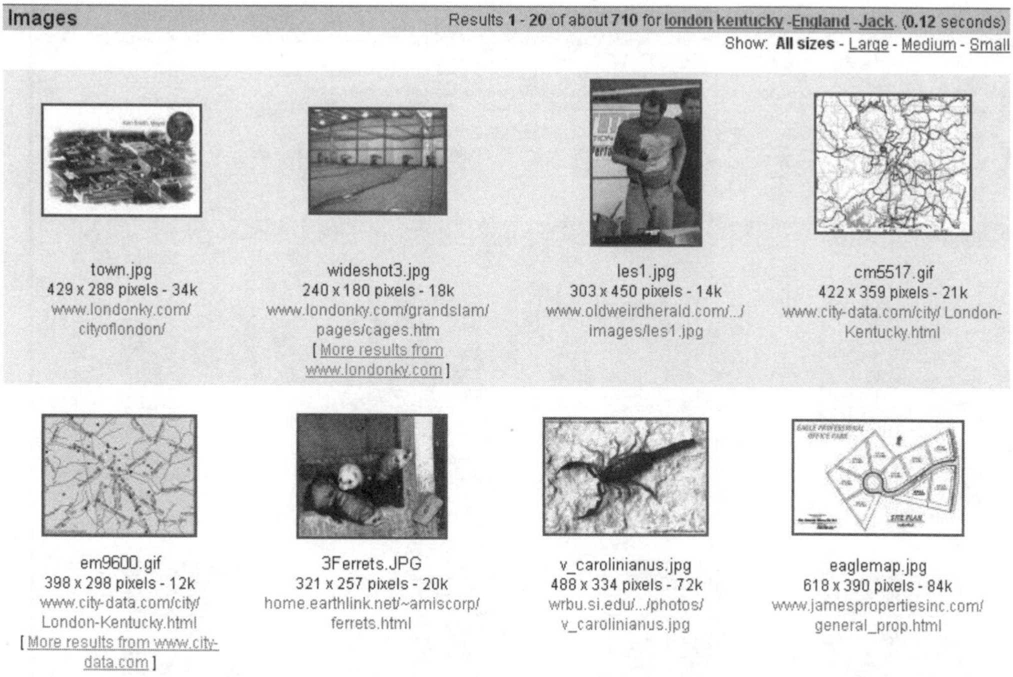

**Images**   Results **1 - 20** of about **710** for london kentucky -England -Jack. (0.12 seconds)

Show: **All sizes** - Large - Medium - Small

town.jpg
429 x 288 pixels - 34k
www.londonky.com/
cityoflondon/

wideshot3.jpg
240 x 180 pixels - 18k
www.londonky.com/grandslam/
pages/cages.htm
[ More results from
www.londonky.com ]

les1.jpg
303 x 450 pixels - 14k
www.oldweirdherald.com/.../
images/les1.jpg

cm5517.gif
422 x 359 pixels - 21k
www.city-data.com/city/ London-
Kentucky.html

6

em9600.gif
398 x 298 pixels - 12k
www.city-data.com/city/
London-Kentucky.html
[ More results from www.city-
data.com ]

3Ferrets.JPG
321 x 257 pixels - 20k
home.earthlink.net/~amiscorp/
ferrets.html

v_carolinianus.jpg
488 x 334 pixels - 72k
wrbu.si.edu/.../photos/
v_carolinianus.jpg

eaglemap.jpg
618 x 390 pixels - 84k
www.jamespropertiesinc.com/
general_prop.html

**FIGURE 6-9**   Excluding nonrelevant words from Image Search queries improves results.

It's important to note that Google often ignores stop words even if you include them in the **all of the words** search box—for example, the words "of" and "the" in the query **seven wonders of the world**. You can force these two words to be included by using the inclusion operator (+) in front of each term, as shown in Figure 6-10.

Google doesn't always ignore stop words. An Image Search for **The Who** (both of which are stop words) returns 800,000 results, with most of the images related to the well-known rock band. The results aren't as favorable for **The The**, another well-known band, even when you use the inclusion operator. Google only looks for a single instance of the word "the," and the results are all over the map, with no images of the band "The The" appearing in the top results.

# Other Advanced Image Search Filters

Google offers a number of additional filters that allow you to limit your Image Search results in more precise ways.

FIGURE 6-10 Use the inclusion operator to make sure important words are not ignored.

## The Size Filter

The **Size** filter lets you limit results to images that are small, medium, or large. It's the same filter that appears on Image Search result pages, but you control it on the Advanced Image Search page using a drop-down menu rather than clicking links.

**POWER SEARCHER TIP**  *The **size** filter defaults to "medium" on the Advanced Image Search page. Be sure to click the **All sizes** link on the result page to see the full set of search results.*

## The Filetypes Filter

The **Filteypes** filter lets you limit results to one of the two file types described earlier: .jpg for photographs and .gif for graphic images. This filter also lets you limit results to a relatively new, less common image format called Portable Network Graphics or .png files. The **Filetypes** filter is especially useful if your search results contain both photographs and graphics, and you want to exclude one format or the other.

For example, the query **silk road** returns both maps and images of the famous trade route between China and the West. Limiting results to **filetype:jpg** eliminates most of the maps, as shown in Figure 6-11.

Why aren't all the illustrations filtered from the search results shown in Figure 6-11? Because some web authors don't understand the difference between the various graphic formats, and they may save a graphic image as a .jpg file, or a photograph as a .gif file. Images saved in improper formats will still display in a browser, although they may look funny. Google can't really tell the difference between a photograph and a graphic illustration. It relies on the file extension, which indicates the file type, so this isn't a perfect filter for selecting between photographs and graphics.

**6**

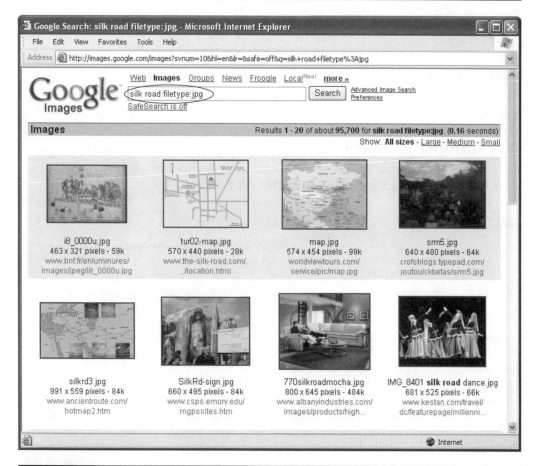

**FIGURE 6-11**    Limiting results to pictures gets rid of most maps and other drawings.

*Most images on the Web are in either .jpg or .gif format. The .png format has not really caught on, despite being an unpatented standard that is free to use.*

## The Coloration Filter

By default, Google Image Search returns results in any color. The **Coloration** filter gives you four options: **any colors** (the default), **black and white**, **grayscale**, and **full color**. Selecting one of these options almost always has a dramatic effect on search results.

Full-color images can be either photographs or illustrations. Grayscale images tend to be photographs, whereas black-and-white images tend to be line drawings and schematics. Although these aren't hard-and-fast rules, they are useful rules of thumb that can really help you narrow search results.

Grayscale photographs were often taken prior to the invention of color photography in the early 1900s. Selecting the **grayscale** option is an excellent way to find historical photographs of a particular subject. By contrast, because black-and-white images are often drawings or schematics, limiting your search to **black and white** can help you find floor plans, drawings in instruction manuals, and so on.

### Domain and SafeSearch

The **Domain** and **SafeSearch** filters work for images in exactly the same way as described in Chapter 4.

## Using Multiple Image Search Filters

In many cases, the best approach is to combine several Image Search filters, especially when you're looking for a very specific type of image. Here are some examples:

| Search Terms | Selected Filters | Results |
|---|---|---|
| **new!** | size=small<br>filetype=gif<br>coloration=full color | Icons for web pages that can be used next to new links or other content |
| **Trifid Nebula** | size=large<br>filetype=jpg<br>coloration=full color | High-resolution photographs suitable for printing or for computer wallpaper |
| **snow leopard** | Site:snowleopard.org | Pictures of the elusive cats from the International Snow Leopard Trust |
| **Bach music** | coloration=black and white | Sheet music scores |

*More information about Google's Image Search capabilities can be found in the FAQ at http://www.google.com/help/faq_images.html.*

# Combining Image Search
# and Advanced Search Commands

In addition to the image-specific filters available on the Advanced Image Search page, you can also use most of Google's other operators to further refine your query. Although Google's Image Search FAQ says that you "can use all operators for image search that you would use in a Google text search," in practice only a few give you meaningful results. Word filters, such as the Boolean AND and OR operators, as well as the inclusion and exclusion operators work well, as seen in the previous examples.

Other operators, such as **cache:**, **link:**, and **related:**, have no effect on Image Search results.

POWER SEARCHER TIP     *You can limit your search results to Macromedia Flash files with the **filetype:swf** operator. Though not all Flash files contain images, many do, and this is one of the few ways to explicitly search for this type of content on the Web.*

6

# Beyond Google: Other Image Search Sites

Although Google's Image Search is one of the best on the Web, it's not the only one. All the other major search services offer image search capabilities, and some go beyond still images to offer video and multimedia search.

## Major Image Search Services

Most of the major search engines also offer image search. These services either crawl the Web in search of images or license image databases from another provider. And just as with web results, image search results will differ greatly across the different services.

### Yahoo! Image Search

Yahoo!'s image search (http://search.yahoo.com/images) is comparable to Google's, displaying 20 thumbnail pages in search results and offering virtually identical advanced search capabilities. Yahoo! image search results also include news photographs, though they're integrated rather than explicitly labeled on the result page.

### AltaVista Image Search

AltaVista's image search (http://www.altavista.com/image/) is essentially the same as Yahoo!'s—both services are owned and operated by Yahoo! AltaVista image search does offer a few nice features not found elsewhere. Though there is no advanced image search page, the basic AltaVista image search form provides check boxes to limit your results to photographs, graphics, or banners and buttons. Color filters are also available. Though you can't limit your search to a specific domain, you can choose from web, news, or movie images, or you can search two specialized image databases provided by Corbis.com and *Rolling Stone*. AltaVista also gives you the most control over the size of images in search results, with the usual small, medium, and large choices, as well as more than a dozen specific sizes related to screen resolutions.

AltaVista also offers a video search service, allowing you to limit results to the five major video formats, with short or longer durations, and from five different sources, including the Web, news, MSNBC, FMITV, and *Rolling Stone*.

*The image search offered by AlltheWeb, at http://www.alltheweb.com/?cat=img, is also powered by Yahoo!, and it offers a few unique features as well.*

## Ask Jeeves Picture Search

Ask Jeeves Picture Search (http://pictures.ask.com) is a simple picture search service, offering no advanced search or filtering capabilities. But it does offer different images for most search terms than Google or the Yahoo!-powered image search engines, so it's a good alternative resource.

## Webseek at Columbia University

Webseek (http://www.ctr.columbia.edu/webseek/) differs from all the other image search services mentioned here because it is a directory of images, organized by subject. Though Webseek offers a search form, a better way to use it is to browse, drilling down through subcategories until you find the images you're looking for. Although this approach isn't as fast as searching, in many ways it makes it easier to find a suitable image because you don't have to guess at the best search terms to find what you're looking for.

## Visual Collections

View more than 300,000 maps, fine artwork, photographs, and other items from over 30 renowned collections, using a special, free browser available at this site (http://www.davidrumsey.com/collections/).

# Chapter 7

## Grokking Google Groups

The Internet has always been a hybrid medium, supporting both publication and communication. We naturally turn to the Web when we are searching for information, just as we use e-mail or instant messaging to communicate with others on the Net.

Internet discussion groups combine the best of publishing and communication, serving as forums that allow people to publish thoughts and opinions and comment on the postings of others. *Usenet* is the largest system of discussion groups on the Internet. Usenet is a global network consisting of thousands of discussion groups (often called *newsgroups*) on just about every imaginable subject. Usenet is an open system, meaning anyone can read and post messages to most newsgroups.

Google Groups was originally created as an archive and interface to Usenet. Recently, Google has expanded the service to allow users to create and manage their own groups independently of Usenet. The name "Google Groups" is a bit of a misnomer, because Google doesn't operate the Usenet network, nor does it decide which groups should be included or excluded. Additionally, the company exercises very little control over the content created by Google Groups members. Rather, in the same way that Google organizes the Web by making it easy to find web pages, Google Groups makes it comparatively easy to find information in the Usenet network—with the added benefit of making it easy to post your own messages to either traditional Usenet newsgroups or to a Google-hosted group through a single interface.

# Knowledge and Hearsay from Experts and Zealots

Usenet originated in 1979 when two Duke University graduate students, Tom Truscott and Jim Ellis, thought of hooking computers together to exchange news with other computer programmers. Steve Bellovin, a graduate student at the University of North Carolina (UNC), wrote a simple version of a "news" program and installed it at UNC and Duke (this is the reason the system is sometimes called "Newsnet" and its discussion groups "newsgroups"). The system was an immediate hit and expanded rapidly, primarily among academic institutions and government agencies, but later to Internet service providers throughout the world that offered subscribers access to Usenet. Usenet discussions are organized by topic, in a set of hierarchal groups and subgroups. Each group has a unique name that's similar to a web domain name. Dots separate each part of a group's name, showing its full hierarchy, as shown here:

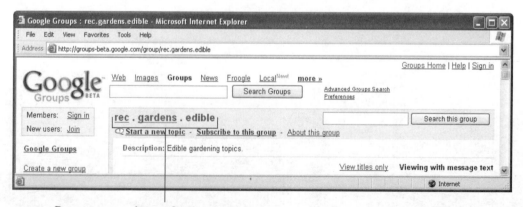

Dots separate each part of a newsgroup's name.

The leftmost part of the name shows the group's top-level category, and each successive name shows subcategories. Most names are descriptive enough that you can get a good idea of the subjects they cover. Here are some examples:

- alt.amusements
- comp.infosystems.search
- humanities.music
- sci.physics.relativity
- soc.genealogy

There are groups dedicated to just about every topic imaginable, from arthritis to religion, drama to seismology, architecture to zymurgy. Just like the Web, groups can be an incredibly valuable source of information. And just like the Web, groups can contain junk, spam, incorrect information, or outright fraudulent posts. Some groups are moderated, which can be a huge advantage if you're looking to avoid garbage. But most newsgroups are open to anyone, and as such, anything goes.

Usenet is not centralized. Rather, Internet service providers around the world maintain Usenet repositories (called "news servers") for their customers. News servers contain all recent postings and are constantly updated with new postings. Older posts, by design, "expire" and are purged from the repositories.

This culling of posts keeps storage requirements reasonable, but poses a problem if you're interested in reading older posts. When you access Usenet through most Internet service providers, you're only able to read a very recent set of newsgroup postings. By contrast, Google has deliberately created one of the most comprehensive archives of Usenet postings available, and never purges anything.

## The Genesis of Google Groups

Over the years, many efforts have been undertaken to establish comprehensive Usenet archives, but most archives were created as labors of love by individual Usenet participants. Until relatively recently, costly storage combined with the noncommercial nature of most Usenet activity made it difficult to impossible for fledgling Usenet archives to thrive, let alone survive. For a time in the 1990s, most of the major search engines offered the ability to search Usenet, though none maintained a comprehensive archive.

The most significant effort to create a comprehensive Usenet archive was undertaken by a company called Dejanews. The company assembled a database of Usenet news postings with articles dating back to 1995. However, during the dotcom madness days of the late 1990s, Deja decided to add other features to its web site in an effort to become commercially viable. Deja added product reviews and dropped the term "Usenet," replacing it with the more generic "discussions." It also changed its name from Dejanews to Deja.com. In May 2000, Deja moved its system to new servers and dropped much of its archive, allowing searches only back to May 15, 1999.

Like many other fledgling Internet companies, Deja.com died, expiring on Feb. 12, 2001. Fortunately, Google stepped in at the last minute and purchased Deja's newsgroup archives and rechristened the service as Google Groups. Initially, users could search only the most recent six months of the archive. At first, the reaction from Deja users was not positive. Google was widely criticized for failing to implement many of the features Deja users had relied on. Gradually, however, Google improved the interface, restoring much of the old functionality and adding new features that were previously unavailable. By May 2001, the entire Deja Usenet archive dating back to March 29, 1995 was searchable. Google expanded the size of the Deja database with an archive of its own and added an advanced search capability.

Google didn't stop there. Google engineer Michael Schmitt undertook a mission to find and restore the private Usenet archives mentioned earlier. Assembling archives stored on magnetic tape, CD-ROM and other sources, Google restored a comprehensive archive of Usenet, dating back to 1981, and made this available to users in December 2001. Although still not totally complete, Google Groups now likely contains more than 99 percent of all Usenet postings ever made.

Perhaps ironically, Google has also added features and enhancements to Usenet in much the same way Deja did. Fortunately, given the strength of the company, it's unlikely Google will suffer the same fate as Deja. The new features and enhancements to Google Groups are described later in this chapter.

**POWER SEARCHER TIP**    *Depending on when you read this book, you may see the word "beta" on both Google Groups pages and in URLs. Google Groups went through a rapid transformation process just as this book went to press. Even if you are seeing the word "beta," you are still seeing the most up-to-date information available.*

Google has compiled a fascinating 20-year Usenet timeline, highlighting some of the most interesting or memorable postings at http://www.google.com/googlegroups/archive_announce_20.html.

**POWER SEARCHER TIP**    *Google Groups has its own special vocabulary. For definitions of the more common words you'll see while using Google's Usenet service, see http://groups.google.com/googlegroups/glossary.html.*

## Mining Google Groups for History and Help

Why would you want to look for information using Google Groups instead of simply doing a Google web search? Well, Google's Usenet archive contains information posted all the way back to 1981. The Web wasn't even invented until 1990, and it didn't really grow into a significant repository of information until the late 1990s. This makes Google Groups an extremely valuable resource for doing historical research. For example, on the 20-year Usenet timeline mentioned earlier, you can find the first review of the IBM-PC in 1981. July 1983 saw the first mention of Madonna. In May 1986, the first discussion about the Chernobyl reactor meltdown began.

It was quite common for people in the computer industry to post announcements to Usenet whenever they had created something new. For example, you can find posts announcing most of the major search engines when they first came online in the mid 1990s. Trawling through Usenet is a great way to pick up "alternate" histories that may have never entered the mainstream.

Google Groups is also a terrific resource for sharing information and asking for help from others. It's very common for people to pose questions to a particular group: "How do I install this software driver?" "What's a good substitute for mayonnaise in a recipe?" "What's known about this new medical procedure?" Quite often, experts who have the answers you're looking for voluntarily step up to help. And often, they'll go beyond providing just a simple suggestion, engaging in a dialog with other participants in the group to fully explore a subject.

In short, Google Groups is an excellent resource whenever you're looking for offbeat history, help, or advice—or when you just want to shoot the breeze with other aficionados of a particular subject that's dear to you.

POWER SEARCHER TIP     *A list of Usenet FAQs receiving very high ratings from readers is available at http://www.faqs.org/topRated.html.*

# Exploring Google Groups

7

When you first start exploring Google Groups, it's important to remember that the service is both an archive and interface for the external Usenet, as well as a way to find and post messages to Google's own groups. These groups are hosted by Google and—unlike Usenet newsgroups—are not found elsewhere on the Web. Both are referred to, somewhat confusingly, as "Google Groups." And you have to be careful when you're searching or browsing Google Groups to "get your bearings" to make sure you're accessing the groups you intend to access.

## Browsing Google Groups

Google Groups is organized by topic into hierarchies, as shown in Figure 7-1. These ten categories organize the groups created by Google members. A separate link allows you to browse Usenet newsgroups; we'll explore that option later in this chapter.

Each hierarchy has a top-level topic, such as Arts and Entertainment, Computers, Regions and Places, with numerous subtopics. Most subtopics live two to four levels below the top-level topic (for example, Computers > Operating Systems or Recreation > Travel). Subtopic pages are organized by Topic, Region, Activity, and Members. The numbers in gray parentheses after subtopics in the Topic or Region category indicate the number of additional subtopics (or groups) in that category. The numbers for the Activity and Members categories give you an indication of popularity.

This hierarchical structure lends itself to browsing, and for groups with relatively few subtopics, browsing the Group directory is a good way to go. Simply click the top-level link, then click each successive subtopic link, until you reach the list of postings for the group that interests you.

Browsing is great for randomly exploring Google Groups, but it's an inefficient method for locating specific content in the more than 1 billion messages available. It's also not a terribly good way to navigate the larger hierarchies. As you browse through group hierarchies, note the **Directory Search** box. This differs from the **Search Groups** box at the top of each page.

FIGURE 7-1   Google puts ten top-level categories on the home page of Google Groups.

**Search Groups** is a broad search that returns group names as well as individual posts. **Directory Search** returns category listings only, and it tends to favor proprietary Google Group messages over Usenet newsgroups as far as I can tell.

## Browsing Usenet Archives

To browse Usenet content, click the **Browse all of Usenet** link on the Google Groups home page. This displays an alphabetically organized list of all Usenet newsgroups, as shown in Figure 7-2. This list isn't particularly useful, because you'd have to click through more than 950 pages to see the full alphabetical list. Fortunately, there's a drop-down menu on this page that let's you get closer, but you'll still have to do a lot of work to browse Usenet.

In previous versions of Google Groups, there was an easy-to-use, intuitive interface that allowed you to efficiently browse Usenet. With the current version of Google Groups, a better approach in almost all cases is to rely on Google's search prowess to locate information.

**FIGURE 7-2**    Use the drop-down menu to navigate to postings in Usenet newsgroup archives.

**POWER SEARCHER TIP**    *Unfortunately, because Usenet is not centralized and open to anyone, there's a lot of porn and other unsavory content posted in just about every unmoderated newsgroup. It's common to stumble upon inappropriate content when you're browsing, so searching may be a better approach if you're concerned about inadvertently viewing spam.*

## Searching Google Groups

There are two ways to search Google Groups. The search box at the top of any Google Groups page is a universal search that gives results from both the Usenet archives and the proprietary Google Groups. Use this search whenever you want the broadest possible selection of choices in your search results. The **Find Groups** search box in the middle of the Google Groups home page is essentially the same as the **Directory Search** function mentioned earlier. Confusing? Yep. As a general rule, stay with the **Find Groups** search function. That's the one we'll focus on here.

When you use the **Search Groups** function, results include links to individual messages in both the Usenet archive and proprietary Google Groups. You'll also see sponsored links and suggestions for related groups, as shown in Figure 7-3. Click the title link to read an individual post. Alternatively, you can view all messages in a group by clicking the category link at the bottom of each search result.

At the top of the search results in Figure 7-3, note that there's a message indicating that results are sorted by relevance. Next to this message is a link that lets you sort results by date. Clicking this link reorders the results, with the most recent posts at the top of the list.

Although the basic search is adequate, results for a search within Google Groups are often not as relevant as web search results. Why? Because Google Groups lacks the all-important link structure that Google uses to determine the most relevant pages for a web search.

Fortunately, Google has created a very good advanced search page for searching Google Groups. For just about any searching you do within Google Groups, you should automatically use these advanced search capabilities. Using the advanced search will save you time and spare you frustration.

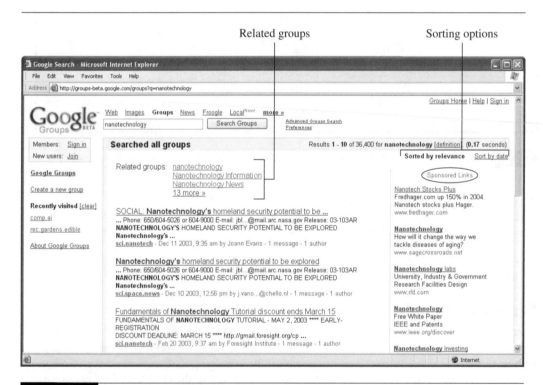

**FIGURE 7-3**    A result page from a search of Google Groups

# Advanced Groups Search

The Advanced Groups Search page, shown in Figure 7-4, is similar to all of Google's other advanced search pages, but it offers specific filters that take advantage of the unique characteristics of Usenet and its structure.

## Word Filters

At the top of the Advanced Groups Search page are the four word filters you're familiar with from Chapter 4. These filters work in exactly the same way with messages in Google Groups as they work with text on web pages. Here's a quick review:

- with **all** of the words = Boolean AND between all search terms
- with the **exact phrase** = search terms enclosed in quotes
- with **at least one** of the words = Boolean OR between all search terms
- **without** the words = exclusion operator (–) placed in front of each search term

7

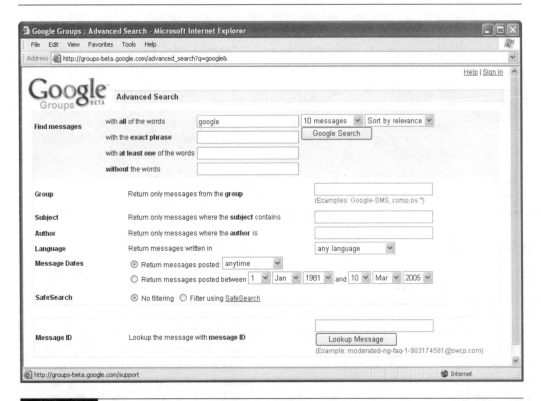

**FIGURE 7-4**   The Google Groups Advanced Search page

Although the word filters give you a greater degree of control over your results than simply running a basic search, it's the rest of the filters on the Advanced Groups Search page that can really help you zoom in on the specific information you're looking for.

## Group Filter

The **Group** filter lets you limit results to a specific Usenet newsgroup, proprietary Google Group or set of groups sharing a common topic.

This filter is most useful when you're already familiar with the structure of Usenet and its various hierarchies. Although this filter can be quite helpful in weeding out extraneous postings from nonrelevant groups, it may also backfire if you use it in a too-restricted fashion. For example, if you're looking for information about a recent security patch for Microsoft Windows, should you limit your posts to microsoft.public.windowsupdate or comp.security.announce? Unless you're familiar with a particular newsgroup, limiting results might exclude relevant posts in a related forum.

Fortunately, you can use the wildcard (*) to expand search results when using the **Group** filter. One approach is to use the wildcard to search for results in newsgroups all located in a specific hierarchy. For example, limiting your search to "rec.arts.*" would include the categories rec.arts.fine, rec.arts.misc, and any other subcategories in results.

The wildcard can also be used to pick up groups on similar subjects that are located in completely unrelated hierarchies. To accomplish this, use the wildcard operator on either side of a keyword.

**POWER SEARCHER TIP** — *Using the wildcard to find all groups using a specific keyword is an excellent technique to discover newsgroups not included in Google's top ten, especially country-specific newsgroups. For example, using the wildcard symbol on either side of the search term "linux" (\*linux\*) turns up fido7.ru.linux, a Russian newsgroup.*

Sometimes using the wildcard as a newsgroups filter returns unexpected results, such as a posting in a newsgroup that does not contain your search term. Often this occurs because Google has found a posting where the name of a matching newsgroup has been used in the text of a message.

## Subject Filter

In many respects, the subject of a newsgroup posting is similar to the HTML title of a web page. The subject typically is a concise description of the message itself, so in theory, limiting results to specific words in a subject can be a very strong filter, eliminating messages that simply use your search terms in the body of a message.

In practice, however, limiting results to postings with your search terms in the subject of messages doesn't always reduce the total number of results by an appreciable number, especially if you use a single-word query. In many cases, using the search term in the **Subject** filter reduces the total number of results, but not by much. To really get the most from the **Subject** filter, use it in combination with one of the word filters at the top of the Advanced Groups Search page.

**POWER SEARCHER TIP**

*In most cases, it's better to use multiple filters rather than put all search terms in the **Subject** filter. Because subject lines tend to consist of few words, you'll sharply reduce the number of results when limiting by multiple terms in a message subject—sometimes to an extreme degree. It's also possible that the subject does not contain the gist of the post. You can miss useful material this way.*

## Author Filter

By convention, anyone posting a message or replying to a Google Groups post must identify themselves with a name and e-mail address. If you've found an author who you find particularly interesting, you can use the **Author** filter to return a set of their Usenet postings. Be careful with this filter: Few names are completely unique, so you'll almost always want to use an additional search term or two in one of the word filters that uniquely identifies the author.

## Language Filter

You've already seen Google's language capabilities in action in Chapter 2. The Advanced Groups Search page's **Language** filter allows you to specify the language in which you want Usenet messages to be written. Currently, this filter lets you limit your results to pages written in up to 30 languages. Its inclusion on the Advanced Groups Search page allows you to construct sophisticated queries in any language and then limit results to one specific language. Figure 7-5 shows an example of a message written in Arabic.

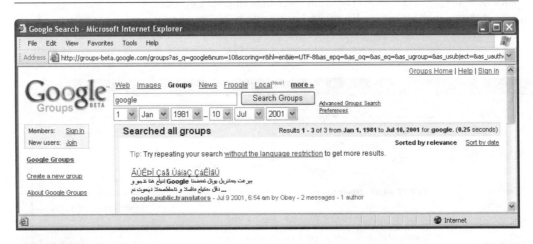

**FIGURE 7-5**    Searching for the term "Google" and limiting results to Arabic returns this message.

## Message Date Filter

In Chapter 4, I wrote that the **Date** filter on the advanced web search page was essentially useless—not through any fault of Google's, but rather because there is no consistent standard for date notation on the Web. In Google Groups, the situation is just the opposite. Whenever someone posts a message to Usenet, the message is given a date and time stamp that is accurate to the second. The **Message Date** filter is particularly powerful when you're searching for messages posted in a relatively narrow range of dates, as shown in Figure 7-6.

## SafeSearch Filter

Because Google Groups does not provide access to any image-oriented Usenet newsgroups, the **SafeSearch** filter in Google Groups will filter out potentially objectionable messages in search results. Remember, though, the SafeSearch filter isn't perfect, and occasionally objectionable content will slip through and show up in your search results. For more information on the **SafeSearch** filter, see Chapters 2 and 4.

## Message ID Filter

The Usenet system automatically assigns each newsgroup posting a unique message ID. If you know the message ID, you can quickly retrieve the post by using it as a search term.

# Message Viewing Options

When a new message is posted to Usenet, it resembles an e-mail message. Each message is clearly identified with a message ID, the author's name, a subject, the date and time posted, and, of course, the body of the message itself. Figure 7-7 is an example of a message that was posted

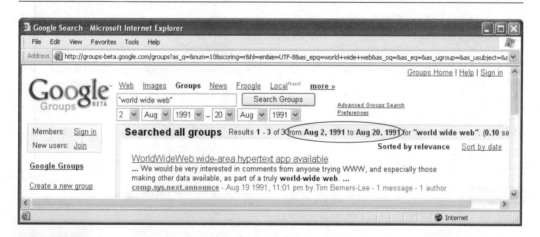

**FIGURE 7-6**    The Message Date filter lets you zoom in on specific events, such as this announcement of a new Internet application called the "world wide web."

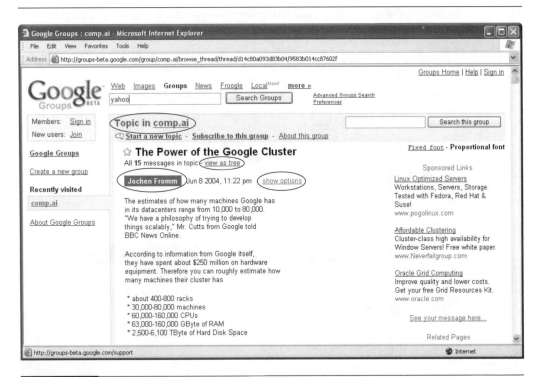

**FIGURE 7-7**    A Usenet message posted to the comp.ai newsgroup

to the comp.ai newsgroup. When you view this message in Google Groups, you have a number of options apart from reading or responding to the message.

Notice the **show options** link in the header area of the message. Clicking this link expands the header to display a number of useful options.

Clicking the **Find messages by this author** link will automatically run a search and bring up a list of all posts by the author. Want to send the author a private message? Click the **Reply to Author** link. Other links let you forward the message, print it, display just the message itself without any other messages in the thread, and show the original message, which displays the message without the ads from Google or the hyperlinks, but displayed with a much more cluttered appearance.

Although these options for viewing messages are useful, the real power of Google Groups is that it assembles all the replies (and replies to replies) associated with a message into a *threaded view*. This lets you easily scan the complete discussion. To see all the messages in a thread, click the **View As Tree** link. This changes the view to a two-frame display, with the message in the right frame and navigation links for the thread in the left frame, as shown in Figure 7-8.

A red arrowhead next to an author name in the left frame shows which message in a thread is currently displayed in the right frame. Each author's name is a link; clicking the link displays that particular message in the right frame. Indentation and post numbers show which messages each

Thread-viewing controls

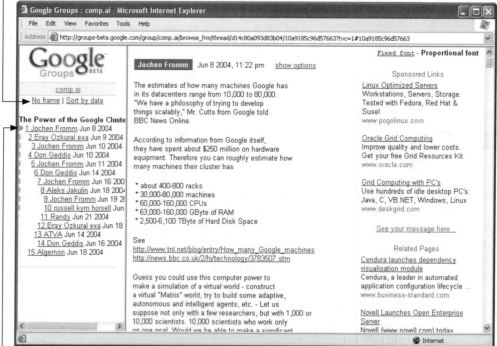

Current message indicator

**FIGURE 7-8**  Viewing a complete thread makes it easy to read and navigate through all the messages for a particular subject.

author replied to. This is the default view; you can sort all posts in a particular thread by date rather than by the hierarchy of replies by clicking the **Sort by date** link in the thread-viewing controls. Another option lets you view all messages in a thread sequentially, one after another, without frames. To view the thread this way, click the **No frame** link.

Spend some time playing with the different display options offered by Google Groups. You'll quickly find the viewing options you're most comfortable with and learn to navigate quickly through Usenet messages, whether browsing hierarchies or perusing search results.

# Posting Messages to Google Groups

To post a new message or reply to an existing message through Google Groups, you first need to create a Google account. Accounts are free—all that's required is a username, password, and e-mail address.

**POWER SEARCHER TIP** *Google takes the issue of privacy very seriously. Nonetheless, you should review its privacy policy before signing up for a Google account and posting to Google Groups. The privacy policy is located at http://groups.google.com/privacy.html.*

Once you've registered and logged in, navigate to a group or search for a particular topic that interests you. To start a new thread, click the link **Start a new topic**. This link appears when you're one level above the actual articles in the group—in other words, when you can see the subject lines and brief descriptions of the messages that have been posted to the group.

To reply to an existing message, click the **Reply** link that appears at the end of every message.

Whether you're posting a new message or replying to an existing message, you'll see a form with three entry fields. The first is for the group to which you want to post the message. The second is for the subject, and the third is for your message itself. These fields are blank for new messages, and they are filled in automatically if you're replying to an existing message. Once you've composed your message, you have the option to preview the message, post it without previewing, or canceling the post altogether.

That's all there is to it. Remember, even though you're using Google Groups, you're posting your message to Usenet, and anyone who accesses the system, whether they're using Google Groups or not, can read what you've posted.

What happens if you decide you want to delete a post? You can delete your own posts using the automatic removal tool at http://services.google.com:8882/urlconsole/controller. You cannot remove posts made by others.

**POWER SEARCHER TIP** *For full instructions on posting to Google Groups, and important points about posting etiquette on Usenet, see http://groups.google.com/googlegroups/ posting_faq.html.*

## Managing Favorites in Google Groups

Google provides two ways to easily access and track messages in Google Groups. You can subscribe to a group, and this group will be added to your "My Groups" list, accessible from any Google Groups page with a click of a link. You can also bookmark individual messages or threads. To bookmark a thread, click the star next to a topic title. Thereafter, all new posts to that topic will appear on your My Groups page. You can view all starred topics by clicking the **My Starred Topics** link in the menu on the left side of the screen.

## Creating a Google Group

Chances are you'll find a community in Google Groups dedicated to any topic imaginable. But in the event you can't, or want to create a private group that also includes a mailing list feature, you can create your own Google Group. It's free and very easy to do.

To start, you need to be a registered Google user. Click the **Create a new group** link on any page, log in, and Google will display a page that lets you create a group. All you need do here is enter a name and e-mail address for the group, write a brief description of the group, indicate whether the group will have adult content, and then specify whether the group will be public, announcement only (a mailing list), or restricted (accessible by invitation only).

Once you've created a group, you need to add users to it. You can add members directly, or you can invite members to join via e-mail. You also need to set subscription options for how members receive notification of new postings. These options range from no e-mail, e-mail of each message as it's added, and abridged or digest versions of messages.

That's all there is to it. Once you've created a group, you'll see a **manage** link appear next to its name in your My Groups list. Management tools let you change settings, set up moderation or review messages, and even delete a group.

*To access the Google Group created to discuss this book, visit http://groups-beta .google.com/group/googlepower.*

## Beyond Google: Alternate Usenet Interfaces and Other Web Forums

Google Groups is just one of many interfaces to Usenet. Some are web based; others are desktop applications that run from your own computer. Most people find no reason to depart from the comfortable and powerful Google Groups interface to access Usenet. But there are alternatives if you find Google Groups isn't satisfying your own particular needs.

## Other Ways to Access Usenet

Although Google Groups is the largest, most comprehensive Usenet archive, it omits a huge and potentially very important part of the system: binary files. These are pictures, audio or video streams, or virtually any other type of nontextual data. The only way you can access binary files that have been posted to Usenet is to use an access tool other than Google Groups.

The easiest approach is to use the Usenet tools that come with your browser. With Internet Explorer, Outlook Express has the ability to access Usenet, using the same familiar interface you use for e-mail. Alternatively, you'll want to consider getting a specialized newsreader program or use a web-based Usenet interface.

POWER SEARCHER TIP

*The Google Directory has good lists of Usenet access tools. For web-based tools, see http://directory.google.com/Top/Computers/Usenet/Web_Based/. For desktop-based tools that work with all popular operating systems, see http://directory .google.com/Top/Computers/Software/Internet/Clients/Usenet/.*

## Yahoo! Groups

Unlike Usenet newsgroups, which have no owner or true "home" on the Internet, Yahoo! Groups (http://groups.yahoo.com) is a self-contained area within the Yahoo! service itself. There are millions of Yahoo! groups, and although many are public, a large number of groups are private, limited to invited members only. In addition, anyone can start a Yahoo! group, whereas existing members of the Usenet community must vote in favor of starting a new Usenet group.

Anyone can view postings in public Yahoo! groups. To post your own messages or reply to postings, you need to be a member of Yahoo!

## MSN Groups

MSN Groups (http://groups.msn.com/home) is similar to Yahoo! Groups, with thousands of discussion groups established on the MSN site. Anyone can browse or search MSN Groups, but to post or reply to messages, or to create your own group, you need to sign up for a .NET Passport account from Microsoft.

## Search Engine Watch Forums

The Search Engine Watch forums (http://forums.searchenginewatch.com/) are dedicated to—you guessed it—discussions revolving around the major web search engines and directories. The forums have two primary focuses. Searchers will find lots of discussion related to searching techniques, specialized search engines, and tools to help with web research. Webmasters and marketers will find numerous discussions related to search engine optimization and search marketing issues.

7

There are 26 public Search Engine Watch forums, including forums dedicated to Google, Yahoo!, Ask Jeeves, and the other major search engines and directories. Most of the forums have subforums dedicated to specific topics. In the Google forum, for example, there are subforums dedicated to Google web search, the company's AdSense and AdWords programs, and other Google issues.

Anyone can view the Search Engine Watch forums. To post or reply to existing posts, you'll need to sign up for a free membership to the forums. (Disclosure: The author of this book is an editor of Search Engine Watch.)

## Finding Web Forums and Discussion Groups

In addition to the millions of forums available via Google Groups, Yahoo! Groups, and elsewhere, there are thousands of other forums on just about any topic imaginable scattered across the Web. Some of these are online forums using discussion board software. Others are Internet mailing lists, where you interact with other members via e-mail. Some are hybrids, combining both online and e-mail components.

A simple way to find these communities is to search Google, using queries like these:

- ■   *topic* forums
- ■   *topic* "message boards"
- ■   *topic* "discussion groups"
- ■   *topic* "mailing lists"

In each of these examples, replace the word *topic* with the subject you're interested in. Be sure to put phrases ("discussion boards") in double quotes. This technique works surprisingly well.

Two search tools help you find online discussions: Lycos Discussion Search and Netscan from Microsoft Research. Both are works in development, so they may have changed (or gone away) by the time you read this.

Lycos Discussion Search (http://discussion.lycos.com/) does a web search for discussion groups, forums mailing lists, and other online communities. In addition to web search results likely to contain forums on your topic, the result page provides links to organizations related to your search terms and the ability to limit results to any site—Yahoo! Groups, MSN Groups, or .org web sites.

Microsoft's Netscan (http://netscan.research.microsoft.com/) is an experimental Usenet search and browse tool that has many similarities to Google Groups. It offers some cool features not available elsewhere, such as the ability to build a list of your favorite newsgroups, authors, and threads, as well as the ability to do detective work on particular Usenet authors and their posting activities.

Two other directories worth mentioning are Tile.net and CataList. Tile.net (http://www.tile .net) is a directory containing more than 75,000 listings of discussion groups, Usenet groups, and other Net resources. CataList (http://www.lsoft.com/catalist.html) is the official catalog of more than 70,466 public Listserv software-based lists on the Internet.

# Chapter 8

## The Essential Google Toolbar

How often have you found yourself viewing a web page, wishing you could search Google *right now,* without leaving what you're reading and calling up Google.com? For most web users, this situation happens constantly. Perhaps you're reading a news article and want to follow up on related developments. Or you're researching an investment and would like more detailed information. Sometimes it's something as simple as wanting to see a picture of the author of the web page you're viewing.

The Google Toolbar embeds the power of Google directly into Internet Explorer. It's a browser plug-in that features a Google search box and an array of useful tools that go beyond Search and improve your overall web-browsing experience. Best of all, it's free, and extremely easy to install and use.

**POWER SEARCHER TIP**   *Although Google has a very forthright privacy policy, enabling certain features of the Google Toolbar causes it to send some information about your web surfing to Google. This isn't the nasty or pernicious type of activity found in spyware or scumware. Rather, the Toolbar sends information to Google so it can provide you with additional information that would otherwise be unavailable. As you read this chapter, be sure to take note of the various Toolbar configuration options so you know exactly what information your computer is exchanging with Google.*

# Installing and Using the Google Toolbar

Installing the Google Toolbar couldn't be easier. From the Google Toolbar home page (http://toolbar.google.com), select your preferred language from the drop-down menu and then click the **Download Google Toolbar** button (see Figure 8-1). Follow the same procedure you would when installing any other software.

When you see the Choose Your Configuration dialog box, notice the message in red: "Please read this carefully: It's not the usual Yada Yada." Google gives you the option to install the Toolbar with or without what it calls "advanced features." Enabling advanced Toolbar features allows you to see additional information about the current page you're viewing. This includes its PageRank and links to see a cached snapshot of the page, to view its backward links, and to view similar pages. To do this, the Toolbar must send the URL of the page to Google.

Enabling advanced features means that Google knows what you view on the Web. Google's privacy policy is explicit, however, stating that "Google cannot collect, for example, your name, e-mail address, telephone number, etc." Information in a URL, such as usernames and IDs, passwords, and account information of any kind are not passed on to Google and are not kept or stored anywhere. Unless you're totally paranoid about privacy, you'll probably want to enable the advanced features because they are very useful.

**POWER SEARCHER TIP**   *If you're browsing "private" web pages you don't want Google to know about, remember that the Toolbar can send the URLs of those pages back to Google, and they may then be crawled and added to its index. To prevent this, either disable the advanced features in the Toolbar or block the page from crawlers with a "no robots" meta tag, described in Chapter 1.*

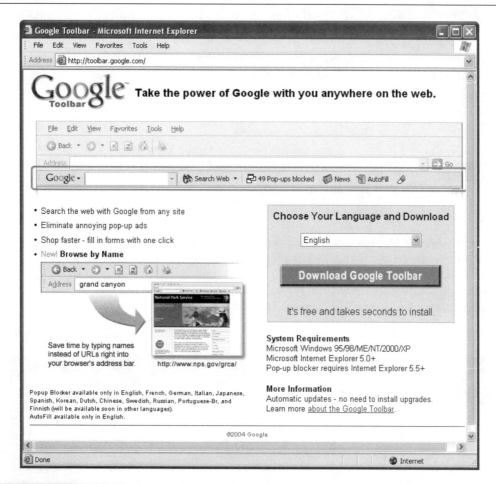

**FIGURE 8-1**    To download the Google Toolbar, simply select your preferred language and click the Download Google Toolbar button.

Three final steps conclude the installation of the Toolbar. First, select your primary Google server. Choosing the location in or nearby your home country will provide the fastest results.

Next, decide whether you want to make Google your default search engine and enable the **Browse by Name** feature in the Internet Explorer address bar. By default, whenever you type anything other than a valid URL into Internet Explorer's address bar, the browser runs a search on MSN Search. You can change this so that you'll get Google results rather than MSN results when you type words rather than URLs into the address bar. The **Browse by Name** feature enhances this capability, working something like the **I'm Feeling Lucky** button, automatically directing you to web sites when you enter words that have implicit destinations, such as "united nations." Table 8-1 shows a few examples of Browse By Name in action.

| Browse By Name Words | Page Displayed |
|---|---|
| itunes | http://www.apple.com/itunes/ |
| new york times bestsellers | http://www.nytimes.com/pages/books/bestseller/ |
| currency converter | http://www.xe.com/ucc/ |
| windows help | http://support.microsoft.com/ |
| rock and roll hall of fame | http://www.rockhall.com/ |
| tv listings | http://tv.yahoo.com/ |
| great wall of china | http://www.travelchinaguide.com/china_great_wall/ |

**TABLE 8-1**    The Toolbar's Browse By Name Feature Makes It Easy to Visit Well-known Web Sites Without Typing a URL

When Browse By Name is working, the cursor briefly changes to an arrow with three colored balls beneath it. If you enter words without a clear match, you'll see ordinary Google search results.

When you complete these steps, the Toolbar installer closes Internet Explorer. When you restart the browser, the Google Toolbar should automatically appear, as shown here:

The Google Toolbar

If you don't see the toolbar, open the **View | Toolbars** menu and make sure there's a checkmark next to **Google**. With some older versions of Internet Explorer, you may not see **Google** in the **Toolbars** menu, and **Radio** may appear twice. In this case, select the second **Radio** option to turn on the Google Toolbar.

Here are the Google Toolbar system requirements:

- Microsoft Windows 95 or higher
- Microsoft Internet Explorer 5.0+
- Pop-up blocker requires Internet Explorer 5.5+

# Search Google from Any Web Page

The Google Toolbar's primary purpose is to provide access to the full power of the search engine at all times while you're on the Web, regardless of the page you're currently viewing. The Toolbar features a search box, two drop-down menus, and several optional features displayed as buttons.

To run a Google web search, simply enter your query in the Toolbar search box and press the ENTER key. Results appear exactly as if you had entered your query from the Google home page. You can also run your search in any of Google's specialty catalogs from the Toolbar by selecting the drop-down menu to the right of the search box, as shown at right. All these specialty search catalogs are described in other chapters.

> **POWER SEARCHER TIP**   *Press ALT-G to move your cursor into the Toolbar's search box without using your mouse.*

With the Toolbar installed, you can also run a Google web search by simply highlighting any words on a web page, right-clicking, and selecting the Google Search option on the right-click context menu. When you highlight more than one word, Google will automatically run the query as a phrase search, enclosing your search terms in double quotes.

Highlight any word on a web page, right-click, and select Google Search, and the Toolbar will search on the highlighted word.

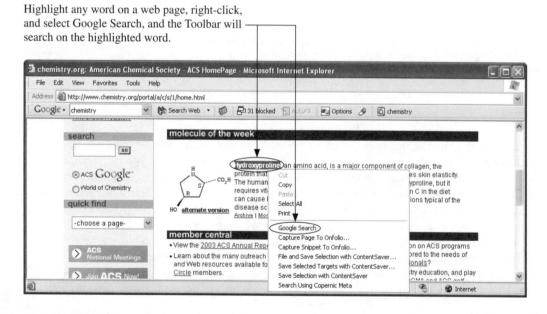

> **POWER SEARCHER TIP**   *For even quicker searching, simply highlight text on a web page and drag the highlighted selection to the Google Toolbar search box.*

8

The Toolbar also provides easy access to Google search pages, via the menu to the left of the search box, as shown at right. The topmost menu items take you directly to the Google home page. From the **Google Links** menu item, you can go to the Google Advanced Search page, or the Images, Groups, Directory, News, or Froogle home page. There are also links to other Google services, such as Google Answers and Blogger, the company's weblog hosting and tools operation. This menu also gives you an option to change your preferences and language selections, as described in Chapter 2.

*If you've selected a site other than Google.com, which is based in the U.S., as your default, the Toolbar will also display an option to search only pages from the country you've selected.*

## Your Search History

When you enter queries into the Google Toolbar, they are saved by default as your personal search history. This makes it easy to run queries again—simply use the drop-down menu to the right of the search box to access your history.

It's important to note that your search history includes not just the queries you made from the Google Toolbar, but from *all* Google search forms. No matter whether you're searching Google.com, Google News, or Google Images, your queries are added to your search history on the Toolbar. Obviously, having access to your search history can be a great help when you repeat searches on a regular basis. But beware: If you have your search history enabled on a public computer, anyone who uses the computer can see exactly what you've searched for.

To clear your search history, click the Google logo to the left of the search box and select the **Clear search history** option from the drop-down menu. You can also turn search history off altogether. From the Google Toolbar **Options** menu, uncheck the **Drop-down search history** box. Then click the **More** tab and uncheck the **Save the search history across browser sessions** box.

*Your Google search history (and all information that you type into any web page form) is also stored separately by Internet Explorer. To clear this history, go to Internet Explorer's **Tools** menu and select **Internet Options**, then select the **Content** tab. Within the **Personal Information** area, select **AutoComplete** and click **clear forms**.*

# The Highlight and Word Find Buttons

When you've run a search from the Google Toolbar and are viewing a result page, two other Toolbar features help you zoom in on the information you're looking for. To the right of the Toolbar, you'll see a highlighter button and a magnifying glass icon next to each of your search terms.

The highlighter button is a toggle—click it, and your search terms are automatically highlighted on the search result page (see Figure 8-2). Each search term is highlighted in a different color. Click the toggle again and the result page returns to normal.

Clicking a word find button jumps to the next occurrence of that word on the page, where it's also temporarily highlighted. Each time you click the button, you'll jump to the next occurrence of the word on the page. To search backward, hold down the SHIFT key while clicking. To find only exact matches of your word (for example, find only the exact word "to," not words that contain "to" such as "toward," "rialto," and so on), hold down the CTRL key while clicking.

**POWER SEARCHER TIP**   *Both the highlighter and word find commands work on any web page your browser is displaying (not just search result pages). To highlight or find words on the page you're viewing, simply enter a word in the Toolbar search box (don't press ENTER) and click the highlighter or word find button.*

8

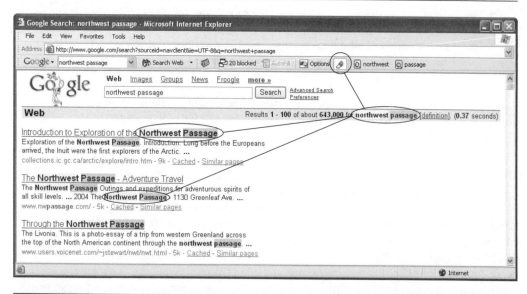

**FIGURE 8-2**   The highlighter toggle reveals the exact location of your search terms on a web page.

## The Google Toolbar Pop-up Blocker

The Google Toolbar includes several non-search features that are indispensable. One is the pop-up blocker, which prevents annoying pop-up windows from opening as you surf the Web. When the pop-up blocker intercepts an incoming ad, your cursor changes briefly, displaying a finger with a star icon. The pop-up blocker button displays a similar icon, as well as a count of the number of pop-ups blocked since the last Toolbar installation. The Toolbar also plays a sound to let you know it has blocked a pop-up.

Google's pop-up blocker is designed to be somewhat intelligent. It doesn't automatically block all pop-ups. Instead, it tries to determine if the content of a pop-up window might be useful—containing a dictionary definition or a registration form, for example. The pop-up blocker will allow many of these benign pop-ups to display without interference.

Occasionally, you may encounter a site with "good" pop-ups that are nonetheless being blocked. You can let a pop-up window display on a one-time basis by holding down the CTRL key while clicking the link that causes the pop-up to display.

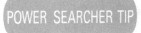

*You can "whitelist" an entire web site by clicking the pop-up blocker button on the toolbar while visiting a page. The pop-up blocker button changes to **Site popups allowed**, and pop-ups from that site will always be allowed. You can remove a site from your whitelist by visiting it and clicking the pop-up blocker button once again.*

The pop-up blocker is available only in English, French, German, Italian, Japanese, Spanish, Korean, Dutch, Chinese, Swedish, Russian, Portuguese-Br, and Finnish, though Google says it will soon be available in other languages.

## AutoFill

The Google Toolbar's AutoFill feature has a single purpose: to help you save time filling out forms on web pages. Figure 8-3 shows the entry form for AutoFill. Enter your name, e-mail address, phone number, street address (with an optional second address for shipping), and credit card number, and whenever you view a page that asks for that information, a single click on the **AutoFill** button automatically fills everything in. All your personal information is stored locally, on your computer's hard disk, and is never transmitted to Google. In addition, you must create a password if you enter credit card information, and you must submit this password either to have AutoFill enter your credit information on a form or to modify it with different information.

AutoFill is currently available only in English.

**FIGURE 8-3**    AutoFill saves you time filling out forms asking for your personal information.

# Toolbar Options

As useful as the default features of the Toolbar are, there are a number of options that can further enhance your search experience. To change your options, click the Google logo and select **Options...** from the drop-down menu.

The basic options menu, shown in Figure 8-4, lets you control Toolbar features for searching, page information, accessories, and configuration. You'll recognize several of these options because they are enabled by default when you install the Toolbar (history, highlight button, word find buttons, pop-up blocker, AutoFill button).

Other options include:

- **Use Google site**    Specify which Google domain to use for your search. You set this option when you selected your location when you installed the Toolbar.

- **Open a new window to display results each time you search**    Opens a new browser window instead of displaying results in the current window.

Basic options for the Google Toolbar

- **PageRank display**   Gives an indication of the PageRank (discussed in Chapter 1) for the page you're currently viewing.

- **Page Info menu**   Gives you access to more information about the page you're viewing. From the button's drop-down menu, you can select four options: **Cached Snapshot of Page, Similar Pages, Backward Links,** and **Translate into English.**

Any of the options on this menu can be enabled or disabled simply by checking or unchecking the box next to the option.

In addition to the basic Toolbar options, the **More** tab provides additional options, a few of which are also set by default when you install the Toolbar. Figure 8-5 shows the **More options** menu. These additional options include additional search options, web buttons, extra search buttons, and a catchall category simply called "extras."

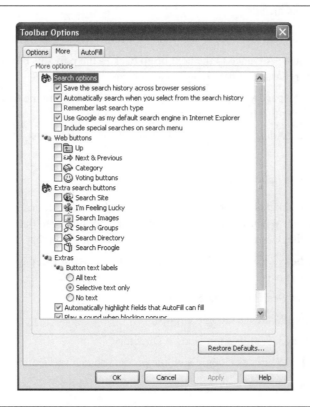

**FIGURE 8-5**   The More options menu for the Google Toolbar

Additional search options include:

- **Save the search history across browser sessions**   Turns history on or off.

- **Automatically search when you select from the search history**   You can run a search again simply by selecting it from your search history list.

- **Remember last search type**   For example, web search, current site, images, news, and so on.

- **Use Google as my default search engine in Internet Explorer**   You can run Google searches from the address bar when words other than URLs are used.

- **Include special searches on search menu**   You can add Google's special searches for Linux, BSD Unix, U.S. Government, Apple Macintosh, and Microsoft searches to the Toolbar menu.

8

**Web buttons** options include:

- **Up**   Navigate up one level in the site you're currently visiting.

- **Next & Previous**   Advance to the next or go back to the previous result for the current search without returning to the Google search results page.

- **Category**   If the page you are viewing has a related category in the Google Web Directory, clicking this button takes you to that category page.

- **Voting buttons**   Adds buttons that allow you to vote for or against a web page that you're viewing.

**Extra search buttons** options include:

- **Search Site**   Click this button to restrict your search to pages found on the site you're currently viewing. When you use this option, remember that even though results are restricted to a site, Google may not have crawled every page on that site.

- **I'm Feeling Lucky**   Click this button to bypass the search result page and directly view the topmost result page.

- **Search Images**   Searches Google Images.

- **Search Groups**   Searches Google Groups.

- **Search Directory**   Searches the Google Directory.

- **Search Froogle**   Searches Google's online product search service, Froogle.

**Extras** options include:

- **Button text labels**   You can select how you want the buttons to appear on your Toolbar. Your choices are **all text**, **selective text only**, and **no text**. To minimize the amount of space used by the Toolbar, select the **no text** option. You'll be surprised how compact the Toolbar becomes!

- **Automatically highlight fields that AutoFill can fill**   AutoFill detects fields it can fill and highlights those fields in yellow. AutoFill is described in detail in the "AutoFill" section, earlier in this chapter.

- **Play a sound when blocking popups**   Additional audio confirmation that a pop-up has in fact been blocked.

All these additional options have value, but they also take up space on the Toolbar. It doesn't hurt to enable these features and try them out. After you've had a chance to play with them, simply open up the Toolbar Options window once again and selectively remove the features you don't use on a regular basis.

# New Features

As this book went to press, Google released a beta version of the Toolbar (version 3.0) that included three new features. These features are:

- **Spell Check**   Whenever you type anything into a web page form the Toolbar will automatically check your spelling. This is especially useful when you're doing a lot of typing, such as composing a web-based e-mail message.

- **WordTranslator**   This nifty feature translates English words into other languages. To use it, simply move your cursor over any word on a web page and a small pop-up window will appear with the word translated into other languages. WordTranslator currently supports translation from English into Chinese (Traditional and Simplified), Japanese, Korean, French, Italian, German, and Spanish.

- **AutoLink**   If a U.S. street address appears on a web page (such as the address of a restaurant or retailer), AutoLink will automatically generate a link to a page that creates a map of that location. AutoLink can also link package tracking numbers to delivery status, vehicle identification numbers to vehicle history, and ISBN numbers to Amazon.com listings.

8

# Beyond Google: Other Search Toolbars

The Google Toolbar is indispensable, but it has a major limitation: It only works for searching Google, and it only works with Internet Explorer. Most of the other major search engines offer toolbars as well. Just like the underlying engines, other search toolbars have strengths and unique features not found in the Google Toolbar. And fortunately, most toolbars play well together, so you can have more than one installed in your browser.

## Major Search Engine Toolbars

Most of the toolbars offered by the major search engines share similar features. Naturally, they make it easy to search their own search engines from the toolbar. Most have pop-up blockers, highlighting of search terms, and the ability to do specialized searches for images, news, and so on. Rather than describing each toolbar in detail, here are the unique features offered by each. All of the toolbars described require Windows 98 or higher and Internet Explorer 5.0 or higher.

### Alexa Toolbar

The Alexa Toolbar can be downloaded from http://download.alexa.com/index.cgi?p=Dest_W_b_40_T1. Unique features of this toolbar include:

- **Google web search**   The Alexa Toolbar uses Google to provide web search results.

- **Alexa site info**   Provides access to contact information, site stats, and user reviews of web sites.

- **Alexa traffic rank**   A popularity measure compared to other web sites.

- **Related links**   Shows similar web pages based on the surfing behavior of other users.
- **Wayback machine link**   You can view archived copies of the current page back through 1996.

Microsoft Windows and Internet Explorer 5.0 or higher are required.

## A9 Toolbar

The A9 Toolbar can be downloaded from http://toolbar.a9.com. Unique features of this toolbar include:

- A "diary" feature to leave notes on any web page, which you can later access from anywhere.
- You can check your browsing and search history from anywhere.
- You can get related links and ratings with Alexa Site Info (both Alexa and A9 are owned by Amazon).

Microsoft Windows, Internet Explorer 5.5 or higher, and an Amazon account are required.

## Ask Jeeves Toolbar

The Ask Jeeves Toolbar can be downloaded from http://sp.ask.com/docs/toolbar/. Unique features of this toolbar include:

- Ask Jeeves Smart Search for news stories, dictionary definitions, weather forecasts, and more.
- You can configure web pages for easy one-page printing using the **Zoom** feature.
- You can instantly e-mail any web page.

Microsoft Windows and Internet Explorer 5.0 or higher are required.

## Dogpile Toolbar

The Dogpile Toolbar can be downloaded from http://www.dogpile.com/info.dogpl/tbar/. Unique features of this toolbar include:

- **White Pages**   Look up residential listings from around the U.S.
- **Yellow Pages**   Access business listings easily from one location.
- **Ticker**   Get the latest news and information delivered directly to your ticker.
- **RSS Tool**   Add any type of ticker feed, including news, summaries, and blogs.
- **SearchSpy**   Watch scrolling terms to see what people are searching for in real time.

Microsoft Windows 98 or higher and Internet Explorer 5.5 or higher are required.

## HotBot Desktop

The HotBot Desktop can be downloaded from http://www.hotbot.com/tools/desktop/. Unique features of HotBot Desktop include:

- **Search your local computer**   Index and search files, e-mail, RSS, and browser history.
- **Subscribe to RSS news feeds**   You can get more content with less clutter from top sites as well as your favorite blogs.
- **Custom Sites "search shortcuts"**   Easy access to site searches from any site on the Internet.

Microsoft Windows 98 or higher and Internet Explorer 5.5 or higher are required.

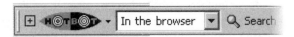

## MSN Toolbar

The MSN Toolbar can be downloaded from http://toolbar.msn.com/. Unique features include the ability to launch MSN Hotmail, MSN Messenger, and My MSN directly from the MSN Toolbar.
   Microsoft Windows 98 or higher and Internet Explorer 5.01 or higher are required.

### Teoma Search Bar

The Teoma Search Bar can be downloaded from http://sp.ask.com/docs/teoma/toolbar/. Unique features of the Teoma Search Bar include:

- **Dictionary**    Allows you to easily perform a dictionary lookup.
- **Email this page to a friend**    You can e-mail any web page with a click of the button.

Microsoft Windows 98 or higher and Internet Explorer 5.0 or higher are required.

### Yahoo! Companion Toolbar

The Yahoo! Companion Toolbar can be downloaded from http://toolbar.yahoo.com. Unique features of this toolbar include:

- You can save your favorite bookmarks online.
- An anti-spyware utility is built-in.
- You have access to other Yahoo services.

Microsoft Windows 98 or higher and Internet Explorer 5.0 or higher are required.

# Other Search Toolbars

By now, if you've tried out all the toolbars described in this chapter, either you've found a favorite or you have so many toolbars installed that the web page display area has become almost too cramped to be useful. Fortunately, there are other toolbars that have many of the great features you're looking for combined with the ability to search more than one single search engine. These toolbars can often take the place of multiple toolbars offered by different search engines.

## Groowe Search Toolbar

The Groowe Search Toolbar (http://www.groowe.com/) lets you choose from a number of major search engines whenever you enter a query. The Groowe Toolbar lets you select from Google, Yahoo!, Teoma, AltaVista, Ask Jeeves, MSN, and other search engines using a drop-down menu. The Groowe Search Toolbar is customized for each search engine, allowing you to take advantage of the special features offered by each, such as image search, audio search, video search, and so on.

The Groowe Search Toolbar also works with a number of specialized search sites, such as Monster Jobs, Barnes & Noble Shopping, Tucows, and Downolad.com, letting you search for jobs, books, and software downloads.

Microsoft Windows 98 or higher and Internet Explorer 5.0 or higher are required.

## Copernic Meta Toolbar

The Copernic Meta Toolbar (http://www.copernic.com/en/products/meta/index.html) is a meta search tool. From the toolbar you can search Google and several other web search engines simultaneously, without the need to move from one to another. You can also search for images, audio, multimedia, news, auctions, and more. As if this weren't enough, you can also add your own favorite search engines to the list of information sources accessible through Copernic Meta Toolbar.

Microsoft Windows 98 or higher and Internet Explorer 5.0 or higher are required.

## Alternatives for Non-IE Browsers

The Google Toolbar has one very big drawback: It only works with later versions of Microsoft Internet Explorer on Windows. If you use another browser, or have a Macintosh, you're out of luck. Fortunately, there are some excellent alternatives.

### Opera Browser

The Opera browser (http://www.opera.com) has a number of toolbar-like features built into the program. The browser's "search panel" searches Google by default, and also has buttons to run Amazon and eBay searches, comparison shopping searches at Shopping.com, and software searches at Download.com, as well as Google News and Google Groups searches. The browser has a built-in pop-up blocker and several other tools, including a "links panel" that provides a quick overview of all the links and linked file types present on the web page you are visiting. The Opera browser is a great alternative to Internet Explorer and works with most major operating systems.

### Googlebar for Mozilla and Firefox

With recent concerns about security problems with Internet Explorer, many people have switched to the free Mozilla/Firefox web browser. The open-source community that developed Mozilla has also built some very interesting search tools for the browser, including the Googlebar, which emulates all the basic search functionality of the Google Toolbar. As such, it's a virtual clone of the Google Toolbar, providing web search and easy access to almost all of Google's specialty searches—including some which are not yet supported by the original Google Toolbar! In fact, if you try to access information about the Google Toolbar using a Mozilla or Firefox browser, Google itself recommends the Googlebar—the highest form of endorsement possible. The Googlebar is available at http://googlebar.mozdev.org/, and works with Mozilla, Phoenix/ Firebird 0.2 or higher, and Netscape 7 or higher. Versions are available for Windows, Linux, and Mac OS X.

### Macintosh SearchGoogle.service

While Apple's Safari browser uses Google as a default search engine, the Macintosh SearchGoogle.service (http://gu.st/proj/SearchGoogle.service/) is a simple little utility that extends this capability to Mac OS X applications. Simply select text in nearly any application and press SHIFT-APPLE-> to launch a Google search for that text. Alternatively, you can press SHIFT-APPLE-< to search Amazon.com or SHIFT-APPLE-* to search the iTunes Music Store.

Mac OS X is required.

# Chapter 9

## Goodies from Google Labs

Google Labs is the company's "playground" for testing new technologies that are not yet ready for primetime. Google encourages employees, in addition to their regular projects, to spend 20 percent of their time working on anything they think will benefit Google. The most promising projects end up on public display in Google Labs (see Figure 9-1), and the best "graduate" and become full-blown services. Google News (Chapter 14) and Search by Location (Chapter 16) were two "20-percent time" projects that have now become integral parts of the overall Google service.

**FIGURE 9-1**    Google Labs is where promising new technologies are showcased and tested.

This commitment to research and development has been a core Google value from the very beginning. In their seminal paper "The Anatomy of a Large-Scale Hypertextual Web Search Engine," Google founders Sergey Brin and Larry Page wrote:

> "One of our main goals in designing Google was to set up an environment where other researchers can come in quickly, process large chunks of the web, and produce interesting results that would have been very difficult to produce otherwise. Another goal we have is to set up a Spacelab-like environment where researchers or even students can propose and do interesting experiments on our large-scale web data."

Google isn't just showing off new technology in Google Labs—they want you to play with the gizmos and gadgets on display, and send feedback directly to the engineers who developed them. You can also discuss the projects with other Google users, in special Google Groups forums dedicated to each application.

**Personalized Web Search**
Get personalized search results based on your interests
3/29/04 - Give us feedback - Discuss with others

All the applications in Google Labs can be found at http://labs.google.com. Remember, all these technology demonstrations are prototypes, and they sometimes may deliver surprising or unexpected results. As the Google Labs FAQ states: "Please, remember to wear your safety goggles while using this site."

POWER SEARCHER TIP

*More information about Google Labs can be found in the FAQ at http://labs .google.com/faq.html.*

**9**

# Personalized Web Search

It's a major challenge for Google and all major search engines to provide first-rate service for everyone, because they know very little about individual users. Google doesn't know if you're a man or a woman, adult or teenager, or whether you prefer broccoli over asparagus. On top of that, most searchers use very few search terms—typically only two to three—to express their information need. Nonetheless, Google must work with this paucity of data and instantly find answers that are suitable for any person searching for information on literally any subject imaginable.

It's a tough challenge, which partially explains why search results often include irrelevant or wildly off-topic suggestions. If you're searching for **Mercury**, for example, are you looking for information about the planet or the automobile? The Roman god or a history of the 1960s space missions? Or are you looking for recent news stories discussing proposed changes to permissible levels of mercury in power plant emissions? Unless you provide additional clues, Google must simply guess at your intent.

It would be far easier for Google to provide completely relevant results if it knew just a little bit about you. That's the whole point behind the Personalized Web Search application in Google Labs. You set up a "profile" containing your interests, and Google Personalized uses that profile to custom tailor your search results.

It's easy to set up your own profile. Click the **Edit Profile** link under the search box on the Google Personalized home page at http://labs.google.com/personalized. This displays your own personal interest profile, which is initially empty, and a list of interest categories for you to choose from. Clicking any category link displays a list of subcategories with check boxes next to them (see Figure 9-2). Simply check off the categories that interest you and Google automatically adds them to your interest list.

When building your list, it's tempting to create a giant list of all your interests. However, Google does a better job at creating personalized results when you select just a few categories, particularly if they're related. The more interests you add to your list, the less weight each is given

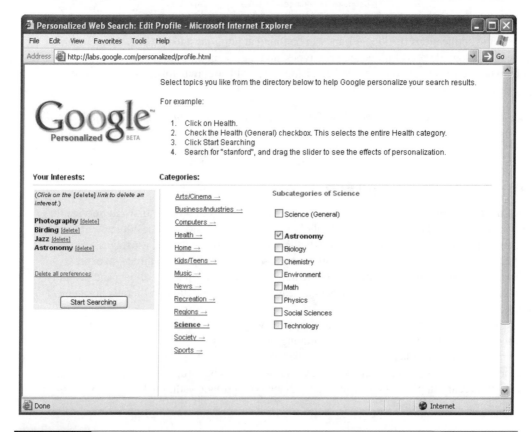

Check the boxes next to categories to add them to your interest list.

when Google considers how to personalize your results. You can always add or delete interests—even change them for individual searches to make them more specific to a particular topic.

Once you've created your interest list, click the **Start Searching** button to begin.

*Google stores your interests in a cookie, so personalization only works on the computer where you created your profile.*

Personalized search results look like regular results, with one exception: A slider bar at the top of the page allows you to rearrange your results from minimum personalization to maximum personalization, or anywhere in between. A colored ball icon next to a result indicates that it is a personalized result based on your interests.

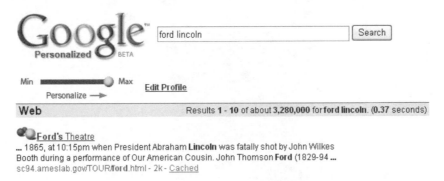

Sometimes personalized results will show little or no difference from standard Google results. In fact, if Google can't find any meaningful differences based on the interests you've selected, you'll see the message "Personalized results not detected for this query." The degree of personalization varies both by what you're looking for and the number of interests you've selected. If you're not getting satisfactory results, try different search terms, or remove or change some of your interests by editing your profile.

This simple application just barely scratches the surface of the possibilities for personalization. Google is keenly aware of the privacy issues regarding personalized search results. You can expect the company to continue to innovate in the area of personalization, gradually adding new features that will make search results even more relevant to you.

*More information about Google Personalized can be found in the FAQ at http:// labs.google.com/personalized/faq.html.*

# Froogle Wireless

How often have you been shopping at the mall, ready to make a purchase, and then found yourself wondering if you might get a better deal online? With Froogle Wireless you no longer need to have any doubts about whether you're getting the best price at your local store.

Froogle is Google's product shopping search service (Chapter 15). If your cell phone has web access, you can use a special interface designed for mobile devices at http://wml.froogle .com/ to search Froogle. Enter your search terms in the box and select the "Search" button.

Your search results show product information, prices, and retailer names. Use your phone's keypad arrows to scroll through the results. Because these results are sparse compared to the product listings on the main Froogle service, you won't want to use this wireless interface as your primary shopping search service. But because prices are prominently displayed in boldface text in search results, it's an easy way to get a simple range of prices from various merchants.

 *The Froogle Wireless interface works only on web-enabled mobile devices. Trying to use it on a standard browser will generate a dialog box to download a file— don't do this!*

# Google Compute

Unlike most of the other goodies in Google Labs, Google Compute doesn't help you find information, nor does it provide you with any insights into how Google works. Instead, it's a program that allows you, via Google, to help advance scientific knowledge. Google Compute is a feature for the Google Toolbar that lets your computer work on complex problems when it's idle. Google Compute "borrows" processing time from your computer to work on a tiny piece of a much larger problem, and it automatically sends the results to a central computer that is coordinating the efforts of thousands of other users' computers just like yours.

This is called *distributed computing*. Google Compute currently works with the Folding @home project, a nonprofit research project at Stanford University that is working to understand the structure of proteins, with an ultimate goal of developing better treatments for a variety of illnesses.

To participate in the Google Compute project, you need to be using the English language version of the Toolbar. If you don't already have the Toolbar, it will be installed automatically when you install Google Compute from http://toolbar.google.com/dc/offerdc.html.

Your reward for donating your computer's spare processing power is the ability to see statistics on the process of the problems it is helping to solve, knowing that in a small way you're helping mankind.

POWER SEARCHER TIP    *More information about Google Compute can be found in the FAQ at http:// toolbar.google.com/dc/faq_dc.html#faqs.*

# Google Sets

9

Google Sets offers a rare inside peek at how Google "thinks." It's a simple idea, but one that's quite complex behind the scenes. Google Sets groups keywords by concept. Enter three or more words, and your results will show words that are "predicted" to be closely related. Enter "square," "circle," and "triangle," for example, and the set returns "rectangle," "star," "oval," "diamond," and so forth. You can request either a large set or a small set (15 or fewer) by clicking the appropriate button.

Why is this useful? One use would be to come up with a larger set of potential search terms when you're searching an unfamiliar subject. Another is simply to observe how Google performs internal "query expansion," a technique that allows it to extract at least a partial contextual framework from just a few keywords in a query. Related words in sets can offer important clues to Google for gaining a deeper understanding of ambiguous or short queries.

A final reason to use Google Sets: It's fun! Try it with people's names or famous dates in history. Sometimes the results are surprising.

POWER SEARCHER TIP    *A fun tool to visualize the relationships among the terms in Google Sets is found at http://www.langreiter.com/space/google-set-vista. Enter a single search term into the box and you'll see a visualization of a set of related terms. Click any of these, and the set will be expanded to include other related terms.*

# Recent Graduates of Google Labs

When programs in the Labs have had sufficient testing, they can "graduate" to official status within Google. Here are some applications that matriculated out of the Labs during the brief time between writing this chapter and publication of the book.

# Google Desktop Search

Google's Desktop Search is one of the newest additions to the Labs, but it's also one of the most valuable. In a nutshell, Desktop Search indexes many of the files on your own personal computer and makes them searchable. The program also automatically stores a cached copy of every web page you view, creating your own personal web archive that you can view whether you're online or not.

Desktop Search is a quick, simple download, and it integrates seamlessly into the standard Google interface rather than running as a separate application. To search, right-click the Google Desktop icon in the task tray and select the **Search** option. This opens Internet Explorer with Google Desktop Search enabled; simply enter your search term and you'll see results that look virtually identical to Google web search results.

## The Google Deskbar

Chapter 8 took a detailed look at the Google Toolbar. The Google Deskbar, shown in the following illustration, is similar to the Toolbar and has many of the same functions. The key difference is that the Toolbar is a browser add-in for Internet Explorer, whereas the Deskbar is an application that runs in your Windows taskbar. The Toolbar works only if you have Internet Explorer open; the Deskbar works whenever your computer is on and you have an Internet connection, regardless of whether you're browsing the Web or not.

This makes the Deskbar a very handy tool for accessing information when you're working in other applications. You can look up information or get a dictionary definition when you're word processing, or you can search for images to include in a PowerPoint presentation, for example. Search results are displayed in a "mini viewer" that appears directly above the Deskbar's search form. Results are shown in the mini viewer until you move the cursor out of the Deskbar's search form, and then the mini viewer hides itself.

Unlike the Toolbar, the Deskbar provides keyboard shortcuts with a number of useful functions:

- To move the cursor from any Windows application to the Deskbar's search form, simply press CTRL-ALT-G.

- To show or hide the mini viewer, press SHIFT-F1 from any Windows application.

- From within the Google Deskbar, most of the search options also have keyboard shortcuts, as shown in the following illustration. To force results into a full browser window, press SHIFT-*SHORTCUT* (for example, you can use SHIFT-CTRL-N to run a news search and display results in a full browser window).

Though the Google Deskbar has fewer overall functions than the Toolbar, it can be extended. In addition to Google searches such as Web Search, Images, and News, the Deskbar also does third-party searches, such as weather by ZIP code, movie reviews from Rottentomatoes.com, dictionary and thesaurus lookups, downloads, and stock quotes.

You can also add custom searches that you perform often, such as looking for items on auction sites, checking TV listings, and so on—though you need to do a bit of fiddling with URLs to get these working properly. To add a custom search, open the Deskbar options from the menu and then select the **Customized Searches** tab. Click the **Add...** button and then enter the name and search string for your custom search.

*To learn more about how to add custom searches to the Deskbar, see the help page at http://toolbar.google.com/deskbar/help/options_custom.html.*

The options menu also allows you to customize other parts of the Deskbar, such as the preferred Google site for searching, adjusting mini viewer settings, and so on.

If you already have the Google Toolbar, do you need the Deskbar as well? Google says that the two complement each other, and that's true, to a degree. Most people will probably be just fine with the Toolbar alone. If you do a lot of work on your computer that's not web related, such as word processing, creating presentations, or working with spreadsheets or databases, then the Deskbar is a good choice. Power users will want to have both.

POWER SEARCHER TIP    *More information about the Google Deskbar can be found in the FAQ at http://toolbar.google.com/deskbar/help/faq.html.*

## Web Alerts

Wouldn't it be nice if Google sent you an e-mail any time it found and indexed something new on the Web that interests you?

Web Alerts, shown in Figure 9-3, do exactly that. Web Alerts are Google searches that you create and save, and then Google automatically runs the searches for you either once a day or once a week. Google looks at the top ten news results and top 20 web results for the search terms, and if it finds something new, it sends you an e-mail alert with a link to the new information.

Web Alerts are excellent tools for competitive intelligence gathering, allowing you to keep tabs on new developments in business or industry. You can also use them to discover new web sites on a topic that interests you. And, of course, you can use them to find out what other people on the Web are writing about you or your company.

To create a Web Alert, simply go to the Web Alerts page at http://www.google.com/webalerts and enter the search terms you would like to track, and whether you want news alerts, web alerts or both. Then provide an e-mail address where you want the alerts to be sent and use the drop-down menu to indicate whether you want alerts to be sent once a day or once a week. Google will then send you an e-mail message that requires you to confirm that you want the alert. You'll need to click the link in the e-mail to confirm the alert before it will start working. You can create up to ten unconfirmed alerts at a time, but there is no limit on the number of alerts you can create once you've confirmed them.

POWER SEARCHER TIP    *To edit or delete web alerts, you'll need to sign in using a Google account, described in other chapters.*

Even though you specify daily or weekly delivery, Google will only send you alerts if it has found something new. If you're tracking a popular or frequently changing subject, you'll see regular alerts. However, if you're tracking something obscure or are monitoring a particular topic or web site that changes infrequently, you may rarely get results. If you find you're getting fewer alerts than you would like or expect, try creating a new alert with different search terms and then compare its performance with the one that's not working as you'd like. Over time, you may decide to delete the first alert if it's not providing the results you want.

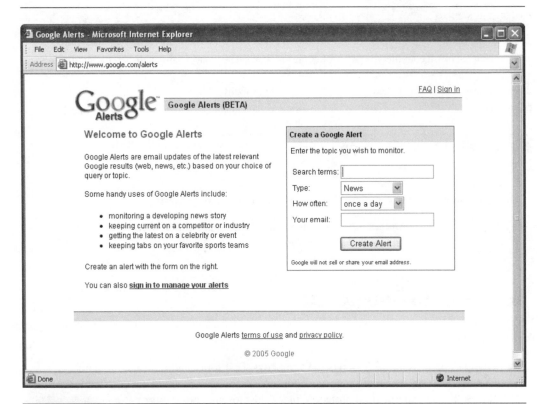

**FIGURE 9-3**    Google Web Alerts automatically run searches for you.

The great thing about Web Alerts is that they support the full advanced Google syntax described in earlier chapters. This means you're not just limited to alerts that find pages related to your search terms—you can use them for a variety of purposes. The best way to construct Web Alerts using advanced syntax is to have two browser windows open—one to the Google Web Alerts home page and the other showing the Advanced Search page at http://www.google.com/advanced_search. Construct your query using your keywords and the controls on this page and then click the **Google Search** button. When the result page appears, copy the text that appears in the search box on that page and paste it into the box on the Google Web Alerts home page.

POWER SEARCHER TIP    *If you only want news articles in your alerts, use Google News Alerts at http://www.google.com/newsalerts.*

| Search Terms | Purpose |
|---|---|
| "Neal Stephenson" | Find new pages related to the author Neal Stephenson. |
| site:research.microsoft.com filetype:pdf | Let me know when new papers are published by Microsoft Research. |
| link:www.searchenginewatch.com | Show new links to my web site. |
| Pfizer "new drug" | Monitor new developments at the world's largest ethical drug company. |

**TABLE 9-1**    Use Google Web Alerts to Track Virtually Any Topic on the Web

Table 9-1 shows some examples of more complex Google Web Alerts.

**POWER SEARCHER TIP** *More information about Google Web Alerts can be found in the FAQ at http:// www.google.com/help/faq_webalerts.html.*

# New Additions to Google Labs

At the time this book went to press, Google added several new applications to Google Labs. These are all worth a look:

- **Google Video**    Google Video is the company's first foray into multimedia search. Contrary to what its name suggests, Google Video doesn't make video searchable. Rather, it's an experimental project to index the closed-caption information from television broadcasts from several San Francisco Bay Area stations. It's an interesting initial effort, but at least for now its usefulness is limited.

- **Google Suggest**    As you type your keywords into the search box, Google offers suggestions in real time, and shows the number of search results the query will generate. You can use arrow keys to scroll down through the results and select your desired search terms.

- **Google Scholar**    This utility allows you to search through academic journals, abstracts, and other "scholarly" literature. Some results are links to full-text documents; others may offer links that help you locate materials in a physical library.

- **Google SMS**    Send a query to Google as a text message on your cell phone, and get phone book listings, dictionary definitions, or product prices as results, formatted as simple text without links or web pages.

# Part II

# Power Searching with Google

# Chapter 10

## What People Search For

First-time visitors to Google's worldwide headquarters in Mountain View, California, immediately realize that they are not in a typical workplace. In the lobby of the Googleplex, a grand piano sits next to the receptionist's desk. Lava lamps, beach balls, and all manner of Google-branded paraphernalia are visible everywhere. Once you've signed in and are sitting comfortably in a bean-bag chair waiting for your host, your eye is drawn to a large scrolling display, showing an endless stream of what appears to be random lines of text:

> *salt river tubing...*
> *why does my cat bite me...*
> *world health organization...*
> *over the hill autograph hound...*
> *camel+toes+pictures...*
> *Harry Potter...*
> *penguin party tea room...*
> 台風情報

After a few moments of staring at this cryptic, constantly shifting word salad, it dawns on you: You're looking through a window into the very core of Google, watching queries submitted by people throughout the world—in real time.

Though the queries seem (literally) all over the map, patterns slowly begin to emerge. Most people use Google to find information in just a few categories. Most often, people are searching for information about other people—celebrities, friends, co-workers, themselves. The phenomenon is so widespread that it's actually entered the language: When you're searching for information about a person, you are "Googling" them.

Other types of queries are also popular. People frequently turn to search engines when researching health issues or medical treatment options. Business research and competitive intelligence is another popular category. And, of course, people are increasingly turning to search engines for news, information about contemporary events, entertainment, shopping, and so on.

This chapter takes a look at how people use Google, and search engines in general. Apart from being a fascinating exercise in social anthropology, observing how people search can teach you a lot about using Google more effectively.

# The Google Zeitgeist

The Google Zeitgeist (http://www.google.com/press/zeitgeist.html) is a snapshot of the most popular queries Google received during the previous month. The term "zeitgeist" comes from the German "Zeit," meaning "time," and "Geist," meaning "spirit." Webster's dictionary defines zeitgeist as "the general intellectual, moral, and cultural climate of an era."

The topmost part of the Google's Zeitgeist (see Figure 10-1) shows the top ten most popular queries from the previous week. Rankings display both gaining and declining queries, giving you a quick snapshot of the issues and people foremost in searchers' minds, as well as those fading from the limelight.

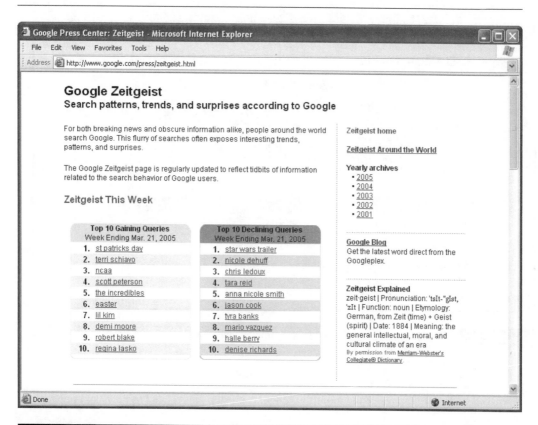

**FIGURE 10-1** The top ten queries in the weekly Google Zeitgeist are often people related.

International search statistics are also available via a link on the main Zeitgeist page. Queries from specific countries often have a local flavor. For example, you may see the top hockey-related queries in Canada, travel-related queries for Spain and Germany, popular airlines for Japan, or popular animals for Australia. These categories change from month to month, providing an ongoing glimpse of what's trendy and popular in countries throughout the world.

The rest of the Google Zeitgeist page is updated monthly with lists, graphs, and other tidbits of information related to Google users' search behavior, highlighting popular topics such as famous men and women, travel queries, entertainment queries, and other categories that vary from month to month (see Figure 10-2).

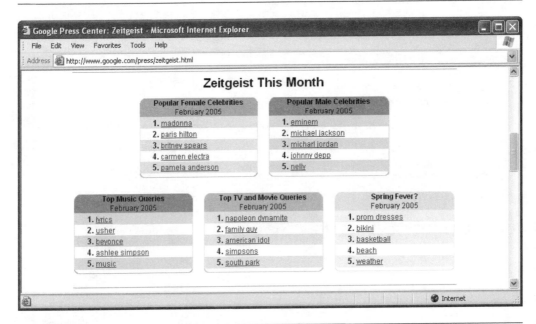

**FIGURE 10-2**    Popular queries on Google are featured each month.

Two other regular features of the monthly Zeitgeist are statistics related to news and image search queries.

Each year, Google also compiles a year-end Zeitgeist, recapping the hottest trends as expressed in the billions of searches handled by the company during the year. Beyond a summary of the monthly Zeitgeists, the year-end Zeitgeists also provide charts showing sharp spikes in search activity triggered by noteworthy events. Figure 10-3 shows several spikes that occurred during 2003, such as a spike on the term "NASA" when the space shuttle Columbia was tragically lost, and another on the date that Operation Iraqi Freedom began.

Google maintains an archive of all Zeitgeist reports, which is a treasure trove of data for mining history and observing how trends change over time. Table 10-1 has a complete list of the various Zeitgeist archives.

## Inside the Searcher's Mind

The search terms people use on Google are just one part of the equation relating to how they interact with the search engine. Just as people tend to use widely varying search terms, they also interact with search result pages in unique ways. Research done by search marketing firm

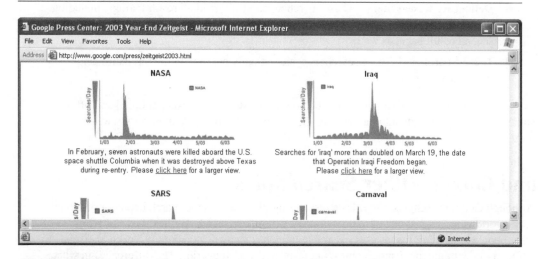

**FIGURE 10-3**    Google sees surges in search activity when a current event triggers massive collective interest in a particular topic.

Enquiro revealed fascinating insights into the searcher's mind. The study concluded that there are four "types" of searchers:

- **Scan and Clickers**    These searchers do a quick scan of the top search results without really reading page titles or descriptions, and they quickly click through to several sites. After scanning a page for 10–15 seconds, they will either stay on the result page or click back to try another result.

- **2-Step Scanners**    These searchers scan the top listings to see if anything "jumps out," and if so, they will click a result. If not, they will do a more thorough scan of the page, and often will deliberately check out many result pages before finally settling on one.

| Zeitgeist Archive | URL |
|---|---|
| Complete Zeitgeist Archive | http://www.google.com/press/zeitgeist/archive.html |
| 2004 Year-End Google Zeitgeist | http://www.google.com/press/zeitgeist2004.html |
| 2003 Year-End Google Zeitgeist | http://www.google.com/press/zeitgeist2003.html |
| 2002 Year-End Google Zeitgeist | http://www.google.com/press/zeitgeist2002.html |
| 2001 Year-End Google Zeitgeist | http://www.google.com/press/zeitgeist2001.html |
| Search Statistics Related to September 11, 2001 | http://www.google.com/press/zeitgeist/9-11.html |

**TABLE 10-1**    Google's Zeitgeist Archives

- **Deliberate Researchers**   These searchers carefully read all result listings, including titles, descriptions, and URLs before making a selection. They will often go on to the second result page, as well.

- **1, 2, 3 Searchers**   These searchers systematically begin with the top listing and investigate all results in turn.

If you're really interested in searcher behavior, this study is an excellent read and offers some outstanding insights into the mind of the searcher. It's available at http://www.sempo .org/research/searcher-mind.pdf.

# Beyond Google: Other Search Spies

Although Google's Zeitgeist provides a fascinating glimpse into the search behavior of Google users worldwide, it's just one of many windows offered by search engines showing glimpses of what people search for. Just as every search engine has its own "personality," each also tends to attract users with unique demographics, interests, and search queries. The differences in what people search for at Google vs. Yahoo!, Lycos, or some other search engine is often striking. Here's a look at some of the other useful "search spies" available on the Web.

## The Yahoo! Buzz Index

Yahoo!'s Buzz Index (http://buzz.yahoo.com/leaders/) is by far the most comprehensive collection of search-related statistics available anywhere. The Yahoo! Buzz Index is published Tuesday through Saturday. All the rankings on the Yahoo! Buzz Index are updated each weekday and reflect the traffic from two days earlier, providing a dynamic view of the constantly changing interests of Yahoo! searchers.

The Yahoo! Buzz Index main page is organized into seven major categories:

- Overall
- Television
- Music
- Sports
- Actors and Actresses
- Movies
- Video Games

For each category, the top three queries are displayed with a number of useful indicators. These indicators include current rank, an arrow indicating whether the query is moving up or down in popularity, its previous rank, and two other statistics: Buzz Score and Move. Buzz Score is a number indicating overall popularity, with each point equal to 0.001 percent of users searching on Yahoo! on a given day. For example, a buzz score of 500 means that 0.5 percent of all users searching on Yahoo! that day searched that particular query. Move is the percentage increase or decrease in the subject's buzz score from the previous day. Yahoo! says that the Move number can indicate a trend, but it's important to remember that people who search Yahoo! on Sunday differ greatly from those searching on Monday, so you can't always draw definitive conclusions from the numbers.

Like the Google Zeitgeist, the actual queries displayed in the Yahoo! Buzz Index are hyperlinks that will automatically run the search so you can view the results.

Every Sunday, Yahoo! publishes the Buzz Index Weekly Report, which recaps the top 20 searches for the week and offers colorful commentary on recent buzz activity. Yahoo! also publishes a weekly World Report, showing the most popular English-language Yahoo! searches that originate from countries outside the U.S. For example, if someone in Brazil (domain .br) uses Yahoo.com to search for "baseball," that data is calculated as buzz for Brazil.

Yahoo! archives the Buzz Index Weekly Report, but the archives are not particularly easy to access. Each weekly page has links to reports from the five prior weeks. You can click your way back in time using these links, but there's a faster way to get to earlier versions. Archived pages all have a similar URL—the only thing that changes is the date string in the middle of the URL. Change the date string to a prior Sunday to directly access that archived page.

POWER SEARCHER TIP *Yahoo! syndicates the Buzz Index via RSS. More information and links to feeds are available at http://buzz.yahoo.com/rss_info/.*

## The Lycos 50

The Lycos 50 (http://50.lycos.com) is another interesting search spy because it offers extensive analysis and commentary in addition to popularity statistics. Each week, the Lycos 50 editor offers an in-depth analysis of the popular topics and shifting trends as reflected in searcher queries.

A unique feature of the Lycos 50 is the weekly "bonus list," which explores a hot trend in more detail. Bonus lists can cover celebrities, food and drink, geography, spelling, sports—just about any topic that catches the editor's fancy. The Lycos 50 also offers a complete archive, including year-end lists (see Table 10-2).

POWER SEARCHER TIP *One of the most interesting Lycos 50 columns is a subjective look at the ten oddest topics ever to appear on the Lycos 50, available at http://50.lycos .com/083002.asp.*

| Lycos 50 Archive | URL |
| --- | --- |
| Complete Lycos 50 Archives | http://50.lycos.com/archives.asp |
| Greatest Hits, "Our best articles and predictions" | http://50.lycos.com/greatesthits.asp |
| Lycos 50 Elite, "Our most popular subjects ever" | http://50.lycos.com/elite.asp |
| Top 100 of 2004 | http://50.lycos.com/2004review.asp |
| Top 100 of 2003 | http://50.lycos.com/2003review.asp |
| Top 100 of 2002 | http://50.lycos.com/2002review.asp |
| Top 100 of 2001 | http://50.lycos.com/2001review.asp |

**TABLE 10-2**    The Lycos 50 Archives

## Ask Jeeves IQ

Ask Jeeves IQ (Interesting Queries, at http://sp.ask.com/docs/about/jeevesiq.html) is a bare-bones peek at what Jeeves users have on their collective minds. The page displays the most popular search terms based on the millions of queries submitted to Ask Jeeves, reported at the end of each week. Jeeves IQ reports on four categories. Three are constant: the top advancing searches for the week, showing topics gaining in popularity; top searches for the week, showing which topics have the most overall interest; and top news searches for the week. The fourth category varies from week to week, focusing on subjects such as pictures, movies, shopping, companies, and so on.

Unlike Google's Zeitgeist, there is no archive of previous Jeeves IQ lists.

## MetaSpy

Metacrawler's search spy (http://www.metaspy.com/info.metac.spy/metaspy/) shows a snapshot of queries being processed by the search engine in real time, updated every 15 seconds (see Figure 10-4). These search queries flash by without any commentary or interpretation, leaving you to figure out what searchers had in mind. MetaSpy is available in filtered and unfiltered versions.

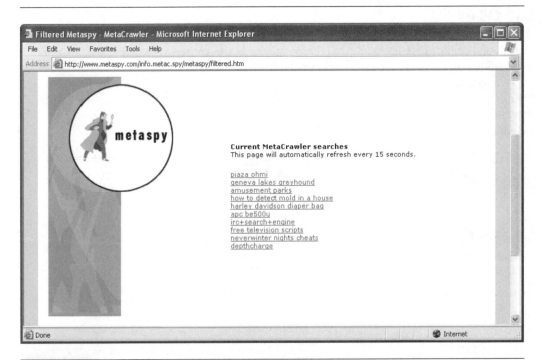

**FIGURE 10-4**    Metacrawler's MetaSpy shows real-time queries, updated every 15 seconds.

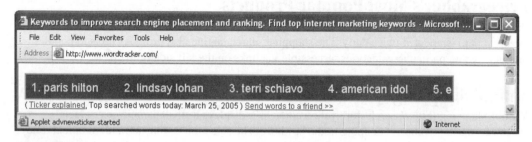

**FIGURE 10-5**   The Word Tracker Ticker reflects a broad range of search engine queries.

## Word Tracker Ticker

All the search engine spies described in this chapter so far report directly on the search behavior of their own users. The Word Tracker Ticker (http://www.wordtracker.com/), shown in Figure 10-5, reveals the top 50 search terms for a variety of search engines over the past 24 hours. Word Tracker collects real query data from a number of meta search engines across the Web, providing a good sense of the most popular queries without regard to the differences in users among the various engines.

# Shopping Search Spies

Occasionally, the Google Zeitgeist or Yahoo! Buzz Index will disclose popular shopping-related queries. But several of the major shopping search engines (described in more detail in Chapter 15) provide regularly updated lists of specific products that are popular with users of their services. If you're looking to get a sense of hot new toys or the latest must-have gadget, these lists are the place to go.

## Froogle

Unlike the Google Zeitgeist, which shows cumulative popular queries on the search engine, Google's shopping search, Froogle (http://froogle.google.com), displays items users recently searched for directly on the Froogle home page.

Click your browser's "refresh" button and you'll see a new list of product-related queries.

## Shopping.com Consumer Demand Index

The Shopping.com Consumer Demand Index (http://www.shopping.com/cdi) offers a weekly snapshot of what's hot on the shopping search engine. The index features the top 20 shopping searches and the top 10 gaining queries, spotlights a particular product that's showing increasing popularity, and also has a list of the top 10 specific items within a particular popular product category. There's also a link to the top 100 searches by category and a drop-down menu providing access to previous weekly consumer demand index reports.

10

## Pricegrabber's Most Popular Products

Pricegrabber.com's 200 most popular products page (http://www.pricegrabber.com/home_ mostpop.php) is updated twice daily. The shopping search engine also provides links to popular products within particular categories, accessible via links on the left side of the page.

## Yahoo! Shopping

Yahoo! Shopping (http://search.store.yahoo.com/OT?) displays a small sample of products purchased through Yahoo! Shopping in the last hour. The selection is done at random in real time from a sample of purchased products. The **Click here to see more items** link refreshes the page with a new set of products.

# Chapter 11

## Tools to Enhance Your Google Searches

Google is great for locating specific web sites or finding quick online answers. But finding information is often just the first step in doing web research, or in keeping up to date with topics that interest you.

Sure, all browsers offer some sort of bookmarking capability, allowing you to save the title and URL of web pages that interest you. If you're compulsive, you can even organize your bookmarks or favorites into folders and subfolders. But inevitably, after you've accumulated hundreds or even thousands of these online markers, you begin to forget what they are or why you saved them in the first place. Worse, bookmarks are fragile, breaking when webmasters move pages or when sites go out of business or simply drop off of the Web.

Alas, as good as Google is at helping you locate information, it does virtually nothing to help you organize that information for later use. For many web sites, that's OK—you'll only visit the site once, never to return. For other web sites, especially prominent ones, it's a simple matter just to run your search terms again and let Google surface the proper links. That is, assuming you can remember the search terms you used to actually find the site. Or assuming Google hasn't reengineered its algorithms, making a search that worked brilliantly for you yesterday return completely different results today—with the site you're looking for nowhere to be found.

Fortunately, there are a number of excellent tools that help you organize your favorite web resources and keep up to date with new information on topics of interest. Whether you're doing serious research, such as sleuthing out a competitor's new marketing strategy or investigating a cutting-edge medical procedure, or simply checking out your best options for a new digital camera or planning your summer holiday, these tools go far beyond Google, in essence allowing you to create your own personal search engine with a private, customized copy of the Web.

# Web Research Managers

Web research managers are essentially bookmarks on steroids. They solve the multiple failings of the simple-minded "favorites" utilities built into browsers by saving full copies of web pages, rather than just a bare-bones page title and link. By saving a copy of a page, you dramatically decrease the risk of not finding it again. Saving complete copies of pages delivers another benefit, as well—the ability to index and search the contents of those pages. Most web research managers also allow you to annotate saved pages with your own notes or keywords, further enhancing the power of their search and retrieval capabilities.

Most web research managers are browser toolbar applications that let you capture web page URLs, page snippets, images, PDF documents—just about any sort of information you find on the Web. Some also let you store non-web information, such as notes, e-mail messages, and so on.

Once you've captured information, your collection becomes instantly searchable. Depending on the sophistication of the search capabilities of the application, you can often sort search results by relevance, name, type, date, priority, category, or any other type of descriptive information that was saved when capturing the documents.

A key feature of all these programs is the ability to share your research with others. How information is shared differs depending on the type of program you're using and whether it's a standalone application running just on your computer or a web service accessible to anyone who has access to an Internet-connected computer.

The two essential types of web research managers are collaborative bookmark managers and standalone web research managers. Here's a closer look at each type, with a comparison of the strengths and weaknesses of each.

# Collaborative Bookmark Managers

Collaborative bookmark managers let you store your web favorites and share them with others. These online services have been around for years, offering rudimentary bookmarking and sharing capabilities. Only recently, as the cost of disk storage has plummeted, have many collaborative bookmark services beefed up their capabilities, allowing you to store complete web pages in addition to page titles and URLs.

Collaborative bookmark managers are obviously a great tool for teams who need to share online research. They also have the advantage of being accessible anywhere in the world, as long as you can get access to a computer with an Internet connection.

Another key advantage is that many are free, supported by advertising or user donations.

## Furl

Furl (http://www.furl.net), which stands for "file URL," solves the "disappearing bookmark" problem—pages that for one reason or another vanish, making your bookmarks useless. Furl does this by actually storing copies of web pages on its own servers. It also makes these pages searchable. Like all collaborative bookmark services, pages stored with Furl are accessible from any web-connected computer.

Using Furl is easy. First, you need to register for the service. Registration is painless—just provide your name, e-mail address, and create a user name and password. Furl has a brief but reasonable privacy policy—they don't share your personal information, but rather use it to keep track of your furled web pages.

The next step is to install the Furl tool into your browser. The **Furl It** bookmarklet, shown in Figure 11-1, is a simple piece of code that works just like a bookmark. The bookmarklet is nice because it doesn't take up additional toolbar space.

Now you can begin saving pages to your own personal cache. When you furl a page, a pop-up window opens up that lets you store additional information about the page (see Figure 11-2). In addition to saving the title and URL, you can give the page a rating from 1 to 5 and assign it to a topic.

Topics are categories, allowing you to organize your furled pages in a simple, Yahoo!-style directory. The ten preset categories include business, entertainment, health, and more. Furl offers the ability to edit, delete, and add topics to your own list. You can also add comments and keywords that can help you find content later. Furl can also clip and store text from a page if you highlight it before furling.

Once you've furled some web pages, it's easy to get back to them. First, click the **View** tab at the top of any Furl page. This displays a list of your own furled pages, with the most recent entries at the top. You can sort these pages by title, date, topic, rating, or the number of views the

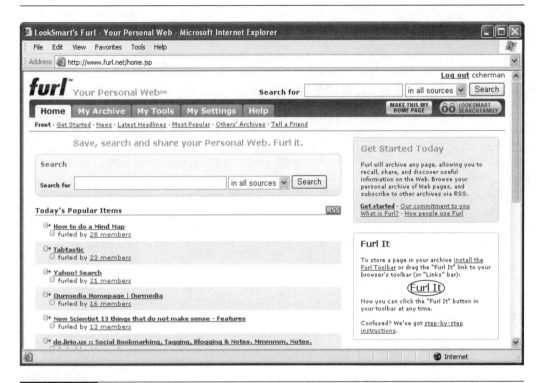

**FIGURE 11-1** Furl's bookmarklet button installs in the browser's links toolbar.

page has had by other Furl users, simply by clicking the respective hyperlink at the top of each column. Figure 11-3 shows the list of furled pages created for this chapter (you can access this list online at http://www.furl.net/members/GooglePower).

Furl will even save non-HTML web content, such as PDF files, Excel spreadsheets, and so on.

Forms on a View page let you filter an archive by topic or date, or you can search for content by keywords.

Perhaps Furl's greatest strength lies with its sharing features. By default, both pages and topics in your archive are public (you can easily designate both individual pages and entire topics as private). You can share your archive with anyone by providing them with the URL that Furl automatically creates for your archive when you register for the service.

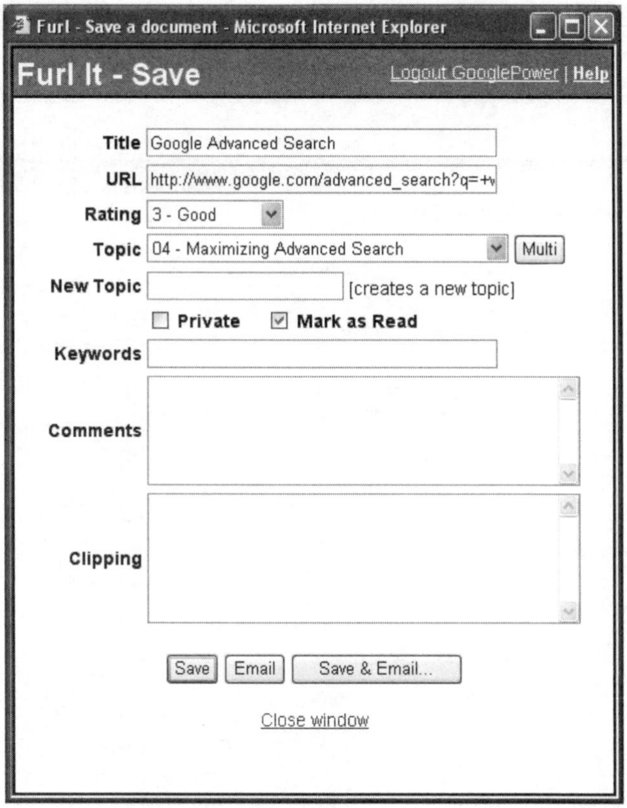

**FIGURE 11-2**   Furl's "save page" dialog box lets you enter several additional pieces of information about a saved page.

You can also share your archive by e-mail. Anyone who subscribes gets a daily e-mail with your top entries. If your colleagues use an RSS news aggregator, they can also subscribe to a Furl feed that's automatically generated when you save new web pages (see Chapter 19 for more information on RSS).

Borrowing a page from Amazon, Furl has a cool feature called "People who furled this, also furled..." that automatically appears when you furl a page previously saved by another Furl user. Seeing related pages saved by other users can be a great way to discover new, related content to the pages you're saving.

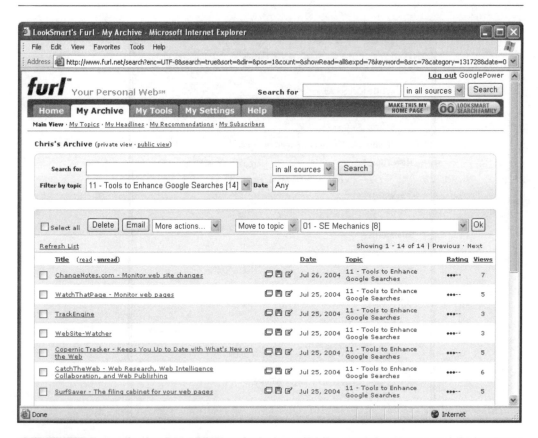

**FIGURE 11-3**    Furl's searching capabilities are basic, but reasonably useful.

Furl works on virtually any computer and with most web browsers, including Internet Explorer (Windows and Mac), Safari (Mac), Netscape, Firebird, Mozilla, and Opera.
Although Furl is free, registration is required.

POWER SEARCHER TIP    *Furl is an excellent tool for keeping track of passwords, login names, and other personal registration information (other than super-private information, such as social security numbers or bank account details, for example). Just furl a page associated with your private information (a login page or a product registration page, for example), enter your login details and registration numbers in the **Comments** or **Clipping** area, and check the **private** box. You'll never lose or forget this important information again.*

## Backflip

Backflip (http://www.backflip.com) was one of the first online bookmark services, starting life back in the Web's wild days of the late 90s, only to flame out along with so many other companies during the dotcom bust. Today, the service is maintained by a team of volunteers who worked on the original service. Offering many of the same features as Furl, Backflip also has an interesting feature called "My Daily Routine" that lets you put together a "slide show" of your favorite web sites, allowing you to simply click an arrow button to visit each in turn.

Backflip works with Microsoft Internet Explorer 4.0 and higher, Netscape Navigator or Communicator: 4.0 and higher.

Although Backflip is free, registration is required.

*Backflip's financial challenges illustrate one of the problems of using an online-only service: If the company goes out of business or is sold, there's no guarantee that you'll be able to continue to access your information. Be sure to keep backup copies of critical information on your own computer.*

## Spurl.net

Spurl.net (http://www.spurl.net/) has a couple of interesting features not found in Furl or Backflip. You can filter public Spurled lists by language, and there's a "safe" filter available to eliminate potentially offensive content. Spurl also offers anonymous registration—simply enter a user name and password (no e-mail address required).

Spurl currently supports Internet Explorer, Opera, Mozilla/Firefox, Netscape, and Safari across Windows, Linux, and Mac OS.

*You can find an extensive list of bookmark utilities in the Google directory, at http://directory.google.com/Top/Computers/Internet/On_the_Web/Web_ Applications/Bookmark_Managers.*

11

# Standalone Web Research Managers

Although collaborative online bookmark managers make it easy to save web pages and share them with others, they lack the industrial-strength searching and reporting capabilities offered by standalone web research managers. These programs create searchable databases of web pages on your own computer and allow you to supplement saved pages with additional information, called *metadata,* that greatly enhances the precision of subsequent searching.

Sharing with collaborative online bookmarks is limited—usually it's just a slightly annotated, clickable list of links you've saved. By contrast, standalone web research managers allow you to create sophisticated reports, culling and highlighting important content and deleting less relevant portions of web pages. Reports can also be formatted to be read offline, obviating the need for an Internet connection.

## ContentSaver

ContentSaver (http://www.macropool.de/en/index.html) is one of the most powerful web research managers. ContentSaver actually has two very different components: an Internet Explorer toolbar, used to capture web content, and a Microsoft Outlook–style application used to view and organize saved information.

The toolbar, shown in the following illustration, lets you easily save web content with one or two clicks. The **Save** button allows you to quickly save pages in a default folder, bypassing the dialog boxes that are typical with other applications. The toolbar has two other notable features that can be helpful: the ability to save individual frames of a framed web page, and the ability to automatically open all the links found on a page and save those as well.

The ContentSaver Toolbar

ContentSaver's organization tool is a separate application from the toolbar, with the look and feel of Microsoft Outlook (see Figure 11-4). The left pane has navigational controls, allowing you to easily navigate in your folders of saved information. On the right are two panes. The topmost pane displays the title, URL, and other information about individual saved pages. Clicking one of these items displays the full page itself in the bottom pane.

ContentSaver's search capabilities are particularly strong. The basic "find" capability is competent and quick, but the advanced search feature shines. You can search by keywords in the content, title, URL, or your own comments. You can also specify categories, document types, the date saved, and file size, or you can search by the importance you assign to a document. You can save searches as templates as well, which can be run again at any time simply by double-clicking a template link.

ContentSaver also has a nifty notepad feature that allows you to create notes and save them along with captured web content. You can assign categories and importance rankings to these notes as well.

The program supports many options for exporting and sharing information. You can transfer documents to Microsoft Word, create a web page presentation that can be opened in any web browser, or export documents in their original file types.

Windows 98 or higher and Internet Explorer 5.5 or higher are required.

ContentSaver comes with a free 30-day trial period and costs $U.S. 39.90.

**FIGURE 11-4**    ContentSaver's organization tool has the look and feel of Microsoft Outlook.

# NetSnippets Professional

NetSnippets (http://www.netsnippets.com) has two parts: a toolbar for Internet Explorer, and a viewing pane that opens in the Explorer Bar on the left side of the browser window. Although the NetSnippets toolbar is quite large, with five buttons spreading across a good chunk of your toolbar space, it offers a quick way to capture content.

If you have the screen real estate, a better option is to open the program in the Explorer Bar and disable the toolbar altogether. All the toolbar functions are available from the **Add** menu in the Explorer Bar, and you can use the toolbar space for other helpful resources, such as the Google toolbar.

To save content, simply click the **Add Entire Page** or **Add Link** button on the toolbar. You can also highlight parts of web pages (both text and images) and select the **Add Selection** link. One other nice feature is the ability to save only the text, links, or images from a page.

NetSnippets' drag-and-drop capabilities are strong. You can capture a link to a page by dragging the page icon from Internet Explorer's address bar to a folder. You can also highlight an area of text or select an image and then drag it to the folder where you'd like to save it. In addition to web pages, NetSnippets can store PDF files, MS Office files, e-mails, and video and audio from the Web or from your local PC. Every snippet is saved along with its source information, and you can add additional comments, source information, keywords, and custom information as well as set an importance level.

A unique feature of NetSnippets is its multifaceted screen capture function. Simply select **Screen Capture** from the **Add** menu and then choose the shape you'd like to save (rectangle, ellipse, triangle, pentagram, and so on). Drag your cursor over the area of the page to be captured, release the cursor, and then drag the area to a folder. That's all there is to it.

Although NetSnippets does allow you to search through your saved content and to create presentations that can be viewed in a browser, these features are not quite as powerful as those found in the other web research managers described in this chapter. One unique feature that will appeal to some, though, is the program's ability to generate bibliography reports in MLA, APA, and Chicago styles.

Windows 98 or higher and Internet Explorer 5.0 or higher are required.

NetSnippets comes with a free 30-day trial period and costs $U.S. 129.95.

# Onfolio

Onfolio (http://www.onfolio.com) is a toolbar application for Internet Explorer that lets you capture web page URLs, page snippets, images, PDF documents—anything that can be displayed in Internet Explorer's browser window. Stored information is kept in folders on your computer for easy retrieval. The Onfolio toolbar has a very small footprint, so it peacefully coexists with your other toolbars, such as the Google toolbar.

Saving content is easy. When you come across a document you want to keep, click the briefcase icon on the right side of the toolbar button (or right-click and select the **Capture Page to Onfolio** option). This activates a dialog box that lets you save the page. When you save content, you have the option of saving a link or a complete copy of a web page. You can also highlight and save just a portion of a page, or you can click an image and save just that image.

When you save something, Onfolio opens up a dialog box that automatically attempts to capture as much information as possible, including the source URL, copyright information, the author's name, keywords associated with the document, and the capture date. You can also add your own comments to saved content.

Onfolio stores captured content in "collections," which are folders with descriptive names. You can have as many subfolders in a collection as you like, and it's easy to drag and drop information between folders to help keep it organized.

To view your saved content, use the "collection browser," which opens up in the Explorer pane on the left side of the browser. On top, your collections are displayed. Click a folder icon, and the contents of that collection are displayed below. Icons show you whether an item is a link, a web page, PDF file, and so on.

Collections are searchable, and you can sort search results by relevance, name, type, date, or "flag," which is an annotation created by you to represent a priority, category, or any other type of descriptive information for items in a particular collection.

The professional edition of Onfolio makes it easy to share your research with others, in several ways. For example, you can publish a report, which wraps up everything in a collection into a single MHT document that can be viewed by anyone using Internet Explorer. You can also publish your research as a web site, with selected links, comments, and content that you've captured. You can also automatically include an RSS feed as part of the output.

Windows 2000 or higher and Internet Explorer 5.5 or higher are required.

Onfolio comes with a free 30-day trial period and costs $U.S. 79.95.

### Ask Sam SurfSaver Pro

SurfSaver Pro (http://www.surfsaver.com) is a browser add-on that lets you save and search all the facts, figures, news, and research you find on the Web. SurfSaver stores your favorite web pages directly from your browser into searchable folders.

Windows 95 or higher and Internet Explorer 6.x and Netscape Navigator 4.x are required.

SurfSaver Pro comes with a free 30-day trial period and costs $U.S. 29.95.

POWER SEARCHER TIP    *You may wonder if you really need a web research manager when you can use Google's cache to view older copies of web pages. The answer is yes, because Google does not cache copies of every page in its index, and never keeps a cached page for more than 30 days before recrawling and storing a new copy of a page in cache.*

11

# Choosing a Web Research Manager

Which of the web research managers described in this chapter is right for you? That depends on your own needs. If you're looking for a quick-and-easy way to save an occasional web page, Furl and Backflip are good choices, thanks to their relatively limited feature set and low cost—in Furl's case, the software is free.

If, on the other hand, you're looking for a heavy-duty tool to help create a searchable archive of hundreds or thousands of web pages, with your own notes, keywords, categories, and other annotations, ContentSaver and Onfolio are good choices. If you're doing academic research and want strong reporting and bibliographic capabilities, NetSnippets is a good choice.

Another factor to consider is whether you want to save local copies of web pages on your own computer, or whether you want online access to your stash from any Internet-connected computer. Although most of the standalone web research managers allow you to publish reports that can be sent to other computers, this isn't as convenient as the direct access offered by an online collaborative bookmark manager. On the other hand, storing pages on your own computer makes them available when you're offline, or in a location where you have limited Internet access.

How you share information is another important consideration. Do you want to provide open access to your cache of web pages to anyone? If so, an online collaborative bookmark manager is your best choice. Do you prefer to create edited, annotated reports, culling only bits and pieces of various information sources? If so, a standalone web research manager provides many more reporting and sharing features than online bookmark managers. Your preferences will determine which program is the most suitable for your own needs.

All the web research managers described in this chapter are excellent tools, each with its own unique set of strengths and features. All are free to try, and if you're serious about web research, you should put them all through their paces before settling on any one application. You may find, as I have, that you use more than one, depending on what you're trying to accomplish.

*If you use a collaborative online bookmark manager, you should also take the time to permanently store your most important pages with a desktop web research manager. This ensures that you'll never lose vital content should one of the online services go out of business.*

## Monitoring Your Favorite Web Sites

Web research managers solve the problem of keeping track of favorite or valuable web sites. But they don't solve another problem faced by all serious searchers: How do you know when your favorite sites have been updated with new information? It's relatively easy to keep track of your favorite blogs and news sites using RSS feeds, as described in Chapter 19. But to keep up to date with changes and new content at most other web sites, you actually have to visit the site itself. The good news is that you can save countless hours by automating the process with software that tracks changes to your favorite web sites—even while you sleep.

These programs—variously called *page trackers, URL monitors,* and other descriptive names—are constantly on the lookout for changes to web pages.

What kinds of pages would you want to monitor on a regular basis? Well, I've got page trackers set up to monitor all the major search engines' press release pages. Even before the folks in the public relations departments e-mail me a new press release, I already know about it, thanks to the page tracker. I also use the software to monitor a number of web pages that update their content infrequently or on an irregular schedule. You can use page trackers to monitor online forums, auctions, social networking services—any web site that adds new content that you want to read as soon as it's published.

Here are some examples of types of pages to track with a URL monitor:

- Product update pages: http://www.mozilla.org/
- Movie trailers: http://www.movie-list.com/
- Favorite blogs: http://www.researchbuzz.com
- Radio program schedules: http://www.npr.org/about/schedules/
- Bestselling books: http://www.nytimes.com/pages/books/bestseller/

## Features of Web Site Monitors

Web site monitor programs all share similar features. First, you create a list of pages you want to monitor, and specify how frequently they should be checked. Next, you determine what kind of changes should be monitored. Finally, you select your notification options.

Selecting pages to monitor is easy. Most programs allow you to add the page you're currently viewing to a list of tracked pages, or you can drag and drop a link to the list. Many also allow you to import bookmarks.

Pages can be checked for changes on a regular schedule, as frequently as every minute or just once every month or two.

With most of these services, you specify the kinds of changes you'd like to be notified about. Do you want to track any change made to a page? Do you only want to be notified when there's new content? Perhaps you're just looking for an image to change. Most of these programs offer flexible content-monitoring options.

When changes have been detected, the programs will notify you by sounding an alarm or by sending you an e-mail alert. For web-based page-tracking services, a notification will be posted to a custom web page.

## Copernic Tracker

Copernic Tracker (http://www.copernic.com/en/products/tracker/index.html) is a desktop-based tool that automatically looks for new content on web pages. One of the nicest features of this program is its ability to keep copies of page revisions, allowing you to compare changes to a page over time. You can also export different page revisions to a single file for all or selected page revisions. In addition, you can add notes to tracked pages and each of their revisions.

When Copernic Tracker detects a change to a watched page, it can notify you by sending an e-mail, including a copy of the web page with the changes highlighted, or by displaying a desktop alert or tray icon.

Windows 98 or higher and Internet Explorer 5.0 or higher are required.

Copernic Tracker comes with a free 30-day trial period and costs $U.S. 49.95.

11

## Web Site-Watcher

Like Copernic Tracker, Web Site-Watcher (http://www.aignes.com/) is a desktop application that allows you to monitor any number of web sites for updates and changes with a minimum of time and online costs. When changes in a web site are detected, Web Site-Watcher saves the last two versions to your hard disk and highlights all changes in the text. You can also archive various versions of the page as well as have page changes (when detected) e-mailed to you.

For serious tracking of an entire web site, the "follow links" feature allows you to monitor complete sites, instead of single pages. For doing competitive intelligence work, this is a very powerful option.

Web Site-Watcher has most of the features offered by Copernic Tracker. It's more flexible in its browser support, however, and is compatible with Internet Explorer, Netscape, Opera, NetCaptor, and NeoPlanet.

Windows 95 or higher is required.

Web Site-Watcher comes with a free 30-day trial period and costs $U.S. 29.95.

## ChangeNotes.com

ChangeNotes.com (http://www.changenotes.com/) is a very basic free service that watches the web pages that interest you and notifies you by e-mail when they change. Tracking options are limited—the service downloads tracked pages once per day, strips out all code, images, and other non-text elements, and looks for changes. Changed pages are assembled into an e-mail and sent to you once per day. You can also log into the service and view your tracked pages online.

You can use any operating system or browser to access ChangeNotes.com, and you can track up to 100 URLs for free.

## TrackEngine

TrackEngine (http://www.trackengine.com) is an online service that's part web page monitor, part online bookmark service. You set up a list of sites to monitor using a bookmarklet, which displays a dialog box that allows you to specify a few options for monitoring frequency, report schedule and format, and so on. At any time, you can sign into TrackEngine and manage your bookmarks online. You can edit the tracking parameters of selected bookmarks as well as delete bookmarks you no longer need.

You can use any operating system and any browser that supports JavaScript to access TrackEngine.

It costs $U.S. 19.95 per year to monitor up to ten bookmarks, or $U.S. 4.95 per month to monitor up to 50 bookmarks.

## Trackle

Trackle (http://www.trackle.com/) is a web-based URL-monitoring service. You select which pages to monitor and specify the monitoring schedule. Trackle sends you a single e-mail (titled "Trackle") consolidating new content portions from all the web sites you monitor. The service keeps a copy of your most recent Trackle online, which is very useful for access via handheld devices such as the Blackberry and Treo.

Unlike other services, Trackle displays changes as plain text, while preserving links, which makes it easy to simply scan for changes or click through to see changes on the actual underlying page itself.

You can use any operating system or browser to access Trackle.

Trackle comes with a 14-day free trial period. A subscription costs $U.S. 1.95 per month or $U.S. 19.95 annually.

**POWER SEARCHER TIP** *Most web site monitors let you specify the type of change you want to track— changes to content, a specific area, or the date of the page. In most cases, it's best to avoid tracking by date, because some sites refresh their content on a regular basis, regardless of whether content has changed or not, leading to false hits with a page tracker.*

## Choosing a Web Site Monitor

The web page monitoring services described in this chapter each offer the same basic tracking features. Each also offers unique features that might fit your needs better than the others. Copernic Tracker and Web Site-Watcher are the most powerful; however, they are also desktop based and lack the flexibility of the other services, which can be accessed via any Internet-connected computer.

On the other end of the spectrum, ChangeNotes.com is a free service, with very basic features. This simplicity may appeal to those who want a quick "heads-up" whenever a site changes.

As with choosing a web research manager, choosing a web site monitor is a personal decision that should be based on your own needs. All the programs covered in this chapter are reliable and get the job done. They differ primarily in the number of features offered, and whether they are standalone applications or online services.

11

# Chapter 12

## The Art of Googling People

"In the fields of observation, chance favors only the prepared mind," said Louis Pasteur. He was talking about discovering new organisms with a microscope, but he might just as well have been talking about searching for people on the Web.

Finding information about people online is often a matter of chance, and isn't always as easy as you might think. Sure, people checking out other people via Google has become so popular that "Googling" a person has become a verb. But if the person you're looking for has no web presence, or has a common name, even Google won't be able to help you track them down. Despite the proliferation of people finders, white pages, and e-mail directories, your chances of finding the person you seek are slim if you approach the task with a casual attitude.

If you're serious about tracking down a long-lost friend or lover, doing a background check on someone you don't know, or just finding accurate information about someone you've just met, take Pasteur's advice and spend some time preparing for your search before you go online. You'll save yourself a lot of time and dramatically increase your odds of actually finding the person or people you're searching for.

# Before You Begin: A People-Finding Checklist

The secret to successful people searching is to have as much information on hand as possible before you begin your search. Then, once you go online, there are a few rules you should follow that will help you hone in on your "e-target."

First, create a "mini-biography" of the person you're seeking. Assemble everything you know about the person before you start. Write down the person's full name (a middle name or initial is very helpful), married and maiden name, and the names of parents and siblings. Write down the person's last known address and telephone number and any other places you know they lived. Make a note of their profession, current and previous employers, hobbies, and memberships. Finally, write down the names of mutual friends who might be able to help you with your search. Table 12-1 is a handy checklist to help you fill in all the relevant details for this mini-biography. Don't worry if you don't know all these details—just fill in as much information as you can.

| Searching for People: A Mini-Biography Checklist |
| --- |
| ❑  Full name (with middle name and maiden name if known) |
| ❑  Last known address |
| ❑  High school and university |
| ❑  Employer(s) |
| ❑  Hobbies and interests |
| ❑  Parents, siblings, children |
| ❑  Awards or other recognition |
| ❑  Web-related work (writing, music, or photos online?) |

**TABLE 12-1**    Prepare This Checklist as Completely as Possible Before Beginning Your Search for a Person

Be sure to check your spelling! As basic as this sounds, proper spelling is crucial—you won't find John Doe if you're searching for John Doh!

With checklist in hand, you're now ready to go online and begin your search.

# The Art of Googling People

When you're searching for people on Google, you'll greatly enhance your chances of success if you follow a few simple rules of thumb:

■ *Always* put a person's name in double quotes, to make Google treat the name as a phrase. If you neglect the double quotes, Google will look for the first name, last name, and/or middle name *anywhere* on a web page, regardless of where the words appear or in which order they appear. By enclosing a name in double quotes, you'll get a dramatic reduction in the number of results, but this is a good thing—it will help you weed out mostly irrelevant pages. The difference in the number of results for a query with and without double quotes is typically striking. For example, a search for **maria garcia** (without quotes) returns nearly a million results. By contrast, the search **"maria garcia"** (with quotes) cuts the number of results down to a much more manageable 34,000.

■ Google ignores most punctuation symbols, which can increase noise in search results. A query for **"john smith"** will return results matching "St. John's, Smith Square." To force an exact match, turn off stemming by putting a plus sign in front of search terms. This will tell Google to ignore plural or possessive versions of a name.

■ Remember, Google is not case-sensitive. It makes no difference if you capitalize a person's name or not. A query for **"Robert Peters"** returns exactly the same results as a query for **"robert peters"**.

■ Google's Boolean OR operator is your friend when searching for people. In Chapter 2, I discouraged the use of the OR operator, because it tends to expand the number of search results for many queries without enhancing the precision of those results. When you're searching for people, however, the OR operator can be used in very powerful ways, as you'll see in the examples in this chapter.

■ When searching for people, take advantage of what I call "magic keywords"—special types of search terms that work particularly well for certain types of searches—particularly when used in combination with one or two advanced Google operators. Magic keywords don't necessarily cause Google to do anything special. Rather, they work as a form of data mining that opportunistically seeks patterns in the Web based on the way people commonly refer to themselves or other people. You'll see what I mean in the examples that follow.

12

- Use the right search service. In some cases, you'll hit pay dirt after a few simple searches on Google. But in many other instances, you're better off using specialized search services, such as e-mail directories or online telephone White Pages. I'll show you a number of specialized people-searching services later in this chapter.

- Use common sense. You may get better, quicker results offline if you've got some good leads. For example, if you have a phone number of a relative or mutual friend, call them and ask for help! Don't waste time snooping around on the Web when a direct approach will give you better results.

**POWER SEARCHER TIP** *The oddly named Clusty search engine (http://www.clusty.com) can be a big help in finding people, if you enter a name and other details such as profession and location. Results are "clustered" into categories that make it easy to quickly sort through results.*

# People-Searching Strategies

When you created your mini-biography for the person you're seeking, you wrote down their name, address, city, school, employer, and any other bits of information you could think of that were relevant to the person. Here's the biography I created for my good friend Michael McClure, who graciously gave me permission to use him as a living example of how to sleuth out personal information hidden away in Google's massive index of web pages.

*Michael McClure attended Orme High School and the University of California at San Diego. He's an accomplished musician (guitar and keyboards) and songwriter. He has worked for Kaiser Permanente and currently works for Disney Feature Animation. He's also an avid photographer, having won several photography competitions, and runs a freelance photography business.*

It helps to write the mini-biography as if you were writing an "about the author" blurb that might appear on the back cover of a book. This will force you to use a variety of words that you might not otherwise think of, providing further ammunition in your quest to find information about a person.

Somewhat paradoxically, once you've created the mini-biography, your first strategy is to run a basic, simple search using only the person's name, providing Google with no additional clues. Why? To surface important details about all the other people with the same name that you want to *remove* from your own queries. Your goal is to build a list of "negative" keywords that you'll eliminate from search results using the exclusion operator.

Figure 12-1 shows the results for a simple query on the name Michael McClure. As expected, Google reports thousands of total results for such a basic query. And it turns out my friend shares a name with a very famous beat poet. We'll add the word "poet" to our list of negative keywords to exclude from search results. Scanning the result list suggests that we may also want to add the words "poem" and "poetry" to our negative keyword list.

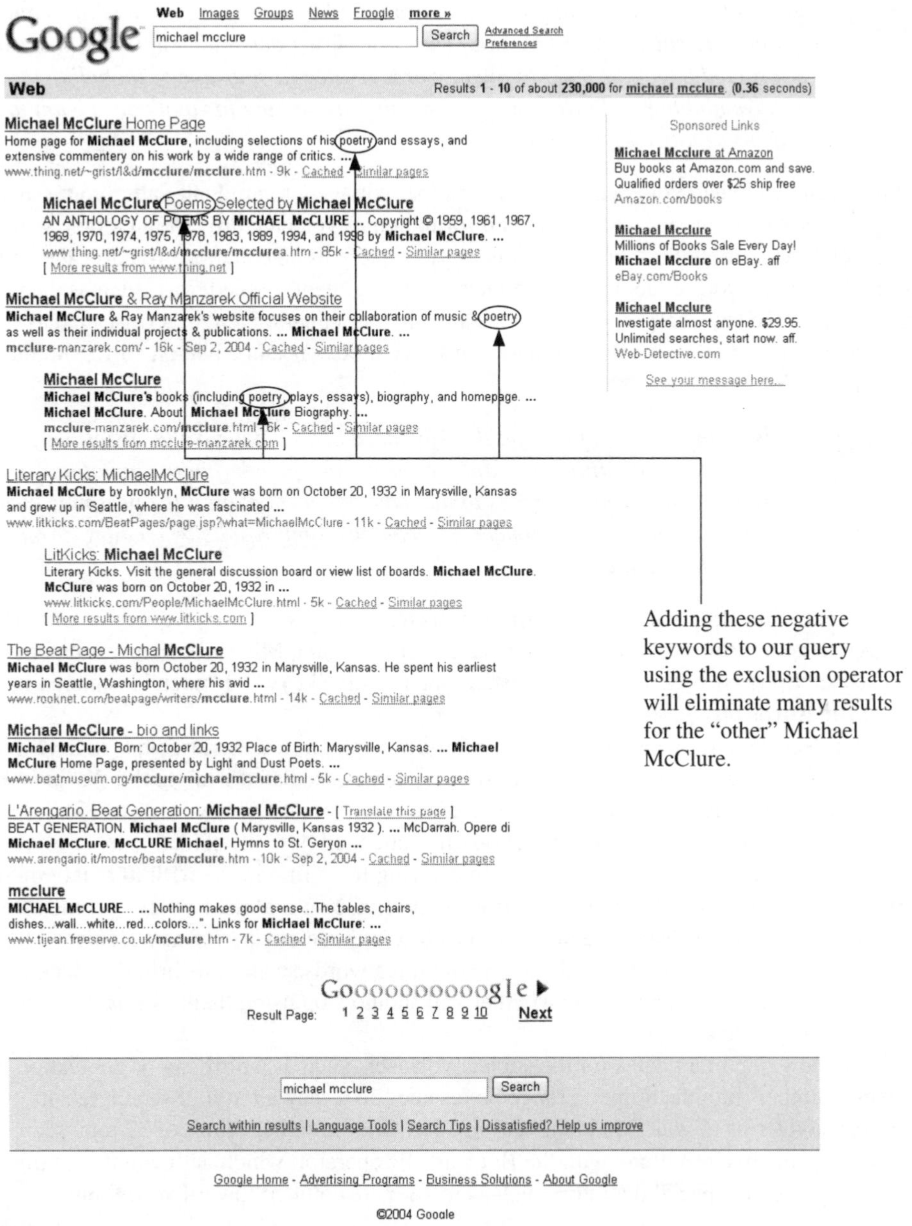

Adding these negative keywords to our query using the exclusion operator will eliminate many results for the "other" Michael McClure.

**FIGURE 12-1**   Search results for a simple query on a person's name help us find negative keywords.

POWER SEARCHER TIP

*A quick way to find negative keywords is to set your Google preferences to 100 results, then copy and paste an entire search result page into a word frequency analyzer such as Word Counter (http://www.wordcounter.com/). You'll see an ordered list of the most frequent words related to your query, including terms that have nothing to do with the person you're searching for that you'll want to add to your negative keyword list.*

Once you've created your negative keyword list, you want to gradually alter your search strategy to pack your queries with as much information as you can, providing Google with multiple clues to work with. It helps to think of your query as an equation. To solve the equation and find the person you're looking for, you need to experiment. Some terms, such as the person's name and negative keywords, should be constants in your equation. Other terms, such as school name, employer, and other words that mark transitory milestones in a person's life, should be treated as variables.

POWER SEARCHER TIP

*Using the multiple fields on the Advanced Search page is the easiest way to experiment with different search terms in your people-finding equations. For example, limit your searches to the .edu or .gov domain if the person is involved with academia or government. You can also limit results by country if you know where they reside.*

Begin experimenting with your person search equation by setting up a query in Google's Advanced Search form, as shown in Figure 12-2. One constant, Michael's name, is entered in the **with the exact phrase** box. The other constant, the negative keyword "poet," is entered in the **without the words** box.

Next, select some of the words from the mini-biography to use as variables. Your best bet is to start with the words that the person is most likely to be associated with on the Web as well as the words that most closely describe the person's current situation. Save words that describe a person's past, such as the name of the school they attended or their maiden name, for later.

Experiment with one or two words at a time, trying them first in the **with at least one of the words** box and then in the **with all of the words** box. You'll almost always get more results when you use the **with at least one of the words** box because this performs a Boolean OR on the search terms. As you experiment, make a note of which words seem to be bringing back a lot of noise or irrelevant results, and decide whether you should stop using them as search terms or add them to your negative keyword list.

If you know important dates for the subject you seek, such as a birthday or graduation year, plug these numbers into the numeric range boxes and see if they alter your search results.

As you add terms to your equation, bear in mind Google's query limit of 32 total search terms. Google gives you a break with the Boolean OR operator, which isn't counted in this 32-word limit. But other special operators such as **intitle:** are counted toward your limit.

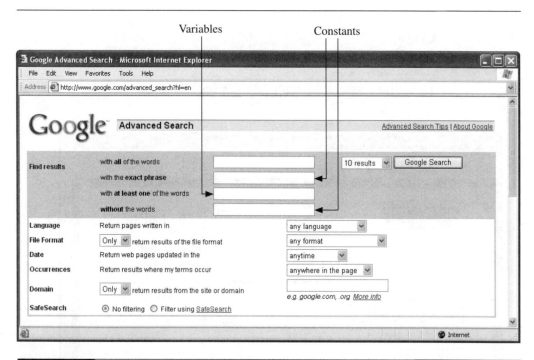

FIGURE 12-2    Begin your search equation with both constants and variables.

Gradually, as you refine your equation, you should start to see a pattern emerge. If you're lucky, you'll find yourself honing in on pages about the person you seek. When you discover new information about a person that might be relevant to your search, add it to your mini-biography and play around with the additional search terms you've found.

 *When you're searching for people, don't overlook Google Groups. You can use the same strategies for finding people on Usenet as you do on the Web—with an added bonus that Google Groups' advanced search allows you to limit your search to author names.*

You'll find that different versions of your search equation are usually required to get comprehensive results for the person you're searching. Figure 12-3 shows the equation that ultimately surfaced a page about my friend Michael's photographic work.

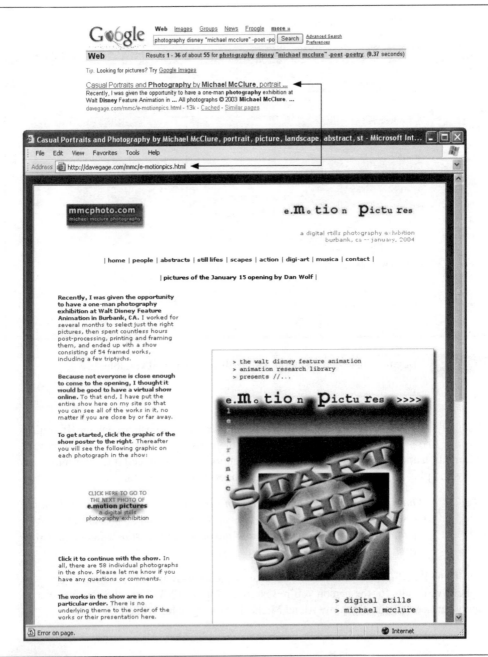

FIGURE 12-3  This combination of constants and variables surfaced a page related to one of my friend's interests.

Figure 12-4 shows another combination that was required to find information about Michael's musical interests. With time and patience, other combinations of search terms may surface even more information.

**FIGURE 12-4**   A different combination of constants and variables was required to surface a page about my friend's musical interests.

12

# Finding People at Work and Home

There are many different ways to find information about people on the Web. Some people are relatively easy to find, through their personal web pages, Usenet postings, blogs, or other online activities. Other people have a more subdued presence—perhaps a few work-related pages that take a bit more sleuthing to find. The hardest challenge for the searcher is to find people who have left few online footprints.

When you set out on your quest to find information about a person, mentally classify the type of information you're seeking. You'll use very different techniques to find information about a person based on where—or how—you expect to find it, as you'll see.

## Finding People at Work

Remember the "fill-in-the-blank" strategy from Chapter 2 that suggests searching for a phrase you think may be written on a web page somewhere? Turns out this is a particularly powerful approach for finding people at work, for two primary reasons: online resumes and "about us" sections of web sites. Finding information about people from these two sources can be tricky, however, because almost nobody links to resumes or personnel information pages. This means they're not likely to rise to the top of search results unless you apply the fill-in-the-blank strategy, using variations of the magic keywords "work for *company name*" as your query. To see an example of how powerful this can be, try the query for any large company.

Figure 12-5 shows the results for the query **"work for Exxon"**. As you can see, there are a number of variations on the way people use the phrase, such as "he went to work for Exxon," "I work for Exxon," "people who work for Exxon," and so on. This suggests we can tweak the query, depending on whether we're looking for current or past employees, groups of employees, and so on.

We need to work additional words into our query to take advantage of these variations. Let's say we're looking for current employees of Exxon. We can use the Boolean OR operator to include synonyms of the word "for," such as "at" and "with." Our query would then expand to **"work for OR at OR with Exxon"**. Figure 12-6 shows the results of this expanded query.

**POWER SEARCHER TIP**  *Google recognizes the "pipe" symbol ( | ) as a shorthand substitute for the Boolean OR operator.*

You can also use the wildcard operator to substitute for the words you want to OR together, but the results will be unpredictable. And unfortunately, Google's "fuzzy" synonym operator, the tilde (~) symbol, does not work when used within a quoted phrase.

Get creative when you're doing fill-in-the-blank searching. Try variations such as "worked for" or "employed by" to see what surfaces. The trick is to put yourself in the position of someone writing a web page—what would *you* write if you were describing your own job or employer?

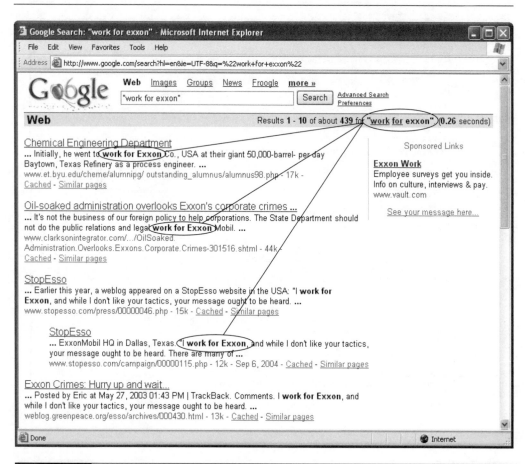

Use the fill-in-the-blank strategy to find people who work at a particular company.

# Finding People at Home

Google has a built-in telephone directory for residences in the U.S., accessed using the **phonebook:** operator. From any Google search box, you can type any of these combinations:

- First name or initial, last name, and either city, state, area code, or ZIP code
- Phone number, including area code
- Last name, city, state
- Last name, ZIP code

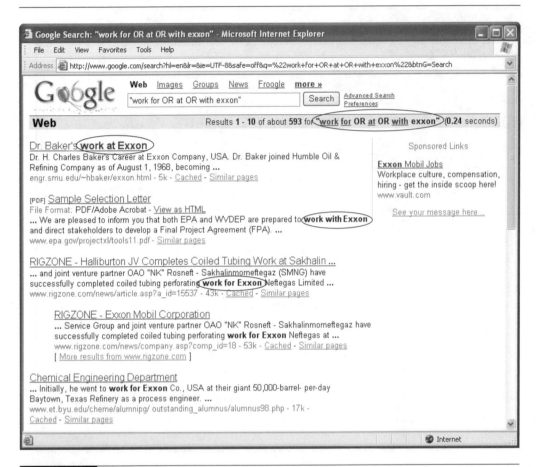

**FIGURE 12-6**    Expanding a query using the Boolean OR operator picks up synonyms that surface interesting variations in search results.

Be sure to type your query using the word order shown in the preceding list. Reversing or mixing up the order of terms—searching for a state, city, and last name, for example—will not give you Phonebook results. Google's Phonebook is described in more detail in Chapter 5.

Google's Phonebook draws information both from its index of web pages and from third-party sources, and, frankly, it's not always the best choice for finding people at home. In many cases, you'll be better off using some of the more sophisticated people-finding services described in the "Beyond Google: Other People-Finding Resources" section, later in this chapter.

## Finding E-mail Addresses

Finding e-mail addresses with Google is tricky, because Google ignores the "@" symbol, even when you use it as part of a quoted string. This makes it impossible to search directly for an e-mail address on Google. However, many companies use a consistent format for e-mail addresses, and it doesn't hurt to guess an address, such as *first.last@companyname*.com.

You can also use Google to take advantage of an increasingly common practice used by people trying to cloak their identities from e-mail spammers. Spammers find e-mail addresses via automated e-mail-harvesting robots that "scrape" e-mail addresses off of web pages. To hide from spammers, many web-savvy people are taking steps to confuse these e-mail-harvesting robots by "munging" (coding or scrambling) their e-mail addresses on web pages. Common practices to mung an e-mail address include:

- Replacing the "@" symbol with the word "AT" and the "." symbol with "DOT" (for example, anselDOTadamsATphotoDOTorg)

- Inserting spaces between names and symbols (for example, "alexei sukarov @ tech haven . com")

- Inserting extra text that the sender removes before sending e-mail (for example, "marikoNOSPAM@REMOVE-boj.or.jp/)

- Typing the e-mail address backward, with instructions to reverse it before sending (for example, moc.egami-rorrim@yrartnoc.yram)

You can search for any of these variations on Google and turn up a surprising number of e-mail addresses. Figure 12-7 shows the result of a search for the query **+at "hotmail dot com"**. Remember, the word "at" is a stop word and ignored by Google unless you put a plus sign (the inclusion operator) in front of it.

## Beyond Google: Other People-Finding Resources

People finders abound on the Web. Some are good; some are stale with out-of-date or inaccurate details. Some specialize in finding particular types of information, such as e-mail addresses, phone numbers, street addresses; others offer combined search options. Some are free; others charge a fee for the services they provide.

When using these directories, bear in mind that some are not frequently updated. You may find a legitimate e-mail address that was abandoned years ago when the person switched Internet service providers. Unlike telephone directories, there is no central authority responsible for keeping e-mail databases current.

Here's a collection of some of the better people-finding services available:

- **Argali (http://www.argali.com)**   Argali is one of the most useful, multifaceted people-finding tools available. See Chapter 5 for a more detailed review of the program.

**12**

FIGURE 12-7  Using "munged" keywords together with an e-mail provider's name often reveals useful clues.

- **ZoomInfo (http://www.zoominfo.com)**    ZoomInfo is a Google-like search engine that crawls the Web looking specifically for information about people. It uses artificial intelligence techniques to link information found on the Web with specific people, and currently has more than 25 million entries online (some more accurate than others).

- **InfoSpace Directories (http://www.infospace.com/)**    InfoSpace provides a number of useful people-finding tools, including U.S. White Pages, reverse phone number lookup, e-mail search, and public records search. All these services, other than the public records search, are free and return results with mostly up-to-date and accurate listings.

InfoSpace offers two very useful features for frequent searchers. The site remembers up to five of your previous searches and makes them available in a search history list. You can also use the "My Locations" feature to save one or more locations and to select which one to use as a default—very handy if you want to do a number of searches limited to a specific geographical area.

■ **Infobel World Telephone Directories (http://www.infobel.com/teldir/)**    Infobel is a directory offering links, ratings, and information for online telephone directories in more than 184 countries. Select a country, and you'll see annotated listings of directory services available for that country, rated from one (worst) to four (best) stars.

■ **Freeality.com Reverse Lookup & E-Mail Search (http://www.freeality.com/finde .htm)**    Freeality is a gateway to many other people-search services on the Web. In the left column are direct links to services such as Addresses.com, SuperPages.com, and so on. In the right column are search forms that you can use to submit your query directly to those services. Midway down this page you'll see a large link that reads "Find People." Click this link, and you'll see a similar tool from Freeality.com that offers direct searching of other people information services.

# Finding Personal Web Pages and Blogs

The Web's creator, Tim Berners-Lee, envisioned an egalitarian environment where anyone could publish pages and easily share their creative output with others. That vision has been realized. Even though large publishers dominate the lists of the most popular web sites, there are countless millions of pages created by individuals, either as personal home pages or, increasingly, as regularly updated blogs.

Google can and does crawl blogs and personal pages. However, because Google puts such a strong emphasis on link analysis in its ranking of pages, most personal pages will never make it into the topmost listings, even when you're searching explicitly using a person's name. The problem is two-fold: Most personal pages are interesting only to a relatively small number of friends and family members. Most of these people won't bother linking to a personal page— they'll bookmark it, or simply type the URL every time they want to visit the page. And even if someone attracts a large following with a particularly engaging blog, other bloggers almost always link to individual postings in a blog, not the blogger's home page. Google sees the blog as an aggregate of pages with a few links pointing to a multitude of posts, rather than dozens or hundreds of links pointing to a single page. As a result, even popular blogs often don't garner sufficient link popularity to rank well in search results.

That's not to say you can't find personal pages or blogs using Google. You can—especially if you take advantage of another set of magic keywords. And you need to use slightly different strategies when looking for personal pages as opposed to blogs. Let's start with personal pages.

**12**

## Finding Personal Web Pages

By convention, most people with a personal web site refer to their main page as the "home page." We can use "home page" as magic keywords for finding personal web sites. However, we need to be a bit more specific—Figure 12-8 shows the result of a simple search for the words "home page" without any modifiers. With more than 15 million results, and the top ten all being major corporations or institutions, we're nowhere near finding personal home pages.

We dramatically reduce the number of results by adding a person's name to the query, as shown in Figure 12-9. However, although the topmost result is a link to an academic's professional home page, other results are for companies, organizations, and so on. We need to get even more specific.

FIGURE 12-8    A simple search for "home page" is much too broad for finding personal home pages.

**FIGURE 12-9** Adding a person's name to the query helps, but still returns too many extraneous results.

What we're really looking for are pages where the phrase "home page" is part of the title of the page. Google's **intitle:** operator does the trick. Figure 12-10 shows the results of limiting results to pages where the magic phrase "home page" appears in the HTML title of the page.

One final refinement will get us the results we desire: Limiting results to pages with both the person's name *and* the phrase "home page" in the title. You can do this in two ways. Remember, most of Google's advanced operators work only on an adjacent word. You could repeat the operator, so your query would become this:

**intitle:"barbara smith" intitle:"home page"**

**FIGURE 12-10**  Close, but still no cigar: The **intitle:** operator limits results to pages with words in the title of the page.

There's an easier way, however. The **allintitle:** operator works much like the Boolean AND command, requiring all of your search terms to appear in the title of the page. Figure 12-11 shows the results of this query.

Two other tips for finding personal home pages:

- By convention, home pages on many web servers use filenames with the word "index," "default," or "home." Use Google's **inurl:** operator to limit results to pages of these types.

- Many basic web page authoring programs use templates with a phrase such as "your title here" or "insert title here" automatically inserted in the title tag as a reminder to authors to change the text to their own title. Many people (especially those creating personal home pages) either ignore or overlook these preconfigured titles. Use Google's **intitle:** operator to search for them in combination with a person's name.

FIGURE 12-11 Use the **allintitle:** operator to require all search terms to be included in the title of result pages.

12

# Fish Where the Fish Are

Many people who want to create a personal page don't want the bother of securing their own domain name and buying complicated web publishing software—they just want a quick-and-easy way to add their pages to the Web. A number of companies cater to these types of people by offering free or inexpensive web page creation and hosting services.

Two of the most popular personal home page hosts are Yahoo!'s GeoCities and Lycos's Angelfire. You can easily search both services for personal home pages by using Google's **site:** operator to limit results to the GeoCities and Angelfire domains, as shown in Figure 12-12.

Both services also have searchable member directories. GeoCities' Member Pages Directory, at http://pages.yahoo.com/, is structured so that you can either browse or search for member pages. You get even more control using the GeoCities Member Pages Directory Advanced Search function, at http://us.geocities.yahoo.com/search/option.

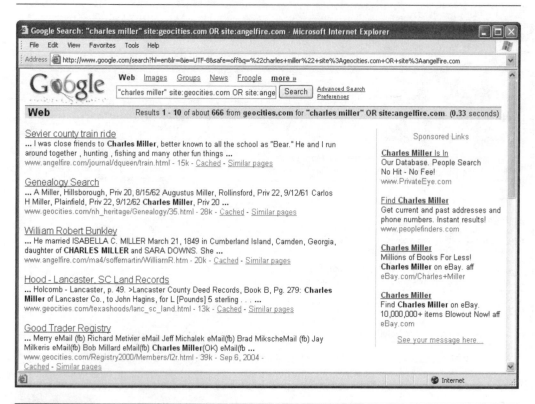

**FIGURE 12-12**   Use the **site:** operator with the Boolean OR operator to limit results to GeoCities and Angelfire.

As you might expect, you get different results from a GeoCities search and a Google site-limited search, as shown in Figure 12-13. Google finds and displays more results from GeoCities pages, but Yahoo! includes premium member sites with non-GeoCities domain names that Google cannot find. You'll want to do both types of searches to make sure you don't miss any important results.

Angelfire also has a search function, but doesn't work as well as simply using Google's **site:** operator to limit results to Angelfire pages, so I can't recommend using it.

**POWER SEARCHER TIP**   *An excellent, comprehensive site dedicated to all aspects of personal web pages is maintained by About.com Guide Linda Roeder, at http://personalweb.about.com.*

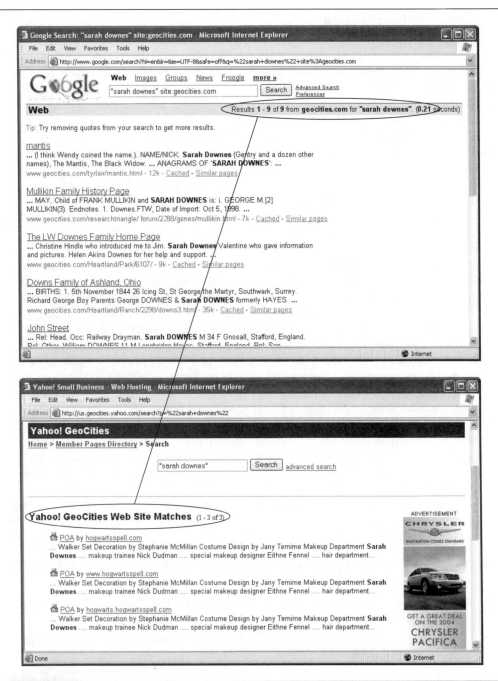

**FIGURE 12-13**   Google and GeoCities searches provide two very different result sets for the same query.

## Finding Personal Blogs

As said, finding personal blogs with Google is a bit more problematic than finding personal web pages. Many of the tricks that work well for finding home pages don't work as well when applied to blogs. For example, the "intitle" trick doesn't work as well for finding blogs as it does personal web pages because many bloggers give their blogs creative or offbeat titles, and often don't use their names in titles.

Searching for a person's name and the words "blog" or "weblog" also typically returns a lot of false hits. Sure, results will often be from blogs, but many blogs allow readers to post comments, so it's often reader names, rather than the blog writer's name, that gets returned in search results.

Somewhat ironically, Google owns Blogger, one of the most popular blogging services, and yet does not provide a specialized blog search function (at least at the time this was written). Despite this limitation, it's possible to locate people using Blogger because Google crawls and indexes thousands of Blogger-powered weblogs.

The simplest approach is to search for a person's name, limiting results to those from Blogger.com or its sister site, Blogspot.com, using the syntax ***"person name"* site:blogger.com OR site:blogspot.com**. Although you'll get many results from this query, it's important to note that you may miss blogs that are created by people using Blogger's editing tools but are hosted elsewhere on the Web. There are a couple of ways to find these sorts of blogs using Google.

When you sign up for a Blogger account, you create a Blogger profile. At minimum, this profile includes basic information such as user name, e-mail, and password information, and is not publicly accessible unless you decide to share your profile with others. Many bloggers add additional information to their user profiles, such as biographical information, interests, a photograph, and so on. Importantly for our purposes, a user profile can also include a list of the user's blogs and a home page URL. Figure 12-14 shows a user profile for Blogger Greg Linden.

We can take advantage of three consistent features of Blogger user profiles to find people. First, all user profiles have the words "user profile" in their title. Second, in the contact portion of the profile, many users will provide a URL for a home page, which always uses the anchor text "My Web Page." This home page can be any page on the Web, so in some cases it will take you to an "About Me" page for further exploration beyond the person's blog. Excerpts from recent posts by the blogger are listed in the middle of the page under the "Recent Posts" heading, and a list of the blogs maintained by the user is displayed at the bottom of the profile page. These consistent features give us a number of options with Google:

- You can find a blogger's profile with ***"person name"* intitle:"user profile" site:blogger .com**.

- You can find a blogger's home page with ***"person name"* "my web page" site:blogger .com**.

- You can find recent posts mentioning *other people* with ***"other person name"* "recent posts" site:blogger.com**.

Click these links to find people with similar interests. ⎯⎯⎯

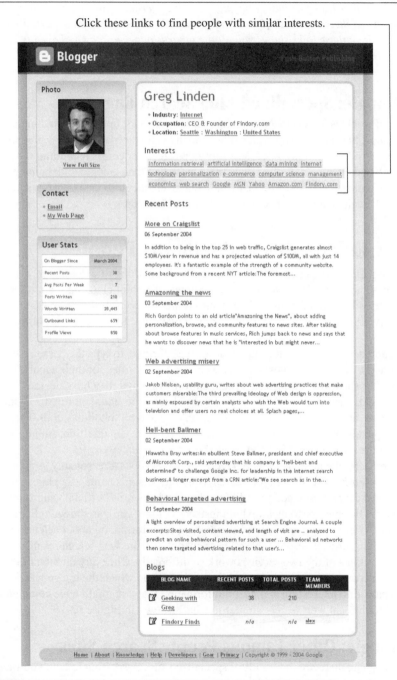

**FIGURE 12-14**   A Blogger user profile that the author has authorized others to read.

 *Another trick for finding people using Blogger user profile pages: If people have listed their interests, Blogger automatically turns these into hyperlinks. Clicking one of these links shows you all the other Blogger users who have also listed that interest.*

## Beyond Google: Specialized Blog Search Engines

As the number of weblogs has exploded over the past several years, options for finding blog content have also expanded. Specialized blog search tools—such as Bloglines (http://www.bloglines.com), Daypop (http://www.daypop.com), Feedster (http://www.feedster.com), Technorati (http://www.technorati.com), and others—will often do a much better job than Google with helping you track down people in the blogsphere. Because many blog search engines also include news sources, these specialized search engines are described in more detail in Chapter 14.

# Sleuthing for Celebrities and Famous People

Although finding "ordinary" people on the Web can be something of a challenge, searching for information about famous people poses a completely different challenge: coping with information overload. Search for virtually any movie star, famous musician, well-known politician, or any other person with celebrity status, and you're likely to be swamped with results.

A simple approach to finding information about a celebrity is to type the person's name as a URL (that is, www.*famousname*.com). Many web-savvy celebrities (or their agents) have created official web sites with authorized, reliable information that they have decided to reveal. But for every official charlizetheron.com or petergabriel.com you find, you run the chance of running afoul of unauthorized sites such as melgibson.com and billieholliday.com. These sites aren't necessarily bad—they just lack the blessing of the celebrity in question. And it may be difficult to tell if the information provided is reliable or accurate.

A better approach, of course, is to search Google. Google does a reasonably good job of locating official celebrity web sites if you search using the person's name as a phrase. It does even better, in most cases, if you add the additional magic keywords "official" and "authorized" using the Boolean OR operator to pick up both instances of the word, as shown in Figure 12-15.

Don't forget Google Images when you're searching for information about celebrities. Google Images often surfaces results that differ dramatically from web search results because the relevance algorithms of the two services work so differently. Click any thumbnail in Image search results and you'll see the underlying web page on which the image was found. Occasionally you'll find interesting and useful information that you might have completely overlooked in a traditional web search, similar to what's shown in Figure 12-16.

## Beyond Google: Other Famous People Search Sites

As you might imagine, there are thousands of specialized sites purporting to help you find information about celebrities and other famous people. Sadly, many of these so-called information resources are little more than hastily slapped together sites, often with content

**FIGURE 12-15**   Adding the magic keywords words "official" and "authorized" to queries using the names of famous people can improve results.

12

"borrowed" from other sources all over the Web. Their purpose is less to help people find information than to generate advertising revenue from hapless searchers. But don't despair—there are several ways to find high-quality, reliable information about famous people on the Web.

## The Google Directory: Arts > People Category

The Google Directory's Arts > People category (http://directory.google.com/Top/Arts/People/—this URL is case sensitive) is a gold mine for finding information about people in just about any creative endeavor. Subcategories are dedicated to actors and actresses, authors, bands and musical artists, and so on—but you'll also find fun categories including clowns, hypnotists, and ventriloquists.

Two other excellent Google Directory categories for finding information about famous people are Reference > Biography and Society > People > Celebrities.

*Virtually every category in the Google Directory has a subcategory dedicated to people. For example, you can locate famous physicists in the Science > Physics category. Browse around in a category that interests you and you'll likely find listings of famous people in that specialty.*

Image search result

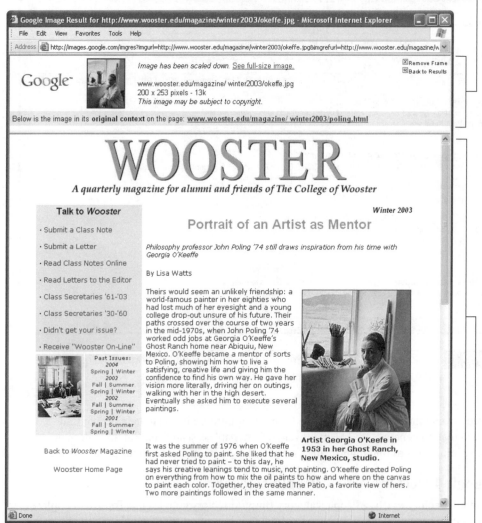

Underlying web page

FIGURE 12-16 Google's Image search provides an alternative means of finding valuable information about famous people.

## World Biographical Index

The World Biographical Index from Saur (http://www.saur-wbi.de/) is widely regarded as one of the most authoritative sources of information about people available. Here you will find:

- Biographies—data and biographical articles—on 1.3 million people

- Brief biographical details on a total of 3.8 million people

- 2.28 million original biographical articles, published from 1559 to the beginning of the twentieth century

Up until September 2004, this index was freely available. Now, it's only available via subscription, but it's worthy of mention because of its comprehensive value.

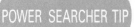 *Many public libraries offer free access to subscription-based databases such as the World Biographical Index—often allowing you to search the database from your own home via your Internet connection. Contact your own local library for more information.*

## Wikipedia Biographies

Wikipedia (http://en.wikipedia.org/wiki/Lists_of_people) is a free content encyclopedia being written collaboratively by contributors from around the world. It is rapidly growing into a comprehensive resource on just about every imaginable topic. Wikipedia features thousands of biographies of famous people and celebrities, and all entries are extensively cross-linked so you can easily read about other people connected with your target.

One of Wikipedia's nicest features is its lists, organized by a central theme. For example, Wikipedia's lists of people are organized by name, belief, nationality, occupation, office held, prize won, and in dozens of other ways.

A caveat with Wikipedia: Though most volunteer contributors are honest and capable, the open nature of the encyclopedia combined with the ability of literally anyone to change listings can lead to errors. If you're relying on something found in Wikipedia, be sure to double-check the information with another source.

## The Dead People Server

OK, I admit it: The Dead People Server (http://www.deadpeople.info) is a goofy link included here just for fun. Yet despite its macabre name, it's actually a well-maintained service that's indispensable for helping answer those "Is so-and-so still alive?" questions. The Dead People Server is a database of "interesting celebrities" who are no longer with us.

# An Offbeat Strategy: Using Google to Set a "Honeypot"

The downside of using Google to find people is that unless the person you're looking for has left footprints or some sort of trace of themselves on the Web, the search engine isn't likely to find any information about them. Lacking a personal web page, a Usenet posting, a blog, or other online presence, many people are all but invisible to Google.

12

That doesn't mean, however, that the person you're seeking doesn't use the Web. In fact, given Google's popularity, it's likely that your e-target is a regular user of the search engine. And most people inevitably end up occasionally "ego searching" for themselves. So why not give them something to find? Create a page *about* the person you're searching for, post it to the Web, submit the URL to Google, and with luck, one day your page will be discovered by the person you're looking for!

Computer security experts call this technique "creating a honeypot." In efforts to track and foil hackers, computer security administrators deliberately create a compromised system, leaving something irresistible for hackers to discover. But honeypots are also "sticky," often snaring hackers in traps, or recording details that allow them to be traced. You can create your own "search honeypot" for Google, designed to attract the attention of the person you're looking for when they're ego searching.

This won't work for all people, of course. Chances of success are much higher if the person in question has an unusual name and spends a lot of time online. You also have to take a bit of care in crafting your page to make sure it has a chance of ranking in results where it will be seen.

Start with the checklist you created when you began your search for the person. If you haven't already, write a mini-biography of the person, up to 500 or so words in length. Be sure to put the person's name in the title of the web page, and repeat the person's name frequently in the text, using nicknames or abbreviated names and initials from time to time. Also, be sure to include the unique details you know about the person—but be careful not to compromise their privacy! Don't include a birth date, mother's maiden name, social security number, or any information that could potentially be used by identity thieves.

At the end of your biography, explain that you're looking for the person and provide appropriate contact details. Who knows—maybe creating a honeypot for someone you're looking for will prove to be a sweet enough temptation to turn the tables, using Google to help them find *you*.

# Other People Searches

A single chapter in a book can hold only so many strategies and links to web sites on a particular topic. For more on other types of people searching, see the following chapters.

- **Chapter 17**  Profiling business executives and company board members
- **Chapter 20**  Lots of additional information about searching for people here, including searching for your roots using genealogy resources, uncovering information in online public records, how to get information about government officials and politicians, and much more

## Ask the Expert

# Expert Tips for People Searching

## Six Questions for Power Searcher Genie Tyburski

**Q: What's your favorite Google search tip?**
**A:** With respect to research about people, searchers should query Google Groups. It consists of a smaller, more well-defined database, which might reveal leads about a person's interests or affiliations. You might also discover e-mail addresses, places of employment, home addresses, and phone numbers. In conducting investigations for Ballard Spahr Andrews & Ingersoll, LLP, I have on occasion found information critical to active litigation.

**Q: What kind of search strategy do you use when searching for people on Google?**
**A:** Unless the name is a common one, I usually start with a phrase search consisting of the first name and last name, like this: "chris sherman". I expand or narrow the search depending on what I find. If the query produces too many Chris Shermans who are not the individual in question, I add one or more keywords based on what I know about the person. The keywords generally include terms that describe hobbies or interests (baseball, body-building), work (dr., doctor, physician), or residence (new york city, manhattan). If the query yields too few results, I enter name variations ("christopher sherman", "christian sherman") or remove the quotation marks around the name. If the last name is particularly uncommon, I combine it with a geographic location or occupation (tyburski "law librarian").

I don't expect to find everything relevant with a single search or by using only one search engine. The limitations of unstructured information make multiple queries in multiple search engines necessary, if the goal is to find all (or most) relevant information.

**Q: Are there specific tools or techniques that lead to best results (for example, operators, filters, special keywords, etc.)?**
**A:** Techniques for finding information about people include searching phone numbers, street addresses, e-mail addresses, and employer or business names. When searching phone numbers, run several queries and change the format of the number (xxx-xxx-xxxx, xxx.xxx.xxxx, (xxx) xxx-xxxx). Use the same strategy for street addresses ("123 main", "123 main" manhattan) and e-mail addresses (user@webhost.com, "user at webhost.com"). For information tied to an employer or the individual's business or business affiliations, enter the person's full or last name and the name of the company ("chris sherman" searchwise, tyburski "ballard spahr").

**Q: When would you not use Google for searching for people?**
**A:** It is difficult—and in some cases, unfeasible—to wade through the results of a search for a common name. Searching for information about someone with a common name is a problem whether you use public web tools such as Google or databases via a premium service such as LexisNexis. Many times, the online information lacks sufficient identifying data—birth date, SSN, or even a current residential address—to know with certainty that you have found information relevant to the subject of the search. Therefore, I would not use Google to search for names such as John Smith or Mary Jones. I would conduct the search, however, if I could combine the common name with descriptive information about the person.

**12**

**Q: What search engines or other web resources do you use to go beyond Google when searching for people?**
**A:** There are numerous free or low-cost resources for conducting research about people. They include book databases, web archives, government databases, article databases, and more. The ones you choose to search depend on what you know about the individual. For example, if the subject of the research were a U.S. medical doctor, I would check:

- The status of his/her license with the state's medical board. A directory of U.S. state medical board web sites is available at http://www.fsmb.org/members.htm.

- Whether he/she defaulted on a Health Education Assistance Loan, through the database of Defaulted Borrowers maintained by the U.S. Department of Health and Human Services at http://defaulteddocs.dhhs.gov.

- For published articles and books by the doctor. Three sources are useful here:

  PubMed, a service of the National Library of Medicine, at http://www.ncbi.nlm.nih .gov/entrez/query.fcgi; a copyright search from the U.S. Copyright Office at http:// www.copyright.gov/records/; and the Library of Congress Online Catalog at http:// catalog.loc.gov. I'd also check Amazon.com for nontechnical publications.

- For pending federal lawsuits, check the U.S. Party/Case Index at http://pacer.uspci .uscourts.gov.

- Finally, check Legal Dockets Online at http://www.legaldockets.com for a database of state civil and criminal lawsuits.

If the doctor or medical practice had its own web site, I would check the Internet Archive at http://www.archive.org for earlier versions. I would also review the domain and web host information provided by Whois Source at http://www.whois.sc, because it can reveal business affiliations.

The People Finder at http://www.virtualchase.com/people/ on The Virtual Chase web site that I maintain provides an extensive list of public records databases and other sources of public information.

**Q: What's your favorite power-searching tip?**
**A:** Rather than a favorite power-search tip, here's a "necessary" one: People searchers should understand that only 35 percent of public records appear online, and most of these lack sufficient identifying data for verification purposes. Consequently, you might have to follow up with phone calls to appropriate government sources, or a trip to the source, to determine whether relevant information exists or to verify that which you have found.

*Genie Tyburski is the author of* Introduction to Online Legal, Regulatory & Intellectual Property Research *(South-Western Educational Pub., 2004) and maintains The Virtual Chase (http://www.virtualchase.com), a web site dedicated to online legal research.*

# Chapter 13

## Hunting for Health Information

According to a recent study by the Pew Internet & American Life Project, many people view search engines as more than just casual information-seeking tools, relying on them to locate what they consider *vitally* important information. Beyond Googling a friend, locating a nearby pizza joint, or looking up a historical date for a homework assignment, 44 percent of searchers said that all or most of the searches they conduct are for information they *absolutely need to find.*

More than 80 percent of people surveyed by Pew said they have searched for health-related information, making this one of the most common search activities. It should be no surprise that people search for what ails them, as the Web has become a veritable gold mine infused with rich veins of health-related information. You can dig up an enormous quantity of high-quality, reliable health information on the Web, *provided* you search with care and a healthy dose of skepticism.

And therein lies the rub. Consider this famous quote often attributed to Mark Twain: "A gold mine is a hole in the ground with a liar on top." That quip, in a nutshell, sums up the perils and hazards of searching for health care information on the Web. Whether you're researching a disease or condition, trying to find information about a pharmaceutical drug, or researching the background of a health care professional, you're searching for information that you may use in making vital— in some cases, life and death—decisions. For that reason, you need to be absolutely certain that the information you find in your online searching is both accurate and reliable.

Unfortunately, that's often easier said than done. Although there's a ton of first-rate health information available on the Web, there's also a vast amount of quackery that is posted by charlatans intent on selling you the online equivalent of snake oil. When you're searching for health information, you need to be skeptical above all else, carefully evaluating the information you find. More than just about any other type of searching, you need to maintain an attitude of "you can't believe everything you read" when you're assessing your health-related search results.

Want an example? Recall that quote attributed to Mark Twain? Figure 13-1 shows the results of a Google search using the first part of the alleged quote. Google reports more than 60 results for this query, and the snippets for many results show the quote attributed to Mark Twain. So what's the problem with these results?

The problem is that Twain never said or wrote "A gold mine is a hole in the ground with a liar on top," according to scholars who are considered experts on Twain's life and writings. Although they can't prove with *absolute* certainty that he's not responsible for the famous aphorism, there's not a shred of evidence supporting the attribution. All those Google search results show pages where people have mistakenly quoted other people without consulting Twain's works directly.

And what does this have to do with searching for health information? Simply that you can search for just about anything on Google, or any other search engine, and you'll likely get results. But just because you find results doesn't mean they are accurate or reliable. And in the case of health information, inaccurate or unreliable results can be deadly if you use the misinformation in making health care decisions.

| FIGURE 13-1 | Did Mark Twain really say it? If Google finds results, can you believe what you read? |

# Finding Reliable Health Information

Google does not evaluate or censor the information it discovers on the Web. That's not the search engine's job (unless it's blatant spam). Rather, Google's mission "is to organize the world's information and make it universally accessible and useful."

Although Google's relevance ranking algorithms will generally favor reliable sources of information, they're not specifically designed to determine whether a particular page is authoritative or totally bogus. Evaluating the quality of the information you find using Google is entirely up to you.

I've talked about evaluating information quality in several chapters in the book. Although it's always important to treat search results with a skeptical eye, it's absolutely critical when you're evaluating health-related information. Think of yourself as a detective, examining search results and the pages you discover via Google for clues that information is credible.

One of the best guides to evaluating information quality is found on the excellent web site The Virtual Chase, maintained by search guru Genie Tyburski. The *How to Evaluate Information Checklist* offers step-by-step instructions for inspecting online content for authority and reliability. For each step, the checklist also links to examples illustrating both high-quality and questionable web pages. Here are a few key items from this checklist that are especially relevant when you're searching for health-related information; the complete checklist is available at http://www .virtualchase.com/quality/checklist_print.html:

- Who is providing the information?
- Discover the source's expertise
- Determine the level of objectivity

## Who Is Providing the Information?

Check domain ownership, using a registry information database such as Whois Source, at http:// www.whois.sc.

Next, read the "about us" part of the web site. Are you satisfied that the people providing the information are qualified to do so?

## Discover the Source's Expertise

Is the source an expert or authority? Particularly with health information, you only want information from an expert. If you're reading an article about a particular subject, look carefully at the author's biography. Remember, though, that just because somebody claims to be an expert doesn't necessarily mean that they are one. A biography is just a starting point—in many cases, you'll want to get some sort of third-party validation of a person's credentials.

Examine grammar and spelling. As basic as this sounds, written information should be both grammatically correct and presented in a logical fashion.

Examine links to and from other web sites. Use Google's **link:** operator (Chapter 4) to uncover other pages that link to a particular page. Do these links look like "good" references?

Look for other publications by the author or publisher.

Independently verify credentials. Does the author have any degrees—particularly medical degrees? What kinds of professional associations does he or she belong to? Is the person cited as an expert in the news or trade literature?

## Determine the Level of Objectivity

Does the source provide a balanced viewpoint? This can be difficult to assess with health-related information. Nonetheless, you still want to get a sense that the author isn't overtly biased.

Examine the writing style. Is it trying to influence your opinion? As Genie points out in the checklist, "Lack of objectivity does not necessarily mean the source provides substandard information. A persuasive writer intends to win your favor. S/he might use good facts and analysis to do so."

Figure 13-2 shows an example of information provided by the National Cancer Institute about a newly approved therapy. Contrast this with Figure 13-3, a page apparently written by a doctor

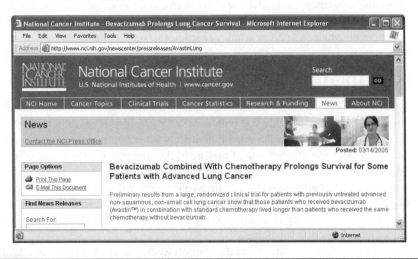

**FIGURE 13-2**   This page from the National Cancer Institute contains timely, accurate information.

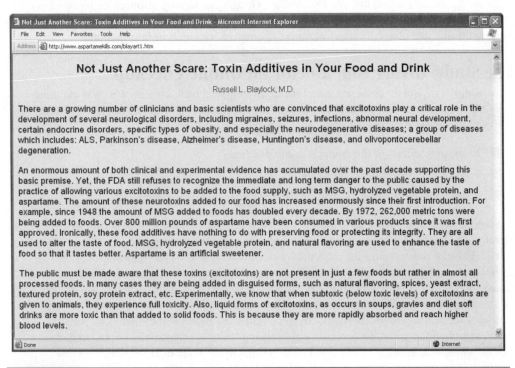

**FIGURE 13-3**   This page, though attributed to a doctor, presents little supporting evidence to back up its claims.

13

(though no supporting biography, credentials, or other personal information is provided). The style is not objective, and many of the claims made are undocumented. Unlike most serious medical information, there are no citations to other articles or studies to support the author's claims.

# Googling Your Health Care Professional

As with any type of people searching, turning to Google to find information about a medical professional may—or may not—provide you with satisfactory results. It never hurts to start with Google to locate information about a doctor, dentist, or other health care professional. But finding information about a specific individual may be tricky, and you'll need to use many of the techniques and strategies discussed in Chapter 12 to get really good results.

In most cases, you're probably better off starting your search with some of the specialized directories of health care professionals described later in this chapter. These directories tend to focus on professionals practicing in a certain country or region, or those specializing in a particular discipline or branch of medicine.

The exception to this "start elsewhere" rule of thumb when you're checking out a health care professional is when you have concerns about the person's past—especially if the person is offering services using a relatively new or controversial technique. Although medical accreditation boards often make disciplinary records public, these records may not be easy to find unless you know specifically where to look. By contrast, Google can turn up information reported in newspapers, find comments by both satisfied and disgruntled patients posted on blogs, personal pages, or forums, and plumb a variety of other "alternative" channels of information.

## Case Study: Giving Your Doctor an Online Checkup

A few months ago, a close associate asked me to investigate a back surgeon who was claiming a very high success rate using a new surgical procedure on patients who had not responded to traditional therapies. We had the following information about the doctor:

■ Name and address of the doctor's group practice

■ Web site address of the doctor's clinic

■ A promotional brochure describing the new procedure in lay terms

Starting with these three puzzle pieces, I followed the checklist described earlier in this chapter to fit together a more complete picture of the doctor and his practice.

The first step was to verify the authenticity of the doctor's web site. Why start with this step rather than trying to determine if the doctor was actually licensed to practice medicine in his state? Because a domain lookup using http://www.whois.sc takes just seconds, and it also provides additional clues for our investigation. By contrast, each state has different licensing procedures for health care professionals. In some states, the health department is responsible for licensing. In other states, an occupational licensing board is responsible. I opted to gather as much information as quickly as possible before turning to the more difficult searching tasks.

The domain check confirmed that the doctor's web site was in fact registered to his clinic—and also provided addresses and telephone numbers that matched those in the promotional brochure.

The next step was to verify the doctor's authority, as claimed on the web site. His curriculum vitae was available on the site (a promising sign) and included the following information:

- Personal information
- Education
- Internships
- Residencies
- Professional associations
- Publications
- Board certifications

According to the web site, the doctor had received his medical degree from a reputable institution and had completed internships and residencies at several hospitals. So far, so good.

The vitae also listed a number of impressive-sounding professional associations. Most medical professionals join associations in their field of expertise as a way to keep up with new developments, network with peers, and, importantly, to demonstrate that they are serious about a commitment to their career.

Notably, this doctor had *not* listed memberships in two of the most prestigious associations that most doctors in his field joined: The American Association of Orthopedic Surgeons and the North American Spine Society. In itself, this omission wasn't a big deal. But doing a Google search on the names of the four associations the doctor *did* list returned surprising results.

For the first association, Google found fewer than 60 results, and several of these results were for pages from the doctor's own web site. Most professional associations have hundreds or thousands of members, so this paucity of results raised a red flag.

The next search was even more surprising: Google found only *one* result for the association name, and that result also happened to be the doctor's curriculum vitae page. In other words, Google could find no trace of this particular medical association on the Web—other than on the doctor's own site. Had this doctor invented his own private association?

**POWER SEARCHER TIP**   *The American Board of Medical Specialties is an organization of 24 approved medical specialty boards that offers a searchable database of its members at http://www.abms.org/.*

Checking the list of publications the doctor claimed to have written also raised warning flags. Although all the articles and papers boasted impressive, technical-sounding titles, many provided no publication details. Searching Google for the titles of two journals where papers were supposedly published produced no results. Although it's rare for Google to find the actual text of scholarly articles published in journals, it's highly unlikely that there would be no mention whatsoever of a prestigious journal title *anywhere* on the Web. And yet this is what Google reported.

13

Our doctor was beginning to look a bit shady. A quick scan of the rest of the web site featured glowing patient testimonials, colorful pages showing photographs of the doctor's clinic, and detailed descriptions of the doctor's innovative procedures and their benefits. A casual visitor to the doctor's web site would likely conclude that he and his new techniques were on the up-and-up. And yet a few pieces of the puzzle just didn't fit. It was time to move beyond "the obvious" and dig a bit deeper.

As stated earlier, each state has different licensing boards and procedures—you may need to hunt around to find the appropriate agency for your state. (*Note: Although the doctor in this case study is based in the U.S., the investigative process described can be easily adapted to most other countries.*) A Google search for **"Florida medical license"** produced the results shown in Figure 13-4. Result #1, the Florida Medical License Search page from the Florida Department of Health, is the site we're looking for.

The #1 result for our query provided the link we needed to check out the doctor's medical license.

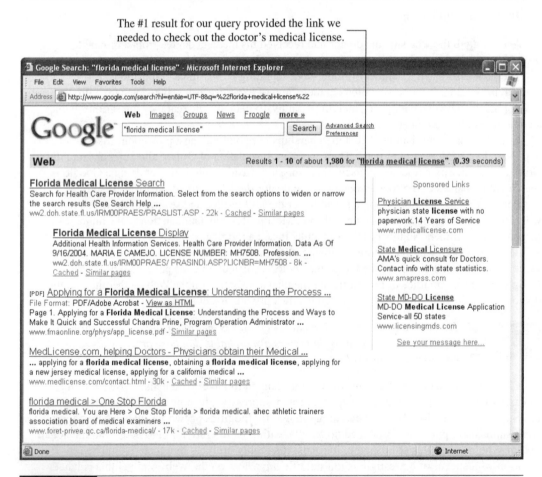

FIGURE 13-4    Use Google to find the appropriate licensing agency for a medical practitioner.

*Once you've found the official site of a licensing organization, it often takes a bit of poking around on the site to find the license search function. A quick way to find it is to do a Google search for **"license search"** and limit results to the licensing organization's web site with the **site:** operator.*

In addition to providing information about the status of a physician's license, the Florida Department of Health also maintains public records pertaining to the doctor's past. This information includes records of disciplinary actions by the board or government agencies, criminal records (if any), and records of malpractice judgments and arbitration awards.

Searching this database returned a record for the doctor, shown in Figure 13-5. This record shows that the doctor is currently licensed in Florida and has been disciplined in the past.

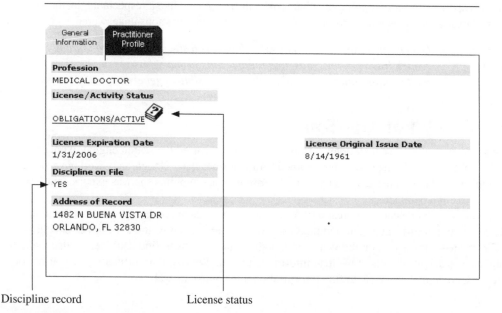

Discipline record                     License status

**FIGURE 13-5**   A record from the Florida Department of Health indicates that the doctor has been the subject of disciplinary actions.

Clicking the **Practitioner Profile** tab provides further details about several disciplinary actions that have been taken against the doctor. However, these details are sketchy and don't provide much in-depth information.

At this point, it's clear that our doctor is, shall we say, somewhat "controversial." The next step is to use Google to plumb the Web for other information gleaned from newspapers, personal web pages, and other sources. As part of this process, you'll want to set your search up on the Advanced Search page, just as with the people search described in Chapter 12. Treat the doctor's name, the word "doctor," and perhaps his state of residency as constants, entering them in the **exact phrase** and **all the words** fields. Then start to play with variable words, such as "complaint," "malpractice," "lawsuit," and any other words that serve as filters to surface potential malfeasance.

**POWER SEARCHER TIP** *The Health Research Group at Public Citizen maintains a searchable database of doctor disciplinary information on state web sites, with direct links to the disciplinary actions taken with health care professionals at each state, at http://www.citizen.org/hrg/forms/medicalboard.cfm.*

If you find additional results, remember to evaluate the quality of the information on those documents using the checklist described earlier. Don't take everything you find at face value—disgruntled patients or professional rivals may be biased in what they write. Although we've surfaced evidence suggesting that a cautious approach to this doctor is warranted, it's important to remember that in these situations there are always at least two sides to every story.

In the end, I reported what I had found to my associate, and she decided against using the doctor's services. A bit of digging on what looked at first glance like a respectable doctor's web site had raised too many questions, and left too many of those questions unanswered.

**POWER SEARCHER TIP** *Quackwatch (http://www.quackwatch.org) is a site focused on combating health-related frauds, myths, fads, and fallacies. Its primary focus is on quackery-related information that is difficult or impossible to get elsewhere.*

# Diagnosing What Ails You

Google likes to showcase testimonials from users who have used the search engine to uncover health information. In one case, a user named "Ann" gushes that "Google may well have saved my life" after she used the search engine to determine that symptoms she was experiencing were likely those of a heart attack.

Although Google can be a great tool for researching medical conditions, it's no substitute for advice and opinions from a qualified medical professional. Certainly, there's a ton of excellent health-related information on the Web, and Google makes it easy to find. But there's also a ton of dubious or outright fraudulent medical information on the Web. And unfortunately, if you're not careful, Google makes it easy to find this questionable content as well.

It goes without saying that you should always apply the information quality checklist to web sites you find when you're searching for information about medical conditions. Even before clicking a result, examine the URL, snippet, and other clues for information credibility and authority. And once you've visited a page, be exceptionally rigorous in your evaluation of the quality of the information you're viewing.

The most important factor you can control to ensure that you get high-quality results when you're researching diseases and syndromes is your choice of search terms. Even slight variations in your query words can dramatically affect the results that are presented. Figure 13-6 and Figure 13-7 show results for two similar, but slightly different queries: **cancer treatment** and **cancer therapy**.

The results for the query **cancer treatment** tend to focus on conventional treatment regimens, and come from authoritative sites such as Science Direct, Cancer.gov, and Family Doctor (from the American Academy of Family Physicians).

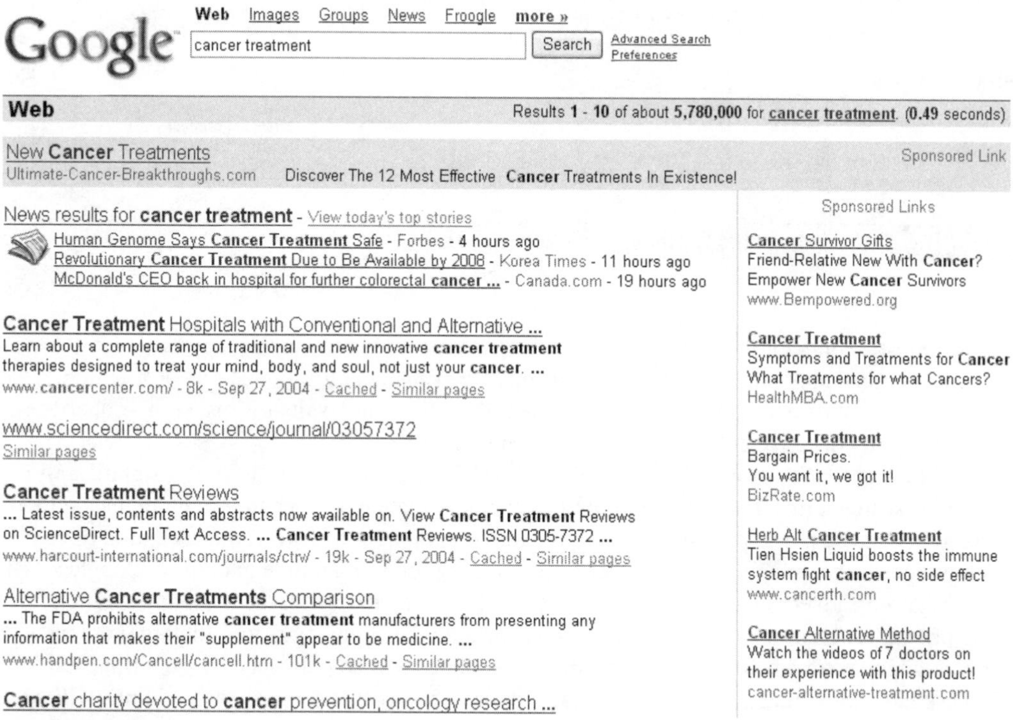

**FIGURE 13-6**   Search results for the query **cancer treatment**

FIGURE 13-7    Search results for the query **cancer therapy**

By contrast, results for the similar query, **cancer therapy**, tend to emphasize alternative and unconventional approaches to managing the disease. That's not to say that the information offered in these results isn't valuable. Rather, it just illustrates that results for two similar queries that are just subtly different can vary widely. Caveat searcher.

Take a look at the **Sponsored Links** section for each query. These links also differ significantly based on the search terms. It's also important to remember that Google's editorial guidelines for sponsored listings do not, for the most part, regulate the content of ads. With the exception of explicit policies concerning pharmaceutical sales and ads promoting online gambling, Google's policies regarding advertising content can essentially be summed up with the company's famous guiding principle: "Don't be evil." As this is being written, the company is formulating more concrete guidelines for advertisers and says these guidelines will be published "soon." But even when these more tangible guidelines are in place, it's safe to say that some sponsored links will fulfill Google's technical requirements and still lead to web sites offering products, services, or information of questionable value.

This is often especially true in the case of sponsored links related to medical search terms. Some of the sponsored links shown in Figures 13-6 and 13-7 are clearly advertisements for unconventional and perhaps unproven therapies. The only way to know for sure is to click a sponsored link and examine the web site you end up visiting.

But ask yourself an important question first: Do you really want to spend your time investigating an unfamiliar source of information and trying to determine whether it's valid and credible when you can easily turn to literally thousands of other sources on the Web that are widely regarded as authoritative and trustworthy? This is not to disparage alternative medical theories or therapies—on the contrary. Medicine is a discipline that's constantly evolving, and today's wild ideas sometimes become tomorrow's conventional practices. But whenever you're researching a topic as complex as a medical condition, the best approach is to start by getting a solid grounding in professionally accepted information that's sanctioned by recognized authorities, and then work your way into alternatives. This approach saves you time and also helps you steer clear of the all-too-unfortunate abundance of quackery and misinformation littering the Web.

Unless you have medical training, in most cases you're probably better off starting your search for information with one of the specialized medical resources described later in this chapter. Then, once you've built a solid foundation of understanding based on authoritative sources of information, use Google to expand and supplement your knowledge via other sources of information.

# Drugs and the Internet

The online sale of prescription drugs is a controversial issue, with governments throughout the world struggling to make laws that protect consumers and yet still recognize the borderless nature of Internet commerce. Google accepts sponsored links for web sites advertising prescription drugs, but it requires advertisers selling drugs or using prescription drug keywords to provide a valid SquareTrade identification number. SquareTrade is an online trust infrastructure company that verifies an appropriate governmental entity has licensed both the pharmacy and its associated pharmacist in a program administered in partnership with the National Community Pharmacists Association (NCPA).

SquareTrade membership is only available for online pharmacies based in the U.S. or Canada. Despite this limitation, Google allows international online pharmacies to purchase sponsored links, but they must exclude the U.S. when they specify which countries their ads should target.

This means that advertisers purchasing sponsored links have complied with SquareTrade policies—but advertisers can be *either* pharmacies or affiliates that advertise on behalf of a member pharmacy. SquareTrade's policies ensure a minimum of compliance focused primarily on four areas: The pharmacy agrees that it operate within compliance of the law, that it is licensed to dispense prescription drugs, that it will not dispense drugs without a written prescription, and that the company owns its own web site. These provisions are reassuring, but remember ultimately you're dealing with an online merchant, and levels of service and customer satisfaction can vary widely.

**POWER SEARCHER TIP**    *Learn more about Google's Online Pharmacy Qualification Program at http://www.google.com/adwords/pharmacy_qualification.html.*

On the other side of the spectrum, Google does not regulate listings that turn up in organic results in any way, other than applying its usual ranking algorithms to attempt to surface the most relevant results for your query. Figure 13-8 shows the results for a search for the best-selling prescription drug Lipitor. Although most of the top results are links to information sites, online pharmacies offering the drug for sale are also included. There's also a link to an online pharmacy in the **Product Results** section from Froogle displayed at the top of the page.

Product (Froogle) listings, because they were found on a crawl of the Web, are not sponsored links and are not subject to the provision that the merchant offering the drugs must be a member of the SquareTrade program.

So is it safe to purchase pharmaceuticals from online pharmacies that you've found by searching the Web? Unfortunately, there's no straightforward answer. Although many online pharmacies are ethical and responsible, others are not. The U.S. Government Accountability Office recently ran a test attempting to purchase drugs from a variety of online pharmacies.

Froogle results

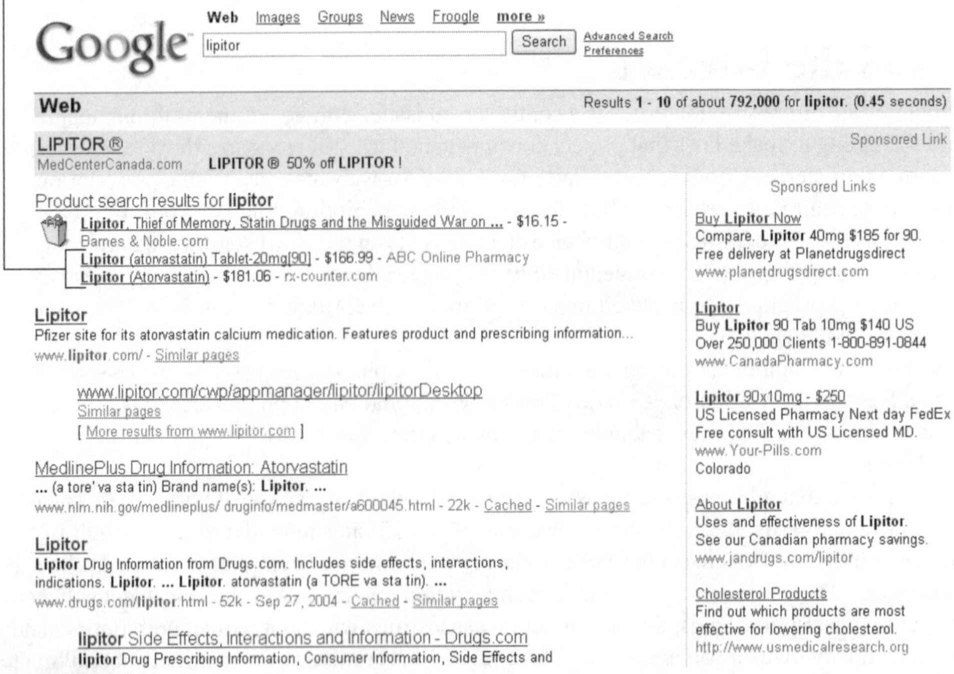

**FIGURE 13-8**    Google search results for the popular prescription drug Lipitor

Whereas some of the pharmacies accurately filled orders, others failed to deliver drugs that the agency had paid for. In other cases, the drugs were counterfeit. Still others arrived in packages with return addresses that were actually private residences.

Filling a prescription online from a known and trusted pharmacist is safe, and you'll get the same service and quality assurances you'd get from your neighborhood pharmacist. But using an unknown source to acquire potent drugs with potential health risks is another matter. This approach is certainly riskier than filling a prescription at your local pharmacy. But for some people, cost savings or convenience may outweigh these concerns. The bottom line is that purchasing prescriptions online is a highly personal choice. In more than any other realm of online ecommerce, buying drugs online is definitely a matter of caveat emptor.

POWER SEARCHER TIP
*Read the full findings of the GAO online pharmacy test,* Internet Pharmacies: Some Pose Safety Risks for Consumers, *at http://www.gao.gov/new.items/d04820.pdf.*

# Beyond Google: Finding Online Health Information

It's easy to get overwhelmed with the vast amount of health information online. Where to start? Which sites to trust? Answers to those questions could fill an entire book. In fact, there is an excellent book that goes deep into the subject of searching for health information on the Internet: *Super Searchers on Health & Medicine,* by Susan M. Detwiler (CyberAge Books, 2000).

I recommend that you take two approaches in going beyond Google for finding health information. The first is to visit an excellent directory of web sites put together by trustworthy information professionals who've vetted the material included in the directory very carefully. The second approach is to visit one of the excellent medical resources maintained by a government agency. There are many throughout the world; I'll describe two of the most popular and widely recognized, based in the U.S. and U.K.

## Librarians' Index to the Internet: Health and Medicine

13

If you're just starting your quest for health-related information, there's no better place to begin than the Librarians' Index to the Internet's Heath and Medicine category (http://lii.org/search/file/health). This directory consists of a categorized list of some of the best health care information sites on the Web, selected and evaluated by librarians for their usefulness to users of public libraries.

All the listings in the LII are carefully annotated with a description of what you can expect to find. Listings are also extensively cross-linked to related subjects, allowing you to easily browse between related categories.

## U.S. National Library of Medicine—MedlinePlus

Ask any information professional which single resource is the best all-around source for medical information, and the majority would likely say MedlinePlus (http://www.nlm.nih.gov/medlineplus/). This comprehensive resource, maintained by the U.S. National Library of Medicine and the National Institutes of Health, is both comprehensive and easily accessible to the non-medical community.

MedlinePlus includes:

- **Health Topics** featuring over 650 topics on conditions, diseases and wellness
- **Drug Information** about prescription and over-the-counter medicines
- **Medical Encyclopedia**, including pictures and diagrams
- **Dictionary**, with spellings and definitions of medical words
- **Health News** from the past 30 days
- **Directories** to help you find doctors, dentists, and hospitals
- **Other Resources**

Another useful resource maintained by the National Institutes of Health is the Health Information Index at http://health.nih.gov/.

## NHS Gateway

Like MedlinePlus, the NHS Gateway (http://www.nhs.uk/) is a comprehensive health information resource. Maintained by the U.K.'s NHS Information Authority, the site provides links to health care provider directories in England, Northern Ireland, Scotland, and Wales.

## VIPPS (Verified Internet Pharmacy Practice Sites) Database Search

This database, maintained by the National Association of Boards of Pharmacy (http://www.nabp .net/vipps/consumer/search.asp), helps you locate a certified online pharmacy based on your own needs. To be VIPPS certified, a pharmacy must comply with the licensing and inspection requirements of their state and each state to which they dispense pharmaceuticals. In addition, pharmacies displaying the VIPPS seal have demonstrated compliance with VIPPS criteria, including patient rights to privacy, authentication and security of prescription orders, adherence to a recognized quality assurance policy, and provision of meaningful consultation between patients and pharmacists.

## Expert Tips for Health and Medical Searching

### Six Questions for Power Searcher Cynthia Shamel

**Q: What's your favorite Google search tip?**
**A:** My favorite Google search tip is to install the Google toolbar. Unfortunately, it only works in Internet Explorer, but once it's there it's very handy and easy to use. I especially like the

"Search Site" capability. This allows you to search through the pages of the web site you are currently visiting. Some web sites do not have a search function built in, so "Search Site" is great for those occasions. Sometimes the site-specific search function is not particularly robust, in which case you can get different results with the Google site search option.

Whenever possible, I like options and the ability to double-check my work. The Google toolbar "Search Site" function gives me options. For example, a search of the Gen-Probe company web site for the term "PCR" (polymerase chain reaction) yields six hits when using either the Google Search Site function or Gen-Probe's own search site tool. Upon closer inspection, however, we see that the six hits are not identical in both searches. The Google search produced a link to the 2004 version of a certain product's package insert, while the Gen-Probe search led to a 2003 version. Neither search result is necessarily better than the other; they are just different and demonstrate the need to verify and double-check.

**Q: What kind of search strategy do you use when searching for medical/health info on Google?**
**A:** My first thought is always to take the simplest approach. This means, whenever possible, choosing search terms that are unambiguous, preferably using as few as possible. For example, professional or patient-based associations often have valuable information on diseases, patient populations, statistics, and cutting-edge therapies. To identify relevant organizations, I will sometimes use Google. Search terms would include the name of the disease or condition of interest, along with a keyword such as "association," "society," or "foundation." I would never use all of these words at once, since Google would look for them all to be on a given page, but I might try them sequentially if one didn't give satisfactory results.

A sample search might focus on prostate cancer. I would begin with the following terms: "association prostate cancer." The first hit leads to the Prostate Cancer Foundation, "the world's largest philanthropic source of support for prostate cancer research." The second hit leads to the Scottish Association of Prostate Cancer Support Groups (a bit specialized for the average search), and the third is for the MedlinePlus page on prostate cancer, which points to a directory of organizations, along with the National Cancer Institute, the American Cancer Society, and the National Foundation for Urologic Disease. So, within the top three hits, there are three very strong sources for information on prostate cancer.

**Q: Are there specific tools or techniques that lead to best results (for example, operators, filters, special keywords, etc.)?**
**A:** When a search is returning so many hits that you begin looking for ways to narrow it down, try using page formats as a limiter. In Google you can specify document type, such as Adobe Acrobat PDF or Microsoft Word DOC. In looking for business information on biomedical companies or products, I like to use the Microsoft PowerPoint format (PPT). This limiter points the search toward presentations given within a company, to analysts, and at scientific meetings or other professional conferences. This can be a good way to locate product data, market share, disease statistics, business strategies, and trends or forecasts. Using Google's Advanced Search page and entering **"drug delivery"** as an exact phrase, including any of the words **"trends forecasts projections"**, and limiting to the PowerPoint format leads to some interesting results. This focuses the search in a unique and useful way.

**13**

**Q: When would you not use Google for searching for health/medical info?**
**A:** I would not use Google if I needed to search the scientific literature for papers or presentation on medical subjects. Although a Google search might yield a few articles through Findarticles.com, there are a number of databases such as Medline, Embase, and Biosis that offer much better coverage of and access to the medical literature. I would definitely choose them over Google for a literature search.

**Q: What search engines or other web resources do you use to go beyond Google when searching for medical/health info?**
**A:** A great deal of the valuable medical/health information I seek comes from commercial, fee-based databases, but there are lots of important sources available on the open Web. I tend to use Google as a general, broad-based starting place. The sites it retrieves can provide context, useful keywords, important organizations in the field, and lead to other sources. If I don't get the background I need from Google, I might try Alltheweb (http://www.alltheweb .com), another general search engine, or Scirus (http://www.scirus.com), which is a specialized science search engine. MedlinePlus (http://www.medlineplus.gov) is a service of the National Library of Medicine and the National Institutes of Health. It is an amazing compilation of medical and health care information with pointers toward additional sources.

**Q: What's your favorite power-searching tip?**
**A:** The most powerful search tip I can offer is to choose your keywords carefully and employ a simple, unambiguous search strategy whenever possible. When I recently tried to remember a song name that Alfalfa used to sing on *The Little Rascals* show (not exactly medical/health, but a good example), I did a Google search for "Alfalfa rascals songs" and the first site on the results list was Alfalfa's Greatest Hits, with each song listed, including the episode in which he sang it. A search on "alfalfa" would have been too broad. Including "rascals" would narrow it some, but there's a lot to know about Alfalfa and *The Little Rascals* beyond the songs that were sung. Adding the keyword "songs" focused it just enough to provide my answer.

*Cynthia Shamel is the owner of Shamel Information Services, a firm specializing in medical and health-related online research, and the 2003-2004 President of the Association of Independent Information Professionals.*

# Chapter 14

## All the News That Fits Online

When Google first launched its News service in September 2002, it completely changed the way many people got their news on the Web. Before Google News, most people bookmarked and visited just a handful of online news sites, such as CNN and the BBC, major newspaper sites, such as the *Los Angeles Times* and the *International Herald Tribune,* and perhaps a local news site or two. Though thousands of online news sources existed prior to the advent of Google News, it was difficult to access more than a few sites without spending hours reading or skipping past duplicate or syndicated stories. Even excellent news aggregator sites such as Yahoo! Full Coverage were somewhat limited, assembled by a team of human editors who could only scan a small portion of the news sites available on the Web.

Google News took the drudge work out of finding news by applying the same basic strategies used to find and organize content on the Web. Google News crawls more than 4,500 English language sources, identifies the most "important" stories of the moment, and aggregates related articles into subject-specific categories. This makes it easy to scan dozens or hundreds of headlines from news sources all over the world and then select those that appear most relevant for reading.

Google News Search is updated constantly, adding new stories and emphasizing important new events as they unfold. For news junkies, the site is about as addictive as they come. For the rest of us, Google News provides an instant way to get a quick update on the current state of affairs throughout the world.

# Inside Google News

Google News was the brainchild of Krishna Bharat, a Google Principal Scientist who realized it would be useful to see news from multiple sources on a given topic assembled in one place. Like many people around the world, Bharat turned to the Web for news after the horrific events of September 11, 2001. Most popular news sites were overwhelmed by unprecedented traffic as people sought to understand what was going on. Many people turned to Google for news, but at that time, Google had no specialized news service of its own. Google did take the unprecedented step of posting this message on its home page:

*"If you are looking for news, you will find the most current information on TV or radio. Many online news services are not available, because of extremely high demand."*

Google also provided links to the *Washington Post,* and a link to a cached copy of CNN (see Figure 14-1). Nonetheless, searching Google for news about the terrorist attacks provided nothing up to date.

The company reacted quickly, however. Within hours, Google created a special "Breaking News: Attacks Hit U.S." page, with links to current news sites and to other sources of previous coverage (see Figure 14-2).

Google also modified result pages for queries related to the attacks, displaying a text message and link to this breaking news page in the area where a sponsored link would normally appear

**FIGURE 14-1**   Google's home page on September 11, 2001

14

(see Figure 14-3). This message directed searchers to the new Breaking News page. Though people could not get news directly from Google, the events of the day planted the seeds of an idea for a new service from the search engine.

Google launched the beta version of its news service just six months later, in March 2002. At that time, Google News searched just 100 leading English-language publications, including *The New York Times,* CNET News.com, and the *Herald Tribune.* It took the company another six months to roll out the categorized, industrial-strength news search service that we use today.

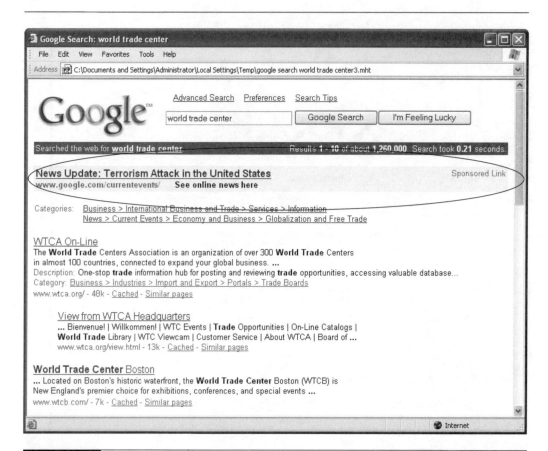

FIGURE 14-2    Google's special Breaking News page, created in response to the events of 9-11

# How Google News Works

Google's philosophy of organizing the world's information relies heavily on powerful
computers carrying out sophisticated tasks with as little human intervention as possible.
It's no surprise, then, that Google's approach to aggregating news is fully automated. The
breaking news events selected for the Google News page (see Figure 14-4) and the individual
articles reporting on those events are selected by a computer program. Unlike most other news
sites on the Web, human editors play no role in the process of what's displayed on the Google
News page.

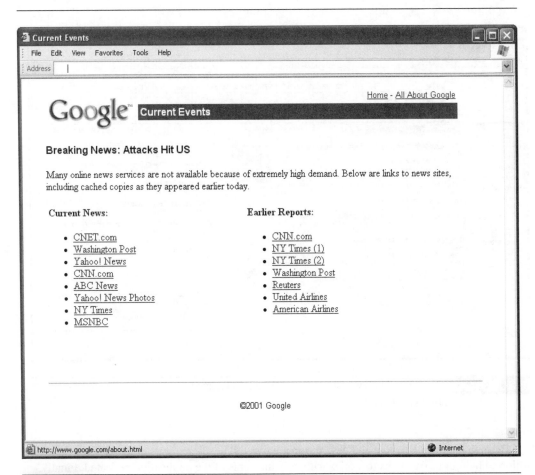

©2001 Google

**FIGURE 14-3** On 9-11, Google presented a special "sponsored listing" directing searchers to its Breaking News page for terrorist attack–related queries.

14

Google constantly crawls more than 4,500 news sources constantly, using real-time ranking algorithms to determine which stories are the most important at the moment, in theory highlighting the sources with the "best" coverage of news events.

"Top stories" are placed first, regardless of topic. Each top story is presented with a headline linked directly to the source. Beneath the headline is a short description, name of the source, and the time when the article was last crawled, ranging from a few minutes to several hours earlier.

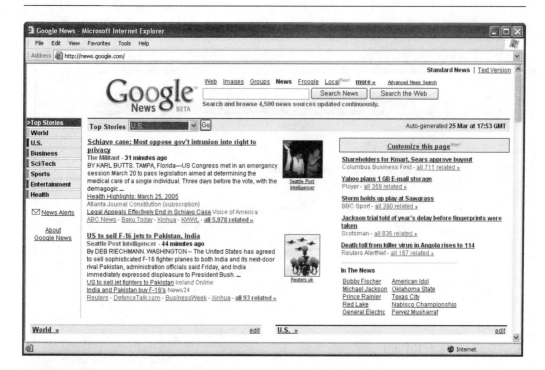

**FIGURE 14-4**    The Google News page is organized into categories, with "Top Stories" placed first on the page.

Beneath the main headline and description are two full headlines from other sources, followed by four or five links to stories with only the name of the publication indicated. Finally, there are links to "related" stories from other sources. This design makes it easy to quickly scan headlines while having the option of reading multiple accounts of a story from different news sources—from literally thousands of sources, for some stories.

Beneath the top stories, the Google News page is organized into seven sections: World, U.S., Business, Sci/Tech, Sports, Entertainment, and Health. An additional section at the bottom of the page provides links to more top stories. Like the Top Stories section, each of these topical sections features a few stories and links to the actual news sources themselves.

Each major category also has its own page. You can access a category page in two ways. Tabs at the upper left of any Google News page let you click through to a specific category page (see Figure 14-5). On the Google News page, each category heading also serves as a link that lets you click through to a category page, as shown in the following illustration.

Links to news category pages

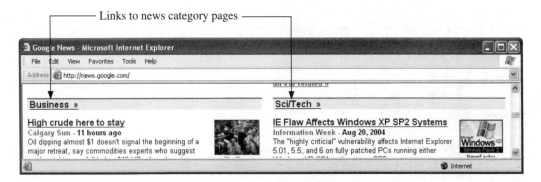

Each category page features 20 major news events, with thumbnail images and links to additional coverage (see Figure 14-6). In addition, text links to top stories from the main Google News page are located in the left column.

POWER SEARCHER TIP *Want to see a visual display of the relative importance of current news stories compared to one another? Newsmap displays a colorful map of the Google News page, at http://www.marumushi.com/apps/newsmap/newsmap.cfm.*

Category links

**14**

**FIGURE 14-5** Use the category tabs at the upper left of any Google News page to access specific topics.

**FIGURE 14-6** Category pages feature 20 topics and links to the most important news stories covering those events.

## Searching Google News

Google's automated approach to discovering news means that most of the major events happening in the world are well represented on the service. Although this is a great way to keep up with the state of affairs throughout the world, you often have to search to find news coverage of less prominent or local events. Fortunately, Google News provides a very powerful search mechanism that makes this process relatively easy. And unlike many news aggregators that simply "scrape" headlines and links from news sites, Google's news crawler indexes the full text of articles.

A Google News search box appears at the top of all Google News pages (see Figure 14-7). This search box provides the option of searching either Google News or the entire Web.

Search result pages resemble a hybrid between Google News category pages and web search result pages (see Figure 14-8). By default, news results are ranked by relevance, using many of the same factors used to determine the relevance of web pages as well as other factors unique to News, such as the recency of the content to help determine which stories get the most prominence.

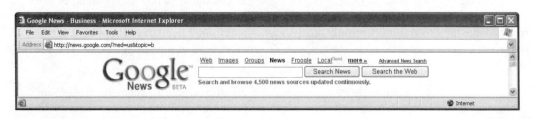

FIGURE 14-7    The Google News search box

With news, timeliness can often be more important than a computed score of relevance—events that happened an hour ago may be virtually irrelevant when major news stories are unfolding with rapidly changing events. Therefore, a link on search results pages allows you to override the default ranking by relevance and order results by date.

FIGURE 14-8    A Google News search result page

14

About the only downside to Google News, if you can call it that, is that it only archives news articles for a maximum of 30 days. This is because most news publishers move content off the Web and into their own subscriber-only archives anywhere from 7 to 30 days after publication. To respect copyright and other legal issues, Google removes news stories from Google News no later than 30 days after articles have been crawled.

*International versions of Google News are available in 20 countries throughout the world. Use the links at the bottom of any Google News page to access these international versions.*

## Advanced News Search

The Advanced News Search page (see Figure 14-9) is similar to all of Google's other advanced search pages, but it offers unique filters that are customized for news content.

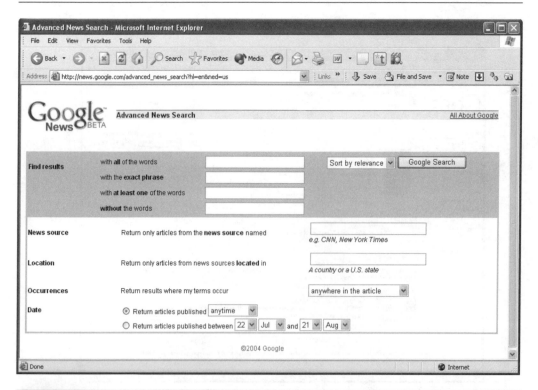

**FIGURE 14-9**   The Google Advanced News Search page

# Word Filters

At the top of the Advanced News Search page are the four word filters you're familiar with from Chapter 4. These filters work in exactly the same way with news stories as they work with text on web pages. Here's a review:

- with **all** of the words = Boolean AND between all search terms
- with the **exact phrase** = search terms enclosed in quotes
- with **at least one** of the words = Boolean OR between all search terms
- **without** the words = exclusion operator (-) placed in front of each search term

| Find results | with **all** of the words | | Sort by relevance ✔ | Google Search |
|---|---|---|---|---|
| | with the **exact phrase** | | | |
| | with **at least one** of the words | | | |
| | **without** the words | | | |

# News Source Filter

The **News source** filter lets you limit results, as you might expect, to specific news sources. Although the filter can be very powerful if it is used properly, it's also one of the finickiest filters on any Google advanced search page.

**News source**          Return only articles from the **news source** named

*e.g. CNN, New York Times*

To use the filter properly you first need to enter one or more search terms in the word filter boxes at the top of the Advanced New Search page and then enter the name of the source you want results from. Simply entering a news source alone won't work—try it and you'll be taken to the Google News home page.

You must also enter the source exactly as it is known to Google, using plain English words with no symbols. This means if you're looking for a story from the *Lexington Herald-Leader,* you must omit the hyphen in your query. Otherwise, you'll get a message saying that the source was not found, as shown in Figure 14-10. A properly structured query is shown in Figure 14-11.

Nor does the **News source** filter recognize partial names or abbreviations. If you're looking for a story from the Scripps Howard News Service, you must enter the full name, as the source **Scripps Howard** alone isn't recognized. Similarly, to find a story from *The Wall Street Journal,* you must enter **Wall Street Journal** as the source, rather than the *Journal*'s common abbreviation, *wsj.* You even need to omit the leading *The* to get the results you expect.

And don't enclose a source name in double quotes. The **News source** filter does not recognize phrases, either.

**14**

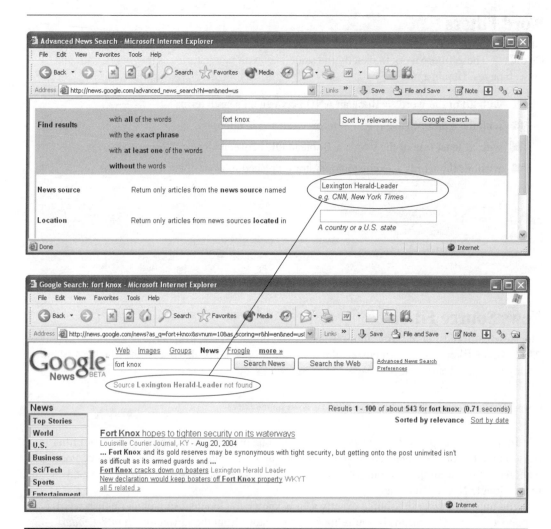

FIGURE 14-10 You'll get an error message if you don't omit all non-text characters from news sources.

Once you've mastered these limitations, the **News source** filter is a powerful way to cull stories to a specific source from the thousands of web sites that Google crawls for news.

> **POWER SEARCHER TIP** *To find the exact name Google uses to refer to a news source, use the wildcard symbol (\*). For example, the query **Lexington** \* \* will return results from the Lexington Herald-Leader displaying the source name used by Google News.*

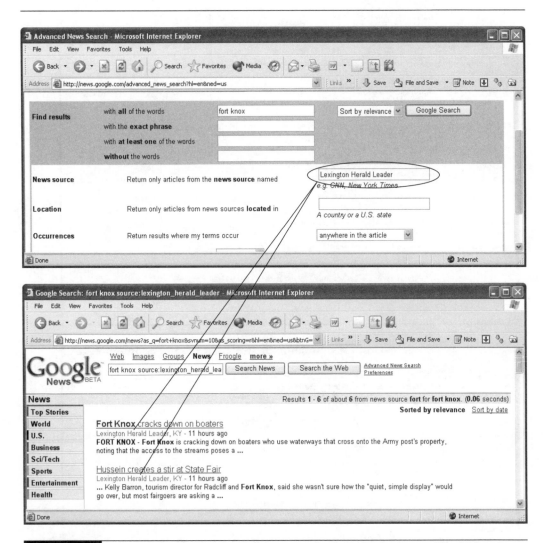

**FIGURE 14-11**    A properly structured query to get results from the *Lexington Herald-Leader*.

The **News source** filter has a corresponding operator that can be used from any Google News search box. Enter your query terms followed by the operator **source:** and the name of the source. The source name must have underscores between each of the words in the name.

# Location Filter

The **Location** filter, shown in Figure 14-12, limits results to articles from news sources located in a specific country or U.S. state.

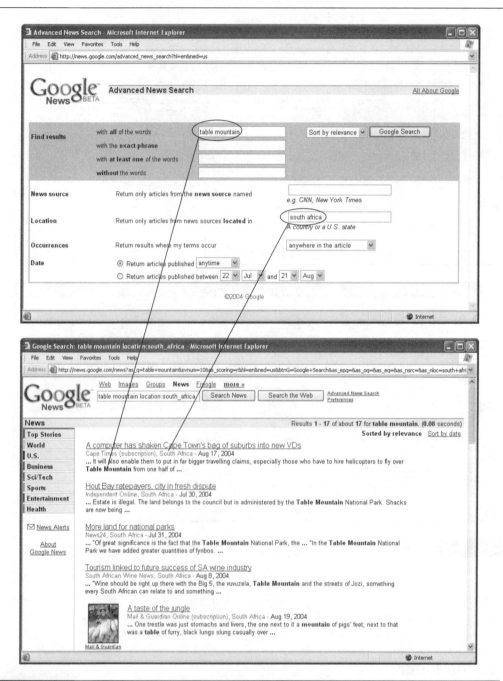

**FIGURE 14-12** The **Location** filter limits results to a particular geographic region.

The **Location** filter has a corresponding operator that can also be used from any Google News search box. Enter your query terms followed by the operator **location:** and a country or U.S. state. Multiword countries must have underscores between each of the words in the name.

## Occurrences Filter

The **Occurrences** filter lets you limit results to articles where your search terms appear in a specific part of the article. These parts include:

- Anywhere in the article, including the HTML title of the article
- In the headline of the article, which may differ from the HTML title of the article
- In the body of the article
- In the URL of the article

Use the drop-down menu, shown next, to activate the filter.

## Date Filter

By nature, news is timely, and it typically loses its value the older it becomes. This makes the **Date** filter, shown in the following illustration, one of the most useful Advanced News Search features, allowing you to limit results to very specific timeframes. Compared to the unreliable and often inaccurate results returned when using the web search **Date** filter, the Google News **Date** filter works quite well.

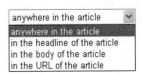

You can use the **Date** filter in two ways. The first option lets you use a drop-down menu to limit results to those found by Google's news crawler anytime, in the last hour or last day, or during the past week or month.

**14**

The other option, shown next, allows you to limit results to those found within a specific range of dates. Remember, Google's news archive only goes back 30 days. Even if you specify a range greater than 30 days using the menu, you'll still only see results for the prior 30 days through the current date.

⊙ Return articles published between [22 ▾] [Jul ▾] and [21 ▾] [Aug ▾]

**POWER SEARCHER TIP**   *To find news stories written more than 30 days ago, your best bet is to use a specialized service such as NewsBank or Newspaper Source from EBSCO. These services are often available through your local public library at no charge—in some cases you can even access them online after signing in with your library card number.*

## Google News Alerts

If you find yourself repeating the same searches on Google News, or if you want a more automated approach to keeping up to date with a particular topic, Google offers news alerts via e-mail. See the section on Google Alerts in Chapter 9 for more information on setting up Google Alerts.

**POWER SEARCHER TIP**   *You can incorporate advanced search features in your news alerts. The easiest way to do this is to use the Advanced News Search page to set up a search. Once you're satisfied that the advanced features you've selected are returning the type of results you want, simply copy the text that appears in the search box on a result page and paste it into the search box on the Google News Alerts page. This text includes all the advanced operators you selected when you entered your search terms on the Advanced Search page.*

# Beyond Google: Best News Search Sites

Although Google News excels at aggregating news from around the world and making it easily accessible, other news search sites offer a variety of interesting features that make them worthwhile alternatives.

## Findory

At first glance, Findory (http://www.findory.com) looks a lot like Google News. The home page features top news stories organized in categories. Like Google News, Findory crawls thousands of sources and offers full-text searching of the news. What sets Findory apart from Google News is that it is a personalized news service, observing the stories you read and automatically emphasizing stories tailored to your interests. Stories that are selected for you are labeled with a "personalized" icon next to a headline, as shown in Figure 14-13.

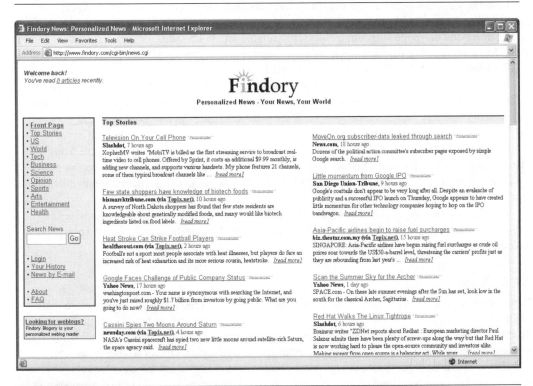

**FIGURE 14-13**  Findory is a personalized news service, automatically adjusting the stories it displays to match your reading preferences.

Findory creates a personalized display of news without requiring you to register or log in. It does this by analyzing the text in the articles you read and then comparing it with other stories you've read, looking for patterns. It also looks for similar patterns in the reading behavior of other users. This approach is similar to Amazon.com's "readers who bought this book also bought..." feature, suggesting content based on similar interests.

Another interesting feature Findory offers is a list of articles you've recently read. You can easily access stories you've read simply by clicking the appropriate link on the "Your History" page.

Although Findory doesn't require you to log in or register, if you do choose to sign up for the service (which is free), you'll have access to your personalized news, your history, and a useful news by e-mail service from any Internet-connected computer.

## MSNBC Newsbot

MSNBC's Newsbot (http://newsbot.msnbc.msn.com/) tracks more than 4,800 news sources around the world and aggregates the top stories into a categorized home page. In both design and sources of information, Newsbot is similar to Google News and other online news aggregators.

14

Like Findory, Newsbot has useful history and personalization features designed to help you easily find news relevant to your own interests. As you read stories, the site tracks the topics you're interested in, suggesting similar stories in related areas. The site captures no personal data other than remembering the stories you've read. Recommendations for similar stories are made based on stories that other Newsbot users have read.

Recommendations are located at the top of each page. Clicking the **why** link next to each recommended story explains the reasoning behind the suggestion. Recommended stories change based on the category you're viewing—you'll see different stories in the "business" category and the "entertainment" category, for example.

Newsbot also displays a list of recently read stories at the bottom of each page in the **Your history** section. Click the **more history** link and you'll see a complete list of stories you've read, with the option to delete stories from your history that may be influencing your recommendations in ways you don't like.

The site also provides a basic news search capability, allowing you to find stories based on keywords. Your search history is also saved and is displayed under the search box on each page, making it easy to repeat a search for a topic that interests you.

## NewsNow

NewsNow (http://www.newsnow.co.uk/) is notable for two reasons. First, it searches more than 17,000 news sources on the Web, more than three times the number included in Google News. Second, NewsNow organizes the news into hundreds of categories (called *newsfeeds*), allowing you to easily scan the current news in a vast number of specialized topics without having to search.

This ability to scan headlines in very narrow categories is important, because NewsNow only allows keyword searching on single words. Why? Because the web site is a showcase for NewsNow's business services software, and the full capabilities of that software are available only to NewsNow customers. Nonetheless, the ability to scan so many newsfeeds makes NewsNow a valuable tool.

To select an individual feed, use the drop-down menus on the left side of the screen. The number of subcategories for each topic is displayed at the top of the menu.

## Topix.net

Topix.net (http://www.topix.net) features an impressive array of features that go far beyond aggregating more than 7,000 news sources. For starters, you can keyword search for news stories. Topix.net is also particularly strong in its categorization of news, with more than 150,000 topix.net pages. These include separate pages for 30,000 U.S. cities and towns, 5,500 public company and industry verticals, 48,000 celebrities and musicians, 1,500 sports teams and personalities, and many others.

Topix.net enhances its news pages with links to partner sites that provide relevant information to a particular topic. For example, a page for a city features not just local news, but current weather information, street maps, aerial photos, movie times, TV listings, restaurants, census info, a Wi-Fi map, and listings for local hotels, as well as links to the topix.net page for nearby cities. Company pages feature news, stock quotes, and other financial information. These enhancements make Topix.net an appealing one-stop source of information.

## Yahoo! Full Coverage

Yahoo!'s Full Coverage (http://news.yahoo.com/fc?) differs from all the other news aggregators mentioned here because it is compiled by a team of human editors. This makes it less comprehensive than the other news aggregators described in this chapter, but the selection of stories, photographs, and other news-related material is first rate, and it should be an essential part of anyone's news search toolkit.

POWER SEARCHER TIP *Yahoo! News (http://news.yahoo.com) is another excellent news search engine. Yahoo! News crawls thousands of newspapers around the world and offers an excellent alternative to Google News.*

## Columbia Newsblaster

Unlike the other news search services mentioned here, Columbia Newsblaster (http://newsblaster .cs.columbia.edu/) crawls only a few (less than 30) major news sites. But rather than simply aggregating links to stories, Newsblaster does something far more interesting: It summarizes the major news stories of the day into a single, lucid paragraph. And it creates each of these summaries automatically, without human intervention, by using a clever combination of linguistic analysis, clustering, and text categorization.

The summaries are typically remarkably well done, and they provide a rounded perspective from multiple news sources that you just don't get from reading a single news story. Links to all the underlying sources are provided, so you can read them directly if you wish. There's also a nifty timeline for many stories, offering links to track a story's development over time.

# Weblogs and Nontraditional News Sources

Weblogs (blogs) are pages maintained by people who typically blend together their own personal anecdotes with commentary on other content (often news) that they've found on the Web. As weblogs become ever more popular, the lines between traditional news providers and less formal but often more immediate sources of news are becoming increasingly blurred. Bloggers have broken numerous news stories before the mainstream media picked them up. And increasingly, respected journalists and news organizations are turning to the blog format as a means of posting news in a timely fashion.

Although Google News does include some blog content, it's not always easy to find. The ranking algorithms used by Google News tend to favor large, established media properties, so it's rare for a blog posting to be listed on the Google News main page or even on a category page. You can search for blog content using the Advanced News Search page, but you need to know the name of the blogs Google News crawls for this to work.

14

Fortunately, a crop of hybrid search engines that crawl both news and weblog content have sprung up over the past couple years. These search engines make it easy to find blog content and explore alternative sources of news and commentary on current events.

## Bloglines

Bloglines (http://www.bloglines.com/) searches and indexes more than 80 million live web articles. To use Bloglines, simply search for the content in which you are interested and identify sources you want to track. Once you "subscribe" to those sources, Bloglines constantly checks them for changes or additions.

## Daypop

Daypop (http://www.daypop.com) searches more than 59,000 news sites, weblogs, and RSS feeds for current events and breaking news (more about RSS in a moment). Daypop also has several unique features, including the "top 40," a list of the most popular links referred to in blogs today, and "top news" and "top posts," which track popular news and weblog entries.

## Feedster

Feedster (http://www.feedster.com) indexes over 800,000 syndicated sources and adds approximately 5,000 new feeds daily. This includes over 50,000 professionally published sources such as *The New York Times,* BBC, CNET, IDG, and *Wired*.

## Technorati

Technorati (http://www.technorati.com) searches more than 3,500,000 blogs. Like Daypop, Technorati has several other interesting collections of statistics, such as "Book Talk," a list of the most frequently cited books mentioned in weblogs.

In a sign of just how significant blogs are becoming, Technorati's founder, Dave Sifry, was invited by CNN to the 2004 Democratic national convention to provide regular on-air commentary on what bloggers are saying about politics and the convention.

# RSS: Essential Tool for the News Junkie

RSS (Rich Site Summary) is a method that automatically creates a *feed* whenever new content is published that can be read by a program called a *news aggregator.* When you subscribe to RSS feeds from news publishers or bloggers (or any web page author, for that matter), new stories are automatically fetched by your news aggregator program, obviating the need to search for stories from your favorite sources.

A full description of RSS and news aggregators is beyond the scope of this book, but if you're a heavy user of news and blogging services, you should definitely look into getting an aggregator and subscribing to feeds from your favorite sources. Information sources that offer an RSS feed typically advertise this capability by displaying a logo. Dragging and dropping this logo into a newsreader is all that's necessary to subscribe to the feed.

> More Articles ...
> or receive news via our XML/RSS feed
> **XML RSS**
> add to MY YAHOO!

Most of the blog search tools described earlier provide basic RSS feed capabilities. Very good, simple RSS news aggregators are available from Yahoo! and Lycos. Yahoo!'s My Yahoo service (http://my.yahoo.com) lets you add RSS feeds to your own, personalized page. Lycos's HotBot Desktop (described in Chapter 8) not only makes it easy to subscribe to RSS feeds, it makes them searchable as well.

 POWER SEARCHER TIP

*A good list of news aggregators is available at http://directory.google.com/Top/ Reference/Libraries/Library_and_Information_Science/Technical_Services/ Cataloguing/Metadata/RDF/Applications/RSS/News_Readers/.*

## Ask the Expert

# Expert Tips for News Searching
### Six Questions for Power Searcher Gary Price

**Q: What's your favorite Google search tip?**
**A:** Place phrases in quotation marks. It can dramatically increase the precision of your results.

**Q: What kind of search strategy do you use when searching for news on Google?**
**A:** I try to vary my terms. I also try to remember that what something is called in one part of the world might be called something else in another part. The classic example is soda, pop, soda pop, soft drink, etc.

If I'm searching for business news, I try to use the jargon of that profession and industry. It can really assist in finding interesting material.

**Q: Are there specific tools or techniques that lead to best results (for example, operators, filters, special keywords) when searching for news?**
**A:** I often find it useful to limit by source if I know a source exists in Google News. Unfortunately, an official list of sources is not available. To find sources, try a search that is not limited and browse the result lists for specific sources. Then, when you've found a source you want to limit results to, rerun the search with the limit in place. It's a good idea to create a simple list of your own most useful sources. This can save you time in the future.

I also like using the advanced search interface and limiting by date. I don't recommend this type of limit when searching the web catalog, but since every news article has an official publication date, using a date limit when searching Google News can work well.

14

**Q: When would you not use Google for searching for news?**
**A:** If I'm looking for an article older than a month or two I would start elsewhere. The majority of the Google News database only contains the most recent material.

**Q: What search engines or other web resources do you use to go beyond Google when searching for news?**
**A:** I use many. In fact, Google News is often not the tool I turn to first. You've already mentioned my favorites in this chapter: Yahoo! News, Rocket News, NewsNow, Topix.net.

A tip I'd offer to your readers is that many public libraries and university libraries offer free access to news databases containing years of new and archived content from thousands of publications. What's even more exciting is the fact that these databases are fully accessible without having to visit the library building. That's right; they're available 24/7/365 from any computer with web access. All you need is a library card.

These databases offer free full-text access and have both simple and advanced interfaces, and have become very easy to search in the past few years. Some databases not only offer the full text but also the full image of the page delivered to your computer in seconds as an Adobe Acrobat file.

So, if you're spending time looking for something that you just can't find on the open Web or paying newspapers for older material, it's very likely that your local library offers the same content for free. Every library offers different databases. My suggestion is to either visit your library's web site and look for this information (to find your local library web site, search for it on Libdex at http://www.libdex.com) or simply call the library and ask about what's available.

**Q: What's your favorite power-searching tip?**
**A:** My favorite power-searching tip is back link searching using the **link:** operator. I find many excellent undiscovered resources by seeing what other people link to. In my opinion, it's more effective than a "find related pages" search. One problem with Google is that when back link searching, you cannot add any other syntax to your query. For example, trying to find pages from Canada that link to Search Engine Watch (**link:www.searchenginewatch .com site:ca**) is impossible. This type of query is possible with other engines, such as Yahoo!

Another tip is to remember that even though we search for just about everything these days, browsing and serendipity are still useful for certain types of searches. I suggest using some of the excellent noncommercial, general-purpose engines out there, including Librarians' Index to the Internet (http://www.lii.org), INFOMINE (http://infomine.ucr.edu), and the Resource Discovery Network (http://rdn.ac.uk). These directories have no advertising, offer excellent annotated descriptions, and stress the quality of the underlying resource versus "having it all."

*Gary Price is news editor of SearchEngineWatch.com and co-author of* The Invisible Web: Uncovering Information Sources Search Engines Can't See (*CyberAge Books, 2001*).

# Chapter 15

## Let Your Keywords Do the Shopping

Shopping search engines have been around in various forms for many years. But only in the past couple years have they evolved into mainstream tools that not only help you find good deals, but also assist with the crucial research and comparison process before you actually make a purchase.

One of the first web shopping search programs was Bargain Finder, developed by Andersen Consulting (now Accenture) in 1995. Bargain Finder was actually a web robot, similar to the crawlers used by search engines. It was a simple program, querying ten online music stores for just one single bit of information: the price each store was charging for a single album. That's it—no artist information, no details about the merchant's shipping or service policies—just price.

In 1995 this was fairly radical. Few online merchants had established a recognizable brand or developed much customer loyalty. Amazon.com wasn't even online until July 1995, and didn't sell music at the time. And the small, scrappy online music pioneers did not welcome the price comparisons Bargain Finder was offering. More than a third of the merchants that Bargain Finder searched took steps to block the robot from accessing their sites. Effectively toothless, Bargain Finder's popularity quickly faded. Shopping search would have to wait for the Web to mature.

Fast-forward to today and merchant attitudes are the polar opposite of what they were in 1995. Today's savvy online retailers do anything they possibly can to attract visitors to their online stores. Merchants have realized that the ease of simply clicking from one online store to another means that people no longer base purchase decisions solely on price. This means it's in the merchant's best interest to work very closely with shopping search engines to make sure their wares are fully exposed and presented in the most favorable light.

Shopping search engines have evolved considerably from Bargain Finder's crude price comparisons. Search results now provide tons of other relevant product information, such as shipping rates, taxes, stock quantities, consumer reviews, and so on.

Google was a relative latecomer to the shopping search arena. Froogle, the company's shopping search tool, was launched just before the holidays in December 2002. Initially, Froogle was designed as a directory, with 15 different product categories. You could browse Froogle by drilling down through a particular category and its subcategories. Today, Froogle has evolved into a powerful tool where the directory structure is less prominent and search is front and center. Google has also launched a U.K. version of the service, suggesting it plans to make Froogle a truly global online shopping service.

 *Froogle and all the shopping search engines described in this chapter are strictly research and comparison tools. Once you've found a product you want to buy, you need to visit a merchant—online or off—to actually make your purchase.*

# Finding Bargains with Froogle

Froogle (shown in Figure 15-1) is available by clicking its link above all the main Google search services, or it can be accessed directly at http://froogle.google.com. Links next to the Search Froogle button lead to the Advanced Froogle Search, Preferences, and Froogle Help screens.

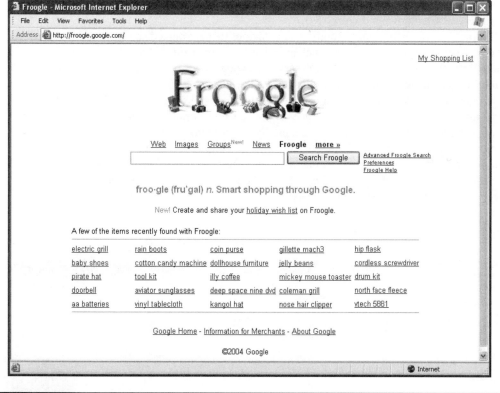

FIGURE 15-1     Like all Google services, Froogle's interface is clean and simple.

What kinds of products can you find with Froogle? A glance at the list of a few of the items recently found with Froogle beneath the search form (see Figure 15-2) reveals the almost astonishing variety of stuff people are looking to buy online (kung fu hamster, anyone?). Click your browser's "refresh" button and the list will update with a new set of search terms. Click any of the links in the list and Froogle will run a search for that particular item.

15

A few of the items recently found with Froogle:

| baby car seat | duffel bag | beef jerky | fish oil | barrette |
| carpet shampoo | driver | kung fu hamster | laser pointer | little tykes kitchen |
| hikers backpack | radio scanner | cpu fan | cuckoo clocks | bath towel |
| spotlight | natural gas grill | luna bars | caviar | ski boots |
| eternity cologne | hip flask | pirate hat | hamper | autometer |

FIGURE 15-2     This list on Froogle's home page shows recent searches from users of the service.

Searching Froogle is easy. Simply type in the name of the product you're looking for and click the **Search Froogle** button. Results look similar to Google web search results, with a few key differences, as shown in Figure 15-3.

Froogle search results contain both organic listings that are ranked solely by relevance to your query, and sponsored links, which are advertisements paid for by merchants. Unlike virtually all other online shopping search services, Froogle does not accept payment from merchants to be included in organic Froogle search results.

Froogle gets product information from two sources: Google's crawl of the Web and product feeds submitted by merchants. Froogle does not have its own crawler. Instead, Froogle relies on the primary GoogleBot crawls, from which product information on merchant sites is extracted for organic Froogle results. Merchants can also submit feeds directly to Google, providing specific structured details about each product the merchant offers for sale. This is the best method for merchants to communicate their product offerings to Google, allowing for precise descriptions of virtually unlimited amounts of inventory.

**FIGURE 15-3**    Froogle search results differ from other types of Google search results in several key respects.

As with organic web search results, product information gleaned from crawling the Web is often imperfect. Some product information in online stores is structured in an "obvious" way. When Froogle is highly confident about the various characteristics of a product, it is listed in the "confirmed results" total.

For other more ambiguous items, Froogle must make an educated guess about a product's price and category based on an analysis of the page on which the item appears. When Froogle can't confirm price or category information for an item, it is included in the "total results" figure, but physically separated on the result page from the confirmed results with a message, as shown in Figure 15-4.

Sometimes Froogle results can seem a bit strange—in some cases, you'll see listings for objects or events that aren't for sale, but that the crawler has associated with a price. In these cases, Froogle is simply "guessing" about the "product" and "price," with occasionally nonsensical results. Remember, though, that Froogle is still in its beta form, and these glitches

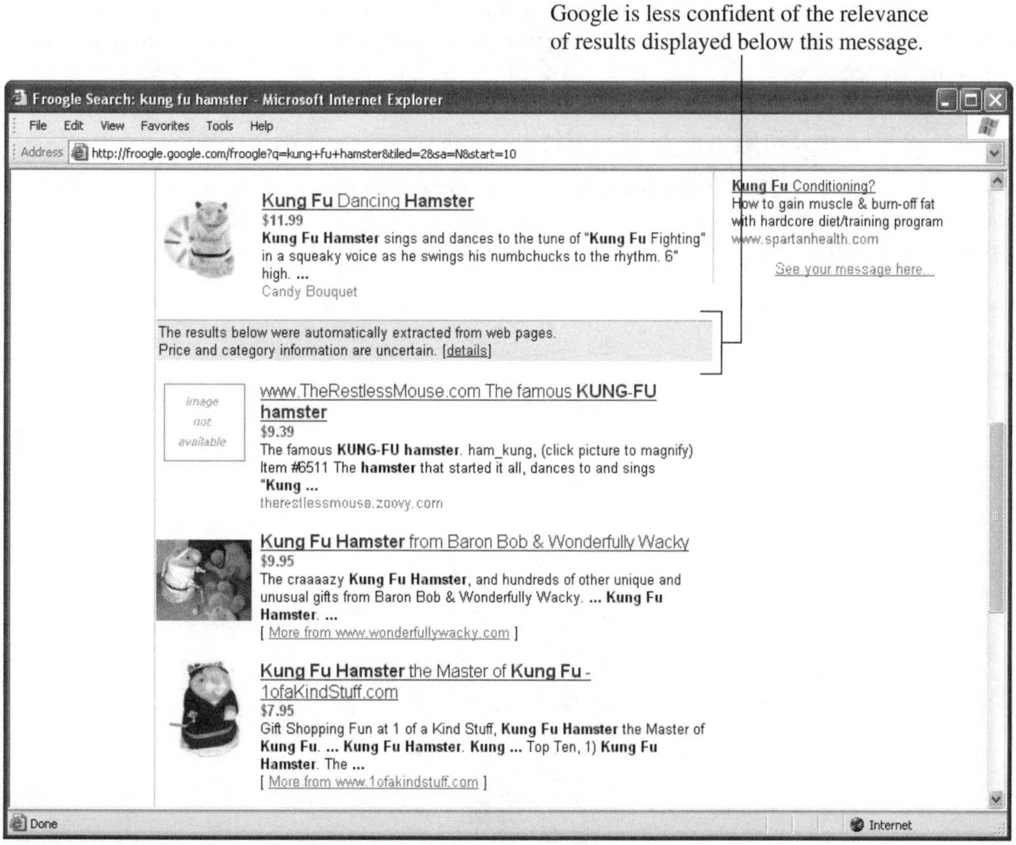

Google is less confident of the relevance
of results displayed below this message.

**FIGURE 15-4**   Results that Froogle is less confident about are displayed lower on search result pages, clearly separated from confirmed results.

15

**Kung Fu Hamster**
$7.95
THE **KUNG FU HAMSTER**.DON'T BE FOOLED BY THIS LITTLE
**HAMSTER'S** SIZE,HE IS THE MASTER OF THE MARTIAL
ARTS!.WHILE THE SONG "**KUNG FU** FIGHTING" PLAYS,HE WILL
MYSTIFY ...
More from Novelty Poster Co., Inc.

| **FIGURE 15-5** | Natural search results are ranked by relevance; Google accepts no payment from merchants for displaying listings of this type. |

are bound to happen. You can expect that you'll see fewer bizarre search results over time, as Froogle gains more experience and confidence in the realm of online shopping.

Froogle search result screens are divided into three columns. Organic search results for your query are displayed in the middle column. Froogle displays only one product offering from each merchant included in results. Each result displays the name of the product, price, description, merchant name, and a photo of the product, if one is available (see Figure 15-5). If Froogle has found more than one result from a merchant that match your query, you'll also see a **More results from *merchant name*** link. The number of results displayed is determined by how you've set your preferences.

## Refining Froogle Search Results

The leftmost column provides several controls to refine your search results, as shown in Figure 15-6. Because product search is still such an inexact science, effectively using these controls typically improves the overall quality of your Froogle experience.

| **FIGURE 15-6** | Froogle offers a number of controls to help refine your search. |

When you first run a Froogle search, results are displayed in "list view." Clicking the **Grid view** link changes the search result listing to a three-column grid displaying just product images, prices, and merchant names, without product descriptions, as shown in Figure 15-7.

Two other controls let you sort results by price, from low to high or high to low. Clicking either of these links reorders the results regardless of whether you're viewing results in list or grid view. A new "best match" link also appears, which will re-sort results by relevance.

Use the **Price Range** filter to filter out results that may not be relevant to what you're looking for. For example, many searches return a variety of results related in some way to your query—the product itself, accessories or add-ons, and even products with similar names. Figure 15-8 shows the results for the query "airport express," a remote wireless networking product from Apple.

**FIGURE 15-7**    Grid view displays product images, prices, and merchant names only.

15

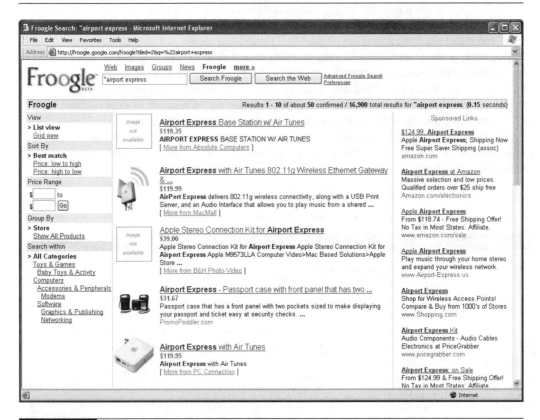

**FIGURE 15-8**   Some Froogle search results include a variety of products related to your query.

The top two results are for the Airport Express product itself, but the third and fourth results are for accessories. You can eliminate results for accessories and focus results on the product using the **Price Range** filter, as shown in Figure 15-9.

The next set of controls allows you to group results by store, either displaying a single result per store (Froogle's default setting) or removing this limit and displaying all results found from all stores.

The final set of controls allows you to refine your search by browsing product categories. Froogle assigns products to categories automatically, sometimes guessing at the best group for a particular product. Sometimes browsing categories can help refine results. On other occasions, you'll get bizarre results that have little to do with your query.

## Don't Overlook Sponsored Links

Results in the rightmost column of Froogle search results are sponsored links, purchased by advertisers. For most products, you'll want to take a close look at these links in addition to natural search results, because in most cases they represent merchants who are both selling

**FIGURE 15-9**    Use the **Price Range** filter to eliminate accessories and other related products from Froogle search results.

a product and actively promoting it with a sponsored link. You may find some great deals through sponsored links that might not appear in natural search results.

Be sure to read the Sponsored Links column carefully. Figure 15-10 shows several sponsored links that all appear to be from Amazon. Look closely, however, and you'll see that only one is directly from Amazon.com itself. The other two have been purchased by an Amazon associate and an affiliate. Clicking any of these links will take you to relevant product pages at Amazon.com. However, the sponsored link purchased by Amazon results is likely to take you to a page where you get the most useful information.

# Advanced Froogle Search

The Advanced Froogle Search page (shown in Figure 15-11) has most of the familiar features of other Google Advanced Search pages. The four word filters at the top of the Advanced Froogle Search page work just like they do on the advanced web search page, with one notable exception.

15

Although all three results appear to be from Amazon, one is an Amazon "associate" and the other is an affiliate.

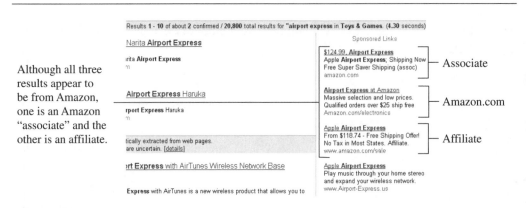

**FIGURE 15-10**    Sponsored links from affiliates or other merchant partners must be clearly labeled.

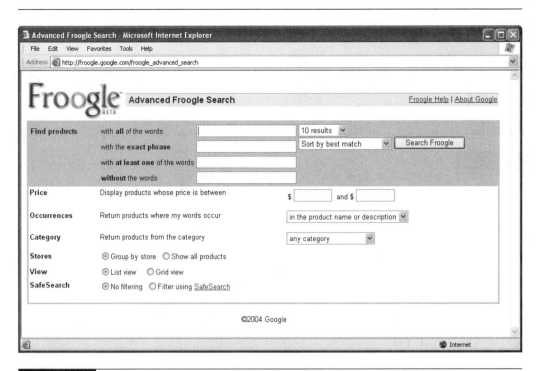

**FIGURE 15-11**    Froogle's Advanced Search page

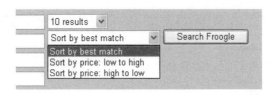

**FIGURE 15-12**   Froogle's Advanced Search word filters feature an additional drop-down menu that lets you control result sort order.

Next to the **Search Froogle** button, note the additional drop-down menu (see Figure 15-12). This menu provides additional control over how your search results are displayed, allowing you to sort results by best match, by lowest to highest price, or highest to lowest price. See Chapter 4 for more details on using these word filters for most effective results.

The rest of the Advanced Froogle Search page (see Figure 15-13) is largely unique, offering many of the same controls you've already seen on Froogle search result pages. The **Price** filter allows you to limit results to products falling within a particular price range. The **Occurrences** filter gives you control over where your search terms must be located in results—in either the product name or description, or only in the product name or only in the description. Remember, because Froogle discovers products by crawling the Web and must often infer product names from surrounding context, this limiter may not always work as expected.

The **Category** filter lets you limit results to one of the 15 different product categories in which Froogle classifies results. These categories include Apparel & Accessories, Arts & Entertainment, Auto & Vehicles, Baby, Books, Music & Video, Computers, Electronics, Flowers, Food & Gourmet, Health & Personal Care, Home & Garden, Office, Sports & Outdoors, and Toys & Games. Products are assigned to categories automatically, using techniques similar to those used by Google to understand the meaning and context of ordinary web pages.

Three final filters allow you to group results in slightly different ways, as shown in Figure 15-14:

- Group results by store, or show all products from all merchants.
- Display results using the List view or Grid view.
- Optionally filter results using SafeSearch.

**15**

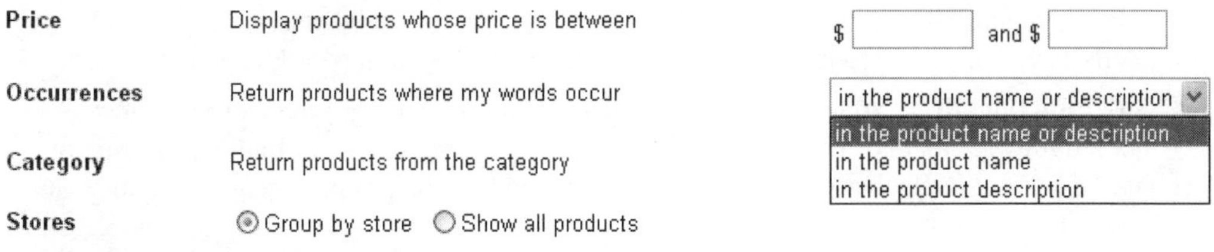

| Price | Display products whose price is between | $ [ ] and $ [ ] |
|---|---|---|
| Occurrences | Return products where my words occur | in the product name or description ⌄ |
| | | in the product name or description |
| | | in the product name |
| | | in the product description |
| Category | Return products from the category | |
| Stores | ◉ Group by store   ○ Show all products | |

**FIGURE 15-13**   Control results displayed by the occurrence of your search term in results.

**FIGURE 15-14**    Filter results by store, by view, or using SafeSearch.

Most advanced search options are available directly from controls in the left column of Froogle result pages. You can also use the exclusion operator and the Boolean OR operator directly in the search form, so whether you choose to preconfigure your search with the parameters you want using the Advanced Search page or adjust the results on the fly after you've run your search is really a matter of your own preferences.

**POWER SEARCHER TIP**    *As with Image search, the SafeSearch filter occasionally misses things, especially when you're using search terms that have multiple meanings. To avoid inadvertently seeing products you might find objectionable, try to use search terms that are as specific as possible, including brand names, product numbers or SKUs, and so on.*

# Getting Your Products Included in Froogle

If you've got an online store, chances are good that Froogle has already crawled and indexed your inventory. If not, or if you want more control over how your products are listed in Froogle, you can register as a merchant with Google and submit a feed with details about your products.

To be included in Froogle, merchants must meet a few basic criteria:

- **Shipping**    You must be able to ship your products anywhere within either the United States or United Kingdom.

- **Product Pricing and Ordering**    You must accept credit card payments (PayPal and other shopping carts are acceptable), the ordering process must be clearly defined and easily navigable, and product pages must list prices in U.S. dollars or UK pounds.

- **Site Functionality**    Your site must be launched and functioning, product pages must not require user login or registration to view, and your site must be in English and cannot have a robots.txt file that prevents Google from crawling the product images directory on your site.

More information about including your products in Froogle, such as Merchant program FAQs, policies, and detailed instructions for creating feeds, is available at https://www.google.com/froogle/merchants/welcome.

# Google Catalogs: An "Undiscovered" Gem

Although Froogle is Google's most prominent shopping search tool, with its own link on Google's home page, the company's seldom-heralded Google Catalogs has actually been around longer. Google Catalogs was launched with little fanfare on December 18, 2001, allowing users to search for products contained in more than 700 popular mail-order catalogs. That's right: Google Catalogs lets you quickly locate products that are otherwise virtually impossible to find in those ever-increasing stacks of catalogs piling up in your bathroom, spare bedroom, or recycling bin.

Today, Google Catalogs (shown in Figure 15-15) searches through more than 5,000 catalogs, focusing on standard U.S. mail-order product catalogs—almost the polar opposite from Froogle, which focuses strictly on merchants that have an online presence.

**FIGURE 15-15**   Google Catalogs searches for products available from mail-order vendors.

One of the more novel aspects of Google Catalogs is how it was created and is currently maintained. Obviously, Google can't "crawl" printed catalog pages in the same way it scours the Web for online product information. Instead, catalogs are torn apart and their content is digitized using scanners. Google uses sophisticated optical character recognition techniques to scan the text in catalogs and "read" product descriptions. This process makes the catalogs searchable and also allows Google to display actual catalog pages as search results.

Figure 15-16 shows a typical search result from Google Catalogs. For each result, you see an image of the cover of the catalog, the specific page on which a product was found (with a yellow translucent box drawn around the product), and a close-up showing product details. Your search terms are highlighted with a yellow background.

Click through on any of these images to view a full-scale scanned image of the page. Above and below these full-page displays, a navigation bar allows you to easily maneuver through the catalog using buttons to move forward or back one page, zoom in or out on a page, or change the view to a single page, double page, or thumbnail view. The navigation bar also provides useful information about the catalog, such as publication date, catalog code, merchant phone number, web site address, and so on. A search box allows you to run another search in the catalog you're currently viewing, all catalogs, or shift your focus out of catalogs altogether to the Web.

As with Froogle, you cannot buy products found in Google Catalogs directly from Google. If the merchant's web site is listed in Google Catalogs search results, you can click the link to visit the site. However, in most cases, this link will be to the merchant's home page, so you'll still have to search the merchant's site to find the product information page. Alternatively, you can call the toll-free number and order the product over the phone.

*Don't bother looking for certain types of content in Google Catalogs. Currently, you won't find any non-U.S. catalogs, travel guides, course catalogs, manufacturers' information sheets, loose-leaf sheets/brochures, or catalogs that are printed with unusually large or small dimensions in Google Catalogs.*

## Google Catalogs Advanced Search

Compared with other Google Advanced Search pages, Google Catalogs Advanced Search page is very basic. In addition to the four advanced search word filters, the Advanced Catalog Search page provides just three additional options. You can limit results to a particular category (these are the same 15 categories used by Froogle). You can limit your search to current catalogs, or all catalogs—including past versions of catalogs from which products may no longer be available. And you can opt to filter Catalog results using SafeSearch.

It's not clear whether Google intends to maintain Google Catalogs as a comprehensive, up-to-date service. As with many projects at Google, Google Catalogs was started as an interesting experiment, and because of its utility the service remains online. Whether it evolves into a fully supported shopping search service like Froogle remains to be seen.

Catalog cover    Catalog page          Close-up of product details

**FIGURE 15-16**    A Google Catalogs result page

**15**

# Beyond Google: Shopping Search Across the Web

Because Froogle is built using the same crawler technology that discovers content for Google's web search index, it's one of the most comprehensive shopping search services on the Web. But a number of other specialized shopping search services are available that offer additional features not available in Froogle.

Unlike Google, which accepts no money for inclusion or placement of organic listings from merchants, most other shopping search services have a combination of paid and free content. Some merchants pay additional fees to become a "featured store" or "featured merchant," thus ensuring that their listings will be featured prominently in search results. Quite often, in addition to having the top rankings, you'll also see the merchant's logo displayed in search results. These pay-for-placement programs are similar to the text-based sponsored links you see in Google and on other search engines. As you scan search results, remember that these top positions are not necessarily an indication that a merchant is reputable, but rather that they've paid to be in the top positions.

Most shopping search engines offer a number of unique features that make them better choices for doing product research and helping you find online merchants than simply searching a general purpose web search engine. Some of these features include:

- The ability to sort your results by store name, price, product rating, merchant rating, and other factors

- The ability to compare several different products by feature and price

- The total price to purchase online, including product cost, shipping, handling, and sales taxes

- Product reviews from professionals or consumers who've actually purchased and used a product

- Reviews and ratings from customers who've purchased products

- Lists of popular products, based on what people are actually searching for or, in some cases, purchasing

- E-mail alerts notifying you of price changes in products you want to track

Just as with web search, it's easy to develop a habit for your "favorite" shopping search service. But no single shopping search service currently has a comprehensive set of features that makes it the "best" choice for all purposes. If you actively use the Web to research and shop for products online, it behooves you to play around with all the services described in this chapter.

## Ask Jeeves Product Search

Although Ask Jeeves (http://www.askjeeves.com) has a specialized product search button, you can search for products directly from the main search box without using any specialized commands or operators. If your query suggests that you might be looking for information about a product, you'll see a set of "related categories" links in a red box at the top of the page, in addition to regular web search results beneath them. Clicking one of these related categories links displays thumbnail images of specific products. This gives you the option to compare both shopping search results and web search results on the same screen.

For example, a search for **digital camera** generates a set of "related categories" such as cameras, lenses and accessories, batteries, and so on.

Clicking the **cameras** link causes Jeeves to replace the related categories links with a new set of thumbnail photographs of actual products (your web search results do not change). The products displayed are the most popular choices for a particular category at Pricegrabber, Ask Jeeves' shopping search partner. Clicking a link beneath a thumbnail image displays a full information page about that product. You also have the option to see all products in a category.

Ask Jeeves offers two other ways to search for product information. If you search for a specific product by name, the refinement process is skipped and you're shown photos of the product itself. You can also select the **Products** radio button beneath the search form, and this will run your search directly in the Ask Jeeves product search, bypassing web results altogether.

## Shopzilla

Compared to other shopping search engines, Shopzilla's scope is huge: more than 24 million products from nearly 50,000 stores. Taking a cue from Google, Shopzilla (http://www.shopzilla.com) created its own proprietary result-ranking algorithm that goes beyond simple product or category keyword matching. "ShopRank" looks at a number of relevance measures, including pricing, merchant reputation, product popularity, and product availability, to determine how results are presented.

Shopzilla also has a unique feature that lets you browse for similar products based on visual characteristics. For example, if you are looking to send flowers to someone, rather than entering keywords such as "long stemmed red roses," you can simply click the **similar products** icon next to an appealing arrangement, and your results will be limited to products that resemble the one you clicked.

> **POWER SEARCHER TIP** *AOL recently launched a shopping search powered by Shopzilla, offering some unique features not found elsewhere. The service is available to anyone on the Web at http://search.aol.com/aolcom/shopping_home.jsp, though it's especially worth a look if you're a registered member of AOL.*

## NexTag

In contrast to Shopzilla, NexTag (http://www.nextag.com) is a comparatively small shopping search engine. However, unlike other shopping search services, which include both paid and unpaid listings, all of NexTag's 2,000-plus merchants pay for listings. The company says this is a quality-control mechanism that ensures that only the most serious merchants with the best quality goods are included in search results.

Like most shopping search sites, NexTag offers a feature that calculates the "true price" of products, factoring in shipping and sales tax charges in addition to product price. NexTag's true price is calculated in real time by taking information directly from shipping tables or formulas provided by retailers.

NexTag also offers a unique price history graph for tech-related products, showing fluctuations in average price over time. Trying to decide whether to buy a product now or wait for a price drop? These charts provide you with valuable clues about the general pricing trends for a product and may make your buy or wait decision easier. The company also offers free price change alerts via e-mail.

15

# Pricegrabber

In addition to powering Ask Jeeves' product search, Pricegrabber (http://www.pricegrabber.com) maintains its own shopping search engine. Boasting "millions of products from thousands of merchants," Pricegrabber features some novel product categories, such as new cars, home mortgages, and other products.

Pricegrabber offers an interesting "shopping list" feature that let's you compare a basket of products among a number of different stores. This helps you with those sometimes tricky calculations about whether it's more cost effective to buy all products from a single merchant or to split up your order among a number of online stores.

Like NexTag, Pricegrabber allows you to set up product trackers and get e-mail alerts whenever prices change for products you're interested in.

# Shopping.com

Shopping.com (http://www.shopping.com) is one of the most popular shopping search and product comparison sites on the Web. The site features more than one million consumer reviews, and you can search for five million products from over 3,000 stores.

Shopping.com is the result of a merger between the former Dealtime shopping search engine and Epinions.com, a consumer review site. This makes it a valuable resource for both product research and price comparison.

Epinions reviews are written by consumers, not professionals, based on their own experiences with products. This hands-on knowledge often provides unique insights into products that you might not get from professional reviews. Epinions review authors are also rated by Shopping. com's user community. These ratings reflect the reputation for credibility and accuracy of each reviewer.

# Yahoo! Shopping

Yahoo! Shopping (http://shopping.yahoo.com) claims to be the largest shopping search engine, combining product listings from the more than 17,000 merchants participating in Yahoo!'s own shopping network with product information gathered by crawling the Web, resulting in more than 150 million product offerings. You can browse categories or search for products across all categories or in one specific area.

Search results display 15 product listings sorted by relevance. You can change this view to display results sorted by lowest price or highest price by clicking a link. You're also presented with a list of "related searches" links that can help you narrow your search. Depending on your query, these might be major brands or even specific product models. You also can compare up to ten products at one time, in a side-by-side chart.

One of Yahoo! Shopping's coolest, most useful features is called SmartSort (see Figure 15-17). If you're looking for computers or electronics equipment, select the product category you're looking for at http://shopping.yahoo.com/smartsort/.

Say you're looking for a television. Rather than typing in search terms you use sliders to specify how important (from not important to very important) certain features are to you. As you move the sliders, search results change dynamically, showing the products that best match your criteria. Even cooler, these results are compared to one another, explaining why a result was ranked third rather than first, for example.

**FIGURE 15-17**   SmartSort lets you play around with sliders to change the parameters of your product search.

## Ask the Expert

# Expert Tips for Shopping Search

## Six Questions for Power Searcher Danny Sullivan

**Q: What's your favorite Google search tip?**
**A:** There are so many, but a simple one many people would benefit from is to switch their preferences to see 100 results at a time. It's all too easy to get locked into viewing only 10 results. Get more, and get more diversity.

Like others, I also love the Google cache links as a way to see what was on a page if it has suddenly disappeared or is no longer available.

**Q: What kind of search strategy do you use when using Google or Froogle for shopping?**
**A:** If it's an unusual or hard-to-find item, I go straight to Froogle, because it does a great job of comprehensively scanning the Web just for shopping items. However, I may then turn to Yahoo! Shopping or Shopping.com to see how a particular merchant was rated, since Froogle doesn't offer this.

**Q: Are there specific tools or techniques that lead to best results? (For example, operators, filters, special keywords, and so on.)**
**A:** There are plenty of commands that can be used, but I'm more into getting people just to word things differently. Think about how the author of the information would have written it. What words might they have used? Use that language—change your query—be specific. Beyond this, I love the exclusion operator (-) as a way to remove words that are obviously bringing up the wrong results.

**Q: When would you not use Google for shopping search?**
**A:** First, if I already know a good merchant. I never buy books via Froogle. I go straight to Amazon. Second, for a really popular product, I might prefer the better features that Yahoo! Shopping might offer.

**Q: What search engines or other web resources do you use to go beyond Google for shopping search?**
**A:** Yahoo! Shopping and Shopping.com I turn to the most for going beyond Froogle. But since I'm U.K.-based, I tend to make use of Kelkoo (http://www.kelkoo.com) and the U.K. Shopping.com site (http://dealtime.co.uk). I also turn to CNET (http://www.cnet.com/) if I want advice on computer-oriented products.

**Q: What's your favorite power searching tip?**
**A:** Beyond thinking differently about queries, I think understanding search engine math commands—the minus sign (–), the quotation marks (""), and the plus sign (+) can be a huge help. Those who want to go a step beyond this should understand how the **site:** command works and how domain names are structured. That can make for some powerful searching.

*Danny Sullivan is the founder and editor of* Search Engine Watch *(http://www .searchenginewatch.com) and chair of the U.S. Search Engine Strategies conferences.*

# Chapter 16

## Google as Your Travel Companion

Google is truly a global phenomenon. By offering local versions in more than 100 countries, and providing access in nearly 100 interface languages, Google has become one of the world's most popular web search engines. Combine this global reach with Google's comprehensive index of the Web, and you have a tool that's ideally suited for helping you tour the world, whether virtually or to help you plan your terrestrial travels.

This chapter is divided loosely into two parts. The first part explores the various incarnations of Google throughout the world and how to use these localized sources to focus in on finding information in specific regions or languages. The second part takes a more practical tack, showing you how to use Google as a virtual travel concierge.

# Google 'Round the World

When you go beyond Google in your own country and language for the first time, it's easy to get a bit confused about exactly what you're seeing, and how to control the search engine to ensure you're getting the type of results you want. Three different variables can come into play when you experiment with Google beyond the familiar trappings of the English-language Google.com. These variables are:

- The Google interface language
- The Google search and result language
- Google's site in your local domain

Let's look each of these variables and how they interact with one another in more detail.

Google's interface language is the language you see when interacting with the search engine. The interface language includes the text, buttons, and links on the Google home page. It's also the language used on other pages throughout the service, such as help pages, frequently asked questions, and preferences. As said, Google supports nearly 100 interface languages, as shown in Table 16-1. Google automatically detects the language your web browser is configured to display and uses this as the default interface language.

You have two options if you want to change your interface language. The easiest is to select your preferred interface language from the Google Preferences page, available via the link next to any search box. You can also modify your browser's language preference, but this will affect what you see from all multilingual web sites you visit, not just Google search results, so use this option with care.

 *To modify your language preferences in Internet Explorer, select **Internet Options** from the **Tools** menu. Click the **Languages** button to view or modify your current language preferences.*

Key point: Changing your interface language changes Google's look and feel, but *changing the interface language does not affect your search results.*

| | | | |
|---|---|---|---|
| Afrikaans | Albanian | Amharic | Arabic |
| Azerbaijani | Basque | Belarusian | Bengali |
| Bihari | Bork, bork, bork! | Bosnian | Breton |
| Bulgarian | Catalan | Chinese (Simplified) | Chinese (Traditional) |
| Croatian | Czech | Danish | Dutch |
| Elmer Fudd | English | Esperanto | Estonian |
| Faroese | Finnish | French | Frisian |
| Galician | Georgian | German | Greek |
| Guarani | Gujarati | Hacker | Hebrew |
| Hindi | Hungarian | Icelandic | Indonesian |
| Interlingua | Irish | Italian | Japanese |
| Javanese | Kannada | Klingon | Korean |
| Kyrgyz | Latin | Latvian | Lithuanian |
| Macedonian | Malay | Malayalam | Maltese |
| Marathi | Nepali | Norwegian | Norwegian (Nynorsk) |
| Occitan | Oriya | Persian | Pig Latin |
| Polish | Portuguese (Brazil) | Portuguese (Portugal) | Punjabi |
| Romanian | Russian | Scots Gaelic | Serbian |
| Serbo-Croatian | Sesotho | Sinhalese | Slovak |
| Slovenian | Spanish | Sundanese | Swahili |
| Swedish | Tagalog | Tamil | Telugu |
| Thai | Tigrinya | Turkish | Turkmen |
| Twi | Ukrainian | Urdu | Uzbek |
| Vietnamese | Welsh | Xhosa | Yiddish |
| Zulu | | | |

**TABLE 16-1**   Google Is Available in Nearly 100 Interface Languages

By contrast, Google's search and result language has everything to do with the type of results you'll see. Google is multilingual—queries can consist of words in any language that Google understands, and your results will include the best results Google can find for those terms. Many of the results are typically in the language of your query terms, but Google's ability to perform multilanguage searching means that it can direct you to any of the billions of pages in its web index—regardless of language—as long as those pages are relevant to your search terms. For pages published in Italian, French, Spanish, German, and Portuguese, Google often adds a **Translate this page** link next to the title on result search pages.

**16**

| Arabic | Bulgarian | Catalan | Chinese (Simplified) |
|---|---|---|---|
| Chinese (Traditional) | Croatian | Czech | Danish |
| Dutch | English | Estonian | Finnish |
| French | German | Greek | Hebrew |
| Hungarian | Icelandic | Indonesian | Italian |
| Japanese | Korean | Latvian | Lithuanian |
| Norwegian | Polish | Portuguese | Romanian |
| Russian | Serbian | Slovak | Slovenian |
| Spanish | Swedish | Turkish | |

**TABLE 16-2**    Google Supports More Than 30 Search Languages

If you don't want multilingual results, you can restrict results to pages written in any of the 30 or so languages Google currently understands. To restrict results to a single language, use the drop-down menu on the Language Tools or Advanced Search pages (see Chapter 2). To restrict results to more than one language, use the check boxes on the Preferences page to select each language you'd like included in results. Table 16-2 lists all the search languages Google supports.

POWER SEARCHER TIP    *Google generally favors result pages in the language that matches your query language. If you want more results in a particular language, use search terms in that language. This will skew results toward that language without eliminating pages written in other languages.*

The third variable in this equation is Google's site in your local domain. Google operates more than 100 country-specific web sites around the world, and it's continually adding new local domains (see Table 16-3). In most cases, when you visit one of these local versions of Google, the interface language is the same as the dominant language spoken in that particular country.

Google doesn't actually have a physical presence in all these countries, despite appearances. The Google domain for a local service always uses that country's top-level domain identifier, such as www.google.ru (Russia), www.google.tt (Trinidad and Tobago), or www.google.pn (Pitcairn Islands). The interface language is also localized, as are the search options, which allow you to limit results to sites within the country's domain. But when you search on any Google site—anywhere in the world—your query is automatically routed to one of Google's global data centers for processing, and your results are drawn from the same index of web pages, regardless of where your query originates.

This doesn't necessarily mean you'll get identical results from a search in your local domain and from Google.com, however. They'll be *similar,* but may have subtle differences, depending on your search terms, the country-specific Google domain you're using, and the IP address of the computer you're using (Google uses this to guess your physical location—whether you're actually searching from within a particular country or elsewhere). To see this in action, try the query **football** on both Google.com and Google.com.br (Brazil). Some results are similar; others are unique. And the total number of results reported is slightly different for each site.

| | | |
|---|---|---|
| **American Samoa**<br>www.google.as | **Anguilla**<br>www.google.off.ai | **Antigua and Barbuda**<br>www.google.com.ag |
| **Argentina**<br>www.google.com.ar | **Armenia**<br>www.google.am | **Australia**<br>www.google.com.au |
| **Azərbaycan**<br>www.google.az | **België**<br>www.google.be | **Brasil**<br>www.google.com.br |
| **British Virgin Islands**<br>www.google.vg | **Burundi**<br>www.google.bi | **Canada**<br>www.google.ca |
| **Chile**<br>www.google.cl | **Colombia**<br>www.google.com.co | **Costa Rica**<br>www.google.co.cr |
| **Côte d'Ivoire**<br>www.google.ci | **Cuba**<br>www.google.com.cu | **Danmark**<br>www.google.dk |
| **Deutschland**<br>www.google.de | **Djibouti**<br>www.google.dj | **Ecuador**<br>www.google.com.ec |
| **El Salvador**<br>www.google.com.sv | **España**<br>www.google.es | **Fiji**<br>www.google.com.fj |
| **France**<br>www.google.fr | **The Gambia**<br>www.google.gm | **Gibraltar**<br>www.google.com.gi |
| **Greece**<br>www.google.com.gr | **Grønlands**<br>www.google.gl | **Guatemala**<br>www.google.com.gt |
| **Guernsey**<br>www.google.gg | **Honduras**<br>www.google.hn | **Hong Kong**<br>www.google.com.hk |
| **India**<br>www.google.co.in | **Ireland**<br>www.google.ie | **Israel**<br>www.google.co.il |
| **Italia**<br>www.google.it | **Japan**<br>www.google.co.jp | **Jersey**<br>www.google.co.je |
| **Kazakhstan**<br>www.google.kz | **Korea**<br>www.google.co.kr | **Latvija**<br>www.google.lv |
| **Lesotho**<br>www.google.co.ls | **Libyan Arab Jamahiriya**<br>www.google.com.ly | **Liechtenstein**<br>www.google.li |
| **Lietuvos**<br>www.google.lt | **Luxemburg**<br>www.google.lu | **Magyarország**<br>www.google.co.hu |
| **Malawi**<br>www.google.mw | **Malaysia**<br>www.google.com.my | **Malta**<br>www.google.com.mt |
| **Mauritius**<br>www.google.mu | **México**<br>www.google.com.mx | **Micronesia**<br>www.google.fm |
| **Mongolia**<br>www.google.mn | **Montserrat**<br>www.google.ms | **Namibia**<br>www.google.com.na |
| **Nederland**<br>www.google.nl | **Nepal**<br>www.google.com.np | **New Zealand**<br>www.google.co.nz |

**16**

**TABLE 16-3**   Google Operates in More Than 100 Countries Around the Globe

| | | |
|---|---|---|
| **Nicaragua**<br>www.google.com.ni | **Norfolk Island**<br>www.google.com.nf | **Österreich**<br>www.google.at |
| **O'zbekiston**<br>www.google.uz | **Pakistan**<br>www.google.com.pk | **Panamá**<br>www.google.com.pa |
| **Paraguay**<br>www.google.com.py | **Perú**<br>www.google.com.pe | **Pilipinas**<br>www.google.com.ph |
| **Pitcairn Islands**<br>www.google.pn | **Polska**<br>www.google.pl | **Portugal**<br>www.google.pt |
| **Puerto Rico**<br>www.google.com.pr | **Rep. Dem. du Congo**<br>www.google.cd | **Rep. Dominicana**<br>www.google.com.do |
| **Rep. du Congo**<br>www.google.cg | **România**<br>www.google.ro | **Russia**<br>www.google.ru |
| **Rwanda**<br>www.google.rw | **Saint Helena**<br>www.google.sh | **Saint Vincent and the Grenadines**<br>www.google.com.vc |
| **San Marino**<br>www.google.sm | **Saudi Arabia**<br>www.google.com.sa | **Schweiz**<br>www.google.ch |
| **Singapore**<br>www.google.com.sg | **Slovenskej republiky**<br>www.google.sk | **Suomi**<br>www.google.fi |
| **Sverige**<br>www.google.se | **Taiwan**<br>www.google.com.tw | **Tchad**<br>www.google.td |
| **Thailand**<br>www.google.co.th | **Trinidad and Tobago**<br>www.google.tt | **Türkiye**<br>www.google.com.tr |
| **Türkmenistan**<br>www.google.tm | **Uganda**<br>www.google.co.ug | **UK**<br>www.google.co.uk |
| **Ukraine**<br>www.google.com.ua | **United Arab Emirates**<br>www.google.ae | **Uruguay**<br>www.google.com.uy |
| **Venezuela**<br>www.google.co.ve | **Viet Nam**<br>www.google.com.vn | |

**TABLE 16-3**   Google Operates in More Than 100 Countries Around the Globe (Continued)

*Occasionally your search results will differ for identical search terms when Google automatically routes your query to a different data center than usual, for load balancing or other performance reasons. This can happen even when you issue the same query from the same computer just moments apart!*

A key difference between Google.com and Google in your local domain: Country-specific Googles have additional controls that allow you to restrict results to pages only in that country, and in some cases, to the local language(s) spoken in the country. Figure 16-1 shows the French

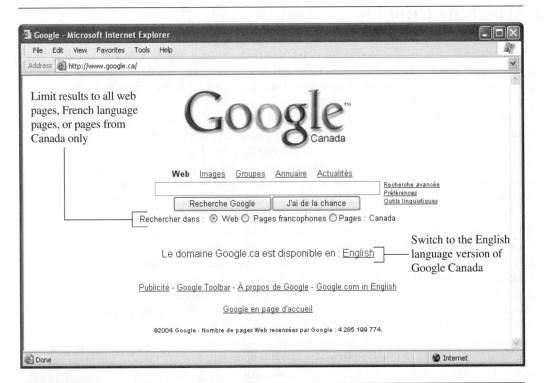

Limit results to all web pages, French language pages, or pages from Canada only

Switch to the English language version of Google Canada

**FIGURE 16-1**   Country-specific Googles offer additional controls for limiting search results.

version of Google Canada. Radio buttons allow you to limit searches to French-language pages or Canadian web sites. A link beneath the search form lets you change to the English language version of Google Canada.

So, what's the bottom line with all these variables related to language and location? The short answer is that in most cases, you're going to get best results using the configuration that Google defaults to for your particular country or language (as determined by your browser settings). Google was designed to be as easy as possible for anyone to use, anywhere in the world. Chances are good that the default configuration for your country and language is the one you'll be most comfortable using.

That said, if you have a need to override the defaults, bear in mind the following rules of thumb:

■ Changing the interface language has *no effect* on search results.

■ Searching on Google.com vs. a country-specific Google will occasionally produce *subtly different* results.

■ Using search terms with identical meanings in different languages (for example, house, casa, maison) will produce *very different* results, in most cases, with *both* Google.com and country-specific Googles.

**16**

# The Armchair Googler

Visiting travel-related destinations on the Web is an increasingly popular activity. Market researcher Hitwise estimates that visits to travel-related web sites accounts for as much as 5 percent of all online traffic. If you've ever used the Web for planning travel, you can understand the attraction. In addition to the vast amount of information about destinations throughout the world, you can also find great deals on travel—if you know where to look for them.

And there's the rub. A 2004 survey by Jupiter Research suggests that a majority of web users believe that there's no single online travel service that always offers the best travel deals. Most people surveyed say they use more than two web sites to find what they're looking for. The large travel sites, such as Expedia, Orbitz, and Travelocity, all offer great information and deals, but they aren't comprehensive. They don't have information from smaller discount airlines, for example. They may also miss special web-only deals available only on a travel operator's web site.

Quite frankly, although Google can help you find travel-related information and web sites, it's not one of the search engine's greatest strengths. It's not that Google falls down on the job when it comes to helping you find travel-related information. Rather, the category is so huge, and in many cases, so ambiguous, that it's difficult for the search engine to understand the intent behind many travel-related queries. Is someone searching for "Turkey" looking for information about the country or about the bird that's an integral part of the U.S. Thanksgiving holiday? Is someone searching for "Cambodia" looking for hotels, or information for a homework assignment on the famous temples at Angkor Wat? The inherent ambiguities in language make it challenging for Google (or any search engine, for that matter) to fathom user intent, especially from just one or two search terms.

Another challenge is that the online travel market is huge, and there are literally tens of thousands of travel-related web sites. Jupiter Research estimates that the global online travel market will reach $79 billion by 2009. With such a lucrative market as travel, it's no surprise that competition is intense for top Google rankings for prime travel search terms. Hotels, airlines, rental car agencies— all of these travel services firms employ legions of search engine optimization specialists to boost the visibility of their web sites—sometimes using tactics that create headaches for both Google and searchers alike.

## Caution! Affiliate Spam Ahead

A particularly popular tactic used by players in the travel industry is to employ affiliates who specialize in capturing top rankings in Google and other search engines. Sometimes these affiliates are so successful that their top rankings displace the listings of the company that employed them! In recent years, it hasn't been uncommon to see affiliate results in top positions push the listings of their employers far down in rankings.

All this jostling for position creates a problem for the searcher. When you're searching for a hotel, for example, even if you use precise, explicit terms, you may end up with what may be politely termed less-than-useful results. Initially, your results will likely appear to be relevant— that is, until you click what looks to be a promising result only to realize that you've landed on an affiliate site or travel aggregator rather than the official page of the firm you were looking for.

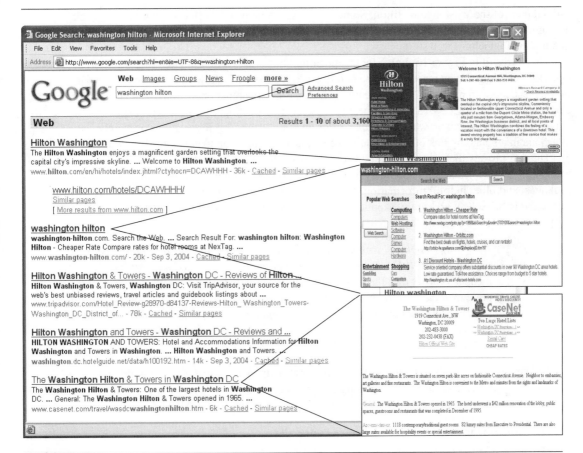

**FIGURE 16-2**    Look closely at these search results—some aren't what they appear to be at first glance!

Figure 16-2 shows an example of search results for the query **washington hilton**. The top result is for the home page of the Hilton Washington hotel on Connecticut Avenue (this is one of several Hilton hotels in Washington, but the only one known locally as the Hilton Washington). You can assume that this is an "official" site by looking at the URL: It's a page from the corporate web site Hilton.com. Google gets an "A" grade for placing this result at the top of the list.

But now look at result #2. At first glance, it certainly looks like an appealing result. The title of the page is "washington hilton." The URL is "washington-hilton.com." What's not to like about a result that Google has determined merits a coveted #2 position?

Plenty. washington-hilton.com is simply a collection of links to *other* travel agencies that offer reservations. Mousing over these links reveals elaborate URLs that undoubtedly contain affiliate tracking and payment codes. Click one of these links and you've just earned the affiliate a fee. And to make matters worse, you also probably ended up at a web site that's not much closer to the

16

official page of the Washington Hilton. Sometimes these "chain-link" effects can go on for click after click after click, fattening the paycheck of the affiliates but leaving the hapless searcher lost in a limbo of unhelpful web sites.

The #5 result in Figure 16-2 also looks appealing, but in this case the URL offers important clues that should give you reason to pause before clicking. The URL shows that this result is a page two levels deep within the site "casenet.com," which has no apparent connection to the Hilton hotel chain. Close scrutiny of a URL is your best defense against wasting your time with pages that are tangential to your search or, worse, that may offer dubious "deals" for reservations or merely serve as a chain in an ongoing link of pages that serve no purpose other than to generate affiliate fees.

This isn't to say that all travel-related search results have links to bogus or less-than-helpful web pages. Some affiliate sites and many travel aggregators do actually offer appealing deals, travel packages, and other helpful information. You can save yourself a lot of time and aggravation by treating search results with healthy skepticism, looking closely at the page title, the snippet, and the URL structure *before* clicking through to a page.

**POWER SEARCHER TIP** *A missing "cached" link in a search result is a sure tip-off that a page isn't what it seems. If Google has crawled a page, the main reason it won't offer a cached link is that the page author has expressly forbidden Google to cache the page with the "noarchive" meta tag mentioned in Chapter 3. Although some web sites use this tag as a mild form of copyright protection, most web authors using the tag (at least at this point) have something to hide—they may be using the "cloaking" spam techniques described in Chapter 4.*

The key to successful searching for travel information is to be as specific as possible with your search terms. Rather than using the single-word queries described earlier, use descriptive, specific queries stating explicitly what you're looking for. Queries that work well include:

- **scuba diving great barrier reef cairns australia**
- **camping blue lagoon iceland**
- **kruger park safari tree lodge**

**POWER SEARCHER TIP** *Using double quotes to search for explicit phrases also helps, especially when you combine phrases with single search terms. For example, the first query in this list could be written as **"scuba diving" "great barrier reef" cairns australia** for even more specific results.*

## The Traveler's Treasure Trove: The Google Directory

Although it's easy to go astray searching for travel information in Google's vast index of billions of web pages, there's another path that offers high-quality, focused pointers to some outstanding resources on the Web. The Google Directory (http://directory.google.com; see Figure 16-3), mentioned several places elsewhere in this book, is tiny by comparison with Google,

**FIGURE 16-3**    The Google Directory offers a wealth of focused pointers to travel-related information.

with just four million listings. But all of these listings have been selected and annotated by human editors who have spent time visiting and evaluating the included sites.

You can find travel-related information in many categories in the Google Directory. Start with the Recreation Category. Numerous subcategories here are worth exploring: The Travel category has more than 8,000 listings, the Outdoor category over 18,000, and the Roads and Highways category sports more than 1,600 listings.

Another excellent category for travel-related information is the Regional category. Here you can dive directly into links to sites with information about specific countries, regions, and cities throughout the world.

The World category is also useful. This category offers links to pages about countries and regions in their native lands and languages.

16

Of course, the Google directory is searchable as well. Start your search by selecting a category or subcategory, and the search form allows you to limit results just to that specific category—a great way to filter out the noise, affiliate spam, and ambiguous results that you might otherwise get with a search of the full Google web index.

# Finding Travel Bargains with Google

Searching the Web for travel information can be like working with a good travel agent—or coping with a surly airline employee. Sometimes you hit pay dirt; other times information overload leaves you frustrated and more confused than before you started your search.

One area where Google really shines when it comes to travel-related information is helping you ferret out deals from sites you're already familiar with. The trick here is to search for specific "magic keywords," limiting your search with Google's **site:** operator to airline, rental car, hotel, or other travel sites that are already known to you.

You can do this in several ways. The simplest is to run a Google search for the words "deal," "special," "lowest fare," and so on, and limit results to a specific travel-services provider. Figure 16-4 shows an example of the kind of results you get for this type of search on the United Airlines web site. Notice that each search term is separated by the Boolean OR ( | ) symbol so that you'll get results using any or all of the search terms.

Of course, not all of the more than 2,100 results shown in this example will be directly relevant to your specific needs, but you get the idea. There's little chance you could have discovered all these offers by stumbling around clicking links on the United.com web site!

You can sharply reduce the number of results by expanding your query to include specific cities or destinations. With an airline site, you can use city names, or get even more specific by adding a three-letter airport code to your query.

To work properly, the query must be constructed so that Google ANDs the destination city or airport code search terms, and ORs the rest of the query. Enclose the OR part of the query in parentheses, as shown, and you'll get the results you expect.

This technique won't work on all travel-related web sites—only those that publish static pages in addition to providing fares extracted in real time from a reservation system database. But it's worth experimenting on any travel-related site that you visit frequently.

Once you've created a query that produces successful results, you can leverage it again and again by saving it as a Google Web Alert, described in Chapter 9. Simply cut and paste your query from the search box into the Google Web Alert form at http://www.google.com/webalerts, and you'll automatically get an e-mail whenever the travel service provider publishes a new deal that matches your criteria.

POWER SEARCHER TIP    *Yahoo! Alerts (http://alerts.yahoo.com) offers a special tool that will notify you by e-mail whenever a specific fare you're interested in tracking increases or decreases. You can even have the alert sent to your mobile phone to take advantage of a particularly good deal before it changes again.*

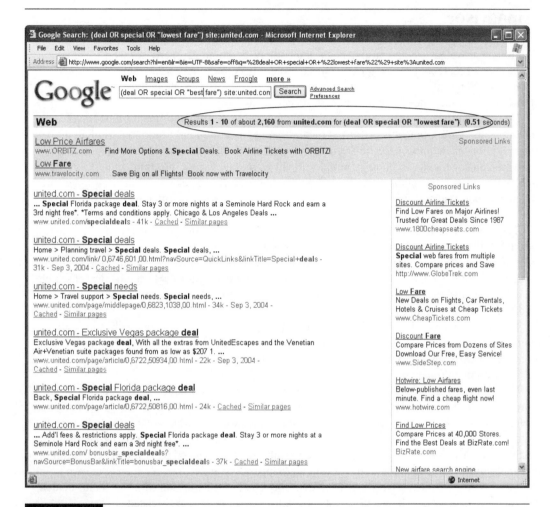

FIGURE 16-4    Finding deals is easy when you limit your search to a specific travel provider's web site.

# Beyond Google: Searching for Travel Online

Travel search is emerging as a promising "vertical," with a number of players offering tools to help you research your trips, find deals, and explore destinations after your arrival. You're probably familiar with large travel sites such as Expedia, Orbitz, and Travelocity. All these sites can help you with your travel arrangements. Increasingly, however, we're seeing a new breed of travel search service emerge—one that's more like a concierge who goes beyond finding good deals to help you find the *best* travel experiences available.

## TripAdvisor

TripAdvisor (http://www.tripadvisor.com) is a specialized travel search engine—with a twist. While some travel sites help you find deals and book reservations, TripAdvisor works like an online concierge, recommending places to stay and things to do once you reach your travel destination. You can't make reservations or bookings on TripAdvisor, though the company does offer links to partner sites that can handle those details for you.

TripAdvisor uses a combination of technology and human editors to find the best travel content on the Web. Content is organized by destination, making it easy for you to find all the relevant information about specific destinations, such as the British Virgin Islands, for example.

The site uses crawler technology to index travel-related web sites, including guidebooks, hotel web sites, tourist information sites, and so on. An editorial team tracks down the best magazine and newspaper articles, reviews, travelogues, and other travel stories written by professional and amateur travelers. Both types of content are blended seamlessly into TripAdvisor search results.

The goal is to provide a comprehensive, high-quality source of information for any place in the world. In addition to this information, TripAdvisor provides ratings for all things travel-related. For example, hotel listings are ordered by popularity. This makes it easy to see which hotels or tourist destinations are favored by other travelers—information not readily available at other travel search sites. You can also read user reviews for hotels and other tourist attractions from fellow travelers who've actually experienced the locations.

If you'd rather avoid crowded tourist spots, TripAdvisor also offers personalized vacation-planning information on hotels, destinations, and things to do. You need to register and create a profile for this, but TripAdvisor requires only a few pieces of information to register, and it has a reasonable privacy policy.

Your profile is used to structure your search results based on your preferences. Creating a profile is similar to working with a good travel agent who asks a lot of questions about your preferences to help you plan your travel. These questions include: Do you prefer to "rough it" or stay in a luxurious hotel? What size hotel do you prefer? Do you prefer off-the-beaten-path destinations or popular tourist spots? Is your ideal vacation focused on rest and relaxation or nonstop activity? Do you prefer to travel with a group, or do you like to explore on your own?

Interestingly, Google itself regards TripAdvisor as a high-quality resource for travel information. TripAdvisor results appear frequently in the top ten listings for many travel-related queries.

*Online newspaper travel sections are also excellent sources of information. For example, the* New York Times, Washington Post, London Times, *and other newspapers all provide a vast amount of archived travel content at no charge. Another excellent resource is the Travel Library at http://www.travel-library.com/.*

## Yahoo! Travel

Yahoo! Travel (http://travel.yahoo.com/) is a hybrid service, offering extensive travel-planning information for 17,000 cities, 80,000 hotels, and what Yahoo! calls "140,000 things to do." Yahoo! has several partnership arrangements in place with travel vendors such as Travelocity, Hotels.com, and others to help you find and book reservations directly through the site. It also features "travel guides" and "interest guides," with content from Gorp.com and other professional travel resources. These guides provide information pages for major cities throughout the world, with lists of popular hotels, recommended things to do, recommended restaurants, entertainment, shopping, links to "sites we like," and much more.

One of Yahoo! Travel's coolest features is user ratings and reviews. Anyone can sign up to simply rate (from one to five stars) or write a review of places, hotels, attractions—anything that's listed on the site. Wondering whether to eat at a particular restaurant in an unfamiliar city? Check out the user ratings and reviews before you go.

## Mobissimo

Once you've researched your trip with Google and sites such as TripAdvisor, you need to make your various transportation and lodging bookings. One option is to use an online travel agency such as Expedia, Orbitz, or Travelocity. But you may find yourself spending a lot of time comparing your results from those sites and visiting the sites of companies that aren't available through the online agencies.

An easier approach is to use a specialized travel meta search engine. Mobissimo (http://www .mobissimo.com) searches the sites of the travel providers themselves, such as HolidayInn.com and JetBlue.com, for their best options. Mobissimo also checks online agencies such as Orbitz and consolidators such as Hotels.com for their best offers.

Mobissimo's design philosophy is similar to Google's, with a Spartan interface that serves a single purpose: to help you find the best travel deals. Unlike other travel search services, Mobissimo searches the sites of suppliers all over the world. Results show the supplier of the ticket (airline, travel agent, and so on), the country in which they're located (the initials in the white oval), and price in U.S. dollars, automatically converted from other currencies. Clicking a **Details** link takes you directly to the provider offering the ticket. There's also an option to e-mail details of the fare to someone else.

Mobissimo plans to expand its services over the coming year, adding hotel and rental car search. The company also plans an ambitious "fuzzy search" that will allow you to express your travel needs in broad terms, such as "I want to travel to Europe this summer." The results will not only suggest economical city connections but will recommend the best time during the season to make your trip.

## SideStep

Like Mobissimo, SideStep (http://www.sidestep.com) is a meta search engine that searches for the best prices directly on the sites of ticketing services providers. SideStep is a free, downloadable program that installs as an Explorer window in IE.

SideStep aggregates the results it finds and makes it easy to comparison shop among popular online travel sites. SideStep's choices are displayed right alongside those from Expedia, Travelocity, and other major sites.

When you've located the most compelling deals, SideStep links you directly with the provider to make your bookings.

16

# Expert Tips for Travel Searching

## Six Questions for Power Searcher Irene McDermott

**Q: What's your favorite Google search tip?**

**A:** When I don't know how to spell something, I type it into Google. I love the way it suggests the correct spelling—usually. Sometimes, so many people misspell a word on their web pages that Google comes up with a wrong alternative spelling.

I also make intense and repeated use of enclosing search phrases in quotation marks. I use this technique to find the names of half-remembered poems that my patrons desperately seek.

**Q: What kind of search strategy do you use when searching for travel and entertainment information on Google?**

**A:** I search for travel and entertainment information on Google in the same way I use it for all information. I usually use Google to search for a known item. If I know the exact title of the thing, I will type it in the search space and enclose it in quotation marks. If I just know the general type of thing that I am looking for, I type several fairly unique keywords into the search box.

**Q: Are there specific tools or techniques that lead to best results? (For example, operators, filters, special keywords, and so on.)**

**A:** The only specific technique that I use is to put a phrase in quotes.

**Q: When would you not use Google for searching for travel information?**

**A:** I would not *start* with Google for travel information. I would first visit subject-specific portals.

If there was something *specific* that I wanted to do or see, I would look it up on Google to find its web page. For instance, when I visited Chicago, I wanted to take an architectural tour. So I visited Google and typed "Chicago architecture tour" and got the web page of the Chicago Architecture Foundation (http://www.architecture.org/). It was just the thing I wanted!

**Q: What search engines or other web resources do you use to go beyond Google when searching for travel information?**

**A:** I start by visit the ticketing sites: CheapTickets (http://www.cheaptickets.com), Travelocity (http://www.travelocity.com), Expedia (http://www.expedia.com), Yahoo! Travel (http://travel.yahoo.com), Orbitz (http://www.orbitz.com), Priceline (http://www.priceline.com), Hotwire (http://www.hotwire.com), Mobissimo (http://www.mobissimo.com), Site59 (http://www.site59.com), and QIXO (http://www.qixo.com) to see what kind of deals are out there. If I find a good price on a particular airline, I will visit the airline's web page to see if I can find out anything further.

For more specific destination information and commentary, I would turn to the online sites of the travel publishers: Lonely Planet (http://www.lonelyplanet.com/), Fodor's (http://www.fodors.com), Gayot.com (http://www.gayot.com), and Let's Go (http://www.letsgo.com/).

For flight tracking, I use both the Cheap Tickets "Travel Resources" (http://www.cheaptickets.com/trs/cheaptickets/content/travel_tools/main_travel_tools.xsl) and the one on the *USA Today* travel site (http://www.usatoday.com/travel/front.htm). Both sites also have good information about the weather around the country and real-time airport delays.

In Los Angeles, we drive everywhere and the traffic is really bad. So when I have to cross town, I check Sigalert.com (http://www.sigalert.com). This site offers a real-time layout of the speeds on the freeways. I just click on a diamond to get the gory details of accidents and traffic jams. It is the same information that the radio and television traffic reporters get. I often use a map site in conjunction with the Sigalert site to plan my best route, either from Mapsonus (http://www.mapsonus.com) or MapQuest (http://www.mapquest.com).

**Q: What's your favorite power searching tip?**
**A:** I use Google mostly for specific, known item searching. When I want to just see what is out there on a particular subject, I turn first to that directory of quality information, the Librarian's Index to the Internet (http://lii.org). If I know of a site and want to find more like it, I go to the Yahoo! Directory (http://dir.yahoo.com/). I type in the name of the site, then look at the other things listed in the same directory category. Also, About.com (http://about.com) often has funky and obscure web site listings on nonacademic topics—like camping, for instance. I usually search that site to fill out my overview of any particular subject.

*Irene McDermott writes the Internet Express column for* Searcher Magazine *and is the author of* The Librarian's Internet Survival Guide *(Information Today, 2002).*

16

# Chapter 17

## Business Information and Competitive Intelligence

Before the Web, finding business information almost invariably meant a trip to the library, a call to the company's investor relations department, or other offline sleuthing activity. Today, there's an abundance of business information online, produced by companies, news organizations, investment banks, and scores of other third-party information aggregators. This cornucopia of knowledge is a boon to anyone doing business research, but it can also quickly lead the unwary searcher into a quagmire of information overload.

This chapter takes a generalist approach to finding information about businesses, focusing particularly on techniques for using Google to surface interesting facts about companies of use to journalists, investors, potential customers, partners, suppliers, and, of course, competitors. If you're looking for information about local businesses in your own neighborhood, you're better off using Google Local, described in detail in Chapter 5.

# Finding Company Information

Today, we take it for granted that most companies, at least the larger ones, have a domain name of the form "companyname.com" or an equivalent, such as microsoft.com, toyota.com, or airfrance.com. It's hard to believe that as little as ten years ago most businesses were so clueless about the Web that literally anyone could purchase a famous company's domain name. In 1994, Josh Quittner, a journalist for *Wired* magazine, purchased the mcdonalds.com domain name and offered to *give* it to the McDonald's corporation, and yet was all but ignored by the company. He recounts that in 1994 there were only "2.5 people" running the official domain name registry for the *entire* Web. It's a fascinating and hilarious glimpse of the Web in its early days (read the story at http://www.wired.com/wired/archive/2.10/mcdonalds.html).

Today, of course, anyone trying to register the domain name of a large business (if it's even available) is inviting a prompt and costly lawsuit. Most businesses have secured not only the ".com" domains with their company name, but the other top-level variants such as ".net," ".org" and so on. Truly web-savvy companies have gone even further, locking up related domain names such as "company-inc.com," "company-corp.com" and a wide range of other variations. Google itself has registered hundreds of domain names, including all of the top-level variations on Google.com, and others such as Googlebot.com, googlegear.com, adultgoogle.com, and even misspelled names such as Goolge.com. The company has also registered some completely unrelated, and in some cases bizarre, names such as totalrequestslive.com, foofle.com, and even 466453.com. (Why? The number spells "Google" on a touchtone telephone pad.)

POWER SEARCHER TIP

*Want to see who Google has an official beef with over a domain name? The WIPO (World Intellectual Property Organization) maintains a searchable database of domain name disputes and actions at http://arbiter.wipo.int/domains/ search/index.html.*

Of course, neither Google nor any other company has the resources or time to register every possible domain name that includes their company name. Even though Google is a trademarked term, company outsiders have registered thousands of domain names that include the word "Google." A small sample of these registered domain names is shown in Table 17-1. The company frowns upon others using its trademark in domain names and in some cases has taken legal

| | | |
|---|---|---|
| audiogoogles.com | bannedingoogle.com | bejinggoogles.com |
| casinogoogle.com | celebritygoogles.com | congressmangoogles.com |
| correogoogle.com | eyegoogle.com | fungoogle.com |
| getpaidbygoogle.com | google86.com | googleaccount.com |
| googleaccounting.com | googleail.com | googleamerica.com |
| googlearabia.com | google-auction.com | googlecash.us |
| googleclassactionlawsuit.com | googledaddy.com | googleemial.com |
| googlefoods.com | google-foundation.com | google-gift.com |
| googlehardware.com | googlehotmail.com | googlemai.com |
| googlemeelmo.com | googlemetop.com | googlepoodle.com |
| googleprofitinfo.com | googleserver.net | googleskills.com |
| googlesoap.com | googlesoffun.com | googlester.net |
| googlestreet.com | googletechnologies.com | googlethebeatles.com |
| googletravels.com | googleturk.com | googlevegetarian.com |
| googlevirus.com | googlewantads.com | googleyed.com |
| googlezoo.com | it-google.com | joygoogle.com |
| justgoogleit.biz | love-google.com | moneywithgoogle.com |
| pcgoogle.org | pricegoogle.net | stgoogle.com |
| szgoogle.net | theantigoogle.com | thegooglesecrets.com |
| thisisgoogle.com | warezgoogle.com | yahgoogle.com |

**TABLE 17-1** Some of the Thousands of Domain Names Containing "Google," Most of Which Are Not Owned by Google (source: Resourceshelf.com)

action to make pretenders take down web sites or even relinquish too-similar domain names to Google (see Figure 17-1).

All these variations on domain names can present a problem for a searcher doing business research. Although it's largely safe to simply visit "company.com" for most large organizations, there's no guarantee that strategy will take you to an "official" web site for many smaller companies.

Fortunately, Google does a good job finding the web sites of most medium-to-large companies when you simply use the company's name as your search term. In many cases, in addition to featuring the company's web site as the #1 or #2 result, Google will also provide up to three headlines with a link to additional current news stories about the company, as shown in Figure 17-2.

Once you've found a company's official site, you have a couple of options for exploring it further. To get a rough approximation of how big the site is, at least in terms of the number of pages Google has crawled, click the **More results from** link that's usually found at the bottom of the indented result. This is the same as running a query of the form **"site:www.companyname .com" companyname**, limiting your results to pages just from the company's site. The number of results reported is generally a good indicator of the number of pages Google has crawled from

17

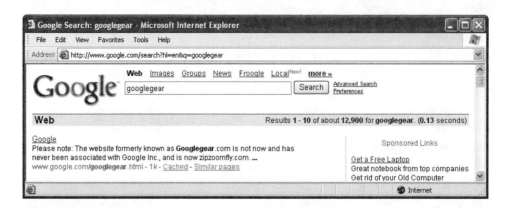

**FIGURE 17-1**  Google filed a lawsuit against the company using the name "Googlegear.com" in 2001 and, as these search results show, won the rights to the name.

the site, because most companies use their name at least once on every page of their site, as shown in Figure 17-3. It pays to experiment with this query, running it without the company's name. In some cases you'll get more results, but in others you'll get fewer results—a counterintuitive effect that illustrates why you should only consider the reported number of results as rough approximations, not absolute totals.

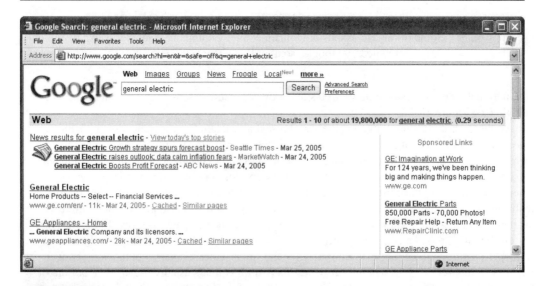

**FIGURE 17-2**  Searching for a company by name generally returns both a link to the company's web site and news headlines.

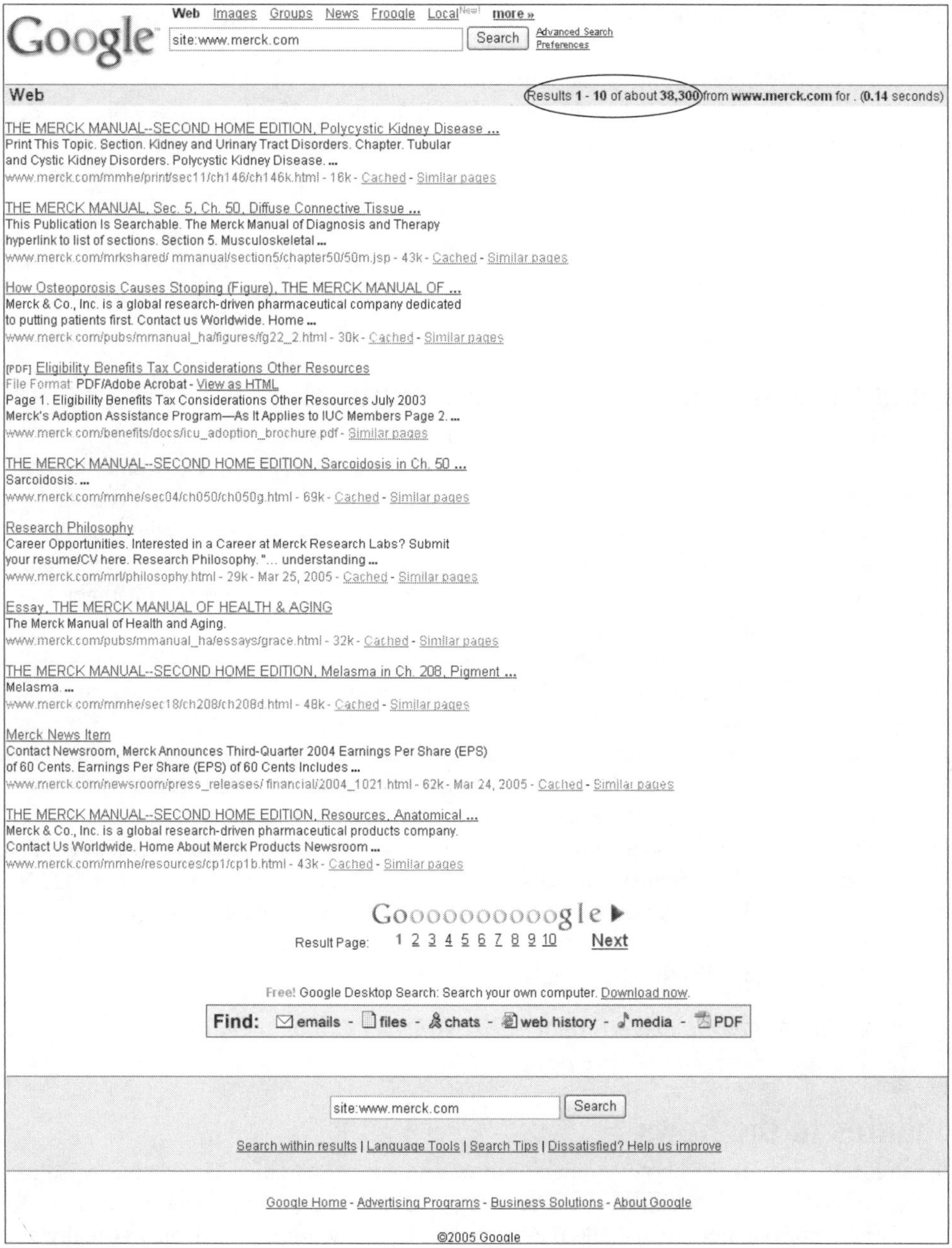

**FIGURE 17-3**    Google has crawled more than 38,000 pages from the merck.com web site.

You can continue searching, limiting your search to the company's web site by simply adding or substituting query terms in the search box of the result page. Another option is to click the **Search within results** link at the bottom of a result page. This will display a new, blank search page that automatically limits results to pages from within the site.

Official corporate web sites are valuable sources of information, but they're very one-sided, presenting the company in the most favorable light possible. For serious business research, you almost always want to use a corporate site as a starting point, and expand your investigation to other sources of information.

*To discover a company's marketing channels, visit its site and click the **for more information** link. Look for a "How did you hear about us?" list—it's usually a checklist where the company is expending marketing dollars.*

## Keeping Up with the Competition: Google Alert

New information is constantly being added to the Web. How can you keep up with it all, particularly if you're tracking a competitor and their new business activities? The web research managers described in Chapter 11 offer one approach. Another is to use Google Alert (http://www.googlealert.com) to monitor new additions to Google. The service lets you automate the process of running regular queries that match specific search criteria (such as information about a company). Any time Google adds something new matching your search terms, you'll get a notification e-mail from Google Alert.

This makes it easy to keep up with any topic you're interested in. Simply create a set of keywords, and Google Alert will run a search each day and automatically send you an e-mail alert when the query produces new results.

Google Alert also lets you take advantage of Google's advanced search options, by clicking the **more** button next to each query. This displays a form with many advanced search features, allowing you to include or exclude terms as well as filter by language, domain, and so on.

Although the service sends you an e-mail every time new results appear, you can also view your results online by clicking **Browse Results**. Google Alert results are also available as HTML or RSS feeds, or via TrackBack (a popular utility that lets your weblog display Google Alert results, among other things).

Google Alert is available by subscription, starting at $4.95 per month.

*Google's own web alerts (described in Chapter 9) don't offer as many features as Google Alert, but they are free.*

## Companies in the News

Google can locate news stories about companies in several ways. Searching Google News is the easiest, most effective way to surface current news stories. Google's news crawler is tuned to retrieve information from more than 4,500 media sources throughout the world, on a virtually constant basis. Even though Google's primary crawlers visit news sites, they do so far less frequently than the news crawler. However, even though you'll almost always have better luck finding the freshest news via Google News, stories are only kept in the News index for a limited time—typically between one and four weeks. If you find a news story that you want to keep, it's important to save it using one of the web research managers described in Chapter 11.

When searching for news about a company, you'll generally get good results simply by searching on the company's name. For more search options, see the description of Google News advanced search capabilities in Chapter 14.

**POWER SEARCHER TIP**   *Some of the most thorough coverage of a company often comes from the local newspaper in the company's home town. You can limit your Google News searches to a specific newspaper with the* **source:** *operator, described more fully in Chapter 14.*

Although Google News doesn't store news stories older than 30 days, the main Google web index often has older stories from news sources that don't remove their articles from general web access. News.com is an example of a site that maintains some of its news stories in a permanent archive available to anyone, as shown in Figure 17-4.

**FIGURE 17-4**   An example of a News.com story from 1999 found through a Google web search

Don't overlook press releases. Even though press releases are invariably spun to portray a company in the most favorable light, they nonetheless contain good factual information that you can rely on, because it's coming directly from the source (that is, unless it's a company like Enron, but that's another story). Press releases are also valuable sources for discovering the names of a company's core management team. Searching for information about a company's executives can often turn up results that are peripherally related, but possibly very valuable, offering different perspectives on a company that you might not find by taking the "straight at 'em" approach.

*An easy way to find press releases is to search for a company name using the Google News Advanced Search page, using the **Return only articles from the news source named** field to restrict results to press release agencies such as Business Wire, PR Newswire, and others.*

## Beyond Google: Other Corporate News Resources

Chapter 14 describes Google News and several other useful general-purpose news search engines in great detail. There are two other sources you should consider when you're searching specifically for company-related news.

### Topix.net: Corporate News Pages

Online news aggregator Topix.net (http://www.topix.net) offers customized news pages for more than 5,500 public company and industry verticals. You can access any of these pages by searching on a company name or by using the URL http://www.topic.net/com/*xxx*, replacing the "*xxx*" with a stock symbol of a publicly traded company. Figure 17-5 shows an example of a company news page from Topix.

### Yahoo! Directory: News Services | Press Releases

The Yahoo! Directory provides an extensive list of online press release distributors (http://dir. yahoo.com/Business_and_Economy/Business_to_Business/News_and_Media/News_Services/ Press_Releases/). Start with the listings in the "Most Popular" section and then use distributors found in the alphabetical listings to find more specialized sources of information.

## Profiling Executives and Board Members

Finding information about executives and corporate board members can be a challenge. Much of the information you can find on the Web consists of sugar-coated "official" profiles, carefully spun by corporate public relations departments. Your best approach for finding this type of information is to use an executive's full name as they use it (including middle initials, but remember that Google ignores periods), together with the company name. Both names should be quoted as phrases.

The company news page for Target, a large U.S. retailer

Often, a better way to find information about executives and board members is to use sources other than Google. Here are a few of my favorites.

## SEC Info

SEC Info (http://www.secinfo.com/) slices and dices the regulatory filings all public companies are required to submit to the U.S. Securities and Exchange Commission. Even though the SEC has its own searchable database (EDGAR), I find SEC Info to be a better search resource, because it provides more flexibility. It's a great resource for finding out information such as executive compensation, stock options, board memberships, and other personal details that must be disclosed—not to mention other general information about companies.

**POWER SEARCHER TIP**   *SEC Info offers free e-mail alerts, dispatched to you any time a company you're tracking files a form with the Securities and Exchange Commission.*

## eComp Online

eComp Online (http://www.ecomponline.com/) has executive compensation data on over 50,000 executives and board members at more than 12,000 U.S. companies. You can get a lot of this information from other sources, but eComp Online puts it directly at your fingertips, searching either by company name or stock symbol.

## The American Society of Association Executives

Associations, by their very nature, are excellent resources for finding information about executives. Executives join associations for networking and career advancement opportunities, and association web sites like to showcase the talents of their prominent members.

With more than 23,000 individual members, The American Society of Association Executives (http://www.asaenet.org) is the largest organization of association executives and industry suppliers in the world. ASAE also serves as the international secretariat of the Global Forum of Societies of Association Executives, a global network for the association management profession worldwide. The number of people who belong to associations represented by ASAE total more than 200 million, though some people have more than one membership.

# Uncovering Business Networks

Businesses, of course, do not operate in a vacuum. They have extensive networks of customers, partners, suppliers, and other organizations or groups that they work with. Sometimes businesses disclose these relationships in press releases, regulatory filings, or elsewhere. But in other cases, working arrangements are not directly disclosed, for competitive reasons.

Even if a company has kept mum about its relationships, clues inevitably turn up on the Web that you can use to weave together patterns and discover who is working with whom. Start with the obvious: Examine a company's web site for links to business partners. There is no magical combination of advanced search operators that makes this easy, unfortunately. You'll certainly want to limit your search using the **site:** operator, but you can't limit your search for all external links using a combination such as **site:boeing.com –inurl:boeing.com**, because the two operators cancel each other out. You *can* use the **site:** operator in conjunction with the **inanchor:** operator (which only looks for text in links) to search for magic keywords, such as "customer," "partner,"

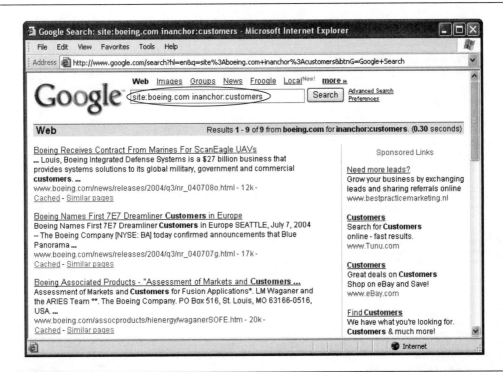

FIGURE 17-6    Combining the **site:** operator with the **inanchor:** operator provides helpful but mixed results.

"supplier" and so on, as shown in Figure 17-6. But this query produces mixed results, with some pages referring specifically to customers, while other pages consist simply of general information about customer service. Ultimately, browsing a web site may be the most efficient way to discover company relationships.

If you broaden your scope from a company's web site to the entire Web, Google's **link:** operator is one of the most powerful tools at your disposal for uncovering relationships. Recall the hoary cliché "Birds of a feather flock together"? On the Web, that truism can be expressed as "Companies of a feather link together." Who considers a company important enough to link to it? You can find out using the **link:** operator, as shown in Figure 17-7.

Remember, you cannot combine the **link:** operator with any other advanced search operator. Also, the number of reported links is an approximation, and Google says that it shouldn't be interpreted as an exact count of links pointing to a particular page.

**17**

POWER SEARCHER TIP    *Can't remember the exact phrasing of a famous quote, saying, or cliché? Try variations in Google as quoted phrases (e.g., "birds of a feather nest together" vs. "birds of a feather flock together"). The version with the greatest number of results is the one found most often on the web, and is likely the correct one.*

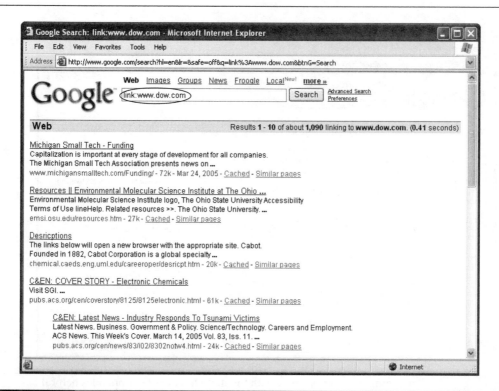

**FIGURE 17-7**    The **link:** operator shows you many of the sites on the Web that have linked to a target site.

Press releases are another excellent source for uncovering business networks. By convention, whenever companies work together, a press release will typically feature quotes from executives of all companies involved. Searching on the names found in press releases often turns up other, often unexpected relationships, as shown in Figure 17-8.

If you spend time following these linkages, a pattern or network will likely soon appear. Indeed, this technique is used by law-enforcement personnel to map out the structure of criminal and terrorist networks. The approach can be equally effective for discovering legitimate—but hidden—business networks.

# Beyond Google: TouchGraph GoogleBrowser

Sometimes the easiest way to discover relationships is to create a linkage map. Although you can do this by hand, the TouchGraph GoogleBrowser (http://www.touchgraph.com/TGGoogleBrowser.html) creates relationship charts from Google search results. This is what

**FIGURE 17-8** Searching for information about the executives mentioned in this press release turns up all sorts of interesting related information.

the Web "looks like" to the search engine, visually displaying the linkages between web sites. The TouchGraph GoogleBrowser uses Google's database to determine and display the linkages between a URL and other pages on the Web, in much the same way the **link:** operator works. However, results are displayed visually, showing relationships between URLs. Figure 17-9 shows the linkage connections between H-P and many other companies in the technology sector.

POWER SEARCHER TIP　*Another useful tool that displays the visual relationships between URLs is Grokker, described in Chapter 20.*

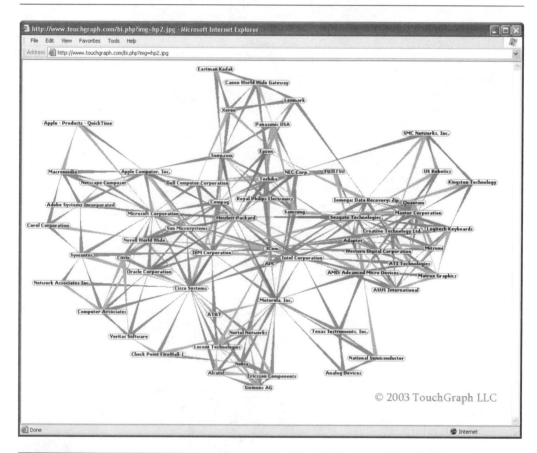

**FIGURE 17-9**　The TouchGraph Google Browser shows visual relationships among URLs.

# Finding What Companies Don't Want Found

Up to now, the focus has been on finding information that companies have deliberately put on the Web, intending it for general consumption. Although this information can be very useful, information that companies *don't* want found can be even more valuable. This can be confidential information that was either accidentally placed on the Web or uploaded by people unaware that once information is put on the Web it's virtually impossible to "erase" it.

The techniques I'm about to describe are all legal. However, in using them, you should think carefully about the ethical issues involved with uncovering "hidden" information. Some of this information, especially straightforward material a company deliberately posted to a public web site, is fair game. Uncovering it is no different than going to a public library. It's only when you start snooping in the shadowier areas that you may have pause for concern. The reason some of this information is available on the Web is because the people who put it there were unaware that the Web has a very, very long memory, or that it could be found by clever searchers. On the other hand, if someone puts sensitive or confidential material in a public forum like the Web, one can argue they should have understood the potential consequences ahead of time.

The most straightforward way to find "hidden" information is to use Google's cache. If a page has changed on a company's web site, the cached copy of that page will still reflect the earlier version, at least until Google recrawls and reindexes the page. Depending on the URL, the cached version may be less than a day old or up to 30 days old. Ironically, as Google gets better and better at frequently updating its index, the usefulness of cached pages will diminish.

## Exploring the Web's History with the Wayback Machine

A far more enduring archive of the Web is maintained by the Internet Archive (http://www .archive.org). This organization has been crawling the Web since 1996, saving copies of web sites in a massive database that's freely available to anyone.

Archive.org's search tool, The Wayback Machine, allows you to enter a URL and displays results showing dates when it took a snapshot of the web site (see Figure 17-10). The archives are not comprehensive—you won't find a complete crawl of every web site on every day in the past. But the records are comprehensive enough to give you a good sense of what previous versions of a web site looked like. Figure 17-11 shows what one of the very first versions of Google looked like, all the way back in November of 1998.

The Internet Archive is particularly useful for finding pages that a company has altered or removed from its corporate web site. Sometimes this information is harmless or insignificant. In other cases, however, it can prove to be a smoking gun. I've heard a number of anecdotal stories about how investigators used the Internet Archive to assist with investigations into some of the corporate chicanery by the likes of MCI, Enron, and others. Apparently, some of these companies published information on their web sites that was later proven to be false or misleading. Although this information was quietly removed from the companies' web sites, copies remained in the Internet Archive.

17

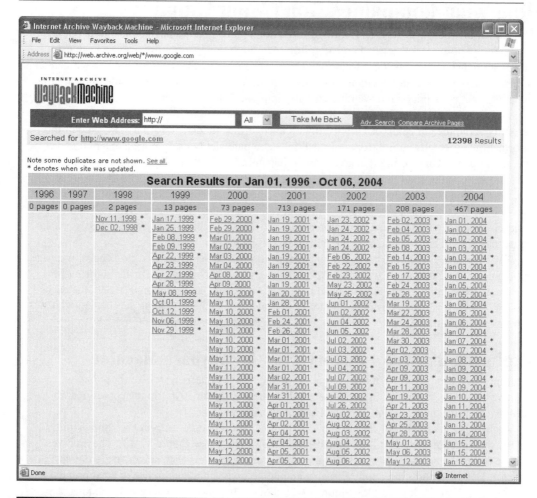

FIGURE 17-10   The Wayback Machine has more than 12,000 archived pages from Google.

 *Looking for legal-related information about a company? Try Findlaw (http://www.findlaw.com), an extensive repository of legal information that uses a Google-powered site search engine.*

## Very Revealing: What You Can Learn from Robots.txt

Chapter 1 touched briefly on the Robots Exclusion Protocol, which allows web sites to block crawlers from accessing content using a special file called "robots.txt." This file serves as a "keep out" notice to crawlers, specifying the files, folders, and directories that the site owner

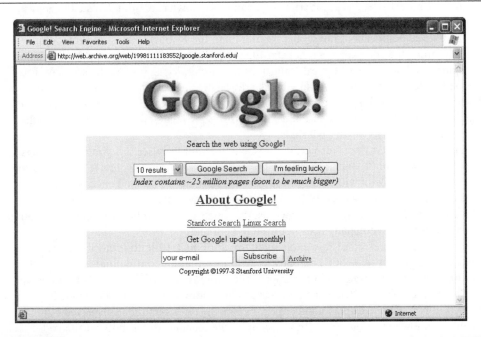

**FIGURE 17-11**    Google, back in 1998, when the search engine emulated Yahoo!'s exclamation
point in its logo!

does not want the crawler to access. Figure 17-12 shows the robots.txt file from a large online
news organization.

This is a fairly simple file, and it's being used to keep the crawler out of just a few directories
on the company's web site. "User-agent: *" means all crawlers; individual crawler names such
as GoogleBot or Yahoo!'s Slurp could also be listed here. The excluded directories are for things

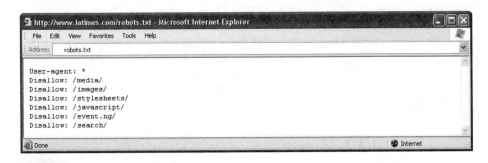

**FIGURE 17-12**    The contents of a robots.txt file tells a crawler which parts of a site are off-limits.

**17**

such as images, stylesheets, and JavaScript—content most crawlers aren't interested in anyway (other than images). The rest of the site is fair game for crawlers to explore.

Two important points about the robots.txt file. First, the Robots Exclusion Protocol is *voluntary,* meaning the contents of a robots.txt file is a *polite request* to keep out. All the major search engines, and indeed most ethical companies that use crawlers, respect the protocol. But a robots.txt file does nothing to physically block crawlers from accessing content on a web site. It's an extremely weak form of protection, and companies that use it to "protect" sensitive information do so at their peril, because there's nothing to prevent a crawler from ignoring the robots.txt file and indexing anything it finds.

Second, the robots.txt file is also easily displayed in your browser. All you need to do is type "www.*sitename*.com/robots.txt" in your browser's address window, and if the site has an unprotected robots.txt file, it will be displayed, just as in Figure 17-12. And once you see the files and directories listed in the robots.txt file, you can easily browse them simply by entering them in the browser's address window. In other words, the robots.txt file *explicitly* reveals the location of files on a web server a company does not want to be found!

Web-savvy companies don't rely exclusively on a robots.txt file to protect sensitive information. The easiest step for a company to keep information confidential is to store it on password-protected web servers that are impossible for crawlers to access. Other companies detect whether the robots.txt file is being accessed by a crawler or a browser, and if it's a browser, will redirect and display another page before the robots.txt file is displayed.

You never know what you might find examining the contents of a robots.txt file and trying to manually access the content that a site does not want crawlers to find. Sometimes it's uninteresting, boring stuff—but on some occasions, you'll turn up some very revealing nuggets of information you won't otherwise be able to find.

## The Fine Art of Googledorking

When Google first began indexing Microsoft Office documents in 2001, a new world was opened up to searchers. Unfortunately, many people who had been using web servers as a convenient online backup system, or who believed that search engines only indexed web pages, were caught off guard. Today, there are literally thousands of files in non-web formats that contain all manner of confidential or sensitive information put online by people who would likely be horrified if they knew Google was crawling and indexing these documents.

People who put unprotected confidential information on the Web are known as "Googledorks." The term was coined by Johnny Long, a researcher and developer for Computer Sciences Corp., and refers to "an inept or foolish person as revealed by Google." "Googledorking" is the process of trolling the Internet for confidential information. Googledorking *is not* hacking in the traditional and often illegal sense of the word. Rather, the fine art of Googledorking involves using a combination of Google's advanced search operators with a set of business-related magic keywords that can surface all manner of interesting information that typically wouldn't be found through most types of searching.

Most confidential information that's not password protected is stored in non-HTML file formats. Therefore, Google's **filetype:** operator is particularly useful for helping you cut to the chase to find specific types of documents stored on a company's web server.

Successful Googledorking requires limiting your search to the file types where the information you're looking for is most likely found, and using magic keywords as your search terms. Table 17-2 shows common types of business information and typical file types.

Here's a list of magic keywords to start with—use your own imagination to come up with other common words or phrases that can be used in conjunction with confidential information:

- total, profit margin, sales projection, forecast
- budget, finances, return on investment, roi
- salary, executive compensation, hourly wages, benefits
- confidential, internal use only, do not circulate, without permission
- marketing plan, product development schedule
- acquisitions, mergers, partnerships, joint venture, agreement, contract

In addition to using the **filetype:** operator, you'll also want to experiment with other operators that limit results to specific parts of a web page, such as **intitle:**, **inanchor:**, and others. Also remember that non-HTML documents make up just a scant fraction of the total Google web index, so you'll often want to use the Boolean OR operator to expand the potential pool of results.

So what exactly can you find through Googledorking? Let's start with a simple example. Many organizations create budgets using Microsoft Excel spreadsheets. A simple search using the query **budget filetype:xls** (see Figure 17-13) returns more than 163,000 results! Not bad, but in these results, the word "budget" can appear anywhere in the spreadsheet. We can get even more specific by looking for files that are named "budget.xls."

| File Format | Types of Business Information |
| --- | --- |
| Word (.doc) | Memos, reports, notes, informal presentations |
| Excel (.xls) | Budgets, expense reports, capital allocation plans, salary information |
| PowerPoint (.ppt) | Presentations |
| Portable Document Format (.pdf) | White papers, reports, brochures, formal presentations |
| Postscript (.ps) | Scientific or academic papers, formal research reports |

**TABLE 17-2**    Common Business Information File Types

17

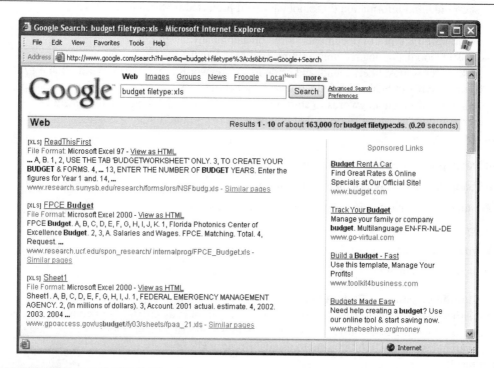

**FIGURE 17-13**     Results from Googledorking for the word "budget" with the limiter "filetype: xls" returned more than 76,000 results in Excel spreadsheet format.

Looking for salary information? The magic keywords "salary" and "compensation" are the best for uncovering compensation information—but we can make this Googledork even more on target by thinking about *other* words that would likely appear in documents containing salary information, such as "confidential," "internal use only," and so on. Figure 17-14 shows the results of a relatively simple Googledork using the word "salary" as the keyword, limiting results to files with the word "confidential" in the title. You can get even more specific by limiting results to particular file types.

Remember, unless documents are blocked using the robots.txt file, or secreted away in a password-protected area of a web site, GoogleBot will likely find them, regardless of what's written on the document itself. Figure 17-15 shows us 39,000 documents that have been placed on the Web with requests not to be cited or circulated without permission. Not the best way to restrict a document to a limited readership!

**FIGURE 17-14**    Results from a Googledork for the word "salary" with the limiter "intitle: confidential" returned more than 24,000 results.

The most powerful form of Googledorking, particularly for competitive intelligence research, is to limit searches to a specific company's web site with the **site:** operator. Although you'll frequently be disappointed, on occasion when you use a fortuitous combination of appropriate operators and magic keywords, you'll be quite amazed at what turns up.

## The Value of Gripe Sites

Want to know the real scuttlebutt on a company? Then pay a visit to one of the countless "consumer complaint" sites on the Web. Here you'll find the first-person stories of disgruntled customers, unhappy employees—even a few nasty asides from competitors. Apart from being the web-equivalent of reality TV, these sites are a valuable source of "buzz" and opinion from unofficial sources. They're a great source for gathering information about problems a company may be experiencing with a product or service, and in some cases, what the company is doing to address the problem.

17

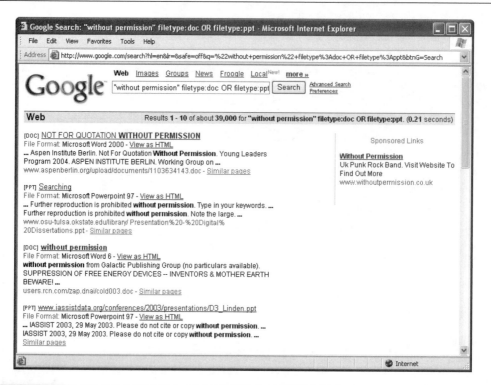

**FIGURE 17-15**     Results for a Googledork on the phrase "without permission" with the limiters "filetype:doc OR filetype:ppt".

An excellent listing of consumer complaint sites can be found in the Yahoo! Directory's Consumer Advocacy and Information | Consumer Opinion category, at http://dir.yahoo.com/Society_and_Culture/Issues_and_Causes/Consumer_Advocacy_and_Information/Consumer_Opinion/.

# Beyond Google: Business Search Engines

Although there are lots of ways of using Google to find business-related information, there are also numerous excellent business-specific search engines and directories. Here's a sampling of some of the best.

# Business.com

Business.com (http://www.business.com) is a specialized directory developed by a team of industry experts and library scientists, containing more than 400,000 listings within 25,000 industry, product, and service subcategories. The directory is categorized by business function, making it easy to browse and drill down to specific business types. Business.com also features both breaking news stories, categorized by industry, and job listings through wholly owned subsidiary work.com.

Business.com achieved notoriety when the service was first launched by paying $7.5 million dollars for its domain name—a record that still stands today.

# Hoover's

Hoover's database of 12 million companies features in-depth coverage of 40,000 of the world's top business enterprises (http://www.hoovers.com). Compiled and maintained by an editorial staff of 80 editors and researchers, information about companies is packaged in a consistent format, including dozens of key metrics and statistics.

Basic business profiles on Hoover's are available free of charge. Much more extensive information is available to paying subscribers.

# Kompass

Kompass (http://www.kompass.com/) offers information on more than 1.8 million companies, in over 75 countries. Listings include more than 23 million key product and service references, 3.6 million executive names, 750,000 trade and brand names, and more than 50,000 "classification codes" developed by the company to facilitate categorization of business services.

Like Hoover's, Kompass is free to search, and basic company profiles are free. Subscribers have access to more in-depth reports.

# MSN Money: Stock Research

MSN's Money site (http://moneycentral.msn.com/investor/research/welcome.asp) is a general-purpose portal for investors. The stock research category has some excellent tools for finding corporate information, including a company report, access to SEC filings, and lots of additional information.

# Yahoo! Finance

Like MSN Money, Yahoo! Finance (http://finance.yahoo.com) is designed primarily as an information resource for investors. The site has extensive resources, including company information, news, industry profiles, and numerous interactive tools for doing more extensive analysis on companies.

17

Ask the Expert

# Expert Tips for Business and Competitive Intelligence Searching

## Six Questions for Power Searcher Mary Ellen Bates

**Q: What's your favorite Google search tip?**

**A:** Use Google to identify *sources,* not necessarily answers. For example, I was looking for trends in the VoIP (Voice over Internet Protocol) market, so I just threw "voip" into the search box. But instead of clicking through most of the links in the search results page, I just looked through the URLs to get ideas of where to poke around next. So, for example, I got pointers to the FCC's fact sheet on VoIP, I identified two newsletters on VoIP, and I learned who the major VoIP conference organizer was. I also scanned the sponsored links along the right margin to identify the VoIP providers willing to pay to advertise.

**Q: What kind of search strategy do you use when searching for business and competitive intelligence information on Google?**

**A:** A lot depends on the kind of research I'm doing. If I'm looking for information on a specific company, I'll use Google to identify the company's web site, if it isn't obvious. If I am researching an industry, I might use the Google Directory to find trade or professional associations pertaining to the industry, which will lead me to reports on trends in the industry. I also use Google to discover industry-specific terms that will help me narrow my query. I've had surprisingly good luck searching Google Groups for industry buzzwords and for pointers to really obscure information. When I was looking for information on 800 MHz public safety radio systems, for example, I found some tremendous material in Google Groups.

**Q: Are there specific tools or techniques that lead to best results? (For example, operators, filters, special keywords, and so on.)**

**A:** The important thing is to use the words that the industry uses. As I mentioned before, one of the first things I do is try to discover the lingo used by that industry, so that my searches will be more likely to find targeted information. Since so much business is now international in scope, I also have to remind myself to use British English spelling and phrases as well as American terminology. If I were looking for trends in the aluminum industry and didn't also include the word "aluminium," for example, I'd miss a significant portion of the information out there.

If the company I am researching is relatively small, I may use the back-link feature of Google (link:www.*whatever*.com) to identify web pages that link to that company's web site. This technique doesn't work well for large companies, of course, because there are just too many links pointing to something like www.starbucks.com.

I tend to use the Advanced Search page when I'm using Google; maybe it's because I've been an online searcher since the 1970s, but I like all that structure. I find it helpful to see exactly what search logic I'm using—I want any of these words, and the results definitely have to have this word. I set my preferences to display 50 results at a time; it's way too easy to ignore what's on the second page of search results, and this forces me to review more than just the first ten results.

**Q: When would you not use Google for searching for business and competitive intelligence information?**
**A:** So much of what I need just can't be found in any search engine—in-depth articles from trade or professional publications almost never appear on the open Web, for example. I never feel that a business or CI search is complete without a search of at least one of the value-added online services such as Dialog, Factiva, or LexisNexis. And when I am looking for government information, I usually go directly to the agency, rather than try to find the information through a general-purpose search engine like Google. Using a search tool like firstgov.gov (http://www.firstgov.gov) that is calibrated to government documents is more efficient and usually finds content that is buried deep in an agency's web site.

**Q: What search engines or other web resources do you use to go beyond Google when searching for business and competitive intelligence information?**
**A:** I can barely remember life before the U.S. Securities & Exchange Commission's EDGAR site (http://edgar.sec.gov) that lets us retrieve the SEC filings of publicly traded companies. Those are truly mother lodes of information about companies, and I cannot imagine doing business research without EDGAR. I also use the market research aggregators such as MarketResearch.com (http://www.marketresearch.com) and ResearchAndMarkets.com (http://www.researchandmarkets.com), and the value-added online services.

   I use Teoma (http://teoma.com) when I think that its Resources list in the search results page will point me to link-rich web pages; Teoma is particularly useful when I am doing research in the consumer goods or services industry. And I use the American Society of Association Executives' Gateway to Associations (http://www.asaenet.org/cda/asae/associations_search) at least once a week, to identify the association that covers whatever industry I'm researching.

**Q: What's your favorite power-searching tip?**
**A:** Always look sideways; use your peripheral vision. Often, the information you're looking for isn't right in front of you, but it's hinted at by a link you see to something else, or perhaps you're reminded to check another source while you are skimming through search results. I call it "creative daydreaming"—letting your right brain get creative as you search. For example, I was looking for information on the efficacy of training programs within *Fortune 500* companies. I figured that the American Society for Training and Development would have

**17**

some useful information, which they did. After reviewing their reports, I realized that the Society for Human Resource Management would also be useful, so I headed over there. After having looked through SHaRM's white papers, I realized that books would probably be a good place to look, so I went to A9.com to search both the Web and Amazon.com's book collection for information. And I also poked around in the FindArticles.com site, to see what magazines were likely to be addressing this issue, and how the topic was most likely described. The point is that you're most likely to find the best selection of information if you move beyond a search engine's search results and start following clues that turn up as you go. It's not always a straight line between you and the answer.

*Mary Ellen Bates is the author of* Building & Running a Successful Research Business: A Guide for the Independent Information Professional *(CyberAge Books; 2003), and six other books about online research, and is the owner of Bates Information Services (http:// www.batesinfo.com).*

# Chapter 18

# Searching for Technical Support

If you've spent any time at all with a computer, it's likely you've also spent time trying to decipher an error message, locate or install some obscure driver, or simply figure out why something that worked yesterday mysteriously refuses to work today. Troubleshooting computer problems isn't fun—but it's inordinately easier now than it was in the pre-Web days, when our only recourse was to phone a tech support line, spend countless hours on hold listening to sappy music, and then facing the ordeal of "working with" surly and often clueless support staff.

Today, we can go online and search for solutions. Searching for technical support information is still a challenging process, but with the right strategies you can generally find solutions on the Web to most computer-related problems.

# Technical Support Search Strategies

Searching for technical support is similar in many ways to searching for people. Before you begin, you should record as much information as possible about the problem you're experiencing. Write down everything—software version or component model number, error message text or number, information about hardware, software, and operating system configurations—literally anything that seems even remotely related to your problem. Why? Hurried searches generally fail to produce useful information. Worse, even slight variations in drivers, versions, or model numbers can lead you to find and apply a fix that's almost—but not quite—the solution to your particular problem. In the worst case, you can end up damaging or even ruining valuable equipment, or losing precious files.

## Searching for Drivers and Software

As with people-related searches, it's best to start with Google's Advanced Search page, and treat your search as an equation. Some of your search terms should be constants, and you should treat others as variables, substituting terms into and out of your equation as you get closer to your goal.

One of the most common technical support tasks is searching for drivers or other software necessary to make something function compatibly with your system. For the sake of example, let's say you found a great deal on an HP LaserJet Model 1012 on eBay. The price was right, but unfortunately the printer came as-is, without drivers. To install the printer, you'll need to search for the appropriate drivers. Figure 18-1 shows the Advanced Search page with our initial search terms placed in the following boxes:

- The word **driver** in the **with all of the words** box. This word is a constant—printer control software is universally called a "driver."

- The phrase **laserjet 1012** in the **with the exact phrase** box. We don't care about any model other than this one.

- The terms **hp** and **"hewlett packard"** in the **with at least one of the words** box. Hewlett-Packard is often referred to by its initials—we'll use both forms and let Google OR them together.

Constants    Variables

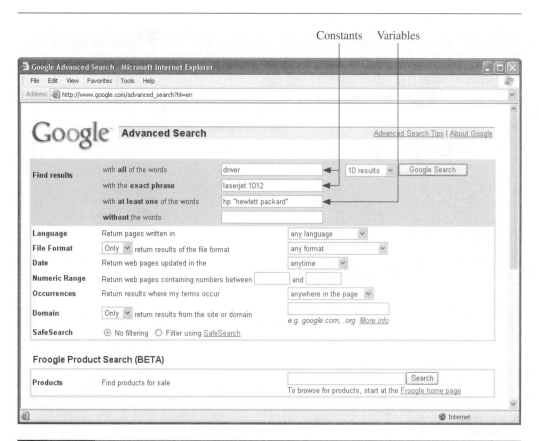

FIGURE 18-1   Our initial query to begin our search for our printer driver

Figure 18-2 shows the result of this query. A quick scan shows that we're close with this query, but most of the results seem to be links to marketing materials or reviews of the printer rather than technical support information or resources.

Result #2, shown in Figure 18-3, looks especially promising—it's a document located on the hp.com web site—but look a bit closer before you click. First, the document type is PDF, suggesting that it contains highly formatted information, rather than links to a software download location. That definitely isn't what we're looking for. Also, the URL indicates that the document is located in a subdirectory called hpinfo/newsroom/press_kits/2003/, indicating that it's a press release, not a technical document.

But look closely at the snippet for this result. The word "support" jumps out, indicating that this is the word HP uses internally for technical support. Click the **View as HTML** link to open the document without firing up the Acrobat reader. Then use your browser's Find command

18

FIGURE 18-2    The first set of results for our query looks promising, but isn't quite what we're looking for.

FIGURE 18-3    The second result offers a number of important clues that can help us refine our query.

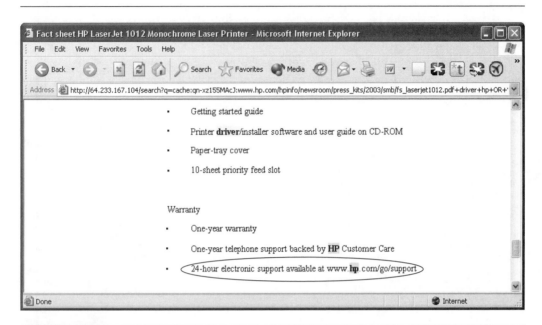

**FIGURE 18-4**   Sometimes looking at a page that we know isn't what we're looking for can nonetheless reveal helpful clues for refining our search.

(CTRL-F) and search for the word "support." Figure 18-4 shows the part of the page from which the snippet was extracted: "24-hour electronic support available at hp.com/go/support." This is helpful, but it's clearly just the URL for *all* technical support at HP. We need to look further.

We have three options at this point. We could add the word "support" to our existing query as a constant and then run the search again. This would narrow our results but still provide a reasonably broad selection of sources of information from around the Web. Alternatively, we could keep our existing query and limit our results to the HP web site. Or we could abandon Google and simply visit the generic HP support site and begin our search anew. We'll try the second approach first, because we know that this is where we will be able to find the "official" version of the driver that fits the exact specifications for our needs. We also know that if Google can crawl the generic HP support site, there's a good chance that with persistence we'll be able to find what we're looking for.

Because we're limiting our search to the generic HP support site, we no longer need to use the search terms "hp" or "hewlett packard." We also want to sharpen our query a bit at this point, adding the word "download" to get us closer to an actual resource that will allow us to get our hands on the software. Figure 18-5 shows the result of this refined query.

18

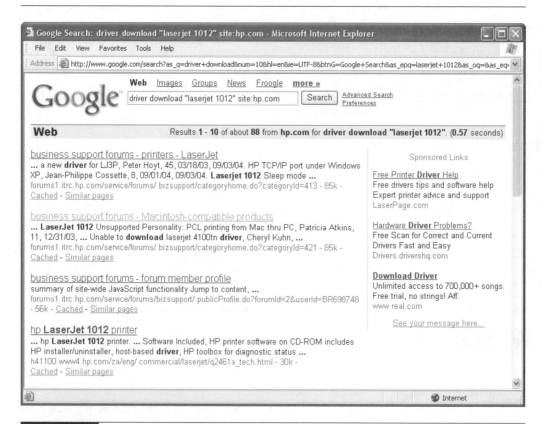

FIGURE 18-5    Further refining our query produces these results.

POWER SEARCHER TIP

*Google's site restrict filter works only with* domain names. *Including directories or filenames after the domain name (for example, everything after the ".com" in "hp.com/go/support") will not work. Google will report that it cannot find any files, even if it has indexed files located in those subdirectories.*

Unfortunately, a quick scan of these results shows we're not much closer to our goal. This is common when you're using Google to limit your search to a manufacturer's web site. Sites like this are typically so huge that even Google has a hard time determining the best results for your search terms. Adding the word "download" didn't help matters much. Why? Clicking through on a result shows that the phrase "download drivers and software" is used in the link text on a menu of the page, but nowhere in the body of the page (see Figure 18-6). Although Google has put us a step closer to our goal, we still have to click an additional link to get there.

**FIGURE 18-6**  Google is picking up the word "download" on this page from a link to another page.

But don't give up just yet. Through a roundabout process involving search and educated browsing of search results, we hit pay dirt when clicking this link. Through this process of trial and error, we've found the download page for the HP LaserJet 1012 (see Figure 18-7). This begs the question, why didn't Google just find this page in the first place? The answer is that Google doesn't know about the page. Even though Google pointed us to a *link* to the page, Google's crawler either did not, or more likely *could not,* crawl the page. Why?

Let's examine the URL for this page. There are several clues that this is an "invisible web" page (mentioned in Chapter 1). The telltale question mark symbol, followed by a string of parameters, indicates either that a script is used to generate the page or that GoogleBot simply

**FIGURE 18-7**   The download page for the HP LaserJet 1012

gave up because of the sheer number of parameters included in the URL. We can confirm that Google has not indexed this page by simply pasting the URL into a search box and checking the results (see Figure 18-8).

If Google has indexed a page, using its URL as a search string performs the same operation as the **info:** operator described in Chapter 4, showing you information about that page. If Google hasn't crawled the URL, you'll see a message similar to that in Figure 18-8.

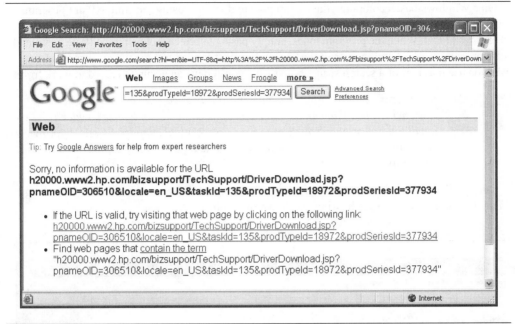

Using a URL as a search string will show you whether Google has indexed that page or not.

*Use the **inurl:** and **intitle:** operators with the magic keywords "support," "download," "FAQ," and others relevant to the specific type of solution you're seeking. Your results might be exactly the page you're looking for.*

# Finding Solutions to Error Messages

I'm convinced that engineers who write error messages must attend a special obfuscation school. Sure, an error message such as "General Protection Fault in Module Dibeng.dll" is meaningful to the two or three people on the planet who can penetrate its meaning, but it leaves a lot to be desired for the rest of us when a deadline looms, a printer is refusing to work, and this cryptic message is the only reason provided.

Fortunately, Google is quite adept at helping locate tech support resources for these kinds of messages.

Writing down error messages, especially when they contain cryptic numbers such as "buffer overrun at 0x400e7f9", can be a pain. It's easy to miscopy these types of messages—and by the way, are those characters "zeros" or "ohs"? Fortunately, there's a simple solution. Although you can't just copy and paste most error messages, you can use your computer's Print Screen (PRTSC) key to take a snapshot of your screen, including the message. Once you've taken the snapshot, you can paste this image into any program that allows you to import bitmap graphics.

18

On a Windows-based computer, the easiest way to do this is using the simple Paint program that comes packaged with the operating system. From the Start Menu, select All Programs | Accessories | Paint. When the program loads, simply paste the screenshot using the Paste command (or by pressing CTRL-V) and then print the image. You'll still need to type the error message when you use it as part of a search string, but at least you'll have an accurate record to work from.

**POWER SEARCHER TIP**    *Some screen capture programs have the ability to capture error messages and save them as text that can be copied and pasted into search boxes, which can be a real timesaver when you're searching for technical support. SnagIt (http://www .techsmith.com/products/snagit/default.asp) is an example of a program with this capability.*

Once you've captured a screenshot of the error message, simply use the entire error message as a quoted phrase as your search string, as shown in Figure 18-9.

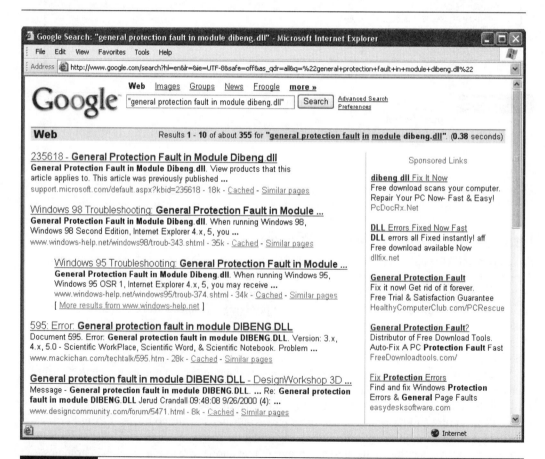

At the very top, results point to pages written by Microsoft support that explains how to resolve this type of problem. Also included are gripe pages from other users who've had the problem—and if you're lucky, the answers they've already found to fix the problem. Links to specialized support forums are also part of the mix.

*Be sure to scan the sponsored links when you're searching for technical support. Many of these paid listings offer very specific solutions to the problem you're experiencing.*

## Google Search vs. Manufacturer Site Search

Since it took so many steps to find what we were looking for using Google, wouldn't it have been better to simply visit HP's web site and used the search tool provided there? That depends. *Site search* tools tend to be very different creatures than *web search* tools. It's easy to believe that a site search tool would be much better than Google at locating information on its own web site. After all, the site search tool has a far smaller collection of pages to deal with, and most site search tools can be tuned to perform well within the context of their own environment.

But site search tools lack some very important features, the most important being Google's ability not only to understand the content of a page, but to understand its relative importance by analyzing the quantity and quality of links on the Web that point to that page. And the sad reality is that many site search tools are simply technologically inferior to Google.

So: Google search or site search? If you're familiar with a web site and know its site search tool works well, then there's really no need to use Google. But if you're looking for something on a manufacturer's site you're unfamiliar with, you might have better results starting out with Google.

# Google's Tech-Related Special Searches

Google has a number of special search pages that automatically limit your search results to web sites related to a specific topic. These were originally created as internal tools to help Google engineers with their own work, but now they're available to all of us. These include:

- Apple Macintosh
- BSD Unix
- Linux
- Microsoft

Each of these special searches is configured to restrict results to web sites focusing solely on its own specific topic.

Each of these special search tools is a great place to start hunting for technical support information. None, unfortunately, have advanced search pages, but you can still use all of Google's advanced operators in your query strings.

**18**

## Apple Macintosh

The Apple Macintosh specialty search (http://www.google.com/mac.html) limits results to sites focusing on Apple computer products, services, reviews, and so on, including Apple itself, and sites such as Apple Insider, We Love Macs, Mac Rumors, Apple-History.com, and many others. Results come from a variety of Macintosh-oriented sites, many of which contain useful information.

## BSD Unix

The BSD Unix specialty search (http://www.google.com/bsd) limits results to sites focusing on BSD, the version of Unix developed at the University of California, Berkeley. These include Bsd.org, freebsd.org, O'Reilly's BSD Dev Center, and many others.

## Linux

The Linux specialty search (http://www.google.com/linux) limits results to sites focusing on the open-source operating system. These include Linux.org, companies that sell Linux (such as Red Hat), online news and discussion forums such as Slashdot, and many others. Although similar to the results provided by the BSD Unix specialty search, these results have their own Linux flavor.

## Microsoft

The Microsoft specialty search (http://www.google.com/microsoft.html) limits results to sites focusing on Microsoft and its products and services. These include Microsoft itself, Windows Annoyances, most of the online Windows-oriented magazines, Security Focus, and many others. If you've ever used Microsoft's own site search tool, you'll appreciate the quality of search results you get with Google's specialty Microsoft search.

# Mining Google Groups and Google Answers

Google Groups and Google Answers are both excellent sources for finding technical support information. As said in Chapter 7, Google Groups is essentially an interface to Usenet, and Usenet was originally created to allow Unix computer programmers to exchange news and information with one another. That legacy continues today. There are literally hundreds of newsgroups dedicated to computer-related topics. And the people who hang out and post in Usenet groups are often highly regarded technical experts, willing to share their time and expertise—especially when it comes to challenging or difficult questions.

Although nowhere near as broad or comprehensive, Google Answers also has a category dedicated to computer-related questions. And the quality of answers provided by Google Answers researchers, as well as comments from users, is generally quite high.

If you're not familiar with Google Groups, your best approach for beginning your search for technical support is to browse the **comp** category, scanning the 96 subcategories for one that's the best match for your needs. The **comp** category is a catchall for discussions about computer hardware, software, consumer information—just about anything related to tech.

Next to each category you'll notice pale blue and green bars. These are activity indicators, allowing you to see at a glance that groups with solid green bars (such as comp.games,.

comp.infosystems, and comp.databases) are highly active, whereas groups with pale blue bars (such comp.hackers, comp.jobsoffered, and jobs.mac) have no meaningful activity at all. Lack of activity doesn't mean you won't find helpful information in a group. Rather, it simply means that few people are actively participating in the group, and you may wait a long time before anyone answers any questions you post, if you get a response at all. But these groups may still have valuable information that was posted in years past when the group was more active.

Also note that many of the groups listed on the **comp** category have subcategories. In some cases, some groups have numerous subgroups, such as comp.ai, comp.databases, and the monster comp.lang categories. An asterisk at the end of a category name indicates that a group has subcategories.

Be sure to check out the second page of groups, using the drop-down menu or clicking the **Next 46 Groups** link at the top of the page.

If you find a promising group, spend some time checking out messages by people who post to that group on a regular basis. This will give you a sense of how well a person knows their subject, and whether you can trust their comments to be reliable sources of information.

POWER SEARCHER TIP *You can limit Google Groups results to posts by a single author using the **author:** operator.*

Once you've familiarized yourself with the various groups of interest to you, it's almost always more effective to search for information rather than browse in Google Groups. You can navigate directly to a subcategory and search within that subcategory, or you can search from the main Google Groups search box to pick up postings that might be elsewhere in Usenet. Of course, you can also construct more detailed, specific queries using the Advanced Google Groups page, described in Chapter 7.

With Google Answers, I've found it's better to begin by searching rather than browsing, limiting results to answered questions using the drop-down menu shown in Figure 18-10. This approach saves a lot of time if an answer to a question also answers your own question. If not,

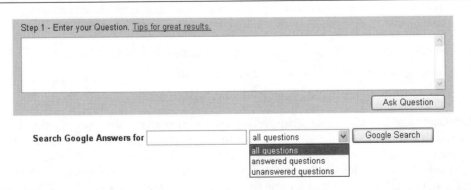

FIGURE 18-10   Begin a search for technical support in Google Answers by limiting results to answered questions.

you can run the search again, relaxing the result filter to include all questions (so that you can see other user comments as well), or you can browse through the categories in the **Computers** group, looking for likely sources of information.

# Beyond Google: Other Technical Support Search Resources

There are so many high-quality, useful technical support resources on the Web that describing them all could fill an entire book in its own right. What follows are some of the resources I've personally found to be helpful in my own quests for tech support.

   *Yahoo! Directory's **Technical Guides and Support** category at http://dir.yahoo .com/Computers_and_Internet/Technical_Guides_and_Support/ is a great source of annotated links to dozens of technical support web sites.*

## Experts Exchange

Experts Exchange (http://www.experts-exchange.com/) is a question-answering service similar to Google Answers but entirely focused on computer-related technical support issues. The site is geared toward information technology professionals, but it's an incredibly rich mine of information for a wide variety of technical support issues.

You can search the question-and-answer database at no charge and without registering for the service. Results show the first couple lines of each question related to your query, and each answer's rating (from one to five stars). To read the answer, you'll need to sign up for a membership, which starts at $9.95 per month, though you can "earn" your membership by answering questions yourself and garnering "expert points" from other users.

## About.com Computing and Technology Channel

About.com is a great place to go trolling for technical support information. About's technology channel is home to more than three dozen expert "Guides" who have built and maintained extensive sites on numerous technology-related topics, including:

- Computer hardware (PCs, scanners/printers, peripherals, and so on)
- Operating systems (Windows, Mac, Linux, and so on)
- Software (databases, graphics, home recording, and so on)

Each Guide writes articles about their specialty and also maintains a directory of links to the best sources of information on the Web about that topic. This combination provides you with a great source of original content as well as excellent pointers to other sites if you don't find what you're looking for. Each Guide site also has its own discussion forum, moderated by the Guide, for users to ask questions and get help from the Guide and other users.

## Windows Annoyances

Windows has more than its share of quirks... um, "features," that can drive you to distraction. Windows Annoyances (http://www.annoyances.org/) is a site dedicated to helping you stomp out those irritating behaviors or settings that often require just a simple tweak to put them aright.

You can browse the site by category, or you can use one of the Troubleshooters for a specific problem. The site also has forums where both users and Windows Annoyances authors participate.

## OldVersion.com

Sometimes the latest and greatest version of a program simply isn't everything it's cracked up to be. Feature bloat, increased system requirements, even changes to the user interface can make new versions of programs all but unusable. OldVersion.com (http://www.oldversion.com/) is an archive of over 480 versions of more than 50 programs. You can download software for free; licensing the program is still up to you once you've installed it on your computer. The site also features forums discussing the merits of older vs. newer versions of the programs available for download.

## MacFixit

MacFixit (http://www.macfixit.com/) is one of the most established and comprehensive technical support sites for the Macintosh community. Maintained by a group of Mac "alpha geeks," the site strives to be the most timely and accurate source of technical support information for the Macintosh. Like Experts Exchange, MacFixit is free to search, but you'll need to subscribe to access the archives. The site also has forums, including numerous troubleshooting forums dedicated to specific topics, that you may browse or participate in without charge.

**Ask the Expert**

## Expert Tips for Searching for Technical Support

### Six Questions for Power Searcher Alexander Holt

**Q: What's your favorite Google search tip?**
**A:** Use the Google Toolbar. After performing a search and getting to a page where the answer may lie, I use the highlighting function to find my terms in the document. This enables me to get to the important parts of the document without reading the garbage found at the beginning of most tech-support documents.

**Q: What kind of search strategy do you use when searching for technical support information on Google?**

**A:** I always quote my search terms as a phrase. If you have a phrase, you are much more likely to get better results. The best search terms to use for software or hardware support are the reported error messages. Copy and paste the entire message, but be sure to include it in double quotes. For other products, such as a digital camera, MP3 player, or other device, using very specific terms related to the product (such as part numbers or SKUs) is very important.

If phrase searching does not work, I use content filters such as the **intitle:** operator. If I think the content is going to be found on a specific site, such as a user forum, I tend to restrict the search to URLs on that site. And if I think the content is going to be recent, such as a problem with a virus or spam, I also use the date restriction on Google's Advanced Search page.

**Q: Are there specific tools or techniques that lead to best results? (For example, operators, filters, special keywords, and so on.)**

**A:** I think the biggest key to getting good results is using good discriminator terms. Also, since Google defaults to a logical AND, sometimes it is important to OR the terms together if there are multiple ways to describe the problem. You may not know how the problems or solutions are described on help pages unless you use variations on your search terms.

**Q: When would you not use Google for searching for technical support information?**

**A:** On some support sites, the content is not crawled by Google for multiple reasons. If I'm getting consistently bad results from Google, and better results from the company's own web site, I am likely to check Google's index via the site filter to see how many pages Google has indexed from a company's support server.

It is also important to make sure you appropriately scope the search, limiting your search to support domains only; otherwise, results might include nonsupport content that has no value.

**Q: What search engines or other web resources do you use to go beyond Google when searching for technical support information?**

**A:** It depends how popular the product is in the marketplace, but user forums are typically the best source for information on many geek toys.

**Q: What's your favorite power-searching tip?**

**A:** Understanding Boolean logic can be especially useful when you have to do a search directly on a corporate web site or database where the relevance ranking is subpar compared with Google. And, of course, I always like being able to stare into the refrigerator thinking there is nothing to eat, typing the contents into Google, and end up getting a decent meal. ;-)

*Alexander Holt is a Technical Strategist in the Web Strategy & Design Group at IBM.*

# Chapter 19

## Other Tools and Services
## from the Googleplex

The word "Google" has become synonymous with web search, and rightly so. Google is one of the most popular search engines with people all over the world. But Google the company is much more than its well-known search engine. And Google the company is also growing rapidly, in search of new markets, products, and ways to achieve its mission of organizing the world's information. In the coming years, you'll likely see Google increasingly expand the horizons of its online business.

This chapter focuses on the services and tools offered by the folks at the Googleplex that aren't directly related to web search. Although most of these services do have a search component, they're described here because they offer useful ways to organize or share information, or to advertise goods and services through Google's AdWords program.

# Google Answers

Google Answers (http://answers.google.com), shown in Figure 19-1, is a service that lets you pose questions that will be answered by skilled online researchers (for a fee). The people answering questions are independent contractors who may not necessarily be experts on a topic for which they provide answers. However, all researchers for Google Answers go through an application process that tests their ability to find high-quality online information and also ensures that they have excellent communication skills.

Google Answers is a useful service for searchers in two ways. Naturally, having a skilled researcher look for information on your behalf can be an invaluable service, particularly if you're looking for hard-to-find information or if you've hit a dead end in your own searching. But even if you don't want to pay for advice, you're free to browse all the questions that have been posted to Google Answers, along with the replies from researchers and comments from other Google Answers users.

This ability to browse Google Answers makes it a close kin to Google Groups—with one very important difference. Anyone can post to Google Groups, and there is no assurance that the information you find there is either literate or accurate. By contrast, because it costs money to get a response to a question from a Google Answers researcher, most people post careful, precise questions. And because the researchers who answer questions have been tested for their information skills, most answers are thoughtful, reliable, and useful. This makes Google Answers a valuable, albeit incomplete, resource for finding online information.

## Browsing Google Answers

Google Answers is structured as a hierarchal directory, as shown in Figure 19-2. To browse Google Answers, simply click a category and you'll be taken to the top-level page for that category.

Top-level category pages have two parts. At the top of the page are links to subcategories. All categories other than **Miscellaneous** are divided into subcategories for easier browsing. Beneath the subcategory links are the most recently answered questions in that category.

You can re-sort the list of answers by clicking the **Date** or **Price** link. Click the **Date** link, and the oldest questions are displayed first. Click again, and the list is re-sorted with recently answered questions at the top of the list. Click the **Price** link, and the list displays questions with the minimum bid of $U.S. 2.00. Click again, and questions with the maximum bid of $U.S. 200.00 are shown first.

**FIGURE 19-1**    Google Answers is the company's "human-powered" search service.

A listing for a question has several parts. In the Subject column, the subject of the question is displayed, along with the questioner's nickname and, if the question has been answered, the nickname of the researcher posting the response. Nicknames are used to protect the privacy of both questioners and researchers.

The Date and Status columns show when the question was posted and whether the question has expired, been answered, or the number of days remaining until expiration (unanswered questions expire after 30 days). You'll also see the number of other Google Answers users who have commented on the question, if any.

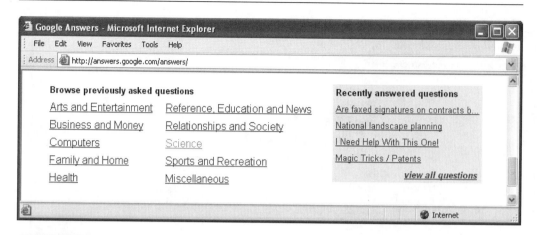

**FIGURE 19-2**  Google Answers is structured as a directory, which makes it easy to browse.

To view a question and its answer or comments, click the subject link. Questions, answers, and comments are clearly labeled. Once a question has been answered, the person posting the question may request clarification of the answer, and the Google researcher is obliged to respond. Requests for clarification and responses are also clearly marked and are indented from the body of the question and answer. Comments by other Google Answers users are displayed at the bottom of the page.

Once a question has been answered, the person posting the question can rate the answer, with one (poor) to five (excellent) stars. Google uses this feedback in evaluating the performance of each researcher, but you can use the ratings as an indicator of the quality of an answer, as well. Be careful, though—some ratings have less to do with the quality of an answer than with another agenda. Also, a high ranking doesn't necessarily mean that the information provided is correct.

Should you question the skills of the researcher based on a negative response? One way to judge the quality of work is to look at some of the other questions the researcher has responded to. Clicking the link for the researcher's nickname shows a list of all the questions answered by this particular researcher, as well as an average rating for all answers.

## Searching Google Answers

The hierarchal structure of Google Answers makes it easy to browse, but sometimes searching is more efficient. The search form for Google Answers is available on the home page and at the top of all category and subcategory pages, as shown in Figure 19-3.

*Be sure to use the **Search Google Answers** form to search for existing questions. It's easy to confuse the **Ask a Question** form directly above with the search box. The **Ask a Question** form won't give you search results; rather, it's used to post a question to be answered by a Google Answers researcher.*

Don't use this form to search Google Answers—it's only for posting questions.

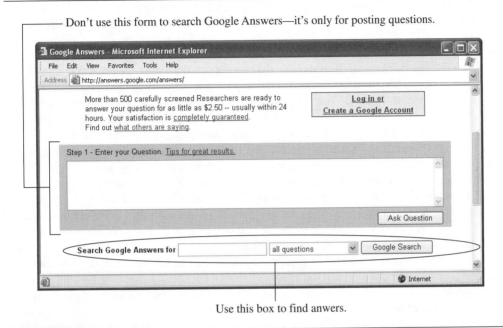

Use this box to find anwers.

The Google Answers search form

To search Google Answers, enter your search terms into the **Search Google Answers for** form and then select whether you want to search all questions, answered questions, or unanswered questions. If you are searching from a category or subcategory page, you'll also see radio buttons beneath the form to limit your search to a particular category or all of Google Answers. Unlike other Google services, there is no advanced search feature for Google Answers.

Google Answers search results look very similar to web search results. Results show the subject of each question, a snippet of text extracted from the question itself, the category where the question was posted, and the questioner's nickname. These results can also be sorted by date and price.

## Posting a Question to Google Answers

To post a question to Google Answers, you need to sign up for a free Google account. You can use the account name you created for Google Groups, Gmail, or any other Google service, or you can simply get the ball rolling by posting your question in the form on the Google Answers home page, and you'll be prompted to either log in or create a new account.

Even if you have a Google account, you need to create a nickname for Google Answers. Your nickname is used to protect your privacy when your question is posted on the public Google Answers site. It's also the only name a researcher will know you by, so you can ask questions that might be private or confidential without worrying about compromising your identity.

To post a question, use the form on the Google Answers home page, or click the **Ask a Question** link that appears at the top right of all other Google Answers pages. When you click this link, you'll see a form with several fields that you'll need to fill in. Enter the subject of your

19

question, the question itself, how much you're willing to pay for an answer (between $U.S. 2.00 and $200.00), and select a category and subcategory (if appropriate) for your question. That's all there is to it.

How much should you be willing to pay for an answer? The Google Answers FAQ offers some guidance: "The more research required to find an answer, the higher the price you should set for your question. Three-quarters of your question price goes directly to the Researcher who answers your question; the other 25 percent goes to Google to support the service. Setting a price too low to compensate for the time required may result in your question not receiving an answer. The more you are willing to pay, the more likely your question is to get answered quickly."

When you post a question, it's helpful to provide as much detail and specificity as possible. Google provides a number of good suggestions for asking great questions, including breaking up multipart questions, summarizing your own findings in the question, and defining the answer you want. Click the **How to ask a great question** link on this page for more detailed suggestions. Google also provides guidance for pricing your question—click the **How do I price my question?** link for these pricing tips. You can change your price at any time as long as your question is not currently "locked" and being answered by a researcher.

Researchers post answers directly to your questions on the Google Answers web site, and anyone can view both the question and the answer. To avoid continually checking for a response, you can request an e-mail notification whenever there is activity on your question. These alerts can be sent whenever there is new activity or once a day.

Researchers may ask for clarification of your question, or they may outline a proposed strategy for answering before undertaking the full process of uncovering information for you. Once a question has been answered, you also have the opportunity to request clarification or further information from the researcher.

When a question has been answered to your satisfaction, Google automatically debits your credit card number for the amount you bid and a $.50 processing fee. If you're not satisfied with an answer, you may request a refund, which is granted in most cases if you provide a suitable explanation.

POWER SEARCHER TIP    *More information about Google Answers can be found in the FAQ at http://answers.google.com/answers/faq.html.*

## Beyond Google: Other Online Question-Answering Services

There are numerous question-answering services available on the Web. Many libraries throughout the world maintain virtual reference desks where you can pose questions that are answered by professional librarians. Other services are similar to Google Answers, with questions answered by nonprofessionals. Some are free; others charge a fee.

### Ask a Question

One of the best known is the Ask a Question service from the Internet Public Library at the University of Michigan (http://www.ipl.org/div/askus/). This service allows you to post questions and get a response within three days from a librarian. Answers provide either detailed information or a list of print or online resources that you can explore yourself. Answers are returned via e-mail.

## Wondir

Wondir (http://www.wondir.org/) is a web-based question-answering service similar to Google Answers—with a twist. Wondir is free to use, and anyone can post questions or answers. This means the questions and answers tend more toward the wild and woolly side than Google Answers. Nonetheless, Wondir is a useful resource for some types of information.

POWER SEARCHER TIP    *An excellent list of question-answering services is found at Google Answers itself, in this post: http://answers.google.com/answers/threadview?id=372087.*

# Gmail

Gmail is Google's free, web-based e-mail system. When Google announced a beta test of this new service on April 1, 2004, many people (including some well-respected journalists) suspected that it was an elaborate April fool's prank. But the joke was on them: Gmail has grown into a robust, highly capable e-mail system that has attracted a near-fanatical following among users who have managed to secure an invitation to try the service.

That's right—when Google rolled out Gmail, it was only accessible by invitation. As you read this, Gmail may no longer be a gated community, though if it is it will undoubtedly open up to all users any day now.

Gmail differs from most e-mail systems in that its core is a high-powered search engine (see Figure 19-4). By contrast, most e-mail programs treat search as a secondary design factor. To organize your e-mail, you create folders as well as rules to filter mail into those folders.

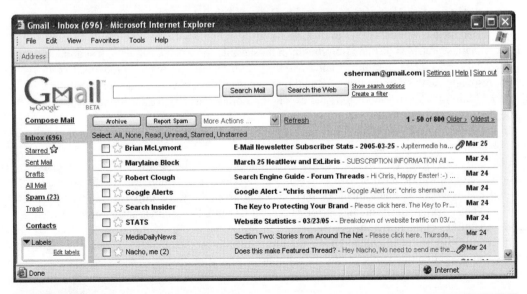

FIGURE 19-4    Gmail provides a very powerful search engine for your e-mail.

19

The search capabilities of most popular e-mail systems, such as Outlook, Eudora, or Hotmail, are poor, slow, and clumsy. By contrast, Gmail was designed to perform at the same level and speed as Google's web search. This means that you no longer need to be concerned about filing or finding e-mail messages once you've received them.

Google took the unprecedented step of offering Gmail accounts with a full gigabyte of storage space—far exceeding the typical 10–25MB offered by most services at the time Gmail was announced. This massive amount of storage also took away the need to manage an e-mail account, deleting old or unwanted messages. With Gmail, you can simply let it pile up as it comes in, confident that you'll be able to find messages any time later thanks to the powerful search capabilities.

Another interesting Gmail feature is its "conversation view" of related messages, which resembles the threaded messages in Google Groups. Replies and replies to replies of all messages sent from your account are threaded together in this conversation view, making it easy to keep track of an e-mail "conversation."

Gmail is free, though Google occasionally includes ads in e-mail messages. Just like the sponsored links in web search results, Google tries to make the ads relevant to the context of the message. In practice, this means that Google's computers are "reading" your e-mail, though no record is kept of the e-mail scan and no person other than you has access to your own mail. Nonetheless, if you're concerned about privacy, it's a good idea to thoroughly read the Gmail privacy policy (http://gmail.google.com/gmail/help/privacy.html) before signing up for and using a Gmail account.

**POWER SEARCHER TIP**    *More information about Gmail can be found in the FAQ at http://gmail.google .com/gmail/help/about.html.*

## Beyond Google: Search-centric E-mail

Google raised the bar when it comes to making e-mail searchable with the launching of Gmail. Prior to Gmail, search was just an afterthought in most e-mail programs. But now, just about all major e-mail services are scrambling to improve the search capabilities in their products. Notably, Yahoo! responded to the introduction of Gmail by dramatically improving the search capabilities of Yahoo! Mail (http://mail.yahoo.com) and expanding storage capacity for free e-mail accounts to 100MB.

If you prefer to read your e-mail on your computer rather than online, Lookout for Microsoft Outlook is an excellent alternative.

For years, users of Microsoft Outlook have complained about the poor quality and sluggish performance of its search function. Not long after the introduction of Gmail, Microsoft responded to user demands by purchasing a small company called Lookout Software (http://www.lookoutsoft .com/Lookout/), which makes an add-in for Microsoft Outlook that dramatically improves the search capabilities of the program.

If you use Microsoft Outlook and don't want to change to another e-mail program, Lookout is an essential addition that you shouldn't be without.

# Blogger

Google's February 2003 acquisition of Pyra Labs, creator of the popular weblog software, did little to contribute to the company's ongoing mission of organizing the world's information. But it followed the pattern established when Google acquired the Deja News Usenet archive and then later transformed it into Google Groups. Although not yet called Google Blogs, Blogger and its companion Blogspot hosting service make it easy for people to post their own information on the Web.

Blogger, shown in Figure 19-5, is a free service. To use it, simply create an account and start blogging using the online "dashboard" or through the companion Blogger Navbar, which also has Google site search built into it. If you've downloaded the Google Toolbar, Blogger has an option to add a **Blog This** button to the toolbar, provided you've already set up a blog.

**FIGURE 19-5**    Blogger provides a free, easy way to create your own online weblog.

Ironically, although Google crawls blogs and includes their content in its index of web pages, it has no specialized weblog catalog and no tab to limit your searches to blog content only. To search for blog content, you still must use one of the specialized blog and news feed search engines described in Chapter 14.

Another useful service available from Blogger is Blogspot. Blogspot is a free hosting service that lets you quickly and easily publish your blog if you don't have access to a server. Your blog will show Google ads.

*More information about Blogger, including an excellent introduction to weblogs and full instructions for creating your own blog, can be found in the Blogger help files at http://help.blogger.com/.*

## Beyond Google: The Weblogs Compendium

Dozens of blogging services are available on the Web. The Weblogs Compendium (http://www .lights.com/weblogs/), created and maintained by Peter Scott, is a one-stop resource for just about all things blogging-related on the Web. The site contains thoughtfully annotated links to blog hosting and tools sites, as well as excellent coverage of RSS and news feeds in general.

# orkut

orkut (http://www.orkut.com/) is a social network. It's an unusual project for Google, because even though it's the creation of a Google engineer (named, appropriately enough, Orkut Buyukkokten), it's not part of Google Labs, nor is it branded with the usual Google logos and sparse design. orkut has its own domain, look and feel, and is labeled as being "in affiliation with Google."

Also, unlike most other Google services, you can't simply fire up orkut and begin using it. orkut is a members-only club, and to join you must be invited by a current orkut member. "That way we won't grow too large, too quickly and everyone will have at least one person to vouch for them," says the site.

So what is this exclusive club? And what's so great about it? Here's the description from orkut's help pages:

"orkut.com is an online community website designed for friends. The main goal of our service is to make your social life, and that of your friends, more active and stimulating. orkut's social network can help you both maintain existing relationships and establish new ones by reaching out to people you've never met before. Who you interact with is entirely up to you. Before getting to know an orkut member, you can even see how they're connecting to you through the friends network."

Figure 19-6 shows an orkut profile page, which serves both as a home page and control console for the service.

Are you missing anything if you're not a member of orkut? Not really. Although orkut is a convenient place to pal around with others online, many people seem to lose interest after the novelty has worn off. If you have a friend who's a member, by all means wheedle an invitation from

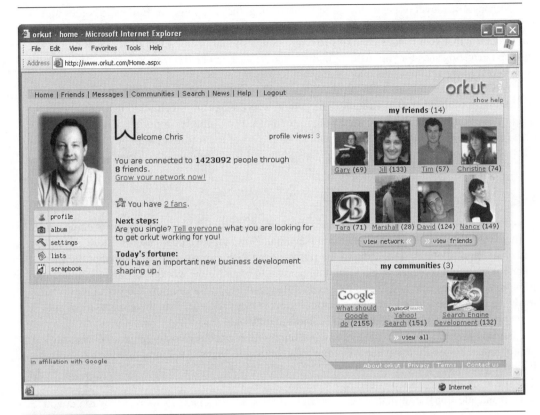

**FIGURE 19-6** The author's orkut profile page

them. If not, check out other community sites such as Friendster (http://www.friendster.com), LinkedIn (https://www.linkedin.com/), and other social networking services that offer many similar features, groups, and opportunities to network with people who share similar interests.

> **POWER SEARCHER TIP** *The Yahoo! directory has an extensive list of virtual communities similar to orkut. It's available at http://dir.yahoo.com/Society_and_Culture/Cultures_and_Groups/Cyberculture/Virtual_Communities/.*

## Beyond Google: Eurekster

Eurekster (http://www.eurekster.com) is an interesting hybrid that blends a search engine with a social network. The search engine is powered by Yahoo!, and when you first start using it your results look pretty much just like they would coming from Yahoo! If you register, the service begins keeping a history of your searches, allowing you to filter results based on your previous search activity.

19

Although this level of personalization is interesting, the real power of Eurekster comes into play when you invite your friends to *share* your respective search histories with one another. The assumption is that your friends are likely to have enough similar interests that their searching might turn up interesting sites for you. Although this is a great idea, in practice your friends typically have such varied interests that results may or may not be useful.

This is where Eurekster's "information nations" comes into play. Information nations are communities focused around a theme. The person who creates an information nation answers a set of questions about the topic they wish to focus on. For example, important keywords, web sites, domains, and information sources can all form part of the information policy for a nation. This policy information is used in a variety of advanced ways to filter search queries.

# Picasa

Google purchased Picasa (http://www.picasa.com), an online digital photo management company, in July 2004. Why would Google buy a company that allows digital camera users to store, manage, and share their photos? At the time of the purchase, a Google press release stated that Picasa's "technologies complement Google's ongoing mission to organize the world's information and make it universally accessible and useful." Google's Blogger also had a relationship with Picasa that made it easy for users to upload pictures from Picasa to blogs. Beyond that, there seems to be little "synergy" between Google's core search business and Picasa.

Nonetheless, the service is elegant and is quite useful for helping you organize and store digital photographs. To use Picasa, visit the home page, shown in Figure 19-7, and download the free Picasa application.

The program itself is well designed and easy to use, and Google provides numerous sources of help and additional information. The Flash tutorial provides an adequate overview to get you started working with the program. For more extensive information, download the Picasa Quick Start guide or scan through the online FAQs.

# Google Site Search

You don't have to be a powerhouse like AOL, the BBC, or other large online destination to have Google-powered search capability on your own site. Google Free lets you install a Google-powered search engine on your personal site at no charge. Google Free is available with three options:

- Google Free web search
- Google Free SafeSearch
- Google Free web search with site search

You don't even need to register to install Google Free on your own site. Simply visit the Google Free page at http://www.google.com/searchcode.html, and cut and paste the code from that page on to your own web site pages. That's all there is to it.

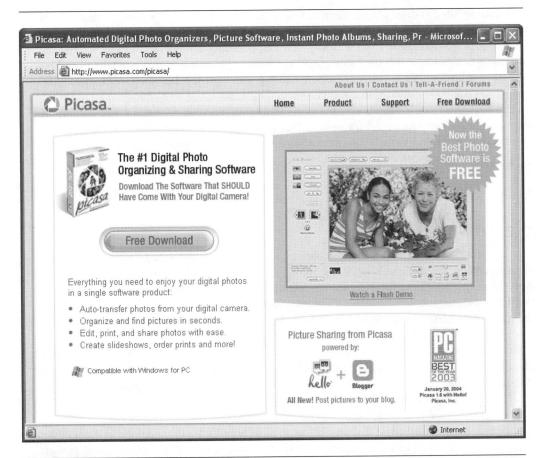

**FIGURE 19-7**    Picasa is a free digital photo management and sharing application from Google.

Want your search results to look more like your site? With a few additional steps, you can customize your results display to include background, text, and link colors you select, and even include your logo on result pages. You need to register for this "upgrade" to customize your Google search results, but even this upgrade is free. To begin the process, visit http://www.google.com/services/free.html and follow the step-by-step instructions. The whole process generally takes only a few minutes.

Google offers another option called Site-Flavored Google Search. As you might imagine, this allows you to provide customized search results based on the content of your web site. Google's Site-Flavored Search uses the same technology behind the Google Personalized tool available in Google Labs, described in Chapter 9.

**19**

To enable Site-Flavored Google Search, visit http://labs.google.com/personalized/customize .html. This displays a Site-Flavored Search profile, which is initially empty, and a list of interest categories for you to choose from. Clicking any category link displays a list of subcategories with check boxes. Check off the categories that interest you, and Google automatically adds them to your profile. When you've finished creating your profile, click the **Generate HTML** button and code will be created that you can cut and paste into your web site.

Site-Flavored Google Search imposes a few restrictions on your visitors. People viewing the site must use Internet Explorer 5 (or newer), Netscape 5 (or newer), or Mozilla 1.4 (or newer), with JavaScript enabled. Google also recommends restricting your search to English only.

**POWER SEARCHER TIP** *More information about Google Free site search can be found in the FAQ at http://www.google.com/faq_freewebsearch.html.*

# Google AdWords

Google is world-renowned for its search technology, and rightly so. But Google isn't really a search engine company. Rather, Google is a vast *advertising network* that happens to use search technology as its delivery platform. In fact, Google's AdWords advertising program (http://adwords.google .com) generates the bulk of the company's revenues and virtually all of its profits. Without AdWords, Google wouldn't have been one of 2004's hottest new stocks, or the darling of the investment community and financial press.

You've already read about Google's Sponsored Links feature in Chapter 3. More than 150,000 advertisers purchase sponsored links through Google's AdWords program. And the vast majority of those advertisers are small and medium-sized businesses, with relatively modest budgets.

If you're selling a product or service and have a web site, Google's AdWords program should be an essential part of your marketing arsenal. A key selling point for AdWords is that it is a *pay for performance* program—Google displays ads at no charge, and advertisers pay Google only when a user actually clicks an ad and visits the advertiser's web page. Most advertisers using Google AdWords report exceptional results, with return on investment that's as good as or greater than that generated from other types of marketing.

Google displays sponsored links through several distribution channels throughout the Web. Sponsored links are prominently displayed on Google search result pages, on the right side of the page. These listings are displayed both on Google's own search results and on those it provides for other services, such as AOL Search (see Figure 19-8).

Google also distributes sponsored links through partners that run their own search services. For example, Ask Jeeves and the InfoSpace search engines Dogpile, Metacrawler, and others display Google sponsored links alongside their own organic search results.

In February 2003, Google further expanded its distribution channels for sponsored links with its AdSense contextual advertising program. The AdSense program allows web sites to automatically display sponsored links from Google that are delivered based on the content of a web page that's

Sponsored links from Google

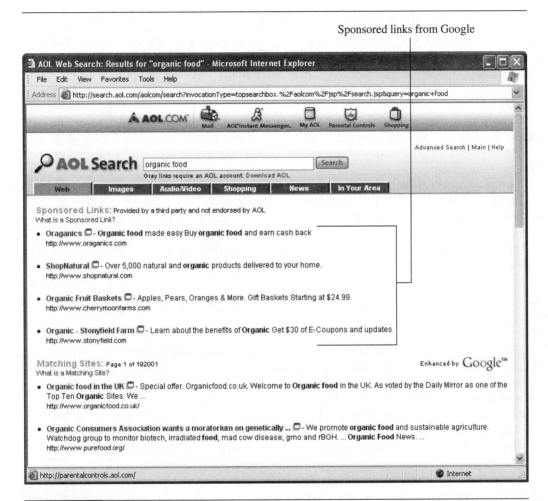

being viewed. In other words, Google figures out the main topic of a web page and serves ads that are, at least in theory, relevant to the context of the page. The AdSense program was quickly adopted by large news, travel, and other heavily trafficked sites, and later by small, niche content providers.

Bottom line: Google's AdWords get exposure all over the Web, often in very desirable locations that would be difficult if not impossible for an advertiser to secure working alone.

## Creating a Google AdWords Account

Anyone who has a web site and a credit card can sign up for a Google AdWords account. You'll pay a modest $U.S. 5.00 activation fee to set up the account, but after that you only pay when an advertising program you've created is actually generating clicks from prospective buyers of your products or services. To create an account, click the button **Sign Up Now** on the AdWords home page.

Creating an account is a four-step process. First, you need to decide where your customers are and the languages you want to target. You can specify whether your ads are displayed throughout the world, in your country, in a region, in a specific city, or even within a specific distance of your business.

Next, you need to create an Ad Group for the product or service you will be advertising, and one or more ads for that group, using simple templates that guide you through the process. Once you've created the ad, you need to select the keywords that will trigger the ad. These are the words a searcher uses in a query, or the words appearing on a content page if you participate in the contextual advertising program. Not sure which words would work best? Google offers a keyword tool that can help you choose the most appropriate words.

**POWER SEARCHER TIP**  *Selecting keywords is as much art as science. One of the best tools available to help you select the best keywords for your ads is Wordtracker, available at http://www.wordtracker.com/.*

The next step is to specify how much you're willing to pay each time someone clicks your ad. Google provides a tool called the Traffic Estimator that can help you make spending decisions. The minimum bid is 5 cents, and the maximum is $U.S. 50.00 per click. Once you've created your ads and set their cost-per-click numbers, you need to specify your daily budget for your advertising campaign. Daily budgets start as low as 5 cents and can go up to whatever limit you are comfortable spending in a given day.

The final step is to create an account and provide Google with credit card and billing information. That's all there is to it!

## Monitoring Your AdWords Campaign

Your ads typically begin running within minutes of their creation. You can track the progress and performance of your advertising campaign with Google's AdWords Control Center, which has three main sections: Campaign Management, Reports, and My Account.

The Campaign Management tab allows you to review campaign status and daily budgets. Statistics are provided for clicks, impressions, click-through rate, average cost per click, overall cost, and average position for each sponsored link.

The Reports section lets you view summary account performance information and create detailed reports about your campaign. The My Account section lets you view your summarized billing history and your detailed payment history as well as access or edit your billing or login information.

Although Google has made the process of creating and running an AdWords campaign easy and painless, there's much more to effective search advertising than simply creating text ads and hoping that searchers beat a path to your virtual marketplace. Unless you're running the most basic type of ad, you'll want to analyze the performance of your efforts and continually fine-tune your campaign to maximize its effectiveness.

Andrew Goodman's *Winning Results with Google AdWords* (McGraw-Hill/Osborne, 2005) provides an excellent, comprehensive look at the art and science of running an effective Google AdWords campaign. Andrew is a noted web search guru, actively writing about search engines and participating in industry conferences since 1998.

POWER SEARCHER TIP    *For an excellent overview of search engine advertising at all major search engines, see Catherine Seda's* Search Engine Advertising *(New Riders, 2004).*

# Chapter 20

## Googling Around the Web

Google powers the web search results at many other sites around the Web. For example, AOL Search is actually Google running behind the scenes. Dozens of sites, such as CNN.com, Amazon.com, and Weather.com, offer web search powered by Google.

Although these sites may tweak Google search results in minor ways, they're all still providing fundamentally the same results that you get at Google.com. By contrast, the sites described in this chapter use Google search results as their raw ingredients and provide lots of useful additional features. You may find after trying some of these services that they end up becoming your preferred way of interacting with Google.

# Google-Powered Web Search Services

Although all the sites mentioned in this section are powered by Google, they each have their own distinct "flavor" or "personality," enhancing Google search results in unique ways.

## A9.com

A9.com (http://a9.com) is a wholly owned subsidiary of Amazon.com, with a tightly focused mission: A9.com, Inc., researches and builds innovative technologies to improve the search experience for e-commerce applications. The company is still in its incubation phase, and at this point in its life is powered by Google, though with many interesting and unique features not available elsewhere.

A9.com's home page (shown Figure 20-1) is even sparser than Google's. The **Search** box is the prominent feature on the screen. But look just below the **Search** box, to the large, blank **Search History** box. This is one of the most interesting features available on A9.com, keeping a record of how you use the search engine and allowing you to easily run previous searches again.

To enable the search history, you need to sign in, using an Amazon.com account. If you already have an Amazon account, simply sign in using your existing e-mail address and password. If you don't have an Amazon account, you can create one without leaving A9.com—and don't worry, you needn't make any Amazon purchases to use the A9.com search engine.

Once you've signed in, you'll see your search history. Your search history is organized to show your recent searches on top, followed by earlier searches grouped into folders below. Clicking a link next to a folder icon expands the history for that time period.

This history feature extends beyond simply remembering your queries and allowing you to easily run them again. A9.com also keeps tracks of search result pages that you've clicked through to read. Look closely at any A9 result page, and you'll see a message next to several of the URLs indicating the last time those particular URLs were clicked from an A9.com result page. If you spend a lot of time searching the Web, it's easy to forget which pages you've looked at, especially when it's been a while since you last viewed a page. This feature not only provides an automatic reminder that you've viewed a page, but also tells you when you last saw it.

A9.com results differ from traditional Google results in other useful ways. On the right side of the page are two vertical tabs: **Open Book Results** and **Open Search History**. Book results come from Amazon, showing books in the retailer's catalog that are relevant to your search terms. Search history displays the same information you see in the **Search History** box on the A9.com home page.

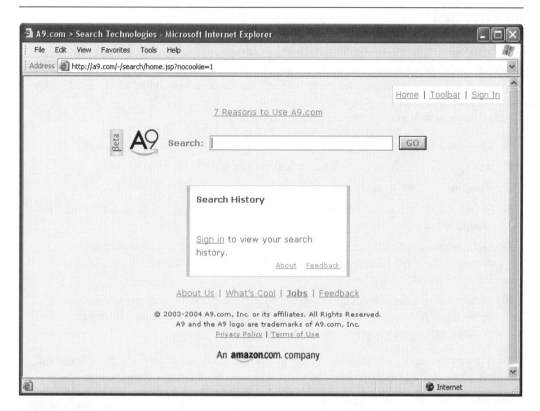

**FIGURE 20-1**    A9.com's sparse home page

You can minimize web results, book results, or search history by clicking the **Close** link in the appropriate window.

> **POWER SEARCHER TIP** *Amazon.com's web search is powered by A9. When you search the Web at Amazon, your queries are automatically added to your A9.com search history.*

A9.com offers another additional feature that you may find useful, though it's only available if you download its toolbar, described in Chapter 8. This is the "diary" feature, which allows you to attach virtual notes to any web page you're visiting. Click the diary button and a small window opens up at the top of the page you're visiting. Type in a note to yourself about the page, and it's automatically saved, reappearing whenever you visit the page again.

> **POWER SEARCHER TIP** *You can search A9.com from anywhere on the Web by simply typing **a9.com/ query** directly into your browser's address bar.*

## FindForward

Imagine Google on steroids, able to answer questions phrased in plain English, find results for "things" (concepts), limit search results to the first half of the twentieth century, leap tall buildings... well, maybe not go that far, but you get the picture. FindForward (http://www.findforward.com/) is an interface to Google that simplifies many sophisticated tasks, making multiple advanced search capabilities available from a simple drop-down menu.

Here's just a sample of the features FindForward offers:

- **Only your language**   This will reduce the result set to pages in your language only.
- **Ask Question**   Ask any question, such as "When was Einstein born?"
- **Amazon**   Search Amazon and return books as well as reviews.
- **Search Grid**   Results are displayed as a two-dimensional grid, with results for phrases created out of two-word couples.
- **Get Questions**   Results are questions related to your query found on web pages. For example, the query "Einstein" finds pages containing questions such as "What was Einstein's estimated IQ?"
- **Person Info**   This search collects information on any person. This may or may not be useful, depending on how common the person's name is, how much information is available on the Web about them, and so on.

FindForward is one of those tools that grows on you the more you play with it. It's an excellent example of how Google's capabilities can be extended with a bit of creative programming.

*FindForward's author, Philipp Lenssen, continually adds new features and improvements. Keep up with these new goodies via his Google Blogoscoped blog at http://blog.outer-court.com/.*

## Jux2

Throughout this book, I've emphasized the point that as good as Google is, it's not always the best search engine for every need. All search engines have their own strengths and weaknesses—their unique "personalities" that make them different from one another. Jux2 (http://www.jux2 .com) shows you exactly how different Google is from Yahoo!, Ask Jeeves, and MSN Search, by comparing the top search results for the same query.

Figure 20-2 compares the query **tokamak** on Google and Ask Jeeves. The two search engines agreed on only four of the top ten results. This is typical: Jux2 says that fewer than 3.5 of the top ten results for any query are common to all engines!

Whenever you want a "second opinion" to Google search results, Jux2.com provides an easy way to get one.

*Another excellent tool that lets you compare results from the major search engines is Thumbshots Ranking, at http://ranking.thumbshots.com/.*

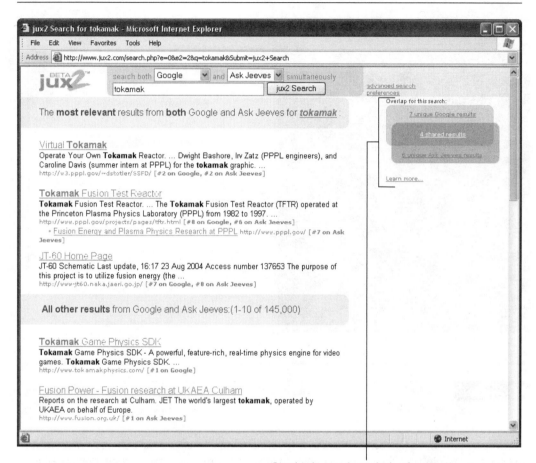

Overlap in search results is often small.

**FIGURE 20-2**    Jux2 lets you directly compare Google results with other search engines.

# Grokker

Grokker (http://www.grokker.com), shown in Figure 20-3, is a unique search tool that creates visual maps of related information, clustered by topics.

Rather than displaying a linear list of search results, Grokker creates colorful spheres in the left pane of the screen that are named by topic. Web results that are conceptually related to one another are clustered together. Mousing over a sphere provides more information about that particular category. Clicking a sphere zooms in, revealing more detail, including the names of subtopics in the category. Individual documents that are part of the web search results are represented by squares—mousing over a square displays a pop-up window with additional details about the document.

20

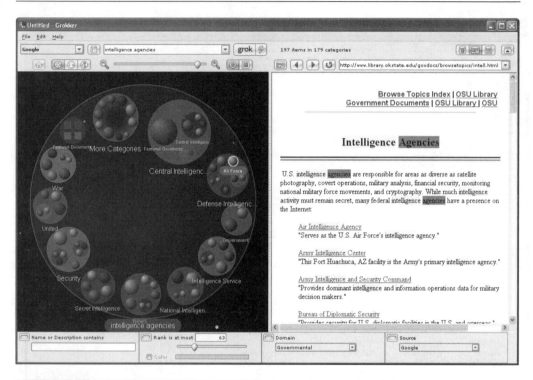

**FIGURE 20-3**  Grokker clusters related search results into conceptually related topics, displayed as a visual map.

Grokker provides a number of filters to help refine results, located at the bottom of the screen. You can filter results so that they must contain a name or description, filter by result rank, or filter by domain (commercial, educational, country, and so on). Another filter lets you select search sources other than Google, such as AltaVista, MSN, Teoma, or your own search source. Grokker also provides a local search capability for the files on your computer.

Windows 2000/XP or Mac OS X 10.2.2 (Jaguar) is required, but Mac OS X 10.3.3 (Panther) is preferred. Grokker is free to try for 30 days, and costs $49 to buy.

 *A web-based tool that visually clusters and displays Google search results is the Anacubis Google Visual browser, available at http://www.anacubis.com/googledemo/google/.*

## MoreGoogle

MoreGoogle (http://www.moregoogle.com) is a simple utility that enhances Google result pages. The most noticeable enhancement is the addition of thumbnail images of the URLs shown in search results. These images come from Alexa, not Google, so not all results have them.

MoreGoogle also provides additional links at the bottom of a search result. These links are **site info**, **archived**, and **more related**, and they also provide access to additional information from Alexa. The **site info** link shows site stats, Alexa's "traffic rank" for the site, and other useful statistics. The **archived** link calls up historical cached copies of the site from the Internet Archives, and the **more related** link shows related sites based on information gleaned by users of Alexa's toolbar.

If your query causes Google to include results from Amazon, MoreGoogle further enhances these results with category, price information, and user ratings, pulled directly from the product listing at Amazon.

MoreGoogle functions much like the Alexa toolbar described in Chapter 8. However, unlike a toolbar, which takes up valuable space on your browser, MoreGoogle works in the background. The author of the program asserts that MoreGoogle contains no spyware, transmits no personal information, and is easy to uninstall if you want to get rid of it.

There is a mild downside to MoreGoogle. There's a slight time penalty to load the thumbnail images and add additional links to search results. This lag may not be noticeable on later model computers, but can really slow things down on older computers.

Microsoft Windows 95 or higher and Internet Explorer 5.0 or higher are required.

POWER SEARCHER TIP *Ggler is a web-based tool that also adds Alexa thumbnail images to Google search results. It's available at http://www.ggler.com/.*

## Pluck

Pluck (http://www.pluck.com/) is a virtual Swiss Army knife for web users. It combines many features found in tools described elsewhere in this book, including a search toolbar, an online bookmark service, a web page clipping tool, an alerting service, an RSS news aggregator, and other services. And even though it boasts such an impressive array of features, Pluck is free.

To use Pluck's online tools, you need to register for a free account. All that's required is a valid e-mail address, and Pluck's privacy policy says that it will not share this information with others.

Pluck installs as both a toolbar and an Explorer pane in Internet Explorer. The toolbar sports a search box and a drop-down menu that lets you search Google, Amazon, eBay, news, or content on your own computer that you've saved with Pluck. The toolbar also has buttons that let you view your selected RSS feeds, see your web folders, and add a link to your online bookmarks. More on each of these features in a moment.

As a search tool, Pluck's toolbar component is basic. But Pluck provides some cool "post-processing" features that make it a very compelling alternative to the Google Toolbar. Results are shown in split frames on the right side of the browser. The top frame displays Google search results; the bottom pane displays web pages. This makes it easy to view search results and their underlying pages at the same time.

The **filter** box at the top of the search result frame lets you refine your results dynamically. Just type in additional words, and all results that do not contain those words are removed from the result list as you type. Icons next to the filter allow you to mark results as read, hide all read items, remove the descriptions from results, refresh the result list, and create a "perch" for the search. "Perch" is the term Pluck uses to describe an automated search alert. You can create a perch to alert you whenever Google adds something new that matches your search terms, similar to the Google Web Alerts described in Chapter 9.

Pluck also has a "power search" feature that provides advanced search options for each of the sources available. These options change dynamically when you change the source. Power search options for eBay and Amazon focus on product and pricing information, for example. A power search for news lets you select headlines, top sources, and so on. In addition, you can also create a perch that monitors an eBay auction, one that tracks a product or author at Amazon, or a perch to follow a news story.

If you're an avid blog reader or a news junkie, an RSS reader is an essential tool. RSS readers (also called *news aggregators,* described in Chapter 14) scan RSS feeds and automatically update themselves with new content virtually as it's posted. Pluck's RSS reader is one of the best designed and easiest to use that I've come across. Links make it easy to add feeds, organize your feeds into folders, and search for new feeds.

Like the web research managers described in Chapter 11, Pluck makes it easy to save web pages in your own collection, allowing you to search for your favorite content regardless of whether you're online or not. Pluck also provides the capability to save pages in your own private online folders, and optionally to share folders with others. Whenever a shared online folder is updated, anyone with rights to view the folder sees the update immediately, making Pluck a very useful tool for collaborative research.

Windows 2000 Home or Professional or Windows XP and Internet Explorer 6.0 or higher are required.

# p-ZOOM

p-ZOOM (http://www.zoomstation.com/prod/p_zoom.htm) is a search engine companion for Microsoft Internet Explorer that clusters search results whenever you use Google, MSN Search, or Yahoo! p-ZOOM results are displayed in an Explorer bar window to the left of regular search results.

Clustered results are useful in a number of ways. With results organized into categories, you can easily avoid nonrelevant results by ignoring categories that don't relate to the specific meaning of your search terms. The names of clustered result folders also provide useful clues for helping you refine your queries. These names are automatically extracted by p-ZOOM from all the search results, and they represent words with the greatest number of occurrences on all pages, indicating that they are popular or "terms of art" for a particular subject. p-ZOOM also goes beyond the standard 10–100 results returned by most search engines, retrieving 200 or more results for your query, saving you time by letting you avoid drilling down through page after page of additional results.

Windows 2000 or higher and Microsoft Internet Explorer 5.5 or higher are required.

# Soople

Soople (http://www.soople.com), shown in Figure 20-4, is an elegant control console for Google's many powerful advanced features, bringing them all together in a well-designed, easy-to-use interface. Soople exposes Google's power with a set of nifty search forms designed to easily exploit Google's advanced search capabilities.

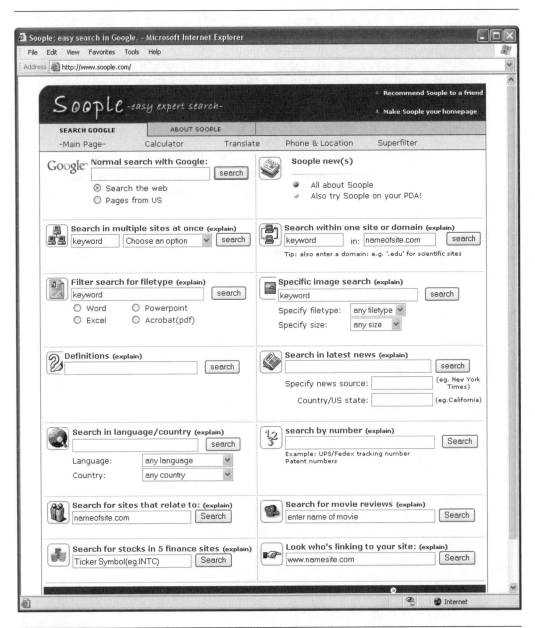

**FIGURE 20-4**   Soople provides a clean, elegant interface to Google's advanced search tools.

From Soople's main page, many of Google's filters are available via simple forms. For example, you can limit your results to documents of a particular file type by simply clicking a radio button. There are also forms that search News, Images, and Google's other specialized catalogs.

The Calculator page does a great job of showcasing just how powerful Google's internal calculator function actually is, by preconfiguring a number of common calculations. Number conversion, percentage, trigonometric functions, square root... all done easily and painlessly, without having to type in symbols or properly structured equations. The Phone & Location page combines Google's residence and business phone directories, a reverse phone directory, and local search functions, all on a single page.

Soople's author, Floris Rost van Tonningen, says that the idea behind the interface was to make Google's full power easily accessible for his mother. He's succeeded—not only does Soople make it easy to use the full power of Google, it also respects Google's minimalist approach with a clean, uncluttered design.

POWER SEARCHER TIP    *Another useful page that assembles multiple Google features on a single page is Fagan Finder, available at http://www.faganfinder.com.*

# Part III

# Appendixes

# Appendix A

## What Google Knows about You

Google obviously knows a lot about the Web. It also, of necessity, knows certain things about you, such as your search terms and the unique IP address of your computer. Google uses other information such as your language or the number of results you prefer primarily to enhance and customize your user experience. Still other types of information Google uses to operate, develop, and improve its services.

Should you be concerned that Google knows these things about you? That depends on your own views of personal privacy. If you look at the range of people using Google, at one extreme are "privacy paranoids" who are irrationally fearful of any kind of computer system monitoring personal information. On the other extreme are those who essentially don't care, sharing the philosophy of Sun Microsystems CEO Scott McNealy who famously said, "You have zero privacy anyway. Get over it."

I believe the best approach to safeguarding your personal privacy lies somewhere between these extremes. You should at the very least be aware of the personal information Google collects about you and what it does with it. That's just prudent, and it gives you the knowledge you need to make your own decisions about what you do—or do not—disclose when using Google services.

Whether you should feel anxious about the information Google collects is another question. More than most other online services, Google goes to considerable lengths to disclose the types of information it collects, and presents its privacy policies in readable, easy-to-understand language. The company also makes its core principles and codes of conduct transparent, accessible to both employees and users alike. Permeating everything is Google's informal code of conduct: "Don't be evil."

Most people who take the time to read and understand Google's personal information policies feel comfortable that there's an implied trust between the company and its users—one that the company works hard to maintain. Speaking personally, in all the interactions I've had with numerous Google employees since Larry and Sergey first started the company, I've never had any reason to doubt the sincerity of Google's principles or its care in exercising them. I believe Google when it says it places top priority on protecting the privacy of its users, and I'm comfortable disclosing the information I need to use all of the company's services.

Other people aren't so sanguine, seeing the specter of Big Brother lurking behind the company's benign public face. They point out—rightly so—that no amount of goodwill and noble intentions can protect users should hackers compromise Google's data centers—or worse, an unaccountable government agency bent on trampling individual rights demands that Google turn over personal records.

If you share these fears, you probably shouldn't be using Google—or any Internet service, for that matter. You should also eschew credit cards, using telephone networks, the postal system, and every other service that collects and stores personally identifiable information. Many of these "offline" services collect far more personally identifiable information than Google, and they share, sell, and otherwise disseminate that information often without your permission or knowledge. If you think that's a wild claim, I'd recommend *Database Nation* by Simson Garfinkel (O'Reilly, 2001) for an eye-opening account of the wide range of personal information that's stored and used by businesses and governments worldwide.

The bottom line is that there's a very real tradeoff between disclosing enough personal information to enable a service to work effectively for you, and the consequences that may occur should that information be distributed to others and be used in a detrimental manner. It's a personal decision, and one that may not be easy for some people.

The best way to make this decision is to learn as much as possible about Google's privacy policies, core principles, and practices regarding using and potentially sharing your personal information.

# "Don't Be Evil"

Google's official code of conduct begins with the following preface: "Our informal corporate motto is 'Don't be evil.' We Googlers generally relate those words to the way we serve our users—as well we should." This theme—"Don't be evil"—resonates through virtually all of the company's privacy policies and public statements. It even had a prominent place in the documents Google filed with the SEC when it filed for its initial public offering.

Google has been mocked by the media and Internet pundits for putting forth such a simplistic, Polyannaish credo as a core principle, but "Don't be evil" has been remarkably successful in defining and unifying the company's corporate culture. It's not uncommon when talking with a Googler to hear them interject "Don't be evil" or 'That would be evil" into the conversation. And as dopey as it may seem to some, Googlers really mean it.

When it comes to the privacy of your personal information, all of Google's actions go through the "Don't be evil" filter. At the most basic level, Google collects only information necessary to perform services you request. To function properly, some Google services require you to disclose more information than others. In all cases where Google collects information from you, it fully discloses what's being collected and how the information is used.

## Information Google Collects about You

Google classifies information it collects about you in two ways, as either "personally identifying information" or "non-personally identifying information." Google defines personally identifying information as "information that individually identifies you, such as your name, physical address or email address." Non-personally identifying information is defined as anything your browser reveals whenever you visit Google or any other web site. As you'll see, your browser reveals quite a bit more about you than you might think.

Whether Google collects personally identifying or non-personally identifying information depends on the service you're using. Let's start with non-personally identifying information, because Google collects this across the board, whether you're searching the Web or using Froogle, Google Groups, or just about any other Google service.

Google collects non-personally identifying information your browser makes available whenever you visit a web site. This information includes your computer's Internet Protocol address, browser type, browser language, and the date and time of your query. Google also sets and reads one or more "cookies," small text files containing information that uniquely identify your browser. Why does Google collect this information? Google's privacy policy states, "We use this information to operate, develop and improve our services."

That doesn't really say much. In practice, Google uses this information to communicate directly with your computer and to make sure you get the search results you asked for, in your preferred language. Google may also aggregate this information to improve overall future search results, by observing which results are clicked most frequently, which results appear most relevant for particular queries (in other words, results that users clicked and stayed on, rather than returning to the search result page to choose something else), and so on. In all, pretty innocuous stuff.

**POWER SEARCHER TIP** *Your browser discloses quite a bit of information to every web site you visit, not just Google. Additionally, your computer may have picked up "web bugs," which are virtually invisible tracking codes that record your complete movements online. To learn more about what your browser reveals about you, visit Privacy.net at http://www.privacy.net/.*

Google collects personally identifiable information for some services such as Google Answers, Gmail, and others that require you to register for an account. When you register for an account, Google asks you to provide personal information such as your name, e-mail address, and a password. Google then uses that information to provide the service—for example, making sure that your e-mail is routed properly to you and not some other user. For certain services, such as Google's advertising programs and Google Answers, you're required to provide a credit card or other payment information. Google stores sensitive personal information in encrypted form on secure servers, and takes what the company calls "appropriate security measures" to protect against unauthorized access to or unauthorized alteration, disclosure, or destruction of your personal information. Additionally, Google restricts access to your personally identifying information to employees who need to know that information to "operate, develop or improve our services."

## About Those Cookies

When you first visit Google, a cookie (a small file containing a string of characters) is sent to your computer. This cookie is "set" (stored) on your computer, and it uniquely identifies your computer and web browser. Any time you or someone using your browser uses a Google service, these cookies record certain types of information. Many web sites use cookies to identify and track user behavior. Compared with others, Google's cookies contain relatively little information.

Google says, "We use cookies to improve the quality of our service and to better understand how people interact with us." Google does this by storing user preferences in cookies and by tracking user trends and patterns of how people search.

Most browsers are initially set up to accept cookies. If you have privacy concerns about cookies, you can set your browser to refuse all cookies or to indicate when a cookie is being sent. Should you change these settings, realize that some Google features or services may not function properly. Indeed many web sites, even including government and noncommercial sites, may not function properly with cookies disabled.

> **POWER SEARCHER TIP** *For more information about cookies and how to manage them, see The Unofficial Cookie FAQ, at http://www.cookiecentral.com/faq/.*

## Google's Information-Sharing Practices and Policies

Google does not rent or sell your personally identifying information to other companies or individuals without your consent. Google does provide personal information to other businesses when it outsources certain tasks, such as processing credit card information. Google has agreements in place that oblige those businesses to process information only on the company's instructions and in compliance with its privacy policy.

Like all online services, Google must provide information to certain groups that request it when required by law. This is somewhat open to interpretation by the company: Google may disclose personal information when the company has "a good faith belief that access, preservation or disclosure of such information is reasonably necessary to protect the rights, property or safety of Google, its users or the public."

If you have a Google account, your personal information may be shared among all other Google services that you use. This sharing among internal Google services enables you to use a single login name for Gmail, Google Answers, and so on.

Google has data centers all over the world and is designed to route information in the most efficient manner possible, regardless of your location. As such, the company can store and process personal information in any country where it has facilities. This means your personal information may be stored in data centers located outside your own country. Nonetheless, Google maintains similar safeguards and precautions concerning your personal information regardless of where in the world it may reside.

Google also shares aggregated information with others—especially advertisers who want to know how popular certain search terms are, or how often certain advertisements were clicked. In these cases, however, no personally identifying information is shared. The key word is "aggregated"—Google shares only information from groups of users that's pooled together without any personally identifying characteristics.

What happens should Google be acquired by another company with a different privacy policy? Google says that it will provide notice before any personally identifying information is transferred, but offers no guarantee beyond providing that notice.

## Updating Your Account Information

Every Google service that requires you to register for an account allows you to update your personal information at any time. In most cases, this just involves logging into the account and clicking a **Settings**, **My Profile**, or other similar link.

# Privacy Policies by Service

Google has one privacy policy that covers most of its services. The company does, however, provide additional privacy information for some of its services, including the Toolbar, Gmail, and orkut.

# Google Privacy Policies

Google's general privacy policy covers all of the company's services. Services that require registration or that collect additional information have their own privacy policy pages, as noted.

## Google Privacy Center

This page covers Google's general privacy policies and practices (http://www.google.com/privacy.html). It also provides links to privacy policies specific to Gmail, the Google Store, and the Google Toolbar, as well as a link to all previous versions of the company's privacy policy.

## Google Toolbar Privacy Policy

When you enable "advanced" features on the Google Toolbar (Chapter 8), you also enable the Toolbar to exchange more information with Google than in a standard web search. There's nothing sinister about this. The advanced features enable things such as the display of the PageRank for the page you're viewing, for example. They also let you view the cached version of a page, other pages linking to the page, and similar pages from menu items on the Toolbar. For more information about the Toolbar privacy policy, see http://toolbar.google.com/privacy.html.

## Gmail Privacy Policy

Gmail's privacy policy (http://gmail.google.com/gmail/help/privacy.html) differs somewhat from other Google privacy policy statements because it relates to your personal e-mail account. When Gmail was first introduced, there was outcry over the company's "reading" e-mail so that it could insert contextually relevant ads. Google computers indeed process the contents of each message, but this process differs little from the processes used by e-mail spam-filtering systems, which analyze content and take action based on a set of rules. Ads are automatically inserted into relevant messages, but advertisers see only aggregate information of the total number of impressions and clicks for each ad. They do not receive any personal information about the person who viewed the ad, or the contents of the e-mails associated with the ad.

However, if you click an ad in a Gmail message, Google *does* send a referring URL to the advertiser's site identifying that you are visiting from Gmail. There is no personally identifying information in this referring URL. It is possible, however, that an advertiser could identify you personally if you've previously visited the advertiser's site or if other cookies or tracking codes associated with your personal information are available to the advertiser. But this is not a privacy shortfall of Gmail—this is also true whenever you click to view *any* online advertisement.

## orkut Privacy Policy

If you're considering joining orkut, it's important to read the privacy policy (http://www.orkut.com/privacy.html) because it differs from the typical privacy policies at Google. And by nature, because it's a social networking service designed to make it easy for people to share *lots* of personal information with others, privacy issues can take on much greater significance than with a simple Google web search. orkut also has a provision in its terms of service agreement whereby you agree to surrender ownership of your own content to Google—so it's important to understand this *before* posting content that you don't want to give away.

# Google as Big Brother?

Some privacy advocates are concerned with the types of information that Google collects and what the search engine does with it. One of the most vocal self-appointed Google watchdogs is Daniel Brandt, president of a nonprofit group called Public Information Research (PIR). PIR operates a web site called Google Watch, describing itself as "a look at Google's monopoly, algorithms, and privacy policies."

Google Watch achieved a level of notoriety in February 2003 by nominating Google for Privacy International's "U.S. Big Brother Awards." These awards are bestowed each year by Privacy International "to the government and private sector organisations which have done the most to threaten personal privacy in their countries." PIR's nomination was something of a publicity stunt, because nominations were open to anyone and were not vetted. Google was not selected as one of the Big Brother finalists, which certainly indicates that Privacy International itself did not see the company as among the major threats to privacy operating in the world at the time.

In its nomination, PIR leveled nine accusations against Google that it claimed supported its contention that Google should receive the Big Brother award:

■ Accusation 1: Google's immortal cookie.

■ Accusation 2: Google records everything they can.

■ Accusation 3: Google retains all data indefinitely.

■ Accusation 4: Google won't say why they need this data.

■ Accusation 5: Google hires spooks.

■ Accusation 6: Google's toolbar is spyware.

■ Accusation 7: Google's cache copy is illegal.

■ Accusation 8: Google is not your friend.

■ Accusation 9: Google is a privacy time bomb.

PIR claimed that it was raising these issues to foster public debate about a service that was becoming an important part of many people's daily lives. "It's not that we believe Google is evil," reads the nomination. "What we believe is that Google, Inc. is at a fork in the road, and they have some big decisions to make. This Google Watch site is trying to articulate and publicize the situation at Google, and encourage more scrutiny of their operations."

*Search Engine Watch* editor Danny Sullivan responded to PIR's claims with a detailed article that objectively examined all the accusations and concluded with "verdicts" on the validity of each. It's an excellent analysis of Google's privacy issues and effectively disputes each claim made by PIR—though with some important points that are well worth considering for anyone concerned about privacy. Read the article, "Google And The Big Brother Nomination," at http://searchenginewatch.com/sereport/article.php/2175251.

POWER SEARCHER TIP    *Read more about Privacy International's Big Brother Awards at http://www.privacyinternational.org/bba.*

# Appendix B

## Inside the Soul of the Machine

With the launch of Google Desktop, which seamlessly integrates a blindingly fast search of files on your own computer with Google's web search, it's easy to think of Google as becoming all-pervasive, much like HAL, the computer in Stanley Kubrick's classic film *2001: A Space Odyssey*. Peter Norvig, Google's Director of Search Quality, once told me, "Search should be like HAL in 2001. It should understand what people say—hopefully without killing anybody."

There's little worry that Google will kill anybody, at least not in its current form. Although Google uses lots of artificial intelligence in the various software systems that power the search engine, Google is not even close to being a sentient being. It is, however, one of the largest supercomputers in the world (if not *the* largest), according to published research by Google engineers.

Google officials send mixed messages when they talk about the actual physical technologies that power the search engine. On the one hand, Google engineers are encouraged to publish papers and work with other computer scientists on interesting projects. Google also opened up its system for others to mess around with, via the Google API discussed in Chapter 9.

But ask a Googler for specifics, such as the number of computers working together in Google's data centers, or how many searchers use Google per day, and you'll almost always get "no comment" or an "approximation," a number that's almost certainly far lower than the "real" number you're seeking.

So it's difficult to paint a precise picture of what goes on behind the scenes at Google. Nonetheless, there are enough clues available to piece together at least a pencil sketch of the workings inside the soul of the machine.

# Inside Google

Google headquarters in Mountain View, California is known as the Googleplex. Currently, the Googleplex is situated in a large building that used to be the headquarters for Silicon Graphics, a one-time computer graphics powerhouse. Wandering around the campus is an interesting experience. Google is much like any other Silicon Valley company, with most employees working in cubicles. But the company allows wide latitude when it comes to how employees decorate their cubes, and the personal effects, photographs, and other miscellany on display have the effect of making Google's offices appear more like a surreal high-tech art gallery than a functional work environment. Especially when you encounter employees sprawled out on a couch, perhaps using a dog as a perch for a laptop computer. Make no mistake, though—the buzz of energy and activity at Google is palpable. And night or day, there's almost always someone hard at work on some project or another.

Although the Googleplex is where most of the creative development and programming work is done, the heart of the search engine lies within the data centers that house the actual computers, routers, and other equipment that carry out the heavy lifting for users. I've had the good fortune of having guided tours of two of Google's data centers in northern California, under the able direction of Jim Reese. Jim is Google's Chief Operations Engineer, and he and his team designed and built the massively parallel server farms that run all of Google's operations. Figure B-1 is a picture of Jim and his team in one of Google's data centers.

Photo by Chris Sherman

**FIGURE B-1**   Google Chief Operations Engineer Jim Reese and team in one of Google's California data centers. Note the fans on the floor to provide additional cooling.

Jim was Google employee #18. Like many Googlers, Jim has an interesting background. He received his A.B. in biology from Harvard and an M.D. from Yale. Just prior to joining Google, Jim was a practicing neurosurgeon at Stanford. Yes, it's true: Google's supercomputer complex was designed by a brain surgeon.

When Jim first arrived at the company, Google consisted of 300 computers, handling several hundred thousand queries per day.

Within his first month, Jim directed the expansion of Google up to 2,000 computers, and from that point forward there was no looking back. Table B-1 shows the rapid growth in both the number of computers and number of queries handled by Google each day.

How big is Google today? The company keeps the exact number a closely guarded secret. The most recent "official" number I've seen is "more than 15,000," but estimates from such notables as *New York Times* technology reporter John Markoff put the number much higher, between 50,000 and 100,000.

The actual number is largely irrelevant. It's tempting to think of Google as 15,000 times more powerful than your computer, but this isn't an accurate comparison. Google does use cheap, commodity hardware that's very similar to the components found in your desktop or

| Date | Computers | Queries/Day |
|------|-----------|-------------|
| Nov. 1998 | 25 | 10,000 |
| Apr. 1999 | 300 | 500,000 |
| Sept. 1999 | 2,100 | 3 million |
| June 2000 | 4,000 | 18 million |
| Nov. 2000 | 6,000 | 55 million |
| Aug. 2002 | >10,000 | 150 million |
| Today | >15,000 | >250 million |

**TABLE B-1**    Google Growth (Source: Presentation by Amit Singhal, Senior Research Scientist, Google)

laptop computers. But it lashes these components together using custom-built software and highly specialized networking components, to maximize the search engine's capabilities and performance.

Google's decision to use cheap, commodity hardware is driven largely by cost—both to acquire and maintain the hardware, as well as the cost involved in running the data centers. Believe it or not, *electricity costs* are an important design consideration for Google engineers. All Google software must not only do the right job quickly, it must also be Scrooge-like in its energy consumption. This is important, because electricity costs can really add up when you have thousands of computers processing hundreds of millions of queries each day.

Not only that, the heat generated by all these machines is intense. Although Google's data centers are located in hosting centers with very powerful air-conditioning systems, the company actually had to make a trip to Home Depot to buy a couple dozen floor fans for supplemental cooling. Walking into the heart of one of the living room–sized steel cages that houses Google's computers, you're hit with a blast of air from these fans—and your hair literally stands on end!

Another advantage to using cheap commodity hardware is that when it inevitably fails, it can be replaced quickly and at a low cost—often with next-generation equipment that's even more powerful. Google is designed to be highly fault-tolerant, and equipment failures are expected. That's OK; when something breaks, a technician simply swaps out the broken hardware in much the same way you or I would replace a burned-out light bulb.

# Technical Facts about Google

What else is known about Google? Here are a few facts gleaned from various sources; most of these sources are listed in the next section so that you can peruse them in more detail:

- Google uses a stripped-down, customized version of Red Hat Linux. "We don't use all the graphical stuff that's not needed for our server," Jim Reese said in an interview in *HP World News.* "We have actually written our own code; we have written our database and back-end servers that do very complicated and complex problem solving and load balancing."

■ Google uses MySQL (an open-source database language) for a lot of development work.

■ Google has also created its own, industrial-strength file system, called, appropriately enough, the Google File System (GFS).

■ Google uses different systems to power web search and to handle parts of its AdWords system, particularly when it comes to billing. Billing systems must be more robust than search, so this information is ultimately handled by Oracle Financial Systems.

# Essential Reading about Google

No book on a subject as complex as Google can be completely comprehensive. Here's a list of other sources of information that I recommend if you're still hungry to learn more about Google.

## Books about Google

■ *How to Do Everything with Google,* by Fritz Schneider, Nancy Blachman, and Eric Fredricksen (McGraw-Hill/Osborne, 2003)

An excellent guide to Google, written by insiders. Two of the book's authors, Fritz Schneider and Eric Fredricksen, are Google employees, and the third, Nancy Blachman, is an experienced technical writer who also runs the useful Google Guide website. In short, these are people who really do know how to do most everything with Google, and they share their knowledge in the book.

■ *Google Hacks,* by Tara Calishain and Rael Dornfest (O'Reilly, 2003)

This book is widely considered to be the "bible" for the Google API, and it's packed with tips, techniques, and code examples using the Google Web API. It also contains some great tips for more effective searching with Google.

■ *Google: The Missing Manual,* by Sarah Milstein and Rael Dornfest (O'Reilly, 2004)

Another good overview of Google, written as the "user manual" that should have been packaged with the search engine.

## Articles and Papers

■ "The Anatomy of a Large-Scale Hypertextual Web Search Engine" (http://www-db .stanford.edu/pub/papers/google.pdf)

The paper that started it all. This is Larry Page and Sergey Brin's overview of their new search engine, Google, presented to the Seventh International World-Wide Web Conference, held in April 1998 in Brisbane, Australia. Though more than seven years old, this paper still ranks as the definitive overview of Google. Despite its technical nature, this paper should be on every serious Google searcher's must-read list.

- ■ "The PageRank Citation Ranking: Bringing Order to the Web" (http://dbpubs.stanford .edu:8090/pub/1999-66)

  Scroll down to the bottom of the page and click the "PDF" link to retrieve the actual paper. Here, Page and Brin discuss the PageRank algorithm they developed in more detail. A great quote from the paper: "To test the utility of PageRank for search, we built a web search engine called Google."

- ■ "Web Search for a Planet: The Google Cluster Architecture" (http://www.computer.org/ micro/mi2003/m2022.pdf)

  This PDF document is a look at Google's software architecture—one of the best technical overviews I've read about the inner workings of the search engine.

- ■ "The Google File System" (http://www.cs.rochester.edu/sosp2003/papers/ p125-ghemawat.pdf)

  A look at how information is sliced, diced, stored, and served, from a very technical, detailed point of view.

- ■ "Efficient Crawling Through URL Ordering" (http://www.csd.uch.gr/~hy558/papers/ cho-order.pdf)

  Written by Junghoo Cho, Hector Garcia-Molina, and Lawrence Page (Page was still attending Stanford at the time), this paper provides insight into how Google crawls the Web, trying to find the "highest quality" documents first.

- ■ Papers written by Googlers (http://labs.google.com/papers.html)

  Want even more? This page at Google Labs features a list of dozens of papers written by Google employees, on a wide range of topics—from web information retrieval and search engine design to artificial intelligence, genetic algorithms, and a variety of other subjects.

# The Future

Google continues to evolve and grow in new and unexpected ways that further enhance our experience as searchers. Will it eventually become HAL? Perhaps. I think the best view of Google's future was expressed by Wayne Rosing, Google's Vice President of Engineering:

*"The day will come when Google won't be a search engine anymore, because everything will be searchable. So, instead, we'll have to algorithmically find you the good stuff. It will be an up-leveling of our ranking function, if you will, from what's the best document to what's the best, most well-formed knowledge on the subject."*

# Index